HOW BIG IS YOUR GOD?

ED BULKLEY

HARVEST HOUSE PUBLISHERS
Eugene, Oregon 97402

Cover by Left Coast Design, Portland, Oregon

HOW BIG IS YOUR GOD?
Copyright ©1997 by Ed Bulkley
Published by Harvest House Publishers
Eugene, Oregon 97402

Library of Congress Cataloging-in-Publication Data

Bulkley, Ed, 1947–
  How big is your God? / Ed Bulkley
    p. cm.
  ISBN 1-56507-558-7
  1. Faith. 2. Christian life. 3. Bulkley, Ed, 1947–
I. Title.
BT771.2.B85 1997   97-2661
248.4—dc21   CIP

Printed in the United States of America.
97 98 99 00 01 02 / BP / 10 9 8 7 6 5 4 3 2 1

I dedicate this book to my parents, Bob and Pat Bulkley,
who are now at home with the Lord.
Their lives of quiet faith in God are still a source of
encouragement and inspiration to me.
From the world's point of view, they were never great successes
because they did not accumulate massive wealth
nor achieve widespread fame.
Yet their consistent godliness, integrity, courage,
and cheerfulness in the face of adversity
left me and my family with a priceless heritage.
Our church's buildings and grounds were initially secured
through their generosity and unselfish sacrifice.
I hope to imitate their greatest success—
that of passing on their faith in Christ
to their children and to countless others.

Contents

Returning to a Faith That Really Works

FAITH IS ESSENTIAL FOR a happy Christian life. Most Christians seem to be aware of this, yet many feel that happiness in their relationship with God has eluded them. That's why they look to certain "faith" teachers who, via radio, television, evangelistic crusades, and healing services, are selling promises of revival, power with God, prosperity, special "anointing," and fire from heaven.

Sincere Christians everywhere are seeking a blessing, not realizing God has already provided everything they need for a joyful, power-filled walk with God. Like the disciples, Christians are crying out to the Lord, "Increase our faith!" (Luke 17:5).

That's what this book is about—real faith—how we have lost our faith in God, and how it can be restored. If you will invest the time to carefully read the teaching sections as well as the narratives, I believe you will clearly understand how the subtle erosion of faith takes place and learn how you can guard your own heart and the souls of your family from the deception of our enemy.

Let me give you a few examples of the tragic consequences of faith destroyed:

A sincere young man sat dejectedly in my office with tears in his eyes. "I accepted Christ as my Savior when I was a boy," he said, "but these last few years, I have had no joy in my Christian life. To tell you the truth, I don't know what I believe—or *whether* I believe anymore." He confessed that his life and language were little different from his unbelieving fellow-workers. The foundation of his faith had been undermined by years of disobedience to God's Word.

A pastor in Michigan wrote and told me the story of how his marriage and ministry had been destroyed by incompetent psychotherapy that led his wife into a swamp of self-pity and bitterness. She no longer believed that God was able to heal her wounded heart and she now flounders in angry loneliness and disbelief. Her husband currently supports himself doing odd jobs and wonders how this tragedy could have happened.

A woman drove to a conference in California to tell me how a major Christian psychiatric clinic falsified her medical records and destroyed her reputation. She has carefully documented her case and contacted numerous religious leaders asking for their assistance, yet there is little they can do. She has asked the clinic to enter conciliation rather than to force her to go to court, but the clinic isn't interested. In deep frustration, the woman asked, "What can I do? How can I get them to do what's right?" She has lost faith in the integrity of this clinic that calls itself Christian.

At the same conference, an elderly prison chaplain told me how his grandson almost fell into the hands of the same psychiatric clinic that damaged the woman. When the clinic was asked what their treatment would cost, they replied, "Nothing, if you have insurance."

"How much will it cost the insurance company?" the family asked.

"Six thousand dollars per week, and he will need at least three weeks of therapy," they said.

"How will you convince the insurance company to pay $18,000?" the family asked incredulously.

Having never yet seen the young man, the representative for the Christian psychiatric clinic told the family that they would simply report that the young man suffered from severe depression. It didn't seem to matter that the young man was not depressed and that the diagnosis was fraudulent. The clinic is now being investigated in California and is the subject of a major lawsuit in Georgia. The founders of the clinic have merged the clinic with another "Christian" counseling service and have since broken up their partnership.

A recent poll indicates that evangelical Christians are getting divorced at a higher rate than the general population. Young people in the church are becoming sexually active at the same rate as unbelievers. Gang members, who call themselves Christians, meet in the balconies of local churches to exchange drugs and to plan battles with other gangs.

A well known evangelical writer left his wife and revealed that he was a homosexual. Not content to stop at destroying his own marriage, he began a campaign to convince other Christians that homosexuality is compatible with Christianity and that the church should be ashamed of itself for its "homophobia."

A group of clergy in Denver recently met at a large synagogue to express their belief that abortion rights have their roots in ancient religion. Hundreds of people at the service bowed their heads and prayed that the right to abort babies would not be taken away from women.

An American president, a professing Christian, vetoed a ban on partial-birth abortions, allowing thousands of babies to be murdered just seconds before they are completely delivered. Were the babies to exit the birth canal and be placed on a table for the brutal procedure, the doctor would be charged with murder. Eight inches makes all the legal difference.

Whether pagan or religious, liberal or evangelical, it seems to make little difference. Professing Christians watch the same television programs, read the same pornography, use the same vulgar language, and depend on the same worldly cures for their psychological woes as those who reject the very notion of a holy God.

What is going on in the evangelical world? How can such outrages take place in the name of Christ? Why is there so much depression, divorce, and dysfunction? Why are Christian wives leaving their husbands and children at an ever-increasing rate? Why has sexual immorality become accepted as normal and purity become viewed as a quaint relic of the past?

The answer is *practical atheism*. Wait! Before you put this book down, I want to assure you that we will do far more than examine the systems and results of unbelief. We are going to discover how to rebuild our wavering faith in a desperately wicked generation. We will examine how to recover the joy and peace that God offers his children, regardless of the condition of the world around us.

You may wonder what unbelief has to do with you, a Christian, but I encourage you to think the issue through with me, because our understanding of God and our attitudes toward Him have a major bearing upon our personal happiness and mental health.

"I'm not an atheist!" you might be thinking right now, and technically, that might be true. We believe that God exists. But are we *acting* like it? If not, we have become practical atheists. Take a moment to think this through with me.

Atheism is a dismal religion seeking to comprehend the universe without a Creator. It is represented in a variety of philosophical arenas: politics (Marxist communism), education (secular humanism), science (evolutionism), and religion (atheism proper).

There is an arrogant hopelessness in atheism mixed with a cynicism which springs from an inevitable worldview of meaninglessness. For the true atheist, all existence is without purpose or design, since he believes there is no Master Designer.

The term *atheist* literally means "one without God" and refers to a person who claims to believe there is no Divine Being. Without being too technical, the term can be applied to people of various philosophical persuasions. Official card-carrying atheists are enthusiastic in their unbelief, having an almost evangelical zeal to convert others to their way of thinking. They gather for meetings, publish magazines, and contribute financially to efforts designed to inform the masses that all religion is a delusion. It is curious that such people deny God with an emotional intensity that could easily be misunderstood as personal hatred for a Being they say does not exist.

Others believe they are scientific atheists. They smugly congratulate themselves on their intellectual objectivity and look down upon lesser-gifted humans with condescension. They draw government grants to create evolutionary dioramas in natural history museums for the purpose of illustrating their patently unscientific beliefs about human origins. They pompously pronounce their theories as scientific fact, blithely ignoring established laws of science which contradict their interpretations of reality. Romans 1:22 describes this sort of atheist: "Although they claimed to be wise, they became fools."

There are intellectual atheists, casual atheists, committed atheists, chemical atheists, business atheists, embittered atheists, and evolutionary atheists. There are temporary atheists, atheists of convenience, political atheists, and national atheists. But there are no *actual* atheists. Think about it: No one spends his life attempting to destroy something he believes is nonexistent. Still, there are some who continue to deny God.

Even in the worst of times, however, atheism has never been very popular. There is something, except among the most blasphemous, that makes a person shrink back from openly declaring "There is no God!" Perhaps it is the sense of one's own finiteness that forces a sincere human to admit that God could indeed exist outside of that person's knowledge and experience. Or perhaps it is the nagging awareness that the empirical evidence in nature for God's existence is overwhelming. It might even be one's concern that there may come a day of accounting for our lives and actions.

Other sincere thinkers have had to admit that in the absence of a sovereign Lawgiver, all moral and ethical standards are mere necessities for civilized continuity. Evolutionary doctrines of "survival of the fittest" and "might makes right" become philosophically acceptable. Racism, Nazi pogroms, abortion, and other brands of genocide become defensible in a relativistic universe void of God.

War, disease, sorrow, or impending death may bring even the most dedicated enemy of God to a moment of reluctant acknowledgment of His existence. When his atheism was questioned, Soviet Premier Nikita Kruschev was quoted as saying,

"I'm an atheist! I *am* an atheist! God *knows* I'm an atheist!" And Chairman Mao commented to Richard Nixon, "When I go to heaven to see God, I'll tell him that for the present it is better to have Taiwan under the care of the United States."[1]

Universally, regardless of location, culture, or century, mankind has found it necessary to acknowledge God in philosophy, organized and casual religion, ethical and moral standards, law, government, and in day-to-day personal living.

In spite of this, there exists a form of unbelief that is more dangerous and pervasive than all others. I call it *practical atheism*. It is a way of life that acknowledges God intellectually, philosophically, and even religiously, but denies His existence in day-to-day actions.

We live in a generation of practical atheism. It has invaded our homes, neighborhoods, schools, stores, courts, and even our churches. Yes, there are *Christian* "atheists," too. These are people who profess to follow Jesus Christ yet in their daily lives they show that they do not believe. Paul writes to Titus about such people: "They claim to know God, but by their actions they deny him" (Titus 1:16).

Practical atheism can creep into all of our lives. It takes many forms, some of which may surprise you. The results of practical atheism are devastating to mental health, marriages, families, children and parents, church fellowships, and the entire Body of Christ. As people of the world see the impact of unbelief in our lives, they will rightfully be compelled to ask, "How big *is* your God?"

A study of weakened faith could be depressing if we simply stopped at that point. But we won't. In this book we will examine some of the deceptions that have swept into the evangelical world, and we will also discover the blessed assurance that results from genuine biblical faith.

If, like me, you desire to live with a faith that really works, you'll find yourself greatly enlightened and encouraged in the pages ahead. You'll see how to reclaim your faith in our mighty

God and experience the joy of a daily walk with our powerful Lord. This study may shake you up at first, but if you read and think deeply, your life can be radically transformed as you learn to know, trust, and obey our loving God.

When Despair Draws Near

Dr. Arthur Wilson sat in his leather recliner as he stared into the fire and listened to the soft rain dripping from the roof to the patio. He was deep in thought as he sipped his favorite Scotch. The sounds of the night and the smell of the fireplace brought a sharp, painful memory. It was on an evening like this five years earlier that his six-year-old son Jimmy had been killed by a hit-and-run driver as he was retrieving a ball from the street.

As he listened to the rain, Arthur's mind went back to that tragic moment five years before. He could still see the dark image of his son outlined by the headlights of a speeding car just before it struck him. He could hear the sickening thud and crunch of the impact that sent Jimmy's body flying limply through the air onto the rain-soaked lawn. Arthur had been haunted by this mournful scene again and again.

How could You allow my only son to die so young? Arthur thought to God in anger. But there was no answer—just the incessant dripping of rain onto the patio. He was actually relieved when he heard the creaking of the garage door as it slowly opened and Susan's car drove in. The car door slammed shut and Susan's keys jingled as she unlocked the door to the family room and stepped in.

"Oh, Arthur," she said as she walked in, temporarily forgetting the tension between them. "I wish you could have heard the speaker at church tonight! He made God seem so real and for the first time in my life I began to understand what Jesus Christ is all about!"

"So tell me, Susan. What *is* Jesus Christ all about?" He picked up the evening paper with a look of irritation. Ordinarily, Susan would have reacted to Arthur's sarcasm with silence, a pained look, and a quick retreat to the kitchen. But tonight she was so excited she failed to read his mood.

"He is the focus of all that's important, Arthur," she said sincerely. "He is God and He loves us. I know He can help us put our marriage back together if we'll let Him."

Arthur looked up from his paper with cold sarcasm in his eyes and said, "Well, isn't that wonderful! Susan has found religion, and now everything is going to be so happy in the Wilson home!" He slammed the paper down on the table next to his chair. "For God's sake, Susan, grow up! Do you really think that an ancient philosopher like Jesus Christ can magically heal this marriage? If He existed at all, He's dead and gone. How can a supposedly intelligent person like you swallow that stuff?" He stomped out of the room furiously.

Susan was genuinely shocked. She knew Arthur wasn't religious, yet she was hardly prepared for the intensity of his anger. But their relationship was so shaky she felt she had little to lose. She followed him through the kitchen to the living room. "Arthur, are you just angry with me, or do you hate God, too?"

"Hate God?" he responded with a smirk on his face. "How can I hate something that doesn't exist?"

"What do you mean, Arthur? How can you say something like that?"

"I can say it because it's true! There is no God. How can anyone possibly believe in a God who allows war and crime and disease in His world? If there is a God why is there cancer, Susan? Why are little children born with defects? Why would God allow our little son to die so young? I can't believe in a God like that!"

Susan turned away sadly and walked back toward the kitchen. Arthur, sensing a victory, followed her and said, "Susan, you studied biology at the university. You know that science has proven that man is the product of evolution. Humans don't need to believe in God anymore to explain the physical world."

She dabbed at her eyes with a tissue. "I can't argue science with you, Arthur. But I also can't believe that this world came about by accident. All I know is that I felt something tonight inside my spirit that I've never experienced before, and it felt good. It's the first time I've known peace since Jimmy died." Tears filled her eyes and she felt her throat becoming tight and dry with a sudden flood of grief.

Arthur's mood softened for an instant, then his eyes hardened again. "So you feel better. I'm glad for you, Susan. But you could have talked with a psychic and you would have felt better, too. All preachers do is tap into the supposed psychological needs of humans to find meaning in a chaotic world. Religion is as old as prostitution. These religious frauds get rich off the pains and insecurities of vulnerable people."

"But God isn't a fraud, Arthur. He's as real as you and I. And I felt His love tonight."

"If He's so loving, why did He kill our son?"

"God didn't kill Jimmy! *You* threw that ball into the street, Arthur." Suddenly she covered her mouth, realizing she had plunged a verbal knife into Arthur's heart.

Arthur cursed her loudly and raised his hand to hit her. He caught himself just in time, turned furiously, and stormed out of the room. Susan stood there for several minutes, shaking with emotion, before she slowly walked to their bedroom.

From that evening onward, Arthur and Susan seemed to grow further apart. As the months passed, Susan began attending church regularly on Sunday and occasionally on Wednesday evenings for a prayer service. She and Arthur never mentioned their bitter argument, for they hardly spoke to each other at all.

One evening Arthur arrived home from work before Susan and found a note that had fallen out of her Bible. The note read, "Susan, we are all praying for you and Arthur. God is still in control, and He can reach Arthur. Just be patient and keep praying. Love, Ellen."

"Oh great!" Arthur muttered as he shook his head in disgust. "Now they're praying for me—Arthur, the Barbarian." He cursed softly and thought, *I can't believe there are people who think they can change somebody else's mind by praying words to a nonexistent God.*

He walked to the family room and sat in his chair. He picked up the remote control and clicked on a television news magazine. A few minutes into the telecast, there was a report on scandals involving some prominent evangelists and their religious empires. There had been sexual affairs, cover-ups, and payoffs.

I knew it! thought Arthur. *All those preachers are frauds! All they want is money—and for what? To buy more TV time to convince more people to send in their money so they can live in mansions and drive their fancy sport cars. I have to tape this for Susan!*

A while later, he heard the garage door open and Susan's car drive in. Arthur could hardly wait for her to come into the house. "Susan, you have to watch this news report! Come here and sit down." He started the tape, eased back into his chair, and watched Susan out of the corner of his eye. She sat silently as the sordid details were unfolded. He could hardly wait for her response. When the report was over, he shut off the TV and asked, "Well, Susan, what do you have to say for your preachers?"

She sat silently for a moment, and then said, "Oh, Arthur, it is so terribly, terribly sad. I'm ashamed that there are preachers like that, but they aren't all frauds. What about scientific researchers who falsify their reports? Does that mean all scientists are phonies? No, it just means that there are some scientists who will do anything to gain prestige and government grants. But it doesn't change what is true about science. And just because there are some false preachers, that doesn't change the truth about God."

"*What* truth about God, Susan? Show me some real proof! If there is a God, why doesn't He come out of hiding? Why won't He reveal Himself in a way that any blind fool could perceive Him?"

"He has, Arthur, but some are just too blind and foolish to see the obvious." She paused, but Arthur had nothing to say. She came over to his chair and sat on the arm. "I'm sorry. I shouldn't have said that, but honestly, Arthur, you make me so mad sometimes. Look, I can't prove the existence of God with a computer or test tubes, but I know that He is and that He loves me . . . and He loves you too."

"Oh, come on, Susan! Don't talk to me about love. You don't even know what that word means anymore. We share the same bedroom—to sleep, that's all. Is your God against sex even between husband and wife?"

Susan felt a quick rush of guilt and embarrassment. She knew she had not been fair to Arthur over the past few months. But their angers were so deep and so constant that she had no desire for him, and she had to admit that she sensed a sort of power over him when she could deny him physical release.

She sighed wearily. "No, Arthur, God isn't against sex. In fact, the pastor at my church was just preaching about the purpose of sex recently."

"Oh! An X-rated sermon. I'd have gone to hear that one."

"Would you really have gone, Arthur? I know you would like our pastor. He's just about your age, and when he preaches he is logical and makes sense. He doesn't just pound the pulpit and scream. Would you be willing to come to church with me some Sunday?" She put her hand on his shoulder, their first physical contact in weeks.

"Are you serious? Get real, Susan. I've heard all the preachers I ever intend to hear. Since you got religion we haven't had one entire weekend together. Maybe if we spent some time together we could remember why we got married in the first place." He pushed her hand off his shoulder, stood up, and walked out on the patio.

She followed him angrily and said, "That's it, isn't it, Arthur? Sex! That's all you see in marriage."

"No, that isn't marriage, but it ought to be a part of it. It used to be."

"And tenderness used to be part of our marriage, too, and understanding, and respect. Where did they go?" she asked loudly.

"Lower your voice, Susan! The neighbors will hear," Arthur said in a near-whisper as he walked back inside.

"I don't care if they *do* hear! I'd like to tell somebody what a miserable husband I have! The great Dr. Wilson, cancer researcher and lecturer, from the National Cancer Institute. Ladies and gentlemen," she said loudly as she came inside and walked theatrically to the oak entertainment center, "one of the truly great intellects of our day is here in our midst. May I introduce to you Dr. Arthur Wilson."

Pretending to have a microphone in her hand, she played the part of a TV reporter. "Here in this cabinet, we have Dr. Wilson's most important research material." She opened the door and pointed to a pile of magazines. Picking up the top one, she held it up to the imaginary camera. "*Playboy* magazine!" Opening it to the centerfold, she said, "Dr. Wilson has carefully examined this patient and can say, without qualification, that she has no cancer—at least in the obvious parts."

"Give me that," he said loudly as he jerked the magazine out of her hand. He threw it back into the cabinet and shut the door.

"What's wrong, Arthur? Does the truth embarrass you? Doesn't it seem a bit childish, a bit immature, a bit unprofessional for a medical doctor to get his kicks from pornography?"

"I wouldn't have to if my wife acted like a lover once in a while!"

"And your wife would act like a lover if her husband acted like a real man once in a while!"

"Will you listen to yourself, Susan? Where is the loving attitude and patience Christians are supposed to have? If this is what being a Christian is all about, count me out." He turned away and walked to his recliner. Arthur knew he had hit home. The one thing Susan seemed to really care about was her newfound religious faith. It gave Arthur a sense of satisfaction to realize that she was still human and not a saint.

Susan ran out of the room crying tears of anger and pain. Feeling awkward and unsure of what to do, Arthur decided to go out for a drink. He stomped out to the garage and pushed the button on the garage-door opener. He got into his Lexus, backed out of the driveway, and squealed the tires as he drove off. The streetlights reflected brightly in the puddles and the rain made it hard to see through the windshield. He headed toward Washington on Wisconsin Avenue, driving too fast. There was a bar near the capitol where he and some old friends used to spend time together. *Who needs Susan and her God?* he thought bitterly.

Some minutes later, Arthur entered the neighborhood in which the bar was located. He had forgotten how run-down and depressing this part of town could be. Traffic was light and he felt vulnerable as he looked from side to side to see what kind of people were out on this stormy night. There were a few ordinary folk on the street, but it was apparent that the bizarre element had crept out of its den after dark.

As he turned the corner, a bedraggled woman appeared briefly in his headlights, then just as quickly she disappeared as he pulled out of the corner. A little further down the street, he saw two men walking together under one umbrella, each with his arm around the other, and Arthur felt a surge of disgust.

Upon passing the two men, Arthur spotted the Playtime Bar ahead on the left side of the street and turned into the parking lot. He carefully parked his car and, before opening the door, looked around nervously. He got out, locked the door, and walked quickly toward the entrance of the bar.

Arthur went inside, stamped the water off his shoes, then wiped his glasses dry. He was surprised at how seedy the old bar had gotten. Even the clientele seemed low class. He sat down at the bar as loud music muffled the voices at the tables and booths.

"What'll you have?" asked the bartender in a raspy voice.

"Scotch and water," he answered. The music, alcohol, and hollow laughter from across the room all blended and seemed to pull Arthur downward into a greater depression as he nursed his anger toward his wife and her God.

. . .

Susan had heard Arthur drive away into the night. She was bitterly angry at Arthur for his moodiness and unreasonable verbal attacks, yet she was genuinely sorry for blaming Arthur for throwing the ball that Jimmy had chased into the street. She knew Jimmy had missed an easy toss and run into the street before Arthur could stop him. She remembered hearing Arthur scream, "Jimmy! Stop!" But Arthur's warning was too late.

She had blamed Arthur then, but as time passed, she realized it had not been his fault and truly forgave him. But Arthur couldn't forgive himself. And his bitterness seemed to grow deeper year by year. Their marriage had begun dying the same night Jimmy was run over.

Susan went into the bathroom to get ready for bed. She began combing her hair. As she looked into the mirror she suddenly remembered the last time she had seen Jimmy; he had been standing on the bathroom stool and looking over her shoulder. He had touched her soft blond hair and said, "Mommy, I know why Daddy loves you. You're so pretty!" Then he had run out to play ball with Arthur.

She began to cry softly, with a sorrow too deep for words. *Oh God in heaven . . . I can't stand much more of this pain. Please show me what to do. Please, please, show me what to do.*

. . .

Arthur took another sip of Scotch. *Susan is right,* he thought. *Pornography is so immature. I'll get rid of those magazines. Maybe that will help Susan. Maybe she feels put down by the pictures. Surely she understands that it's just harmless fantasy. I don't know why I get such a kick out of them. Susan is a beautiful woman in her own right. She works hard at keeping her figure.*

Arthur looked down at his drink and sighed. He wondered how his parents had kept their home together for so many years.

Mom and Dad had such a great marriage. And Mom was no fitness freak, that's for sure. He thought back to his childhood and the warm security he had felt when his mother put her fleshy arms around him and gave him a hug. He remembered her silky old dress with the pink and purple flowers and her apron sprinkled with flour. He could almost smell the fresh bread she would take hot out of the oven and put on the table with a slab of butter and grape jelly.

He remembered how his father had made his mom feel like a queen in her own home—elegant, graceful, and loved. Arthur had always thought of his mother as beautiful until he went away to college. Everything changed then. When he came back home, the house seemed small and tacky. He realized his dad had been old-fashioned and ignorant and his mother was heavy and unkempt.

He remembered how ashamed he had been to invite his friends to visit his home. His mom had said, "Arthur, why don't you invite some of your friends to come home with you some weekend?" He had promised to do so, but never did. Until Susan.

Arthur blinked. The bar came back into focus. *Why would I want a home like Mom and Dad had? They were poor, uneducated, religious, and . . . happy. Yeah, they were happy.*

Arthur paid his bill and walked back out into the rain. *Maybe it wouldn't hurt to visit the church with Susan,* he thought. He started toward his car when suddenly two men lunged from the shadows at the edge of the parking lot. He tried to run, but before he could turn, one of the men hit him hard in the stomach, and he crumpled to his knees in pain.

"Give me your money, quick!" an ugly voice demanded. Arthur looked up into the barrel of the largest pistol he had ever seen. All his fantasies of heroism had focused on just such a moment. He had imagined how he would swing his head to one side, and with blinding speed, grab the pistol with his thumb between the firing pin and hammer. With a deft kick, he would disable the first man and fire with deadly accuracy at the fleeing partner. Arthur Mitty would be on the front page of the morning paper as a hero.

But now his courage drained into his shoes. *God, help me!* he prayed in terror. "Here, take my wallet," he groaned. "Just don't hurt me." The man grabbed the wallet, then swung the pistol viciously at the back of Arthur's head, knocking him unconscious to the asphalt. Laughing, the muggers ran off into the night.

A man came out of the bar a few moments later and saw Arthur lying in the parking lot face-down in a small pool of blood. He ran back inside and shouted to the bartender, "Louie! Call the police! There's a dead man in your parking lot!" Moments later, a police car swung into the lot, with lights flashing. The officer stepped out into the rain cautiously with his gun in hand and scanned the darkness with his flashlight. Seeing no one, he hurried to Arthur's side, knelt beside him, then spoke into his portable radio, calling for an ambulance.

. . .

Susan slept fitfully through the night. She kept dreaming hazy images of Arthur reaching out toward Jimmy as he ran in slow motion into the street. She tried to scream, but no sounds would come. She sat up suddenly, sweating with terror and grief. Then she cried herself to sleep again.

When she finally fell asleep, she was so exhausted she didn't hear the phone ring. A few minutes later it rang again, but Susan slept on. Morning finally came and Susan got up wearily. Her eyes were red and swollen. As her mind cleared, she began devising a plan. She knew what she would do. She quickly showered and put on her makeup. She fixed her hair, got dressed, and then packed a small suitcase. She closed it and carried it into the kitchen. Picking up the phone she dialed her office. No one was in yet, but she spoke when the answering machine came on: "Martha, this is Susan. I won't be in today. I have some personal matters to take care of. I'll give you a call later. Thanks."

She took a notepad from the cupboard and wrote a short message. She tore off the top sheet and put it on the dining room table where Arthur would be sure to see it. With a heavy heart, she grabbed the suitcase and walked out the door to the garage. She got in her car and drove in the morning traffic toward her church. *Pastor Miller can help me. I know he can*, she thought to herself.

. . .

Arthur woke up in the emergency room at the Washington Hospital Center. It took him a few moments to remember what had happened. His head was bandaged and pounded in pain with each heartbeat. He groaned loudly, and the privacy curtain was pulled back by a nurse. "Now maybe we can find out who you are and who we should call," she said.

Arthur gave her his name and telephone number. "Call my wife and let her know where I am. Her name is Susan."

The nurse left for a few moments. When she returned, she said, "Mr. Wilson, no one answers at that number. Are you sure you gave me the correct number?"

He repeated the number and she tried again, but still no one answered.

Arthur stayed overnight in the hospital. As the morning light filtered through the curtains, the doctor arrived to remove the bandage. Looking at the back of Arthur's head, he said, "Well, you have a nasty lump and a little gash, but the X-rays don't show anything serious. No concussion. I think you can go home as soon as the paperwork is done."

After the doctor left, Arthur called his office to let them know what had happened, and asked his secretary if she had heard from Susan. "No, she hasn't called, Dr. Wilson."

"Listen, Jenny," Arthur said, "could you bring some insurance papers over to the hospital and drive me back to my car? The guys who hit me took my wallet and I can't prove who I am or that I have insurance."

"Sure, Dr. Wilson. I'll be there as soon as possible." Arthur hung up the phone and slowly dressed himself. He wondered about Susan and why she hadn't called the office to see where he was.

About an hour later, Jenny arrived with the papers and drove Arthur back to the bar to get the Lexus. She wanted to ask him why he had been at a bar in this part of town, but decided she should mind her own business. "Are you sure you should be driving, Dr. Wilson?" Jenny asked.

"Oh, I'll be fine. Thanks for coming, Jenny. Tell George I won't be in to work until tomorrow. I still have quite a headache."

Arthur drove home, worried that something might have happened to Susan. She had been pretty upset when he left. As he drove up the driveway, he pressed the garage-door opener and the door slid up. Susan's car was gone.

He unlocked the door and went inside the house. "Susan?" he called, but there was no answer. *She must be at work,* he thought as he walked through the kitchen into the dining room. There on the table was a note. He picked it up and read it: "Arthur, I can't go on like this. I am so tired of the fighting. I have to get away for a while. I'll call you in a few days to let you know where I am. Susan."

For the first time in months Arthur really missed his wife. The house felt empty, and the note seemed cold and final. He wanted to apologize for having been such a jerk. *She'll be back,* he thought. *She'll get over this like she always does. I'll tell her I'm sorry and maybe I'll go to church with her once in a while.*

Arthur shook his head sadly and dropped the note on the table. It was still raining and the house was cold. A feeling of loneliness swelled in his chest like a physical growth and he quickly wiped away a tear as though someone might see it. He walked into the family room and sat in his recliner.

A sense of frustration and anger swept over him and he slapped the arm of the chair as he muttered a soft curse. *God,* he thought, *what has happened to my life? Why is there so much pain?* The faces of Jimmy and Susan came into focus at the front of his mind.

Muffled sobs began to shake his whole body. Tears streamed down his face and he swore again. *Curse you, God! You don't even exist, but I hate you for letting life be like this.* He tilted his head back and tried to breath deeply. Now he felt silly and a little guilty. *I'm sorry,* he thought. He shook his head as though to clear his mind. *Who am I apologizing to? Not God, that's for sure! Maybe Mom.*

He stood up quickly and walked to the hall closet to get his umbrella. *I have to get out of here.* He opened the side door and walked out on the patio and listened to the rain for a moment. *Let's take a walk, Susan,* he thought sarcastically. The walks down the quiet side streets near their home in Bethesda had been some of their favorite times together. *We did have some good times. Why did she have to go crazy over religion? I let her go to church. Why can't she leave me alone? Why is she so intent on converting me?*

He stepped out into the rain, forgetting to open the umbrella. He walked briskly down the street. The cool drops felt good, like an ointment for his soul. He tried to put the thoughts of Susan out of his mind by thinking about the experiment he was doing at the National Cancer Institute. His specialty was DNA and he was beginning to unravel some of the genetic code which he felt was responsible for the cancer that had killed his father. *I am a success. I am respected for my knowledge and my work. I speak at seminars all around the world. I make good money. Who needs Susan?*

He stepped in a puddle up to his ankle. *Oh God! Not my new shoes!* His mind went back to when he was nine years old, back in Winfield. He had been playing with a friend across town and was late for supper. Dad always got sore if he was late for supper, so he was running home as fast as he could. He didn't even notice the wet look on the sidewalk in front of him, nor the man kneeling next to it. He ran right into the wet cement, leaving his new cordovan loafers in the prints. The man stood up and began screaming at him, "You little creep! Look what you've done! I ought to . . ."

Little Arthur began crying. "I'm sorry, mister. I didn't see it. I was in a hurry, and now my dad's gonna kill me, especially when he sees my shoes! Can I have them back?"

The man was still red-faced with anger, but when he realized Arthur hadn't meant to do it, he started to calm down. "Stop crying, kid," he said, "I'll get your shoes. Here. And next time, watch where you're going. It'll take me an hour to fix this."

"I'm sorry. Really I am, mister! Can I go now?" And he ran off carrying two gray loafers, leaving cement footprints all the way down the street.

When Arthur arrived home, he sneaked around the side of the house to the faucet. He quietly washed the cement off his shoes and tiptoed toward the garage to look for a rag to dry them off. Just then his dad came out on the front porch and yelled, "Arthur! Where are you, boy? It's supper time! Oh, there you are. Where have you been—and what have you done to your shoes?!"

"I'm sorry, Dad," he cried. He told his dad what had happened, and to his surprise, his dad began to chuckle and shake his head.

"Just try to wash as much off as possible, and come in to eat. We'll dry them off as best we can and put some saddle soap on them to keep them soft. Don't worry, Arthur. It was an accident."

Arthur knew his dad couldn't afford any more new shoes this year. Money was so tight his dad had taken a second job as janitor of their little Baptist church down the street.

His mom and dad had attended the First Baptist Church of Winfield for as long as Arthur could remember. Sunday morning, Sunday night, Wednesday night—every time there was a meeting his folks were there, and so was Arthur.

"Why do I have to go to Sunday school, Dad?" he once asked.

His father looked at him with genuine surprise. "Because we are Christians, Arthur. We go to church to learn more about the Bible and what God wants us to do and to be."

"But my teacher is so boring! All she ever does is read out of the teacher's manual and ask us silly questions."

"I know it can be boring, Arthur. Sometimes I feel that way about my class. But I still think it is important for us to go. Regular attendance is part of self-discipline." So they went, week after week, year after year.

"I hated Sunday school!" Arthur said out loud, and the distant memories faded back into the haze. He was nearly home, and his clothing was soaked. As he walked up the street, he felt a chill coming on. The rain was falling harder.

When Arthur got home, he knelt before the fireplace and started the fire. After a few minutes, the flames crackled merrily. He poured himself another drink and sat in his chair, his mind drifting to the past once again.

. . .

Susan drove into the parking lot of Community Bible Church. The building was plain but functional. There were no stained-glass windows or fancy columns, but the surroundings were attractively landscaped and well maintained. The church had not yet opened, so Susan parked near the entrance, turned off the engine, and listened to the soft patter of the rain on the roof as she leaned back in the seat, closed her eyes, and prayed, waiting for Pastor Miller to arrive.

FAITH FOR OUR PERSONAL LIVES

1

Faith to Change the Way We Think

PSYCHOLOGISTS ARE FOND OF asking their clients, "How does that make you feel?" They may be referring to a statement by an insensitive mate, a suggestion from "controlling" parents, the irritating behavior of an uncontrollable child, or the painful discovery of a troubling secret. The question still rings out, "How does that make you *feel*?" Rarely do therapists ask, "How are you *thinking* about this?" or "What do you *believe* God would have you *do*?"

Jennifer[2] visited her psychotherapist complaining of depression. He quickly and expertly analyzed her problem as suppressed anger and encouraged her to give vent to her feelings. She learned to scream and to curse so that she could eventually *feel* better.

Brenda was instructed by her Christian psychologist to beat a pillow as she visualized her parents so she could rid herself of inner hostilities. This, she was told, would help her to *feel* better.

Mary is part of a group that focuses on childhood sexual abuse. She wasn't even aware she had been abused until she underwent therapy for low self-esteem. Her support group told her that she needed to open up and feel her pain. When she questioned the memories she had "recovered" in therapy, the other group members told her she was in denial and that she needed to "let it all out" so that she would *feel* better.

As the tragic old song goes, "Feelings . . . nothing more than feelings . . . ." For some, life is nothing more than feelings. For these individuals, objective facts are of less concern than subjective sensations or emotions. As one incompetent therapist said regarding his client's questionable memories of abuse, "I don't care whether her memories are true or not. All I care about is how she feels. I'm not a detective. All that matters is whether it is true to *her*."

Dr. Tana Dineen, a licensed psychologist and former head of a psychiatric care unit, disagrees. She writes, "Absorbed in their own world of feelings, and believing that they both should have and do have the right to feel better, psychologically-prone persons accept psychological explanations of their emotions and adopt psychological suggestions of how to free themselves from these feelings."[3]

Psychology feeds the erroneous concept that feeling is all that matters, then proceeds to make a person feel worse while promising to eventually make him feel better. And even when it occasionally succeeds in making a person *feel* better, psychotherapy is rarely able to help a person to *be* a better person.

Realizing that ultimately, therapy doesn't actually make a person better, Dr. Dineen has left her profession. She now believes psychotherapy creates victims who become patients, resulting in more profits for the clinics. She wisely suggests, "Would it not be better to let them turn to God or to each other? But grieving and mourning are no longer within the domain of either family or religion. They have been bought up by the Psychology Industry."[4]

THE PROCESS OF THOUGHT

What we *are* determines how we *think*. How we *think* determines how we *act*. How we *act* determines how we *feel*, and because the primary focus of modern living is on how we feel, we would do well to consider the process and consequences of our thought lives.

The process of human thought has fascinated priests, philosophers, and scientists since the beginning of time. Priests have sought to guide human thinking in order to lead people to an awareness and worship of God. Philosophers have tried to analyze the implications of the thinking process as they attempt to make sense of our existence. Some scientists have reduced the definition of all thinking to organized electrochemical impulses within the nervous system—a biomechanical process explained by evolutionary theory.

John B. Watson, for example, "rejected the concept of 'mind,' believing it was useless to speculate on the question of whether such a thing existed."[5] As the founder of behaviorism, Watson adopted a mechanistic view of human behavior— a view that assumes "we are at the mercy of stresses and strains imposed by the environment and by processes built innately into our nervous system and other biological structures."[6]

Watson's concept was based not upon genuine science, but upon his atheistic philosophy which assumed that the mind and the brain are synonymous, that thought is simply a description of electrochemical brain activity, and that free will is merely behavior under the control of the brain. According to this view, the soul or spirit of man is nonsense.

Others, however, have acknowledged that there is more to human consciousness than electrical and chemical activity. "Seymour Kety, a leading investigator of the biological foundations of behavior . . . maintains that biology is not able with its tools alone to unravel the mysteries of human personality and experience."[7]

Another prominent brain scientist, John Eccles, says that understanding the brain as a physical entity "doesn't explain me, or human choice, delight, courage, or compassion. I think we must go beyond . . . . There is something apart from all the electricity and chemistry we can measure."[8]

What *is* that "something" which stands apart from the physical reality of the brain? When God is removed from the equation, there is no satisfying explanation for human consciousness, emotions, will, or thought. Personal experiences, observations, sensations, reasonings, and subjective feelings force most people to acknowledge that there is a nonmaterial component to human existence which cannot be examined or explained by scientific method. There is something *spiritual.*

Still, mankind is uncomfortable with the concept of God because acknowledging His existence requires accountability for thoughts, words, and actions coupled with the uncomfortable fear of future judgment. Not willing to accept the reality of a righteous God, man looks for an alternative explanation of human thought and behavior.

THE NEW EXPERTS ON THE INNER MAN

As a direct consequence of rejecting God, a new hybrid of expert on human thought has arisen. Psychologists and psychiatrists have assumed the mantles of all three of their historical predecessors—priests, philosophers, and scientists—and have established themselves as the experts on the inner man (mind/heart/soul/spirit/emotions).

Claiming near-divine ability to understand, interpret, and heal the spiritual part of man, these new high-priest social scientists have led the way toward functional atheism. They skillfully shuffle the theological, philosophical, and scientific cards into one new deck, making up the rules of their mind-game as they move through the corridors of power.

It is little wonder, then, that psychology is the most popular major in many colleges, universities, Bible institutes, and seminaries. There is an intoxicating sense of power in believing we are able to explain why our relatives and neighbors act the way they do. We comfort ourselves, thinking that we will finally understand and cure our own dysfunctions by studying the theories of

Freud, Jung, Skinner, and Rogers, and yet the final resolution always seems just beyond our grasp. We find that the heart of man is secretive and illusive and cannot be measured nor analyzed by scientific methods.

In contrast to psychology's popular but mistaken image of omniscience, the Bible tells us that the human heart is unavailable for empirical study. Jeremiah writes, "The heart is deceitful above all things, and desperately wicked: who can know it?" (Jeremiah 17:9, KJV). The answer, of course, is found in the following verse: "I the LORD search the heart and examine the mind, to reward a man according to his conduct, according to what his deeds deserve" (Jeremiah 17:10). Only God is able to understand the inner man.[9]

It is ironic, then, that many Christians have accepted the idea that psychology is better able to deal with the soul of man than the truths of Scripture alone and have come to believe that to find true healing for our inner wounds we must integrate psychological "findings" with biblical principles.

I recently sat in the office of the president of a well-known conservative seminary. He was upset with me for having reported on our national radio broadcast, "Return to the Word," that the seminary was moving away from biblical orthodoxy as psychology progressively displaced the role of biblical theology in its curricula. Our conversation went something like this:

"You're saying that we're becoming liberal," the seminary president said in a hurt tone of voice. "I assure you, that is not the case!"

"Well, then," I replied, "let me ask you a question. Do you believe that the Bible is the inspired, inerrant, and infallible Word of God?"

Without hesitation he firmly replied, "Absolutely."

"Let me ask another question," I continued. "Do you believe that the Bible is sufficient to meet every inner need of man?"

He hesitated for a moment, then with a tinge of embarrassment replied, "We believe that it is thoroughly sufficient for salvific issues."

"And what about issues of sanctification?" I pressed. "Is the Bible, by itself, sufficient to bring the believer to wholeness—to heal the deepest wounds of the human heart?"

He looked down. After a long pause, he finally looked up at me and said, "No. We also need other truths that God has revealed through nature and research."

Having admitted that his institution no longer believes that God has provided sufficient information in His Word to sanctify the believer, the president's stated position is that psychology is *essential* for the healing of the inner man. In terms of biblical sanctification, this sincere leader of a formerly conservative seminary has become a practical atheist. And worse, yet, he was unwilling to consider the biblical alternative or to even think it through.

THE THOUGHT LIFE

What does it mean to *think*? The very concept of thinking implies the existence of intelligence, but even that is an illusive notion. One encyclopedia states:

> Because no one can observe or measure the mind as such, one can only infer a person's intelligence from his or her behavior in various situations. No consensus exists among psychologists on the definition of intelligence. . . .[10]

Yet it is in the mind that we are aware of existence itself. "I think, therefore I am," French philosopher Descartes wrote, thereby acknowledging the existence of the physical universe which he had come to doubt. At one point, he had questioned the reality of existence and rational thought.

> For example, he asked himself whether he could be certain he was not dreaming. His most powerful skeptical hypothesis, that there is an evil genius trying to deceive him, challenges not only the belief that the

physical world exists, but also belief in simple statements of fact, and thus would seem to call into question the validity of reason itself. But not even an evil genius could deceive someone into believing falsely that he existed.[11]

The mere reality of existence does not explain for us what it means "to think." We intuitively understand that thought is the process by which we control our bodies and interact with the physical world, yet we are at a loss to fully comprehend the very entity required to think—our own mind. It is as though a microscope were called upon to examine itself but cannot. Rather, another tool separate from the microscope is necessary to examine it. Confused? *Think* about it: Without a mirror or reflective surface of some kind, you would not even know what *you* look like.

It is even more difficult to know what we actually *are* on the inside. That is why our thinking must be guided by a source outside and superior to ourselves.

Still, what does it mean to *think*? The dictionary defines thinking as:

1. To have or formulate in the mind.
2. To decide by reasoning, reflection, or pondering.
3. To judge or regard; look upon.
4. To believe; suppose.
5. To expect; hope or to intend.
6. To call to mind; remember.
7. To visualize; imagine.
8. To devise or evolve; invent.
9. To bring into a given condition by mental preoccupation.
10. To concentrate one's thoughts on.[12]

To verbally define thinking hardly clears up the issue for us, does it? We need to know in *practical* terms what thinking does to our personal reality and experience. We need to understand how our thoughts affect our actions, attitudes, relationships, beliefs, day-to-day lives, and destiny.

What Does the Bible Say?

Evil Thoughts   What does the Bible say about our thought life? The first use of the word *thought* is in Genesis 6:5: "The LORD saw how great man's wickedness on the earth had become, and that every inclination of the thoughts of his heart was only evil all the time."

These are strong words, but they explain why we humans are inclined to the "dysfunctions" we have identified and labeled and why, as a result, we feel so miserable. The way we *are* determines the way we *think*. The way we *think* determines the way we *act*. The way we *act* determines the way we *feel*. *But the way we feel doesn't tell us much about anything except that something is terribly wrong.*

Our natural inclination toward evil is not necessarily passive. According to the psalmist, our human pride leads us toward practical atheism: "In his pride the wicked does not seek him; in all his thoughts there is no room for God" (Psalm 10:4).

Instead, we fill our conscious moments with sounds and visual images that distract us from perceiving the reality of our miserable condition apart from God. We flood our minds with entertainment, books, videos, games, comedy, sports, and music—none of which are innately evil, but all of which serve to divert our attention away from our misery.

If the only result of these diversions were the inordinate waste of time, we might not need to be so concerned. But the consequences are much greater than that. *Much* greater.

Dark and Foolish Thoughts   The tragic consequences of a person leaving God out of his thought life are intellectual darkness and emotional confusion. The apostle Paul wrote about the results of willfully ignoring God: "Although they knew God, they neither glorified him as God nor gave thanks to him, but their thinking became futile and their foolish hearts were darkened" (Romans 1:21). What follows is a downward spiral of ever-increasing depravity: "Furthermore, since they did not think it worthwhile to retain the knowledge of God, he gave them over to a depraved mind, to do what ought not to be done" (Romans 1:28).

What sort of consequences follow the intentional rejection of God? According to Paul, those "who suppress the truth" (verse 18) deny the obvious facts of creation (verses 19-20) and thereby become "fools" (verse 22). Evolutionists, of course, fit this description because they must employ an endless variety of pseudoscientific mental gymnastics to support their unscientific theories.

Impure Thoughts The personal consequences, however, extend far beyond the intellectual hypocrisy of evolutionism. There are moral and physical repercussions of suppressing the truth: "sexual impurity" and the "degrading of their bodies with one another" (verse 24), "shameful lusts" (verse 26), and unnatural sexual relations (verses 26-27). Homosexuality, lesbianism, and other such abominations are among the repulsive fruits of removing God from man's thoughts. The physical diseases that accompany these "indecent acts" (verse 27) are the "due penalty for their perversion" (verse 27). AIDS is no accident of nature.

Pornography is a fitting symbol for the decadence of our day and it contributes to the destruction of marriage, family, and society. For those who deny God, there is no convincing argument against the feeding of lustful passions. What is surprising, however, is the growing acceptance of pornography among Christians.

A radio station manager once told me that hotels and restaurants look forward to the annual convention of the National Religious Broadcasters because the sale of liquor and pornographic movies is so high when the conference attendees are in town. In another case, after a large convention of youth pastors, it was reported that the in-room rental of pornographic videos was at an all-time high.

Radio and television talk shows discuss "sexual addictions" and suggest that the cure is long-term intensive therapy. This is just as true of "Christian" psychological programs as secular ones. I listened one night to a former pastor who had become "addicted to pornography" explain on national television how he had been caught up in "moral indiscretions" that had ruined his ministry and nearly destroyed his marriage. He and his wife now speak around the country about building strong family foundations. I winced as this seemingly sincere man spoke the neoevangelical psychobabble of "addictions" and "indiscretions," wishing he would simply alert his audience to the fact that trust and purity are being destroyed by old-fashioned lust and adultery.

Are we really to believe that we simply *can't* keep from immoral thoughts and behavior? Are these truly addictions over which we have no control? If so, then the Bible is mistaken when it says that "no temptation has seized you except what is common to man. And God is faithful; he will not let you be tempted beyond what you can bear. But when you are tempted, he will also provide a way out so that you can stand up under it" (1 Corinthians 10:13).

In their thoughts, many Christians have become morally impure and have acted as though God does not exist when it comes to the realities of the sexual aspects of life.

A professing Christian man came to my office asking for advice about a relationship with a woman he loved. "I began dating her when she was married yet separated from her husband," he said. "We prayed together and went to church together because my faith is so important to me.

"We have broken up and gotten back together several times, but recently I've discovered that she has been unfaithful to me—with my best friend! Now I know that she is extremely promiscuous. She's been with at least ten men that I know of this year. But I can't get her out of my mind. I really believe that God will get a hold of her heart and maybe we will get back together someday."

Ignorant of the Scriptures, this baby Christian could not see the irony of the situation. He was sexually involved with a married woman and felt betrayed because she was now unfaithful to him as well!

"Where is her husband?" I asked.

"Well, their divorce was final about a month ago. What do you think I should do?"

I leaned forward and said, "You need to run away from her as fast as you can." I opened my Bible to the book of Proverbs and read these words to him:

> These commands are a lamp, this teaching is a light, and the corrections of discipline are the way to life, keeping you from the immoral woman, from the smooth tongue of the wayward wife. Do not lust in your heart after her beauty or let her captivate you with her eyes, for the prostitute reduces you to a loaf of bread, and the adulteress preys upon your very life (Proverbs 6:23-26).

I don't think he had ever read that passage before. He sat back in his chair, nodded, and said, "That's her exactly." Now he knew the truth, and it was up to him whether or not he would obey God's Word.

When I was a child living in a small midwestern farm town, my parents would never go to a movie theater, even though in those days the films were relatively innocent. Today, however, Christians see no compromise in their walk with God when they go to R-rated movies that contain cursing, vulgar language, and repeated scenes of explicit immorality. And those few Christians who worry that their testimony might be damaged in the eyes of friends and relatives if they are caught at X-rated movies can view pornographic videos in the privacy of their own homes. Cable and satellite television have made vile images instantly available and the internet can deliver every imaginable perversion through the phone lines onto the computer screens of those who claim to be followers of Christ.

Why are humans drawn toward unfaithfulness and sexual impurity? Jesus said that this ugly tendency is rooted in our own hearts: "For from within, out of men's hearts, come evil thoughts, sexual immorality, theft, murder, adultery" (Mark 7:21). All of these destructive practices come not from what has happened *to* us, as our society has come to believe, but what has happened *in* us.

You Are What You Think

What does the thought life have to do with our mental, emotional, and spiritual health? *Everything.* You probably know the expression, "You are what you eat." It would be more accurate to say, "You are what you *think.*" Paul wrote to Titus, "To the pure, all things are pure, but to those who are corrupted and do not believe, nothing is pure. In fact, both their minds and consciences are corrupted" (Titus 1:15).

How we think determines whether our marriages grow more secure as the years pass or end in divorce. It controls whether our business ventures prosper or fold. It strengthens friendships or causes them to wither away. It controls the way we relate to fellow-workers, neighbors, relatives, and friends.

The way we think about God, His character, and His plan for mankind will affect our values, behavior, relationships, and how we deal with the pressures of living in an imperfect world. Some Christians, experiencing minor discomfort and inconvenience, fall apart emotionally and seek out psychiatric help. Rather than learning how to retrain their minds, they prefer to numb their pain with Prozac. Others, however, find consistent comfort and relief by taking "captive every thought to make it obedient to Christ" (2 Corinthians 10:5).

May I ask you what you are filling your mind with? Are you saturating your thoughts with the colorful seductive images of television as you surf through the channels? Are you reading sensual romance novels, creating discontent in your heart toward your mate? Are you lingering on pornographic pictures you purchased off the magazine rack or downloaded from the internet, inflaming lustful passions? If so, you cannot please our heavenly Father, who tells us to be pure.

Peter writes to us:

> Prepare your minds for action; be self-controlled; set your hope fully on the grace to be given you when Jesus Christ is revealed. As obedient children, do not conform to the evil desires you had when you lived in ignorance. But just as he who called you is holy, so be holy in all you do; for it is written: "Be holy, because I am holy" (1 Peter 1: 13-16).

Some Christians have come to believe that it is impossible to live a pure life in our modern age. They have accepted the widely held view that it is necessary to provide sex education and contraceptives for our children because it is unreasonable to expect them—even Christian adolescents and teens—to refrain from sexual activity until marriage. But the Bible tells us to prepare our minds, be self-controlled, and be holy like our Father in heaven.

It would be of little surprise to see members of liberal churches deny the power of God's Word, but now there are many Christians in conservative Bible churches who have bought into the hopeless psychological theories of behavior which tell us that we have no choice in how we behave and that deliverance from our mental dungeons is to be found in professional counseling and psychoactive medications.

David writes, "May the words of my mouth and the meditation of my heart be pleasing in your sight, O LORD, my Rock and my Redeemer" (Psalm 19:14). That's a wonderful goal, but *how* can we retrain our minds in this sin-polluted age in which we live?

How We Can Change Our Thoughts

Do you remember the old gospel song that said, "Turn your eyes upon Jesus/Look full in His wonderful face/And the things of earth will grow strangely dim/In the light of His glory and grace"? That's exactly what we are told to do in three vital passages in the New Testament.

In Colossians 3:1-2 we read, "Since, then, you have been raised with Christ, *set your hearts on things above*, where Christ is seated at the right hand of God. *Set your minds on things above*, not on earthly things" (emphasis added). In direct contradiction of the psychological counsel that tells us to dredge up the pain of the past, Paul instructs believers to focus their emotions and intellect on Christ and eternity rather than the troubles of this life.

The writer of Hebrews echoes this inner-healing principle when he says, "Holy brothers, who share in the heavenly calling, *fix your thoughts on Jesus*" (Hebrews 3:1, emphasis added).

Hebrews 12 expands on this concept. Read it carefully:

> Since we are surrounded by such a great cloud of witnesses, let us throw off everything that hinders and the sin that so easily entangles, and let us run with perseverance the race marked out for us. *Let us fix our eyes on Jesus,* the author and perfecter of our faith, who for the joy set before him endured the cross, scorning its shame, and sat down at the right hand of the throne of God. *Consider him* who endured such opposition from sinful men, so that you will not grow weary and lose heart (Hebrews 12:1-3, emphasis added).

In the spiritual battle for inner peace, we are told how to complete the course. Note the italicized words in the passage above: "Let us fix our eyes on Jesus. . . . Consider him." Why? "So that you will not grow weary and lose heart."

Weariness and discouragement are the preconditions for depression and defeat. God has given us the answer for depression in Christ. Do you want to find healing for your emotions, your mind, your spirit? You do not have to drain your financial resources to rent a friend, spending years in therapy. Instead, you can retrain your thoughts to experience daily peace and joy.

The process is found in Philippians 4:4-9:

Rejoice in the Lord always. I will say it again:
Rejoice! Let your gentleness be evident to all. The Lord
is near. Do not be anxious about anything, but in everything, by prayer and petition, with thanksgiving, present
your requests to God. And the peace of God, which
transcends all understanding, will guard your hearts and
your minds in Christ Jesus.

Finally, brothers, whatever is true, whatever is noble,
whatever is right, whatever is pure, whatever is lovely,
whatever is admirable—if anything is excellent or praise-
worthy—think about such things. Whatever you have
learned or received or heard from me, or seen in me—put
it into practice. And the God of peace will be with you.[13]

Sometimes crude individuals will ask one another, "How's
your love life?" The suggestion, of course, is sexually oriented.
But there is a far more significant question we Christians should
ask ourselves as we examine whether or not we are acting like
practical atheists: "How is my *thought* life?"

Do you want to experience genuine victory in your day-to-
day walk with God? Are you hungry to find real peace and contentment in a world full of confusion and misery? Do you want
to strengthen and vitalize your weakened faith? Set your heart
and mind on things above. Fix your thoughts and eyes on Jesus.
It's all in how and what we think.

Rebel Heart

Still alone at home, Arthur sat in the darkened room, drinking a
cocktail he had made to take his mind off his loneliness. He
began thinking about the faith he had once had as a child and
how he had gradually been freed from its superstitious nonsense. Images of his childhood flitted through his mind.

Arthur had been interested in science since second grade, when
his teacher showed a film about dinosaurs. There was something

fascinating about the huge beasts that had roamed the earth millions of years ago roaring and crashing through dense tropical forests. He was amazed when the teacher told them that the dinosaurs were distant relatives to people and that all living things had come from one common ancestor.

One night, at supper, his dad asked, "What did you learn at school today, Arthur?"

"I learned that we evolved from fish and dinosaurs."

"We what?"

"Evolved—you know, we came up from dinosaurs. But don't worry, Dad, that was millions of years ago."

"Do you really *believe* that, Arthur? What does the Bible say?"

"I don't know. What?"

"It says that God created man. Do you remember the story of Adam and Eve?"

"Oh, yeah. Now I do. But the teacher says we evolved."

"Well, your teacher is wrong, Arthur." And that settled that . . . for a while. But the older Arthur grew, the more he questioned his parents' simple faith. They didn't seem to have any solid answers. They just believed.

For a time Arthur still attended church with his parents, but he found Sunday School unspeakably boring. He felt ugly with his new glasses and he tried to divert attention from his awkward appearance by being the class clown. He managed to liven each session with witty comments and pranks, but Mrs. Frazier, his eighth-grade teacher, didn't fully appreciate his imagination. Once, when she was trying to tell the story of Daniel in the lions' den, she asked, "Who can tell me why the lions didn't eat Daniel?" Arthur's hand shot up. "Because they didn't like kosher food!" The kids all laughed, but Mrs. Frazier didn't see anything funny about his joke, and she made him sit in the back of the room. "When you think you can be serious, Arthur, you may join us again."

But Arthur didn't want to be serious. Nor did he want to join the others. He pushed his glasses back up on his nose and doodled in his Sunday school quarterly with the half-pencil he had taken from the communion rack the week before. When Mrs. Frazier saw what he was doing, she was furious. She grabbed him by his ear and marched him to the superintendent's office. Arthur was embarrassed as the other kids saw him being dragged down the hallway like a prisoner on his way to execution.

Mrs. Frazier pulled him into the Sunday school office and complained, "I can't teach a class as long as Arthur Wilson keeps disrupting it every week!"

"I'll talk with his parents," said old Mr. Phillips, frowning at Arthur through glasses so thick his eyes seemed like gigantic saucers.

Turning to Arthur and shaking his head, he said, "Arthur, Arthur. What are we going to do with you? Your parents aren't going to like this, you know."

No kidding, thought Arthur as he pushed his glasses higher up on the bridge of his nose with his forefinger. *I thought they'd just love it.*

When Arthur's parents came to get him after church, his mom looked like she had been crying, and his dad was angry. "Let's go, son," was all his dad said. Arthur knew he was in trouble. When his dad was this quiet, he was really mad, and a spanking was inevitable.

To Arthur's surprise, when they got home, his dad said, "Let's take a walk, son." They walked down the sidewalk, under the tall old elm trees, toward the city park, three blocks away.

"Son, I'm disappointed in you. You know better than to embarrass us at church. But worse than that, you were making fun of the Bible."

"I wasn't trying to make fun of the Bible, Dad," Arthur said meekly. "It's just that Mrs. Frazier is so dry. I could give a better lesson."

"Maybe so, Arthur, but you showed disrespect for Mrs. Frazier and I can't allow that." They walked on for a few minutes in silence. When they got to the park, Mr. Wilson sat down on a bench in the shade. Arthur sat down on the far end, his head hanging, and scuffed his shoes into the dust.

"Arthur," his dad said softly. "You're fourteen now and you know right from wrong. You're not too big to spank, but I don't think it's called for this time. What I expect you to do is to apologize to Mrs. Frazier and the class, and behave yourself from now on. Do you understand?"

"Gosh, Dad, couldn't you just spank me and get it over with?"

"No, Arthur, I think it's time you grew up and faced your problems."

Arthur stood up and faced his father defiantly. "I won't do it! I'm not going to apologize to her. And I'm not going to go to Sunday school anymore, either!" He turned and ran toward the town square.

His father stood up, pointed at Arthur and started to shout, but stopped. His shoulders slumped as he slowly turned and walked back toward home.

. . .

That day was a turning point in Arthur's life. He made up his mind that he wouldn't go to church any longer. "Maybe you can force me to go, Dad, but you can't make me listen."

"I'm not going to force you to go, Arthur. If you won't go willingly because we ask you to, we won't make you. But you're breaking your mother's heart."

Arthur was tall and gangly by the time he was in high school, and his folks had a hard time keeping him in clothes that fit. His pants seemed to shrink higher above his ankles every day. In addition to the glasses he hated, he now had to deal with the humiliation of wearing braces to straighten his teeth. He resented being automatically classified as a nerd because of his appearance and his intellect. *Is it my fault I'm smart and my folks are poor?* he thought as he walked to class.

"Hey, Nerdbreath!" Bob Jackson yelled at him one day. "When are you gonna buy some new clothes? Or are knickers coming back in style?" All the kids laughed, and Arthur's face turned red. Bob was on the football and basketball teams and held the school track record in three events. His dad owned the main grocery store downtown.

Bob hated Arthur for some reason. Maybe it was because Arthur had straight A's and Bob's grades were so poor that he barely remained eligible for sports. One night after school, as Arthur was walking home, he saw Bob and his pack of friends lounging at the corner ahead. Arthur knew they wouldn't let him pass without a humiliating encounter, so he crossed over to the other side of the street, hoping they wouldn't notice him. But Bob saw him.

"Hey, Chromeface! You scared of us or something?" Bob motioned for his friends to cross over, some in front and some behind Arthur. Arthur looked around and saw that there was no place to run. So he stood there as Bob approached with a wicked grin on his face.

"What do you think we ought to do to Four-Eyes here? Should we beat him up?"

"Let's tear out his braces!" little Tommy Schier squeaked as he stood safely behind Bob.

"Naw, let's pants him," Ron Baker suggested.

"I tell you what, Nerdness," Bob said as he poked Arthur in the chest with his huge fingers. "You and I are gonna fight. Right now."

Arthur's eyes became huge with fear and he felt a rush of adrenaline hit his bloodstream. His voice shook with terror as he said, "I don't want to fight you, Bob. Plus, you have your whole gang here. What kind of guts does that take? Are you afraid you'll need six guys to take me on? Why not fight me by yourself?"

Arthur had no idea where those words came from and immediately he thought, *I'm dead.*

Now it was Bob's turn to squirm. He couldn't sic the pack on Arthur without looking like a coward himself. A memory hit Arthur at that moment: it was back in seventh grade. Bob was sitting next to him holding his geography book when his nose suddenly gushed out a stream of blood, for no apparent reason. The teacher had quickly run to the sink for paper towels and held them to Bob's bloody nose as she sent a student to get the school nurse.

Arthur knew he had only one chance. When Bob walked forward to shove him again, Arthur suddenly swung his right fist with all his might. He connected right at the base of Bob's nose. Bob stumbled backward, stunned by the unexpected blow, and then . . . Old Faithful! Bob's nose erupted with twin geysers of blood, covering his new white shirt with crimson.

Bob was bleeding so profusely that he became frightened. "Oh!" he cried. "Oh, I'm bleeding! Get me home, guys!" But his friends started walking away, shaking their heads. Bob ran off toward home, leaving a trail of blood like a wounded deer. Little Tommy Schier came over to Arthur, patted him jovially on the back, and said, "I knew you could do it, Arthur! Nice hit!"

Bob never pushed Arthur around after that. He told everyone that Arthur had gotten him with a sneaky punch, but he never asked for a rematch. And neither did Arthur.

. . .

As his interest in science grew, Arthur became fully convinced that his parents were wrong about God, the Bible, and science. His teachers seemed so wise and were able to give solid answers to his questions. They had charts and pictures, science books and fossils, and the full weight of scholastic authority. His parents seemed so weak, ignorant, and old-fashioned.

When Arthur was in eleventh grade, an evangelist visited the Baptist church. One evening as Arthur came into the living room, his father put down the newspaper and said, "Arthur, I have a challenge for you."

"What kind of challenge?" Arthur replied defensively.

"I dare you to come hear the evangelist tomorrow night. He's speaking on why he believes in creation and not evolution. If you're so sure man has evolved, why don't you come listen?"

"All right, Dad," he said. "I'll come. It ought to be good for a laugh."

It was late September, but the old auditorium was hot that night, and it was packed with people. Arthur had never seen the church so full. He was surprised to see a classmate, Calvin Johnson, sitting in the third pew from the front. "I'm going to sit with Cal," Arthur told his mother as he nodded toward his friend.

"All right, Arthur, but you behave!"

"I will, Mom." *What does she think I'm going to do in church—smoke?* He walked down to the third row and climbed over two little kids and sat next to Cal.

"Hi, Cal! How long have you been coming to church here?"

"About a year, now. I didn't know you went to church, Arthur."

"I don't usually. But my folks come every week."

The song leader stepped to the pulpit to begin the service. "Let's all stand and turn to hymn 478, 'This Is My Father's World.' Let's all really put ourselves into it!"

As the congregation sang, Arthur didn't want to admit it to himself, but he found himself enjoying the service. It had been a long time since he had been in church. He had forgotten the familiar sounds of creaking pews, the old piano, the rustling of pages as people opened the hymnals, and the heavy breathing of old Bud Ellis. Bud kind of whistled through his nose when he breathed, and you could hear him five rows back.

The choir got up to sing, and Arthur noticed in the second row a new girl about his age. *I've never seen her before,* Arthur thought. "How long has she been coming?" he asked Cal.

"I'm not sure. About a month, I think. She's cute, isn't she?"

"Cute? She's gorgeous!"

When the choir had finished their song, the pastor came to the pulpit. "As you all know, Dr. Robert Arnold was a biologist before becoming an evangelist. He earned his doctorate in biology from Harvard University before he found Christ. He taught for several years at Gordon College. Now, folks, it costs money to pay for transportation and lodging for a guest speaker, and we want to have enough to give a special love offering to this man of God. So, before Dr. Arnold comes to speak, as the choir sings one more special number, the ushers will receive the offering. Please give generously. Thanks."

Arthur always hated the offering. He was embarrassed when the plate came by him and he passed it on without putting anything in. But he wasn't about to give his hard-earned money to a preacher!

When the choir finished, Dr. Arnold walked to the pulpit and began to speak.

"Evolution is a theory, but it is more than that. It is a religion." He had Arthur's full attention. "What you believe about the origin of the universe and all life forms is more than an intellectual exercise, because what you believe about evolution will ultimately determine what you believe about God, man, sin, salvation, and eternity. It will affect your ethical decisions and your morality.

"Huxley once wrote, 'It is clear that the doctrine of evolution is directly antagonistic to that of Creation. . . . Evolution, if consistently accepted, makes it impossible to believe the Bible.'

"H.G. Wells wrote, 'If all animals and man evolved. . . then there were no first parents, no Eden, no Fall. And if there had been no Fall, then the entire historic fabric of Christianity—the story of the first sin and the reason for atonement—collapsed like a house of cards.'

"What is this doctrine—as Huxley rightly calls it—the doctrine of evolution? Well, to put it in nonscientific terms, evolution is a general theory that states that all living things arose by a naturalistic, mechanistic process from a single living source which itself arose by a similar process from a dead, inanimate world."

Arthur hadn't expected this. He thought the preacher would quote a few verses from Genesis and tell people not to question the Bible. This man sounded like he was familiar with scientific ideas.

Dr. Arnold continued, "Aaron Wasserman wrote in his book, *Biology*, 'The present scientific explanation is that life came from an aggregation of non-living substances, by means of random events that brought the right combinations of chemicals and energy together.' Please note Mr. Wasserman's term 'random events.' We will see that this vague concept is the foundation upon which the temple of evolution stands."

Arthur was surprised to see people taking notes. *Mom and Dad will never be able to follow this*, Arthur thought.

"Why is evolution accepted almost universally as a fact instead of a theory? There are several reasons. The media promotes evolution as a proven fact. In an article on evolution in *Time* magazine, anthropologist Thomas Leakey stated, 'It now seemed indisputable that modern man had evolved from more primitive ancestors.' *Reader's Digest* condensed an article from *Tuesday Magazine,* in which it says, '. . . from the evidence it seems clear that modern man evolved on earth. . . .'

"When people on television report on the creationist movement, they portray us as a few ignorant fundamentalists who still believe that the earth is flat and who want to force the public schools to teach religion. The media ignores the fact that many highly qualified scientists have abandoned the Darwinian theory of evolution because of its inconsistencies and intellectual hypocrisy.

"Another cause of the near-universal acceptance of evolution is the vast amount of popular books which push evolution as a fact. The Time-Life series of science books has titles such as *Evolution, Early Man,* and *The Missing Link.*

"Desmond Morris wrote a book entitled *The Naked Ape,* in which he states that man is one of 192 species of monkeys and apes. What does Mr. Morris offer as proof? Nothing. Instead, he says, 'It would take too long to present all the tiny fragments of evidence that have been painstakingly collected over the past century. Instead, we will assume that this task has been done and simply summarize the conclusions that can be drawn from it. . . .'"

Dr. Arnold paused, removed his glasses, and leaned forward on the pulpit to look directly into the eyes of the audience. "Did you notice three vitally important words written by Mr. Morris? These three words represent what many pass off as science. Those three words are 'we will assume.'

"A few pages later, Mr. Morris writes, 'If we accept the history of evolution as it has been outlined here, then one fact stands out clearly: namely, that we have arisen essentially as primate predators.'"

Dr. Arnold slapped his forehead and rolled his eyes back. "I can't stand it!" he thundered. "First the man says 'we will assume' and then he has the gall to claim that he has outlined the history of evolution. Without a shred of evidence, he shamelessly repaints an impoverished theory as an established fact!

"I could quote from book after book that mislabels the theory of evolution as fact. Siegfried Mandel's *Dictionary of Science,* Cox's *Prehistoric Animals,* Huntington's *Mainsprings of Civilization* all teach evolution as fact.

"*The World Book Encyclopedia* and *The Young People's Science Encyclopedia* teach evolution as fact."

Arthur looked down in disgust and shook his head slightly. *And all those people are wrong, I suppose,* he thought.

The speaker continued, "The educational establishment is committed to teaching evolution as the only possible explanation for life in the universe. If a student dares to question a teacher in class, he is quickly silenced. I challenge you students: Look at the evidence before making up your mind. Your public school is not going to give you both sides of the argument."

Again Arthur shook his head. Dr. Arnold seemed to think that there was a national conspiracy to deceive the population. *Oh, come on, Dr. Arnold. There is so much evidence that only a fool could doubt evolution. I've got to talk to you,* Arthur thought as he pushed his glasses back up on his nose, folded his arms, and tried to tune out the preacher's arguments.

When the service concluded, Arthur made his way to the front to talk to Dr. Arnold. People were talking excitedly and several had grouped around the speaker to ask questions. Arthur noticed that the pretty girl from the choir was standing there listening. When there was a pause, she asked, "Dr. Arnold, if evolution is just a theory, why do most educated people believe it?"

"That's a good question, young lady," Dr. Arnold replied. "What is your name?"

"Kathy Olson," she said. Arthur moved closer to her, as though he wanted to hear Dr. Arnold's answer.

"Well, Kathy, when authorities say that something is true, people tend to accept it. This is especially true of scientists.

They are supposed to be objective in their research, but they do not like to be challenged. They expect people to agree with them because they are the 'experts.' There is a great deal of professional arrogance and intellectual insecurity in the scientific community.

"Here, Kathy, let me show you some quotes I have with me." He pulled a file out of his briefcase. "Here's one from Henry Osborn in his book *The Origin and Evolution of Life*. He says, 'In review, we need not devote any time or space to any fresh arguments for the truth of evolution. The demonstration of evolution as a living law of nature is the greatest intellectual achievement of the nineteenth century. Evolution has outgrown the rank of a theory.'

"Nothing could be further from the truth, and the deliberate misrepresentations given by some of these men are incredible! Isaac Asimov wrote in *The Intelligent Man's Guide to Science, Volume 1*, 'Scientists turned more and more to theories involving evolutionary processes following Newton rather than the Bible.' Asimov fails to mention that Newton was a believer in Christ and a student of the Bible. Why? Because Asimov is emotionally committed to the atheistic philosophy of secular humanism.

"Sir Julian Huxley wrote in *Evolution After Darwin, Volume 3*, 'The first point to make about Darwin's theory is that it is no longer a theory, but a fact. No serious scientist would deny that evolution has occurred, just as he would not deny the fact that the earth goes around the sun.' With that statement, Huxley perpetrates two gigantic lies, Kathy. He says that the theory is now fact, when it never can be, and he ridicules all who disagree with him as nonscientists."

Arthur raised his hand as though in school. "Dr. Arnold?"

"Yes, young man."

"You keep saying that evolution is a theory only. What is the difference between a scientific theory and a proven fact?"

"Let me ask you, young man—what's your name?"

"Arthur."

"Arthur, let me ask you, how *does* a theory become a fact?"

"Well, when a scientist has a theory about something, he has to prove it by experiments, doesn't he?"

"Precisely! And in order to establish proof, his experiments must be repeated over and over with the same results. Do you see why that is impossible when we come to the theory of evolution?"

"No, I don't," admitted Arthur.

"I do!" Kathy said with real excitement. "You can't prove evolution because it can't be repeated. We can't go back in time and duplicate all the conditions of millions of years ago."

"Right, Kathy, good for you." Turning to Arthur, Dr. Arnold said, "If you come back tomorrow night, I will show you that many scientists admit that evolution is not really scientific, but religious."

"Religious?" Arthur said in disbelief. "How can evolution be religious?"

"You come tomorrow and see," Dr. Arnold said as he turned back to the pulpit and collected his notes.

Kathy started to walk away, and Arthur hurried to catch up with her. "Hi. I couldn't help overhearing your name, Kathy. Are you new in town?"

"Yes," she said with a smile, "we moved here about a month ago from Illinois. Dad wanted to be near the coast, but not too close to the big cities."

"That was pretty interesting tonight, wasn't it?" Arthur said.

"You bet! I can hardly wait to hear Dr. Arnold tomorrow night."

"I'm going to come, too. I don't really agree with him, but I'm willing to hear what he has to say. Are you going to be in the choir tomorrow night?"

"No. We're just singing once this week."

Arthur's pulse increased. "Could I sit with you . . . uh . . . and your friends?"

"Sure, Arthur. If you don't mind sitting with a bunch of girls. I'm going to invite some of my friends from school."

"Okay, Kathy. See you tomorrow!" He walked away as casually as he could and went outside. When he was far enough from the church, he let out a whoop and ran toward home.

2

Faith to Change the Way We Act

"ACTIONS SPEAK LOUDER THAN words" is an old saying which has become trivialized by overuse, yet it is as true today as when it was first spoken. Paul wrote to Titus, "They claim to know God, but by their actions they deny him" (Titus 1:16).

There are many people who claim to be followers of Christ, but their lives reveal their heartfelt disbelief. Instead of the fruit of the Spirit, their actions demonstrate the fruit of sin. They may be regular in their church attendance, they may faithfully pay their tithe, they may even be elders, deacons, or pastors, but their actions show that they are, at least to some extent, practical atheists.

Jesus reserved his harshest words for religious atheists when he said, "Woe to you, teachers of the law and Pharisees, you hypocrites! You give a tenth of your spices—mint, dill and cumin. But you have neglected the more important matters of the law—justice, mercy and faithfulness. You should have practiced the latter, without neglecting the former" (Matthew 23:23).

Before we smugly agree and picture in our minds the hypocrites we have met, may I remind us all that we each have a bit of the atheist in our hearts. Our actions prove it. For example, Paul writes about one of our most profound problems—an undisciplined tongue—in Ephesians 4:

Do not let any unwholesome talk come out of your mouths, but only what is helpful for building others up according to their needs, that it may benefit those who listen. And do not grieve the Holy Spirit of God, with whom you were sealed for the day of redemption. Get rid of all bitterness, rage and anger, brawling and slander, along with every form of malice. Be kind and compassionate to one another, forgiving each other, just as in Christ God forgave you (Ephesians 4:29-32).

UNKIND WORDS

Language is a wonderful gift from God, enabling humans to communicate ideas, abstract concepts, feelings, emotions, and beliefs from one person to another. Think about the miracle of words. With sounds or writing we can transfer images and meaning. We can cause another being to experience joy or sorrow, courage or fear, love or hatred, peace or terror—all by the combination of sounds or letters we choose to use.

Learning another language is an exciting and yet frustrating experience as we try to link mental images to new combinations of sound. We laugh as we discover that the same sound for "we" means "yes" in French and that the sound for our number "9" means "no" in German. As we listen carefully to different languages, we can easily distinguish the guttural sounds of the Germanic and Slavic tongues from the melodic tones of French and Spanish. We can quickly discern the sing-song patterns of Oriental speech from the clipped sounds of Indian dialects or the clicking words of some African tribes. We delight in the innocent-sounding speech of the Scandinavians and the British and we are absolutely fascinated with the lilt of the Irish and Australian accents. Sounds identify, distinguish, and group tribes and nations.

Were you aware, however, that there is a language of unbelief? It is a bitter and cynical tongue, and it is not limited to a single nationality, for it is spoken on every continent. It is described in Psalm 10:7: "His mouth is full of curses and lies and threats; trouble and evil are under his tongue."

I heard this language clearly spoken my first day in a biological psychology class at the University of Colorado when the professor looked at his students and asked in a tone dripping with arrogance, "Are there any of you who still believe in the myths of the Bible?" The bitterness and cynicism that projected from his heart filled the room.

Was there any direct connection between his theological perspective and biological psychology? Of course. If you deny the reality of God, it affects your entire view of reality—including origins of the universe, the source of life, the understanding of biology, and the meaning of psychology, which for many is the foundational philosophy for their lives.

My professor's attitude is well described in Psalm 10:4, where David wrote, "In his pride the wicked does not seek [the Lord]; in all his thoughts there is no room for God."

Just as you can detect a person's nationality by his speech, so can you recognize a practical atheist by his words. When a person speaks of "evolutionary processes" or says that the universe is "billions of years old" you have heard a functional atheist communicate his mind. The Bible describes such a person this way: "The fool says in his heart, 'There is no God.' They are corrupt, their deeds are vile; there is no one who does good" (Psalm 14:1).

What's surprising these days is that many professing Christians have begun to speak in the same bitter tones which characterize the atheist. Over the years I have counseled numbers of Christians who have admitted that when they become angry, they lose control of their tongues and use vulgar language and speak obscenities and curses toward their mates and children. Though they would rarely come out and say that they no longer believe in the reality of God, that is what they communicate to others. In effect, they have become functional but religious atheists.

One of the most difficult character changes we as Christians are called to make is in the area of our words. James warns us, "No man can tame the tongue. It is a restless evil, full of deadly poison"

(James 3:8). He points out the inconsistency of Christians who claim to love God and yet their mouths prove that they are still full of sin and rebellion: "With the tongue we praise our Lord and Father, and with it we curse men, who have been made in God's likeness. Out of the same mouth come praise and cursing. My brothers, this should not be" (James 3:9-10).

A wicked tongue is especially damaging in the home. As James said, "The tongue also is a fire, a world of evil among the parts of the body. It corrupts the whole person, sets the whole course of his life on fire, and is itself set on fire by hell" (James 3:6).

Marriages are crippled and destroyed by abusive language. Children are as twisted by the harshness of unrelenting criticism and continual belittling as they would be by physical beatings. Instead of experiencing the security, encouragement, and warmth of gentle words, a growing mass of Christian young people seethe with rage, longing for the day they can leave their homes forever. It is no wonder, then, that they spend as little time as possible at home, preferring the company of other angry teens at the local arcade or mall. I am constantly amazed at the number of young people from Christian homes whose deep anger is written clearly on their faces as they walk into church or a youth group class.

I remember a Christian family who drove from the other side of our metroplex for counsel. They were an affluent family living in an upscale neighborhood. They had every possible "thing" that defines "the good life" from the world's point of view—a beautiful home, new cars, video games, expensive clothing—everything. Yet the children were constantly getting into trouble and were becoming involved in gangs.

The father was an ex-marine who ran his family like a drill sergeant ordering his platoon on maneuvers. He attempted to control the family with a loud voice, barking out angry orders. But the children were reacting with rebellion and his wife was about ready to call it quits.

Paul wrote to Christian fathers, "Do not exasperate your children; instead, bring them up in the training and instruction of the Lord" (Ephesians 6:4). The King James Version puts it a bit stronger: "Provoke not your children to wrath." The Greek term for "wrath" is *parorgizo;* which means "to anger alongside" or to enrage. It perfectly demonstrates the power of an ungodly tongue to create deep and abiding hatred within the home.

Did you know that God says an uncontrolled tongue is an indicator of practical atheism? James said, "If anyone considers himself religious and yet does not keep a tight rein on his tongue, he deceives himself and his religion is worthless" (James 1:26). What a convicting phrase—"his religion is worthless." A worthless religion means nothing to God and ultimately, it means nothing to the world either.

I am convinced, however, that if you are reading this book, you have a genuine interest in cultivating godly speech. You want your home to become a reflection of heaven, a place of joy, comfort, and peace. You want your life to be happy and you're tired of the constant friction and tension which seem to remove all the enjoyment life has to offer. Peter wrote, "Whoever would love life and see good days must keep his tongue from evil and his lips from deceitful speech" (1 Peter 3:10).

Changing Our Speech

How can we change our speech from unbelief to godliness? Ephesians chapter 4 provides a framework for a transformed tongue. The first point to understand is that Christians must abide by a different standard than the world does. Paul wrote, "I tell you this, and insist on it in the Lord, that you must no longer live as the Gentiles do, in the futility of their thinking" (verse 17). If we do not grasp this foundational principle, we will never experience genuine change.

Paul explains the process of sanctification this way: "You were taught, with regard to your former way of life, to put off your old self, which is being corrupted by its deceitful desires; to be made new in the attitude of your minds; and to put on the new self, created to be like God in true righteousness and holiness." (Ephesians 4:22-24). It's the P-R-P system: Put Off, Renew, and Put On.

We cannot do this on our own, however. This kind of transformation is a direct work of the Holy Spirit. Even the Old Testament saints understood this when God told them, "I will put my Spirit in you and move you to follow my decrees and be careful to keep my laws" (Ezekiel 36:27).

The word *sanctify*[14] simply means "to set apart for sacred use; to consecrate, to make holy or to purify." God requires that we be holy if we want to experience the joy and peace He offers. This does not happen mystically, however, as some think. The Holy Spirit does not work primarily through our emotions, feelings, or intuition, though that is what some people teach. According to Jesus, sanctification takes place in direct relationship to the Word of God: "Sanctify them by the truth; your word is truth" (John 17:17).

As we study and meditate on the Scriptures, the Holy Spirit does his powerful work, helping us to "put off" our old way of thinking, speaking, and acting. It takes more than making New Year's resolutions to be different. Putting off comes as a natural by-product of genuine repentance, something we hear too little about in this age of churches that are more concerned with pacifying people's desires than they are about teaching truths that people need to hear.

God describes repentance as "return[ing] to me with all your heart, with fasting and weeping and mourning" (Joel 2:12). True repentance involves genuine sorrow for the sins we have committed against God and man. Paul wrote that God desires for us to have the kind of sorrow that leads to repentance (2 Corinthians 7:9).

Repentance does not merely end in sorrow, however. It produces what we are longing for: peace with God and joy in our hearts. Peter called it refreshment from God. He exhorted his countrymen to "repent, then, and turn to God, so that your sins may be wiped out, that times of refreshing may come from the Lord" (Acts 3:19).

How can we know whether we have truly repented or not? There will be a *change* in the way we *act*. Paul said, "to those in Jerusalem and in all Judea, and to the Gentiles also, I preached that they should repent and turn to God and prove their repentance by their deeds" (Acts 26:20).

The Process of Renewal

Repentance is the "putting off" portion of the transformation we seek. We must then move to the next part of the process, which is "to be made new in the attitude of your minds" (Ephesians 4:23). Fortunately, this does not require years of expensive psychotherapy to achieve, but it is the natural result of a heart filled with the truth of God's Word.

Paul explains renewal this way: "I urge you, brothers, in view of God's mercy, to offer your bodies as living sacrifices, holy and pleasing to God—this is your spiritual act of worship. Do not conform any longer to the pattern of this world, but be transformed by the renewing of your mind. Then you will be able to test and approve what God's will is—his good, pleasing and perfect will" (Romans 12:1-2).

But *how* do we learn what God's will is? Does He reveal it to each one of us individually or has He given us objective, propositional truth to guide us in the renewal process? Paul, writing to Timothy, gives us the answer: "All Scripture is God-breathed and is useful for teaching, rebuking, correcting and training in righteousness, so that the man of God may be thoroughly equipped for every good work" (2 Timothy 3:16-17). We can learn God's will for us only by understanding His written Word.[15]

It is important to realize that God works in us not because we deserve it, but because of His love for us. "He saved us, not because of righteous things we had done, but because of his mercy. He saved us through the washing of rebirth and renewal by the Holy Spirit" (Titus 3:5). It is the work God promised through Ezekiel when He said, "I will give you a new heart and put a new spirit in you; I will remove from you your heart of stone and give you a heart of flesh" (Ezekiel 36:26). It is the work that transforms us from practical atheists into victorious children of God.

The final part of genuine transformation is "put[ting] on the new self, created to be like God in true righteousness and holiness" (Ephesians 4:24). This is the "training in righteousness" that Paul speaks of in 2 Timothy 3:16. Growing spiritually mature is much like developing a skill—it involves practice and repetition.

A person who wants to be a star athlete trains daily for years to condition his body and mind so that he can perform almost automatically. The football place-kicker spends countless hours kicking and kicking and kicking so that he can accurately launch the ball between the goalposts. The basketball star practices shooting the ball into the hoop from every spot on the court, training his eyes, arms, hands, and feet to work in perfect coordination so he can successfully complete the shot with nothing but net.

The pianist practices those boring scales over and over again, up and down, up and down, up and down, driving the rest of the family crazy. He practices chord combinations and rhythm patterns, learning to read music with his eyes and translating the notes through his fingers onto the keyboard to produce glorious music.

The process of putting on the new self is like that. We must *practice* righteousness daily until it becomes an integral part of our very character. Jesus put it this way: "Everyone who hears these words of mine and puts them into practice is like a wise man who built his house on the rock. . . . But everyone who hears these words of mine and does not put them into practice is like a foolish man who built his house on sand" (Matthew 7:24,26).

Paul explained the path to inner peace as a process of repetition: "Whatever you have learned or received or heard from me, or seen in me—put it into practice. And the God of peace will be with you" (Philippians 4:9).

There is no shortcut to spirituality. You will not gain control of your tongue through a charismatic experience. There is no magic verse that will suddenly transform your character unless you obey it. James wrote, "Prove yourselves doers of the word, and not merely hearers who delude themselves" (James 1:22 NASB).

I once counseled a man who was suffering from what the world calls OCD—obsessive compulsive disorder. He had been controlled by senseless fears and pointless ritualistic behaviors for most of his life. He was a genuine believer in Christ, but could not seem to gain victory over his obsessions. He had undergone psychological counseling, psychiatric therapy, strong medication, and other interventions without success. Now he was desperate, wanting release from the bondage that was making his life and his marriage miserable.

He came to me, hoping I would have a flash of insight that would instantly provide healing for his problem. He was disappointed when I explained to him that his problem was rooted in wrong thinking and disobedience. I pointed out that his obsessions were long-term habits of behavior that had to be rooted out with repentance and the daily, even hourly, practice of righteousness.

I shared with him that obedience is a moment-by-moment choice that each Christian must make in any given circumstance. A person who has given himself over to alcohol must learn to continually submit his thirst to God in order to be delivered. One who has illicit sexual desires must focus his mind on purity and willfully avoid sexual thoughts as he fills his heart and mind with God's Word instead. Rarely does God free us from the life-dominating sins without effort on our part; that is why the writer of Hebrews says, "Let us throw off everything that hinders and the sin that so easily entangles, and let us run with perseverance the race marked out for us" (Hebrews 12:1).

It has taken time, but I am thankful to see real change taking place in this man's life as he is applying the Word on a daily basis and practicing new ways of thinking and behaving.

The same principle applies to unkind words. We will never learn how to control our tongues until we have been radically transformed on the inside by the daily practice of righteousness. That's where healthy communication begins.

BROKEN TRUST

Another reason many people ask us the question, "How big is your God?" is because they've found that they can no longer trust many Christians. The dictionary says that trust is a "firm reliance on the integrity, ability, or character of a person or thing."[16] We are given several examples of trustworthiness in the Bible. Joseph, for example, had proven himself totally worthy of the trust his master placed in him, to the point that the master "left in Joseph's care everything he had; with Joseph in charge, he did not concern himself with anything except the food he ate" (Genesis 39:6).

When King Joash determined to repair the temple of God, he found governmental administrators who were so dependable that "they did not require an accounting from those to whom they gave the money to pay the workers, because they acted with complete honesty" (2 Kings 12:15). Can you imagine government officials today being worthy of that sort of trust?

Daniel is another model of personal integrity. How wonderful it would be if we could say about our elected officials what was said about Daniel: "The administrators and the satraps tried to find grounds for charges against Daniel in his conduct of government affairs, but they were unable to do so. They could find no corruption in him, because he was trustworthy and neither corrupt nor negligent" (Daniel 6:4).

Before we get too indignant about our government, however, we would do well to examine our own hearts. God says, "It is required that those who have been given a trust must prove faithful" (1 Corinthians 4:2). One of the most fundamental of all trusts is that of marriage, a relationship in which we solemnly covenant with our mate that we will remain faithful, loyal, and pure so long as both remain alive.

Proverbs paints a repulsive picture of the unfaithful wife "who has left the partner of her youth and ignored the covenant she made before God" (Proverbs 2:17). An equally ugly image is presented of the hard-hearted husband. We are told that God removes His blessing from such a man. Why is this the case for unfaithful husbands and wives? "It is because the LORD is acting as the witness between you and the wife of your youth, because you have broken faith with her, though she is your partner, the wife of your marriage covenant" (Malachi 2:14).

Some of the people who have been caught in an affair come into a counseling office in great agony because their mates have left them after discovering their unfaithfulness. Sometimes the separation takes place months or even years after the discovery of the affair. "I don't understand why she can't forgive me," a husband wails. "I told her I was sorry and that it would never happen again." Or a wife weeps, "He just can't seem to put it out of his mind, even though it happened only once."

The problem is, once trust has been broken it is difficult to repair. When a counselor probes for the cause of the unfaithfulness, some people reply, "I just couldn't help myself. It happened so suddenly. I never planned to be unfaithful—it just . . . well . . . it just happened. The temptation was just more than I could handle." That is the cry of the practical atheist.

It is the same excuse offered by the drug addict, the drunkard, the homosexual, the glutton, or any other person who is in bondage to a life-dominating sin. "I can't help myself," he says, and in a very real sense, he is right. That is why the Lord has given us a resource greater than ourselves and our sin—the Holy Spirit! John writes this encouraging word to us: "You, dear children, are from God and have overcome them, because the one who is in you is greater than the one who is in the world" (1 John 4:4).

Even in the Old Testament, God gave the promise of this supernatural power: "I will put my Spirit in you and move you to follow my decrees and be careful to keep my laws" (Ezekiel 36:27). Paul explains the process of victory in Romans 8 when he writes, "You, however, are controlled not by the sinful nature but by the Spirit, if the Spirit of God lives in you. And if anyone does not have the Spirit of Christ, he does not belong to Christ" (Romans 8:9).

Perhaps you are saying right now, "I am a Christian, but I *still* don't have the power to overcome my sin." Then perhaps you need to examine your heart. Are you *really* a Christian? Paul writes, "Examine yourselves to see whether you are in the faith; test yourselves. Do you not realize that Christ Jesus is in you—unless, of course, you fail the test?" (2 Corinthians 13:5). While it's true that Christians will sin from time to time, sin should not be a regular pattern of life for the believer. Is your faith only an intellectual agreement that Jesus died on the cross for your sins? James writes that such faith is not really faith at all. Read carefully what he says:

> In the same way, faith by itself, if it is not accompanied by action, is dead. But someone will say, "You have faith; I have deeds." Show me your faith without deeds, and I will show you my faith by what I do. You believe that there is one God. Good! Even the demons believe that—and shudder. You foolish man, do you want evidence that faith without deeds is useless? (James 2:17-20).

In that passage, James is talking about religious atheism. It is a dead faith that has no power to produce righteousness in our daily lives. Remember, though, that even if this describes you, there is still hope. Find a godly pastor, elder, or lay person who knows the Bible and has demonstrated Christian maturity over the years. Ask that person to show you how to make certain that you are truly born again. Then ask to be discipled so you can grow as God intended.

If you have broken trust with your mate, what can you do about it? You can genuinely repent before God, humble yourself before your mate and ask for forgiveness, and begin the long process of rebuilding trust. Remember, forgiveness and trust are not the same thing. Your mate may indeed forgive you in obedience to the Lord, but trust cannot be commanded. It is the by-product of a long history of trustworthy behavior.

Commit yourself to the long haul. It may take years to fully rebuild the trust you have so carelessly destroyed, but, dear friend, it will be worth it. Don't give up. Just keep proving in every way possible that your word is true. If you say you are going to be at the office late, be sure that is exactly where you are and that there are witnesses so no doubts can arise. Never be alone with a member of the opposite sex without others around. Be sure that you have no unaccounted-for time that can raise suspicion all over again.

ANARCHY AND SELFISHNESS

Considering the state of many Christian homes today, it should come as no surprise to us that unbelievers wonder how big our God really is. I'm talking about domestic atheism, where we refuse to follow God's ordained organizational plan for the family. One reason that marriage is out of order in our generation is the feminization of virtually every institution—politics, education, business, the church, and the home.

Let me hasten to assure you that I am not anti-woman in any sense of the word. I have three wonderful daughters who are the delight of my heart. My wife has been my trusted partner and my closest friend for nearly 30 years. I believe in equal pay for equal work, and I am absolutely opposed to physical or verbal abuse in any form.

Yet I still believe that God has set up a chain of command within the home as is necessary for any organization, no matter how small. Scripture is abundantly clear on the issue of order within the home.

> Submit to one another out of reverence for Christ.
> Wives, submit to your husbands as to the Lord. For
> the husband is the head of the wife as Christ is the head
> of the church, his body, of which he is the Savior. Now as

the church submits to Christ, so also wives should submit to their husbands in everything.

Husbands, love your wives, just as Christ loved the
church and gave himself up for her (Ephesians 5:21-25).

It's very simple: We are to lovingly submit to one another as a
part of our devotion to the Lord. In the rare event when a married
couple cannot arrive at agreement on a course of action, wives are
to defer to the leadership of their husbands, who are to use their
authority with the gentle love demonstrated by Christ. The husband, in turn, is to submit himself to the clear instructions of Scripture, since Christ is over the husband as head of the church.

Any man who interprets this passage as a license for brutality,
harshness, or dictatorship is misapplying the Scripture and will be
held accountable for such sin. He is acting as an unbeliever of the
worst kind, since he is not providing what his family so desperately needs—loving leadership.

On the other hand, the wife who refuses to submit to her
husband's leadership is acting the part of the domestic atheist as
well, since she refuses to trust God to work His good for her in
her unpleasant situation.

Peter writes about this in his first epistle:

> To this you were called, because Christ suffered for
> you, leaving you an example, that you should follow in
> his steps. He committed no sin, and no deceit was found
> in his mouth. When they hurled their insults at him, he
> did not retaliate; when he suffered, he made no threats.
> Instead, he entrusted himself to him who judges justly
> (1 Peter 2:21-23).
>
> Wives, in the same way be submissive to your husbands
> so that, if any of them do not believe the word, they may
> be won over without words by the behavior of their wives,
> when they see the purity and reverence of your lives. Your
> beauty should not come from outward adornment, such
> as braided hair and the wearing of gold jewelry and fine

clothes. Instead, it should be that of your inner self, the unfading beauty of a gentle and quiet spirit, which is of great worth in God's sight. For this is the way the holy women of the past who put their hope in God used to make themselves beautiful. They were submissive to their own husbands, like Sarah, who obeyed Abraham and called him her master. You are her daughters if you do what is right and do not give way to fear (1 Peter 3:1-6).

I am not suggesting a system of Oriental obeisance where the wife meekly follows seven steps behind her husband, nor do I believe that a godly wife has no right to disagree or to appeal the decision her husband makes. However, the Lord has given clear instructions for the believing wife that she is to trust the Lord to work in her behalf and to submit whole-heartedly and confidently to the leadership of her husband, knowing that her hope is in God. That is the message of 1 Peter 3:1-6.

Why, then, is the issue of "submission" so emotionally charged? Because of selfishness. Women fear that their husbands will abuse their authority because they have seen them do just that, over and over again, due to the selfishness of man's heart. Men have, on the whole, abused their office, their physical strength, and the loyalty of their wives to get their own way. It is no wonder there are so many angry feminists determined that no man is going to push them around.

At the same time, however, there are wives who selfishly refuse to give in to their husbands' authority because . . . well . . . just *because!* Feminism has crept into the way we read the Bible, the way we raise our children, and the way we interact with our mates. And the result is unhappiness.

When we remove God's order from the home, the inevitable result is discord, disrespect, confusion, and spiritual destruction. Husbands who are passive and lacking in spiritual and practical leadership have removed the structure for happiness in the home. And if a husband is harsh in his leadership, he likewise damages his home. "A kind man benefits himself, but a cruel man brings trouble on himself" (Proverbs 11:17). Though he may technically be a Christian, this kind of man is acting no differently in his marriage than an atheist would.

The wife who refuses to work within God's plan is spotlighted in Proverbs 14:1: "The wise woman builds her house, but with her own hands the foolish one tears hers down." She, too, has become like an unbeliever in the way she acts in the home.

Pity the children who grow up in a home that is in such disarray. It is understandable when they declare that they have no interest in spiritual things since they have seen little joy or peace in their family. In all my years of ministry, I cannot recall a rebellious teen who had grown up in a biblically ordered home where the father was the loving head and the mother was the respectful second-in-command. The children I have seen emerge from disordered homes are described in 2 Timothy 3:2: "lovers of themselves, lovers of money, boastful, proud, abusive, disobedient to their parents, ungrateful, unholy."

LACK OF COMMITMENT

Is God big enough to help us keep our word? Many do not seem to believe so. But in Ecclesiastes 5 we read, "When you make a vow to God, do not delay in fulfilling it. He has no pleasure in fools; fulfill your vow. It is better not to vow than to make a vow and not fulfill it" (Ecclesiastes 5:4-5). This is especially true for those who call themselves Christians.

God expects us to fulfill our commitments in our business dealings, in our interactions with others at school, in the neighborhood, at church, and especially in our homes.

A major cause for miserable marriages is the lack of commitment to the sanctity of the wedding vows and to the marriage itself. God takes marriage very seriously, as He makes clear in Malachi 2. Our godless modern culture has reacted to the abuses of marriage in the only way it knows how—divorce. Jesus explained why this is the case: "Moses permitted you to divorce your wives because your hearts were hard. But it was not this way from the beginning" (Matthew 19:8).

Divorce is a natural consequence of unbelief. Nearly every pastor has listened to estranged couples as they say, "God wouldn't want us to stay together like this, would He? We don't love each other any more!" This is the cry of the emotional atheist who bases his life and values on his feelings rather than forcing his feelings to comply with a biblical foundation of faith.

Emotionally dependent faith is doomed to failure. It collapses under the weight of unpleasant circumstances, unsatisfying sex, business failure, unexpected disease, financial pressures, boredom, jealousy, the death of a child, imprisonment, governmental social policies, incompetent psychotherapy, or any number of other problems of living.

Let me ask you, dear reader, what kind of commitment do you have toward your promise to God that your marriage would endure, no matter what? Are you looking for ways to bail out? Are you hoping your mate will file for divorce so you won't have to? Think deeply with me for a moment. What acceptable reason will you give to the Lord for ending your marriage when you stand before Him in eternity?

I heard of a former pastor who decided to leave the ministry, divorce his wife of many years and marry a younger woman. He was quoted as saying, "I'd rather go to hell with [his second wife] than go to heaven with [his first wife]!"

A pastor from Michigan wrote to me the tragic story of his wife's involvement in psychotherapy and how their marriage ended in divorce because she became increasingly enraged at him as her therapist led her deeper and deeper into an imaginary past of abuse. She became committed to her fable, rather than clinging to the truth of actual events and how God would have her handle them biblically. Instead of holding on to the commands of God's Word, she chose rather to believe psychological lies. Their ministry, family, and marriage became the casualties of misdirected commitment.

I have heard the same story countless times from every region of the nation. The names and minor details vary, but the essential outline is the same.[17] No longer committed to their marriage, to their vows, to their children, or to the Lord, emotional atheists have opted to follow their hearts rather than the Word of God. The tragic results have devastated churches and families across the nation.

IMAGE WORSHIP

In Galatians 5:20, Paul mentions idolatry as a natural consequence of denying God by our actions. The Greek term he uses, *eidololatreia*, means "image worship." What could be more appropriate to describe practical atheism in our day than image worship? An image is an artificial representation of the real thing, and many modern-day Christians are falling on their knees before a pantheon of worldly deities.

We spend more time with the colorful moving images of television, videos, and movies than we do worshiping our Lord. We idolize television and movie actors, athletes, and a host of other celebrities as though they were gods while we give little thought to God Himself. David wrote, "Turn my eyes away from worthless things; preserve my life according to your word" (Psalm 119:37).

I'm not saying we must destroy our television sets, but we *should* carefully evaluate our viewing habits. I am always convicted when I read Psalm 101:3, especially the New American Standard translation: "I will set no worthless thing before my eyes; I hate the work of those who fall away; it shall not fasten its grip on me." The King James Version puts it even stronger: "I will set no wicked thing before mine eyes."

When we allow the evil images of the world, with its lust, greed, violence, perversion, and mockery of God and all that is good to fill our minds, haven't we set worthless and wicked things before our eyes? Haven't we allowed it to fasten its grip on us?

Am I overreacting? I don't think so, yet I know that even in conservative Christian groups, television and movies are a non-issue. May I suggest a simple guideline for our viewing decisions? We need to ask ourselves, as honestly as possible, "Would I be comfortable viewing this if Jesus were sitting next to me?" (Well, He is!)

The same question can be applied to any form of entertainment we choose: music, novels, magazines, games, athletics, and so on. "Would this be pleasing to Jesus?" In some cases, the answer would be yes. But oftentimes we would have to hang our heads and admit that we are allowing the world to take God's place in our hearts.

Paul knew about this tendency when he wrote, "Do not conform any longer to the pattern of this world, but be transformed by the renewing of your mind. Then you will be able to test and approve what God's will is—his good, pleasing and perfect will" (Romans 12:2).

DRUG THERAPY

A further description of the downward spiral of sinful actions is found in Galatians 5:20, where we find the startling term *pharmakeia*, which was derived from the word *pharmakoān*—a spell-giving potion, or a drug used to induce a trance for the purpose of sorcery or witchcraft. Our modern word *pharmacology* comes from the same root, but we use it to mean legal and medicinal drugs. That is not what Paul was talking about, however. Remember, he was warning Christians about the natural consequences of ignoring God, and addiction to mind-altering substances is one of the most damaging consequences possible.

We are all aware of the pitiful destruction that inevitably accompanies the use of highly addictive drugs such as alcohol, heroin, and cocaine, but many are unaware of the drugs being administered by modern-day witch doctors. At least that is what Dr. Peter Breggin, the director of the Center for the Study of

Psychiatry and himself a psychiatrist, calls those who misprescribe psychotropic drugs.[18]

Christians have also fallen prey to modern shamans who pretend to understand our hearts and minds and who offer us their spell-giving potions to calm us and give us an artificial peace. They do not wear feathers in their hair, nor do they sport bones through their noses. No, they are more sophisticated than that. They are more likely to wear a white medical smock and display a Ph.D. diploma on their clinic wall. Nonetheless, they exercise the same soul-numbing power over their patients that the witch doctors of the steaming jungles have over terrified natives.

How do these "experts" acquire such power over their victims? By creating a foggy climate of fear and mystery they alone can penetrate with their incantations and magical skills. The modern experts of the soul—psychologists and psychiatrists—make a living by convincing themselves and their patients that they know what is going on inside their clients' hearts. They believe they understand subconscious motivations which control the behavior, feelings, and destinies of the suffering humans who come to them.

Some even practice "therapeutic touch," a technique now being taught in medical schools around the world. In this innovative therapy, the practitioner moves his or her hands slowly over the patient's body, not actually touching, but merely smoothing out the aura, or energy field, which they believe surrounds every person. Ironically, this is *exactly* what witch doctors have done for centuries to unsuspecting natives.

Believing they are in safe hands, many Christians have accepted diagnoses of mental illnesses that may not even exist and have ingested the potions prescribed. We may never know how many Christians are continuing to suffer in sin while trying to dull their pain with tranquilizers, anti-anxiety medications, and personality pills, but the numbers are staggering.

Many no longer believe that God is able to heal their inner wounds and have become pharmacological atheists, hooked on Prozac, Ritalin, and Lithium.

WISE ACTIONS

How big is God in the way that we act? If He truly is God, and we are His children, surely our lives should show it. The key is very simple, according to Jesus. He said,

> Everyone who hears these words of mine and puts them into practice is like a wise man who built his house on the rock. The rain came down, the streams rose, and the winds blew and beat against that house; yet it did not fall, because it had its foundation on the rock. But everyone who hears these words of mine and does not put them into practice is like a foolish man who built his house on sand. The rain came down, the streams rose, and the winds blew and beat against that house, and it fell with a great crash" (Matthew 7:24-27).

The key, of course, is hearing God's Word and putting it into practice in our daily lives. When we do, God will heal our broken marriages, restore the love between parents and children, and make our homes a preview of heaven while we await the return of our Lord.

God Allowed Him to Die!

Dr. Arthur Wilson still sat alone in his den. The fire had long since died out, but he didn't even notice. He was thinking back to the time his faith had been destroyed by a favorite teacher. It was as clear as though the memory were being projected on the wall in front of him.

His thoughts returned to the morning after the creation lecture at church. Arthur had gotten up early to hurry to school. He wanted to talk to his biology teacher before class. *I have to get some ammunition for tonight,* he thought.

His teacher, Lewis Jones, was in the classroom at his desk. Arthur knocked and Mr. Jones looked up. "Come in, Arthur. What can I do for you?"

"I have a few questions, Mr. Jones. They're about evolution. Do you have a couple of minutes?"

"Well, just a couple. I'm grading papers. What kind of questions?"

Arthur told Mr. Jones about the speaker at the Baptist church. "He sounded like he knew what he was talking about, Mr. Jones. I mean, he was quoting scientists and documenting every statement. I need some answers."

"Arthur, you already have all the answers you need. I showed the class that evolution is indisputable. No qualified scientist even questions evolution. Creationism is just another arm of the religious fundamentalists. No one takes them seriously."

"Would you be willing to come hear the speaker, Mr. Jones? I'm telling you, he's throwing out some stuff I've never heard."

Mr. Jones looked irritated. "I'm not going to waste my time listening to some ignorant preacher, Arthur! I can't believe you will either. You're too smart for that. I've got to finish these papers now. See you later."

Arthur walked out of the classroom disappointed. *He sounds just like those scientists Dr. Arnold described last night.*

He walked down the hallway to his locker and hung up his jacket. As he closed the door, Kathy Olson walked by. "Hi, Kathy!" he said loudly.

"Oh, hi, Arthur," she replied as she kept walking. Then Arthur noticed the boy beside her. His letter jacket said it all—basketball, football, baseball.

Great! The cutest girl I've ever talked to, and she already has a boyfriend. A jock, at that. Wouldn't you know it? Arthur slowly turned toward his first-hour class. He shoved his hands deep into his pockets as he frowned angrily. *I'm not going to that service tonight. Mr. Jones is right. I'm too smart to be fooled by religious propaganda.*

That night, as Arthur's parents were ready to leave for church, his mom asked, "Aren't you coming, Arthur?"

"No. I've heard all I want to hear. Mr. Jones set me right about that stuff at school this morning. See you later."

"What about that cute blond I saw you talking to?" his dad teased. "You don't want to disappoint her, do you?"

"What cute blond?" Arthur replied as though he couldn't remember. "Oh. That new girl. She'll probably be sitting with a bunch of her friends. No, you go on. I need to do some homework."

When the Wilsons got to church, they saw Kathy sitting with several of her girlfriends near the front of the auditorium. She kept turning around in the pew, looking for someone.

The service started and Dr. Arnold was even more convincing than the night before. Kathy was impressed, and so were her friends. Especially when Dr. Arnold said at the conclusion, "High school and college students, listen to me. I want to make you an offer you can't refuse. I hereby challenge your biology professors to debate me on evolution and creation. Anytime, anyplace. I only live a few hours away by car, so I can return at a convenient date for your professors. I promise you that I will not quote from the Bible. I will only talk science and quote from science texts. I will prove from evidence alone that evolutionism is as religious as creationism and creationism is more scientific than evolutionism. I doubt that any of you will be able to find even one professor that will have the courage to debate me publicly."

Kathy turned to her friends. "I'm going to ask Mr. Jones."

The next day, Kathy walked toward Mr. Jones's classroom. She saw Arthur at his locker. "Hi, Arthur. I missed you last night."

"Hi, Kathy," he said with a frigid tone. "I decided I'd heard enough. I thought it over and realized that Dr. Arnold is a good speaker, but he's wrong in his facts."

"Oh, really?" said Kathy as she pushed her hair back from her face. "Why don't you come with me to talk to Mr. Jones right now? I'm going to challenge him to debate Dr. Arnold."

"Debate?"

"That's right, debate! If Mr. Jones is so sure about evolution, let's see if he's willing to prove it publicly."

"All right. I'll go with you. He'll put that preacher in his place."

They walked quickly to Mr. Jones's room. As they walked in, Mr. Jones looked up and said, "Yes? What can I do for you?"

"Mr. Jones," Kathy began, "I've been attending some meetings at the Baptist church where a Dr. Arnold is speaking. He has his doctorate in biology, and last night he made the most amazing offer."

Mr. Jones looked at Arthur as if to say, "Did you put her up to this?" Arthur shrugged his shoulders innocently. Looking back at Kathy, Mr. Jones said in a curt voice, "What was his amazing offer?"

"He offered to debate any scientist on the question of evolution and creation. He told us to invite our teachers to debate him publicly. Would you be willing?"

Mr. Jones swallowed involuntarily. "Uh, I don't know, uh, Kathy," he stuttered. "I'm awfully busy this week. I'd love to debate him, but I can't this week. Too bad, though," he said shaking his head as though really disappointed.

"But Dr. Arnold said he would come back anytime we could set up a debate. Would you really do it?"

"Well, I don't know, Kathy," Mr. Jones hedged. "I hate to get into a religious argument, especially in public."

"But he said he wouldn't quote the Bible and that he would debate from a purely scientific point of view."

Arthur noticed that little beads of sweat had formed on Mr. Jones's forehead.

"Now look here, Kathy," said Mr. Jones firmly, "I don't have time to debate every preacher who comes into town. Now you'll have to excuse me. I have to turn in the attendance forms to the office." He walked out of the room and down the hall.

Kathy's mouth hung open and she turned to Arthur. "I can't believe it. It's just like Dr. Arnold said. He's *afraid* to debate. He's afraid he'll lose."

"He is not! He's just too smart to waste time on a preacher, Kathy!" Arthur turned on his heel and walked out. But he knew that Kathy was right. Mr. Jones was afraid.

That afternoon in biology class, Mr. Jones began his lecture by saying, "I understand that some of you have been attending religious meetings at a Baptist church where the speaker claims to be a scientist. He also claims that evolution is an error. Isn't it strange that this error is accepted by such intellectual giants as Stephen Gould of Harvard and Dr. Carl Sagan and Dr. David Duncan of Cornell University? If the religious fundamentalists had their way, Copernicus, Kepler, Galileo, and Darwin would be stricken from history and their works burned in the fires of intolerance. I'm sure that few of you are foolish enough to be taken in by religious attacks on intellectual freedom."

Kathy's hand shot up. "Mr. Jones?"

He ignored her. "Mr. Jones," she insisted, waving her hand high above her head.

"What is it, Kathy?" he said with tight lips.

"Mr. Jones, if intellectual freedom is what the issue is all about, why do the public schools refuse to discuss both theories of origin?"

"Because, Kathy, one is science, and the other is religion. And because of the separation of church and state, we cannot discuss religion in class."

"But you just did, Mr. Jones. You brought up the subject of religion. You were making fun of the fundamentalists, as you call them."

"That's enough, Kathy," Mr. Jones commanded. "We're not going to debate theology in this classroom." Others in the class started to mutter under their breaths.

"What was that, Calvin?" said Mr. Jones as he looked angrily at Cal Johnson in the second row.

"I said I think Kathy has a point."

"Well, I really don't care what you think, Calvin. I said we aren't going to debate theology in my class."

"Sure. You can say what *you* want to, but *we* can't respond. That's real intellectual freedom!"

"That's enough! You, Calvin, and you, Kathy, will remain after class and will accompany me to the principal's office!"

Now the class was in an uproar. "That's not fair!" one voice shouted. "That stinks!" said another.

"Class! I'll put you all on report, if necessary! And I'll assign three chapters for tomorrow if I hear another word!"

Silence settled in, but Mr. Jones had lost the day. He assigned the class a worksheet and tried to look in control, but he was clearly upset. Finally the bell rang and the students filed out, except for Calvin and Kathy, who walked up and stood in front of the teacher's desk.

"I'm not going to punish you this time," said Mr. Jones. "But if you ever speak to me that way again in my class, I'll give you an F so fast your head will spin! Do you understand?"

Cal started to respond, but stopped as Kathy nudged him.

"Now, get out of here," Mr. Jones muttered as he stood up and faced the blackboard behind his desk.

As they walked down the empty hallway, Kathy told Calvin, "I'm sorry if I got you into trouble, Cal."

"Don't worry about it, Kathy. I think Mr. Jones is scared."

"Of what?"

"Of the truth."

That evening was the concluding service of the science and creation series at the church. Cal and Kathy went early to talk with Dr. Arnold. They told him what had happened at school. "I'm not surprised," said Dr. Arnold. "The average science teacher is unable to defend his position logically. Quite frankly, most of them have not given serious consideration to the creation theory. When someone challenges a teacher, he usually responds defensively. Your Mr. Jones is no exception."

People were starting to arrive for the lecture. "Well, we'd better let you get ready for your message," said Cal.

Dr. Arnold nodded, then said, "Cal, there is one other thing. You may have been technically correct in your confrontation with Mr. Jones, but by embarrassing him, you have forced him into a corner. Now he will be more determined than ever to support the evolutionist point of view."

"I know. I wish I hadn't gotten so angry, but the way he was picking on Kathy really bothered me." He paused momentarily, then said, "Well, we'd better get a seat."

Cal and Kathy walked to the front row and sat down. They didn't see Arthur and Mr. Jones when they came in a few minutes later and sat as far back as possible, under the balcony.

Dr. Arnold began his lecture. "Last night, I showed you that the theory of evolution is actually a religious faith, and not a true scientific discipline. That point is so important that I want to reinforce it with additional statements from some leading authorities.

"Loren Eisely has written in *The Immense Journey,* 'With the failure of these many efforts, science was left in the somewhat embarrassing position of having to postulate theories of living origins which it could not demonstrate. After having chided the theologian for his reliance on myth and miracle, science found itself in the unenviable position of having to create a mythology of its own: namely, the assumption that what, after long effort could not be proved to take place today had, in truth, taken place in the primeval past.'

"In writing about the theory of evolution, R.H. Peters said in *The American Naturalist,* 'These theories are actually tautologies and, as such, cannot make empirically testable predictions. They are not scientific theories at all.'"

Arthur leaned over to Mr. Jones and asked, "What is a tautology?" Mr. Jones put his finger to his lips to silence Arthur and nodded impatiently at Dr. Arnold.

"Some of you may not understand what Mr. Peters is saying," continued Dr. Arnold. "A tautological statement is one which uses circular reasoning. For instance, a paleontologist might find a rock and say, 'This rock is four million years old.' If you were to ask him how he knows that the rock is four million years old, he might say, 'Because it contains these four-million-year-old fossils.' You could reply, 'How do you know the fossils are four million years old?'

And using circular reasoning, the evolutionist would say, 'Because they are in this four-million-year-old rock.' Admittedly, that is an oversimplification, but you get the idea."

Mr. Jones shifted uneasily in the pew.

"L. Harrison Matthews wrote in his foreword to the 1971 edition of Darwin's *Origin of the Species*, '[The theory of evolution] forms a satisfactory faith on which to base our interpretation of nature.' Isn't that amazing? A renowned evolutionary biologist is saying in writing that the theory of evolution is a faith. Yet, when a creationist wants to present his theory in the public schools, he is told that his point of view is religious, and that the evolutionary side is pure science. The simple truth is, both systems are based on faith and the scientific establishment is afraid that if you get both sides of the argument, you will choose creationism."

Mr. Jones leaned over and whispered to Arthur, "I've heard enough of this trash. I'm leaving. If you're smart, you will, too."

Arthur followed Mr. Jones out into the evening. They walked silently toward the parking lot. When they reached the car, Arthur looked at Mr. Jones and asked, "Why did you want to leave, Mr. Jones?"

Mr. Jones looked down for a moment, then unlocked the car. "Get in, Arthur. Let's talk for a few minutes." Arthur opened the passenger door and sat in the bucket seat of Mr. Jones's red Mustang convertible.

"I left because I don't want to listen to religious fundamentalism. If they have their way, they'll get control of our schools and they'll force creationism down our throats. It would be a return to the Dark Ages."

"But, Dr. Arnold was not quoting the Bible. He was quoting evolutionists."

"Sure, Arthur. But out of context. If you take a person's quote out of context you can make him say anything you want."

"Well, then, couldn't we get copies of Dr. Arnold's notes and check out the quotes? I mean, we could nail him if he is misquoting the scientists."

"Arthur," Mr. Jones said wearily, "I don't have time to check out every little quote this preacher comes out with. If you're smart, you'll forget this creationism stuff and get on with serious studies. You told me that you want to be a doctor someday, right?" Arthur nodded. "That means you need to understand biology and chemistry and the human body. Those are scientific disciplines, not religious doctrines. If you want to be successful in this world, you had better get religious fiction out of your mind."

"But can't a person be religious and scientific at the same time?"

"Of course, Arthur. I'm religious, to some extent. I believe that Jesus was a good man and that he taught some good principles, like treating others the way you want them to treat you. I go to church sometimes."

"You do?" Arthur said with surprise. "Where do you attend?"

"Sometimes I go into Baltimore. They have a church there called Science of the Mind. They teach how people can feel better about themselves by realizing that each of us is divine and that we are all part of the one universal force."

"That sounds more like science fiction than church."

"Maybe science fiction isn't so far off in its philosophy," Mr. Jones said. "Science has definitely proven that there is a unity in all living matter. I'm not against religion, Arthur. Just the kind of religion that says that human beings are sinners and need a Savior to get in touch with God. I believe that God is all things and that you and I are a part of that life-force. I think that evolution is the universal principle and that mankind is evolving even now into higher and more intelligent forms. Fundamentalist Christians could hold back that development, Arthur. That's why I get so upset when I hear them attacking the obvious truth of evolution."

"How can they hold back evolutionary development?" Arthur asked with a confused look on his face.

"Well, their constant emphasis on sin, for one thing," said Mr. Jones. "All they seem to talk about is sin and damnation. It is such a put-down of the essential nature of man. They seem to have this fixation against sex, that it is dirty and sinful. Anything enjoyable seems to be on their hit list—movies, books, television, smoking, alcohol, you name it."

Arthur nodded and said, "I know what you mean. That's why I quit going to church."

"It isn't just their outdated views on science, Arthur. It's their entire outlook on life that I object to. They are so narrow and negative. I don't want to poison my mind with their kind of thinking. I want to help make our world a better place by removing superstitions and myths. I want to help push mankind into the future. There is nothing we can't accomplish if we release our minds to work. Someday, Arthur, man will travel to Mars. And that will just be the beginning!"

Mr. Jones slammed his door and started the engine. "Want to go for a ride?"

"Sure! It beats sitting in a church service," Arthur said with enthusiasm.

Arthur had never been in such a beautiful car. The seats were leather and still smelled new. Mr. Jones pulled out of the parking lot onto the street by the church. They could still hear Dr. Arnold's voice echoing in the auditorium. Mr. Jones looked over at Arthur, who was smiling broadly as he ran his hand over the dashboard. Mr. Jones pushed a button and the top folded away.

"Gee, Mr. Jones, I've never seen a neater car!"

"I'm glad you like it. Buckle up and I'll take you out on the highway and show you what it can do." They drove out to Highway 27 and then to I-70 east toward Baltimore. "Hold on, Arthur," Mr. Jones said as he pushed the accelerator to the floor. The powerful engine roared and Arthur was thrust back against the bucket seat. He swallowed hard. The wind in his face and his nervousness brought tears to his eyes, which blew out and ran backwards past his ears onto his neck.

"What's the matter, Arthur? Scared?" Mr. Jones laughed good-naturedly.

"No, it's just the wind," Arthur said, a bit embarrassed.

The speedometer quickly moved past 55, then 65, then 75. The wind pulled Arthur's hair straight back and the air rushed past his ears so loudly he couldn't hear Mr. Jones.

"What?" Arthur shouted.

"I said this is fun, isn't it?!" Mr. Jones shouted back with a laugh. He looked in the rearview mirror, shut his eyes as though in pain, and moaned, "Oh, no!"

"What's wrong?"

"The police." Mr. Jones cursed loudly and looked over at Arthur. "You want to outrun them?"

"You mean it?" Arthur said. "Aren't you afraid you'll lose your license?"

"Not if they don't catch me! Hold on!" Mr. Jones pushed down on the pedal and his Mustang began pulling away from the police car. They sped past a line of cars, then the road curved to the right just long enough for them to get out of view of the police car. Mr. Jones saw an exit sign, and had just enough time to cut between two cars and off to the highway below. He quickly pulled into a service station and stopped by a gas pump.

The police car sped right past the exit and continued across the overpass and soon the sound of the siren faded away. Arthur looked over at Mr. Jones, who sat with a victorious look on his face. He looked over his left shoulder and calmly drove out from the gas station, under the overpass, and turned onto the onramp that would take them back to Winfield.

Arthur felt guilty. He knew what had just happened was wrong, but he didn't say anything. They drove back to Winfield under the speed limit. Neither spoke a word, and when they came to Arthur's house, Mr. Jones said, "What's wrong, Arthur? Did I scare you?"

"No, it isn't that."

"What, then?"

"Well, I guess I feel a little guilty. Mom and Dad have tried to teach me to obey the laws and—"

"I know, I know," Mr. Jones interrupted. "But see, Arthur, that is what I have been talking about. Laws are just man made rules. We didn't hurt anybody. I was in control the whole time. Guilt is just one more thing that churches have used to keep people in line. But in this modern day, guilt is becoming a thing of the past. We are here to enjoy life, Arthur! Live a little!"

"I suppose you're right, Mr. Jones," Arthur said, nodding his head slowly.

Later that night, as Arthur sat alone in his room, he thought to himself, *Mr. Jones understands where I'm coming from. Mom and Dad are so backward and old-fashioned. I have to sneak around to go to the movies I want to see. They are always trying to get me back into church. Why can't they just understand that I want to enjoy life like any other kid? They are so negative! And why? Because of church and all the dusty old doctrines about everything being sinful.*

Arthur's mind was made up. He wanted to be like Mr. Jones—successful, intelligent, worldly. *He seems so sure of himself. He knows what he wants in life and he is determined to get it. I want to be like that.*

. . .

Arthur never returned to the Baptist church after that evening with Lewis Jones. He hardly spoke to Kathy or Cal, except to nod in the hallway when he couldn't avoid their eyes. His mom and dad grieved that Arthur had no spiritual interests, and they continued to pray for him night after night.

In his senior year, Arthur finally had his braces taken off. He smiled into the mirror and couldn't believe how straight and beautiful his teeth had become. Now he actually liked to smile. *If I could only get rid of these glasses,* he thought. *Then I wouldn't be a bad-looking guy.* All his money was being saved for college and he knew he couldn't afford the luxury of contact lenses.

One evening in his last semester of high school, Arthur came in late from studying for finals at the library. He heard his mother crying softly in the bedroom as his dad awkwardly tried to comfort her. "Now, now, Doris. We have to keep trusting God's Word.

Maybe when Arthur is older, he will understand his need for God. Remember what Proverbs says? 'Train up a child in the way he should go, and when he is old, he will not depart from it.'"

"That's just it, Harold. We haven't trained Arthur in the way he should go. We didn't insist that he keep attending church with us. We let him decide, and see where that has taken him? Away from God! Oh, Harold!" She began to cry sadly. Arthur resisted the impulse to run into their room and promise to attend church regularly. Instead, he shook his head sadly, hardened his heart, and tiptoed to his room.

. . .

In his senior year, Arthur wasn't sure what to expect when one day he was suddenly summoned to the school office. When he got there, he knew something was terribly wrong. His mother and her pastor were waiting for him.

"Mom, what's wrong?" Arthur asked.

"Oh, Arthur," she said with a quivering voice. Then she broke down in tears and couldn't speak. She sat down in one of the chairs by the office door.

"It's your father, Arthur," Pastor Stewart said softly as he put his hand on Arthur's shoulder. "He went to be with the Lord."

Arthur felt like someone had punched him full-force in the stomach. "No!" he exclaimed. "He couldn't have!" He tried to keep the tears back, but suddenly, his legs felt weak and he sat down next to his mother. He closed his eyes, leaned his head back and breathed deeply. Finally, he reached over and took his mother's hand, and they cried together.

Arthur looked up at the pastor and asked, "How did it happen?"

Pastor Stewart looked at Mrs. Wilson as though to say, "Is he serious? Doesn't he *know*?"

Arthur's mom shook her head. "He didn't know, Pastor. Harold didn't want to worry him. He wanted Arthur's senior year to be special, and with Arthur working so hard to earn a scholarship . . . well, Harold just thought it best not to say anything."

"About *what,* Mom?" Arthur asked.

She paused for a moment, then took Arthur's hand. Looking into his eyes, she explained, "Your dad had cancer, Arthur. It was a fast-growing type that the doctors simply couldn't do anything about. Surgery would have been no use."

"But Dad seemed so healthy. A little tired, but basically . . ." Arthur stopped, then hung his head. "How could I have been so stupid? Dad lost a lot of weight these last few months. I thought he was just on a diet, or something." He shook his head in self-disgust. "I've been so focused on my studies . . . I haven't thought about anything else!"

"That's all right, dear," Mrs. Wilson said, trying to comfort Arthur. "Your dad didn't want to worry you."

Arthur started crying. "But, Mom! I never got to say good-bye! I didn't get to tell him . . ." Arthur choked with deep emotion and his voice failed. He finally whispered with a husky voice, "I didn't get to tell him . . . that I loved him."

. . .

A few months later, Arthur graduated from high school with honors. Lewis Jones helped Arthur apply for scholarships, and with his high grades, Arthur was accepted at Georgetown University in the pre-med program, with nearly all of his expenses paid.

At first, after his father's death, Arthur felt intense guilt. He knew he had caused his dad a lot of pain by refusing to go to church and by saying that he didn't believe God existed. But now he was angry. *If God really existed,* he thought, *He wouldn't have let Dad die. No one loved God more. No one was more faithful. No, if this is the way God is, I don't want anything to do with Him!*

With that, Arthur determined to put God out of his mind once and for all. He was going to make something of his life that his father would have been proud of. He was going to find a cure for the cancer that claimed his dad's life. *If God couldn't take care of it, I will!*

Lingering self-doubts plagued Arthur. His glasses still made him self-conscious, so he took some money from his dad's insurance settlement and purchased a pair of contact lenses. Looking into a mirror one night, Arthur thought, *I look so much better! Dad would be proud.* He felt ready to enter college with a new sense of confidence.

That fall, Arthur and his mother stood by their old car in the dorm parking lot at Georgetown. She hugged him for too long, then stepped back with tears in her eyes and got into the car. Arthur thought about how his dad would have clumsily stuck out his hand and said, "Son, remember what we've taught you. Make us proud."

"I will, Dad. I promise," Arthur would have said, and for that moment, he would have meant it. He was surprised at the emotion that caught in his throat. "I'd better go in and get unpacked, Mom," he said with a husky voice. Then he turned and quickly walked into the dorm without looking back.

3

Faith to Change the Way We Feel

Remember our key verse, Titus 1:16? "They claim to know God, but by their actions they deny him." In Galatians 5, Paul lists some of the actions that have the practical effect of denying the existence of God:

> The acts of the sinful nature are obvious: . . . hatred, discord, jealousy, fits of rage, selfish ambition, dissensions, factions and envy; drunkenness, orgies, and the like. I warn you, as I did before, that those who live like this will not inherit the kingdom of God (Galatians 5:19-21).

As we examine this passage, let's look at some of the things people *feel*—the emotions which grow in people's lives when they take their eyes off the Lord. These, by the way, are the very emotions that eventually lead people into psychotherapy, and ironically, psychotherapy often increases the very pain which it claims to relieve.

HATRED

The first of the negative emotions Paul lists is "hatred," perhaps the strongest of the dark passions. It is a violent animosity that wishes evil upon another. It is what leads people to commit deliberate and violent acts.

Hatred is more than intense dislike of another person. It is a seething caldron of loathing and revulsion that can motivate a person to do things he believed himself incapable of, such as being brutal or killing someone. John warns us, "Anyone who hates his brother is a murderer, and you know that no murderer has eternal life in him" (1 John 3:15).

Hatred can lead to physical illness in the person who hates: hypertension, severe headaches, and heart disease are just some of the possible results. Hatred can also result in mental and emotional problems, such as anxiety, suspicion, and depression. Hatred is rooted in bitterness, and it will always affect one's spiritual life.[19] That is why we are warned in Leviticus 19:17, "Do not hate your brother in your heart."

John wrote, "Anyone who claims to be in the light but hates his brother is still in the darkness" (1 John 2:9). Hatred is a form of practical atheism; "if anyone says, 'I love God,' yet hates his brother, he is a liar. For anyone who does not love his brother, whom he has seen, cannot love God, whom he has not seen" (1 John 4:20).

DISCORD

Discord is seldom discussed as an emotion, but it comes from the same source as the hatred mentioned above—a heart full of bitterness. The Greek term, *eris,* speaks of willful contention, arguing, or love of strife. Romans 1:29 describes people who have this condition: "They have become filled with every kind of wickedness, evil, greed and depravity. They are full of envy, murder, strife, deceit and malice."

When Paul wrote to the Corinthians, who were proud of their "spiritual gifts," he told them that they were acting like unbelievers. "You are still worldly. For since there is jealousy and quarreling among you, are you not worldly?" (1 Corinthians 3:3). In his second letter, he warned them about the results of such discord: "quarreling, jealousy, outbursts of anger, factions, slander, gossip, arrogance and disorder" (2 Corinthians 12:20). Hardly a glowing recommendation for a self-proclaimed Spirit-filled church!

The English word *discord* has an interesting etymology, coming from the Latin *discors—dis*, meaning "apart," and *cors*, meaning "heart." Discord happens when hearts are far apart—apart from the Lord and the truth of His Word, and apart from fellow-believers, family, and friends.

Discord can take many forms: a casual statement of unhappiness with the youth pastor; a sarcastic comment about the music; whispering in the foyer about an offense between two brothers; criticism of the pastor's sermon, his style, his personality, or his work habits; or the fact that not all of the elders showed up for a specially designated work day at the church.

Discord can take the form of neighborhood or office gossip, where long-term friendships are broken. It can divide loving families as daughters are turned against parents by incompetent therapy which creates false memories of childhood sexual abuse.[20] It is one thing when families separate over the truth of the gospel. As Jesus said, "They will be divided, father against son and son against father, mother against daughter and daughter against mother, mother-in-law against daughter-in-law and daughter-in-law against mother-in-law" (Luke 12:53). It is something else altogether when families are divided by false teachings and petty disagreements, and that is what is happening in our day.

Discord is rampant among Christians as churches split over politics, race, power struggles, personality clashes, disappointments, hurts, and insignificant issues such as the color of the nursery wallpaper. We may think that churches tend to split over serious issues such as Bible doctrine, but oftentimes that's not the case.

I recently spoke with some pastors who were forced out of their churches through in-house political discord in their local congregations. I listened carefully to the charges that were leveled against them, but I didn't hear that these pastors were preaching heresy. In fact, in two cases, the churches were growing at an amazing rate, with many decisions for Christ. Still, there was discord in the churches. It appears that some of the members simply didn't like the leadership style of their pastors. Subsequent to the ejection of their pastors, these churches have begun a downward slide that will be difficult to reverse.

DOCTRINAL DIVISION

Doctrine, however, is another matter altogether. Some people have taken the biblical call for unity to the extreme, believing that Christians should never speak out against sin or false teaching in the church. Our church's radio and television ministry, *Return to the Word*, has been accused of being divisive because we gently point out that much of what passes for biblical teaching in our day is clearly false doctrine. For example, we try to expose psychological teaching for what it is, a "hollow and deceptive philosophy, which depends on human tradition and the basic principles of this world rather than on Christ" (Colossians 2:8).

We have been encouraged to ignore these false teachings in the interest of Christian unity, yet Jude warns us that "In the last times there will be scoffers who will follow their own ungodly desires. These are the men who divide you, who follow mere natural instincts and do not have the Spirit" (Jude 18-19).

It is rarely truth that divides fellow Christians. Rather, error is the main culprit. Jude describes those who introduce doctrinal discord into the Body of Christ: "These men are grumblers and faultfinders; they follow their own evil desires; they boast about themselves and flatter others for their own advantage" (Jude 16). We must guard our churches against doctrinal error, for it is only biblical truth that will set us free.

Prominent radio ministries with proud histories of solid biblical teaching have begun to introduce psychological teachings about spirit guides, dream interpretation, "sexual addictions," repressed memories, and other unscriptural subjects. When confronted about these new teachings, the leadership have either denied that certain guests even appeared on the programs (though they later admitted the truth), or cried out that they have been misunderstood and unfairly criticized.

What has happened to these wonderful ministries that once preached the simple truths of God's Word with fearlessness, confidence, and power? Somehow they have become convinced that the world offers a better way to produce inner peace.

Doctrinal deviation and wicked practices must be exposed and reproved. Paul writes, "Have nothing to do with the fruitless deeds of darkness, but rather expose them" (Ephesians 5:11).

JEALOUSY

Paul moves on in his list of destructive emotions: "jealousy, fits of rage, selfish ambition, dissensions, factions" (Galatians 5:20). Jealousy is a resentful emotion which stems from selfishness, envy, and fear. A person who is jealous is primarily concerned with his own desires and he envies the success or possessions of another or perhaps he fears the loss of his own status or position.

While husbands and wives biblically have the right to expect loyalty and faithfulness in their mates, jealousy is often the result of broken trust. This can happen in a variety of ways. One young husband I knew years ago thought it was funny to flirt with other women as he sat next to his wife at ball games. "It was just innocent fun," he assured his friends, but it wasn't amusing to his wife. His little suggestive comments created questions in his wife's mind concerning his trustworthiness, and I'm doubtful that she has full trust in her husband to this very day.

A young wife approached me hesitantly after I had spoken at a family retreat. She told me a story of heartache and betrayal by her husband. "He's away on a business trip right now," she said, "and I'm worried that he's being unfaithful. With AIDS and other sexually transmitted diseases, it's more than just his unfaithfulness that worries me. I'm actually afraid that he could be risking my life." Her trust was broken and she had reason to wonder whether her husband was in the arms of another woman.

Others have come to my office admitting to sexual immorality, but wondering why their mates can't forgive and forget. "I don't get it," the husband might say. "I told her I'm really, really sorry." But he doesn't understand that when trust has been broken in a marriage, it normally takes a long time to rebuild it.

Paul writes that "Love is patient, love is kind, and is not jealous" (1 Corinthians 13:4 NASB), yet many mates act in such a way that makes it virtually impossible for their spouses to trust them.

Real trust is possible only when there is a mutual love that "bears all things, believes all things, hopes all things, endures all things" (1 Corinthians 13:7). Why is this lacking in a large percentage of Christian marriages? Because we have stopped living like believers in Christ and have learned to live like the world. As I mentioned earlier, a recent Barna report stated that evangelical Christians now divorce at a higher rate than the general population. This can give unbelievers the impression that Christian marriages are no better than non-Christian marriages.

FITS OF RAGE

The term *rage* in Galatians 5:20 signifies an emotion of great violence or intensity. It may last but a few moments, but the consequences can last a lifetime. Our English word has an interesting connection through the French to the Latin roots *rabia* and *rabere,* meaning "rabies" and "to be mad." Rage is an uncontrolled storm of violent anger that results in deep emotional wounds and even physical harm. The Greek word for rage or wrath is *thumos,* or "deep passion." *Thumos,* in turn, comes from *thuo,* which means "to breathe hard," as from intense exertion.

I recently received a fax of a newspaper article from the Chicago area which exposed an incredibly foolish and embarrassing "therapy" that was taking place at a Christian men's retreat. The story ran on the front page of the *Daily Herald* and told of a former teaching pastor of one of America's largest and most influential churches who "now runs retreats that incorporate nudity and shouts of obscenity in anger therapy."[21]

The retreat included "inviting men to disrobe and discuss their shame or guilt about their bodies, using obscenity, and 'anger work' in which men speak angrily and hit a punching bag with a bar or tennis racquet."[22]

While the leaders of the church moved to distance themselves from these sinful and bizarre practices, an even more shocking accusation emerged: that it had taken 17 months for the church to respond to complaints about the retreat, and even then only because offended members went to the media after being ignored by the church leadership.

The report stated that the church's elders issued a statement after receiving "complaints from a participant at a retreat in 1994 where [the retreat leaders] encouraged attendees to use obscene language and roar like animals at one another." Another report said that at one retreat, hotel officials had to demand that the shouting of obscenities be stopped because it was bothering the other guests in the hotel. Isn't it an embarrassment to the church at large that *secular* hotel managers had to admonish *Christian* men for the shouting of obscenities?

Is it any wonder that the world laughs at Christians? Where is our power to live a life of self-control that honors our Lord? Are we no different from the world? Then it is true that we have become practical atheists in the way that we live. Peter laments this fact when he writes that Christians who follow false teachers "will bring the way of truth into disrepute" (2 Peter 2:2).

SELFISH AMBITION

"Selfish ambition" is rendered "strife" in the King James Version. The Greek term, *eritheia,* means "intrigue, faction, or strife." It is manipulative discord rooted in selfish desire to get one's own way. James writes, "Where you have envy and selfish ambition [*eritheia*], there you find disorder and every evil practice" (James 3:16).

I frequently hear of "blended families" where chaos rules, threatening their testimonies and marriages. While the details will vary, a common complaint is that the children are unruly and disrespectful, and in many cases the husband or wife encourage their children's rebellion, telling them they do not have to obey their step-parent.

In such cases, it is clear that control is a primary issue. The warring parents have failed to come to an agreement on who is to be the head of the home. James precisely describes this miserable experience: disorder and every evil practice.

What's amazing about selfish ambition or strife is that it never produces the result a person is seeking—personal satisfaction and happiness. Instead, it ends in violence, isolation, and emptiness. The person who is consumed with selfish ambition is an emotional atheist. He is afraid to trust God and believes he must get what he wants by his own efforts and manipulative schemes.

Peter writes about the need to trust God for justice and protection:

> Christ suffered for you, leaving you an example, that you should follow in his steps. He committed no sin, and no deceit was found in his mouth. When they hurled their insults at him, he did not retaliate; when he suffered, he made no threats. Instead, he entrusted himself to him who judges justly (1 Peter 2:21-23).

This concept is especially important for wives who have unbelieving husbands. In the next chapter, Peter writes these words: "For this is the way the holy women of the past who put their hope in God used to make themselves beautiful. They were submissive to their own husbands . . ." (1 Peter 3:5).

This may sound like unreasonable and archaic advice in our egalitarian era, yet the biblical message is clear: We must trust God to bring justice into our lives rather than seeking our own way through selfish strife.

DISSENSIONS

The next fruit of sin seems repetitive. After all, isn't dissension the same as strife? In one sense, perhaps, but it would be more accurate to think of dissension as the poisonous fruit of selfish ambition. The word translated "dissension" is *dichostasia*, which means "two positions" or "division." Paul uses this word when he writes, "I urge you, brothers, to watch out for those who cause divisions and put obstacles in your way that are contrary to the teaching you have learned. Keep away from them" (Romans 16:17).

While Paul was primarily addressing division in the church, the principle is applicable to divisions in the home as well. As a pastor, I am particularly distressed when I hear that a "Christian" psychotherapist has come between a married couple, encouraging one or the other to separate or divorce because of "irreconcilable differences." Ignoring the power of God to heal a damaged relationship, such counselors set themselves up as authorities who supersede the Scriptures.

One well-known Christian counselor encouraged a young man to "divorce" his own parents, since they were so controlling in his life. When the parents asked what they had done to offend their only son, they were told to leave him alone. They asked their church to intervene, but the pastoral staff sided with the counselor and refused to explain what the parents had done. The therapist had come between the parents and their son to such an extent that when a grandson was born, they were not even allowed to see him.[23]

The counselor had caused division in the family, put obstacles in the way of unity, and caused the son to dishonor his father and his mother, contrary to the plain teaching of Scripture. Paul is clear when he says, "Keep away from them [those who cause such division]" (Romans 16:17).

When he wrote to the carnal believers in Corinth, Paul lamented the fact that the church was acting like a convention of practical atheists, since there was "envy, strife, and divisions among you."

He asks this question: "Are you not carnal and behaving like mere men?" (1 Corinthians 3:3, NKJV). His conclusion was that the Corinthians were worldly and not spiritual.

It is important to note in this context that God is not at all impressed with spiritual veneers. Christians can speak in tongues, prophesy, sing praise choruses to the mind-numbing beat of drums, cast out demons, wave hankies, laugh uncontrollably, and fall over unconscious, yet remain filthy with sin. Such external "motions" won't change the fact that they are acting like divisive atheists.

HERESIES

The last fruit of worldliness mentioned in Galatians 5:20 is "factions," or as translated in the King James Version, "heresies," a transliteration from the Greek, *hairesis. Heresy* is used to speak of doctrine which differs from the Word of God. Peter warns about false prophets who will infiltrate the church by "secretly introduc[ing] destructive heresies, even denying the sovereign Lord who bought them" (2 Peter 2:1).

If you study 2 Peter chapter 2 in the light of Christian psychotherapy, you will find some interesting descriptions. Verse 2 says, "Many will follow their shameful ways and will bring the way of truth into disrepute." Secular newspaper articles openly scoff at weird practices that masquerade as Christian therapy. Journalists such as Mark Pendergrast point out that Christians are at the center of foolish practices.

> Unfortunately, many of the [false memory syndrome] characteristics . . . have appeared in mainstream Christian counseling, particularly in the national chain of Minirth-Meier New Life Clinics (formerly Minirth-Meier Clinics) [and now New Life Clinics]. Until the '70s "Christian counseling" generally meant going to confession or talking with a pastor about marital difficulties. But in the late 1970s and 1980s, pop psychology invaded the field, and Christian psychologists such as

Larry Crabb, James Dobson, Frank Minirth, and Paul Meier began their lucrative psychological ministries through counseling centers, radio programs, newsletters and organizations.[24]

After mentioning specific cases of therapeutic abuse, Pendergrast again names James Dobson, Fred and Florence Littauer, and Dan Allender as some who have helped spread the belief in recovered memories. "All too many Christian counselors have taken such books to heart and it is usually good Christian families that are being blown apart as a result."[25]

Today, as more and more Christians rush to the psychologist's office for advice rather than seeking out a godly pastor or elder, the world might well be tempted to wonder why Christians are always in need of psychotherapy. Are Christians crazy by definition?

One of the most influential Christian organizations in America believes that pastors and elders are simply incompetent to deal with real problems of living. On its national broadcast, a well-known Christian psychiatrist stated that critics of psychology and psychiatry are "pharisees, hypocrites, and legalists."[26]

What motivates the Christian psychological industry? While I personally believe that many psychologists have a sincere desire to help hurting people, it is difficult not to allow money to compromise their motives. When licensed professional counselors are able to bill insurance companies large sums for treatment of their patients, the temptation to keep clients in therapy for a few more weeks can be overwhelming. Repeated reports from across the nation prove this point as time and again, callers have told us that the moment insurance funds were cut off, patients were miraculously cured.

Peter wrote, "In their greed these teachers will exploit you with stories they have made up" (2 Peter 2:3). Psychotherapists who specialize in repressed memory recovery are experts in making up stories. Through hypnotic techniques, they convince vulnerable clients that they were so horribly abused in their childhood they can't even remember the traumatic events which led to the repression.

Repressed memory recovery is a "no lose" situation for a therapist because if there was actual abuse, the client may indeed recall some traumatic events, and if there was no abuse, the fact that there are no memories is viewed as proof that such abuse must have taken place, causing memory repression.

One of the common results of psychotherapy is the emotional support it provides for giving in to our sin nature. We are told that we need greater self-esteem and that we must assert our rights. We are encouraged to resist spiritual authority within the church since most conservative churches are, by definition, controlling and abusive. There is even a support group called Fundamentalists Anonymous for those who have been abused by repressive churches. Peter warns us against false teachers who lead Christians to "follow the corrupt desire of the sinful nature," for these teachers cause people to "despise authority" (2 Peter 2:10).

This contempt for pastors and elders is evident throughout the psychological industry and the legal system. I was once asked to testify as a character witness at a hearing for a legal separation, but the judge ruled that I could not testify because I am not a psychologist and am, therefore, not considered an expert witness. A pastor is viewed as categorically unqualified to testify regarding character, emotions, and needs.

Marriage and divorce are supremely spiritual issues, yet even Christians view pastors with a mixture of condescension and contempt in matters related to marriage and divorce while they view psychologists and psychiatrists with awe, believing them to be the true experts on the soul.

Another frightening result of heretical teaching is sexual impurity. Peter warns about false teachers "with eyes full of adultery, they never stop sinning; they seduce the unstable" (2 Peter 2:14). Those who enter counseling are vulnerable to the suggestions, personality, and authority of their counselor. This often leads to sexual involvement, with tragic consequences.

Some of the most vulnerable individuals are those who are recent converts. They are still new in the faith and may have little understanding of the Scriptures, but are trusting and easily led. As a result, a counselor who does not have a firm commitment to and understanding of God's Word can do great harm to a new believer. Peter warns, "By appealing to the lustful desires of sinful human nature, they entice people who are just escaping from those who live in error" (2 Peter 2:18). What a sad picture! Here are spiritual infants trying to move away from the wickedness of the world yet are sucked back toward wickedness by false teachers within the church itself.

Peter says that the false teachers "promise them freedom, while they themselves are slaves of depravity" (2 Peter 2:19). Look at the terrifying consequences of heresy:

> If they have escaped the corruption of the world by knowing our Lord and Savior Jesus Christ and are again entangled in it and overcome, they are worse off at the end than they were at the beginning. It would have been better for them not to have known the way of righteousness, than to have known it and then to turn their backs on the sacred command that was passed on to them. Of them the proverbs are true: "A dog returns to its vomit," and, "A sow that is washed goes back to her wallowing in the mud" (2 Peter 2:20-22).

We dare not allow our lives to get out of control by unbiblical thinking and actions. The consequences are too severe. If we want to find the peace that God offers, we will have to learn how to reclaim a living and powerful faith. If that's what you long for, then continue reading; we're coming to that soon.

Loss of Hope

One morning as he hurried to Biology 101, Arthur bumped into a beautiful young woman. "Oh, I'm sorry," she apologized sweetly. "I didn't see you." Arthur's eyes followed her as she walked into the classroom. He noticed that his mouth was dry and his hands were sweaty. As he walked into the room, he looked to see if there might be a seat near the beauty he had just seen, but the chairs around her were already occupied.

He couldn't concentrate the entire hour. Though he was five seats away from her, he was unaware of anyone else in the room. He carefully observed her every feature. She had long blond hair pulled back behind her ears and kept in place with gold barrettes. She was wearing a powder blue sweater and matching skirt. Her unblemished skin looked clean and soft and he could still smell her perfume on his sweater from when she had bumped into him. He liked the fact that she didn't appear to need makeup to enhance her beauty.

After class, Arthur waited outside the door for what seemed forever. Finally she walked out. Just as she walked by him, Arthur stepped in her way and said, "Excuse me. Aren't you the one who bumped into me before class?"

"Yes," she said hesitantly. "I did apologize."

"Well, that's just it. I think you owe me more than an apology," Arthur said sternly.

"What do you mean?" she said, looking around with embarrassment to see if anyone was watching. No one was, for the hallway was already empty.

"I mean, I think you owe me a dinner," he said with a hint of a smile.

"Dinner? I should buy you dinner for accidentally bumping into you?" She said indignantly.

"No. You should let me buy you dinner," he smiled and turned to walk with her. "Would you mind?"

"I don't know if I should. I don't even know your name."

"And I don't know yours, but I was hoping we could solve our mutual ignorance." Arthur stuck out his hand and said, "I'm Arthur Wilson and I'm the sort of young man your mother hopes you'll marry someday. I'm going to be a famous doctor and . . . I'm also a gentleman."

"Well, Arthur," she replied with amusement, "I'm Susan Aldrich and my mother warned me about young men like you.

She said I shouldn't trust the first guy who showed too quick an interest in me."

"Oh, I hope I'm not the first. How about it? Dinner tonight?"

"Maybe, but on one condition."

"What?"

"You have to find someone for my roommate."

"Your roommate? I was hoping it would be just the two of us."

"Nope. I just found out your name. How do I know if I can trust you alone?" she said with a hint of laughter.

"Well, I don't smoke or chew. I rarely spit, and I have very few disgusting habits. I can give you references. My mom likes me and there's Lewis Jones, my high school biology professor, and . . ." he counted them off on his fingers.

"Not good enough, bucko. Find my roommate a date and the four of us can go out. Say about 6:00 this evening?"

Arthur rolled his eyes in resignation. "Okay, Miss Aldrich. Six o'clock it is."

"With a date for Melissa?"

"What does she look like?" *I bet she's a dog!* he thought.

"She's cute! Come on, Mr. Wilson. Now it's your turn to trust me."

"Okay. Where should I pick you up?"

"I'll be at the library studying, like you should be," she said as she walked off.

"What section?" he called after her.

"Business. You'll find out, Arthur, I'm all business."

Arthur hurried to his dorm to find someone for Susan's roommate. Most of the guys were in class. *Man, I've got to find somebody. I have a date with the most beautiful girl on campus!* His heart pounded with excitement. He knocked on several doors and got no reply until he came to George Ramsey's room.

"Just a minute!" George called as Arthur knocked loudly. George opened the door and saw Arthur standing there red-faced and anxious.

"What do you need, Arthur?"

"I need a big favor, George."

"Sorry, pal," George said, starting to close the door. "I don't make loans to friends."

"I don't want a loan, George. I need someone to double date with me tonight. I have a date with a dream, but she won't go without her roommate. What do you say?"

"No way, Arthur. If this girl is so ugly her roommate has to set her up, count me out!"

"Susan says she's cute. Come on, George. If she's even half as cute as Susan she'll be gorgeous."

"Who is this Susan?"

"Her name is Susan Aldrich and she's a goddess. I can't believe she said yes. Don't mess it up for me. Please, George," Arthur begged.

George sighed. "What's it worth to you, buddy?"

"What do you mean?"

"I've heard you're pretty smart in biology. That's my worst subject. How about tutoring me?"

"Just for going on one date?"

"It's your choice, Arthur. Otherwise, I'll have to stay here and study all evening."

"All right, George. But if her roommate is as pretty as Susan says, I don't owe you anything. Deal?"

"Deal."

. . .

Arthur and George walked toward the library at 5:45. Both were sharply dressed and smelled of fresh aftershave. "I still bet she's a dog," George complained.

"You'd better hope she is, if you want me to tutor you in biology," Arthur said as he playfully shoved George off the sidewalk.

They walked into the library and found the business section. There in a study booth, Arthur saw Susan. She looked even more gorgeous than he remembered. He motioned for George to stay put and then tiptoed behind her. Leaning over, he whispered, "Excuse me, Miss Aldrich, but there's a handsome young man asking for you."

"Tell him I already have a date with you," she whispered back as she turned to face him, with a smile of welcome on her lips.

Her beauty erased the snappy comeback from his mind and he stood there dumbly, staring at her in awe. He finally blinked and regained his composure. "Where's your roommate?" he asked.

"She went to the reference section. She'll be back any minute. Where's her date?"

"Right over there," Arthur pointed toward George, who stood self-consciously by the stacks.

"Oh, he's kind of cute, Arthur. What's his name?"

"George Ramsey, and don't get any ideas. You're with me tonight, remember?"

"Of course, Arthur," she said as she watched George walk toward them. "I think Melissa will like him."

"Well, I hope she's as cute as you say. Otherwise, I've got a long semester of tutoring ahead."

"Well, decide for yourself," Susan said as Melissa appeared in the doorway. Arthur looked up to see a dark-haired model approaching. She walked with a grace and confidence that forced Arthur to stare wide-eyed.

George smiled at Arthur and whispered, "You're home free, pal. Maybe I'll owe you the favor."

. . .

When Susan and Melissa got back to their dorm that night, they compared notes. "George is so handsome!" Melissa gushed. "I bet you are jealous that he was my date."

"He's cute, all right," Susan agreed, "but I really enjoyed myself with Arthur."

"What do you see in him?" Melissa asked sincerely. "I mean, he's not really all that gorgeous, do you think?"

"I think he's kind of sweet. And I like his sense of humor. I'm not sure what it is, but I want to see him again. Do you think he's bad-looking?"

"Not bad-looking at all," Melissa said as she began to pin up her hair. "But I'll take George any day."

As Susan lay in bed that night, she thought to herself, *I guess he's not all that handsome, but I like him. He has dignity, and he can have fun. I like it that he makes me laugh. And he's a gentleman. He makes me feel secure. And he's smart.* She nodded in the dark a smile playing on her lips. *Yeah, I want to see him again.*

. . .

Soon Arthur and Susan were seeing each other regularly. They usually met at the library because both were serious students. One night, as Arthur walked Susan back to her dorm, he put his arm around her and felt her soft body draw close to his. His heart rate increased and his breathing deepened. They stopped under a large oak tree that blocked the streetlight, producing a dark shadow.

Susan turned toward Arthur and looked into his eyes. She leaned ever so slightly toward him as he bent down. Their lips met and Arthur felt a warmth surge through his entire body. Susan linked her hands around his neck and kissed him again. She felt safe and loved as she lay her face against his shoulder and felt his strong arms hold her tightly against him. Neither spoke for several minutes. Finally, Susan whispered, "I think I love you, mister."

Arthur's heart seemed to flip inside his chest. "Oh, Susan!" he sighed. "How can it be true? How did a guy like me get a goddess to love him?"

"I couldn't help myself," she teased. They began to walk again, hand in hand. After a few minutes of silence, Susan asked, "What attracted you to me, Arthur?"

"Everything. The way you walk, the way you wear your hair, your smile. I have never seen anyone so beautiful."

"Oh, Arthur," she sighed as she stopped and kissed him again.

"Now it's your turn. What did you see in me?" Arthur chuckled.

"Well, the first thing that attracted me was your self confidence and sense of humor. The more I got to know you, the more I realized how brilliant you are. And Arthur, you make me feel safe and loved."

Arthur put his arm around Susan and felt her body become tense. "What's wrong, Susan?" he asked. "Oh, nothing," she said, but Arthur sensed a fear in Susan he didn't understand.

"Tell me, Susan," he said gently. "What's wrong?"

"I . . ." she hesitated. "I can't tell you right now, Arthur. It's too soon. Come on, I'd better get to the dorm."

. . .

That night, Susan lay in her bed crying bitterly into her pillow. Melissa was asleep and Susan didn't want to wake her. Susan had known too much sorrow in her nineteen years. No one knew the terror she had experienced since she was fourteen. That was when the doctors found cancer in her mother. She was confined to bed for longer periods of time after each round of chemotherapy.

Susan's father, Jarvis Aldrich, had made a fortune in the stock market and was an executive used to getting what he wanted. He felt helpless and angry as he watched his wife wasting away, and he became physically and emotionally frustrated.

One awful night, Mr. Aldrich had come home drunk. Susan was sleeping in her room down the hallway from the master bedroom. She awakened to hear her door open and saw her father swaying drunkenly from side to side.

"Come here, Susan," he said slurring his words. "Come kiss your daddy." Obediently, she got up and came to him to kiss his cheek. "No. I want a real kiss!" he demanded. He pulled her close to himself and felt her developing body against his.

She tried to resist. "No, Daddy! Stop!" But he didn't stop, that night or on many nights that followed. Each time he said he was sorry and it would never happen again. He warned her not to tell anyone. "They'll never believe you, anyway. It's your word against mine. It would kill your mother, if she knew what you've done with me. If the authorities did believe you, they'd take you out of our home and put you in foster care."

Susan's school work began to deteriorate in the months that followed. She lost weight and often thought of killing herself. She hated herself and knew that no man would ever want her if he found out what had happened to her.

When Susan was seventeen, her mother was rushed to the hospital for the last time. Susan watched as the heart monitor beeped slower and slower until it stopped, and her mother was gone. Susan sat beside the bed and stared out the window until the nurse came and led her out of the room.

At the funeral, Susan sat next to her mother's sister Millie. As they left the burial plot, Millie took Susan by the hands and said, "Child, you've lost so much weight! Is it just your mother's death?" Susan saw her father look over in their direction and frown. Susan nodded sadly and said, "Yes, Aunt Millie. I just don't have an appetite anymore."

"Are you sure that's all?" Millie asked.

Susan looked into Millie's eyes and sensed that she knew. She drew strength from her aunt's touch and stood straight.

"No! That's not all! Aunt Millie, you have to help me make Daddy stop what he's doing to me." Susan told her aunt everything, weeping hysterically. Her aunt held her and rocked from side to side. "There, there, child. I'll never let him hurt you again."

Millie confronted Jarvis that night, but he denied everything. "She's lying through her teeth! I've never touched her, Millie. I swear it! Why would she say such a thing?" But Millie didn't believe him, and a physical examination proved that Susan had been violated. To spare Susan additional trauma, Millie demanded that Susan be allowed to come live with her and that Jarvis would be responsible to provide financial support until Susan married.

"You'll put it in writing, Jarvis," she said ominously, "or I'll go to the authorities."

Jarvis agreed to Millie's terms and Susan moved away from her nightmare to live in safety with Aunt Millie.

. . .

Susan awoke with a start and found herself back in the college dormitory. Even after two years of psychiatric therapy, she still felt empty and worthless. She had difficulty sleeping until her psychiatrist prescribed a strong anti-anxiety medication. She was afraid of men, in general. Yet, she felt drawn to Arthur. Maybe he was different. Maybe she could trust him.

. . .

After a couple of months, Arthur asked Susan to travel home with him for the weekend. He wanted his mom to meet the girl he planned to marry. Mrs. Wilson and Susan hit it off right away. Susan didn't seem to notice the old wallpaper and the worn carpet. When Mrs. Wilson asked her that Saturday night if she would be going to church with her the next morning, she responded, "I'd love to."

Arthur looked at her in surprise, but didn't argue. Later, as they sat in the old swing on the front porch, Arthur said, "I didn't know you were interested in religion."

"I never have been, actually," she replied as though in deep thought. "But I've always wondered about it. I mean, why do so many people find an inner need to worship? What causes people to sing about an ancient teacher like Jesus? What motivates them to give a large part of their money to their churches? I guess I'm just curious, that's all."

"Oh. I'm glad," Arthur said, relieved. "I mean, I'm glad you're curious and that's all. I grew up with all that Jesus stuff, and I decided a long time ago that I don't need religion to help make sense of my world."

"But don't you ever wonder?"

"About what?"

"About life itself. Where did the world come from? Why are we here? How did that first living cell manage to survive and duplicate itself? How did those cells group together and special-ize their functions in order to create living organisms? What force directed evolutionary progress? What makes something right and another thing wrong? Why is there love and hatred? What makes people hurt others?"

Arthur saw in Susan an intellectual depth he hadn't recog-nized before. "Where'd you come up with all those questions, Honey? You sound like a philosopher."

"I guess I never thought much about such things until my mom died. Then I began to wonder what happened to her. Did she just die like an animal and totally cease to exist? Or do we have an immaterial part that continues to exist after we die? I some-times wonder if she . . . ." Tears filled her eyes as she remembered her mother.

"Come here, little one," Arthur said tenderly as he put his arm around Susan and pulled her close. "It's okay. Everyone asks those questions at one time or other. It's part of the mystery of the cosmos. Some things we just don't understand yet."

Susan regained her composure as she wiped her tears away and asked, "Will you come to church with us tomorrow?"

"For you, my love, I'd go anywhere," he said as he gently kissed her.

. . .

The next morning, Mrs. Wilson left for Sunday School while Arthur and Susan stayed behind until it was time to go to the worship service. A little later, they walked, hand in hand, toward the little Baptist church Arthur had rejected several years before.

Susan seemed to enjoy the singing of the congregation. She sat listening, unfamiliar with the tunes, until they began to sing "Amazing Grace." *I know that one,* she thought. The congrega-tion stood and Susan began to sing with them, "Amazing grace, how sweet the sound that saved a wretch like me! I once was lost, but now am found, was blind, but now I see."

Arthur didn't sing with her. In fact, he was irritated. She didn't notice because her eyes were closed and a tear escaped and wandered down her cheek as the congregation sang, "Through many dangers, toils, and snares, I have already come; 'tis grace hath brought me safe thus far, and grace will lead me home."

As they were returning to the university, Susan said, "I like your mom, Arthur. She's real, you know?" *That's what a home should be*, she thought. *Simple, ordinary, and full of love.*

. . .

As Susan's involvement with Arthur deepened, she was terrified that he might leave her. For the first time in her life she felt loved by a man for her own sake and she desperately needed Arthur. She had not planned on giving herself to Arthur physically until they were married, but one night, as they embraced in his room, passion overcame him.

Susan protested mildly. "Stop, Arthur," she said. But as he held her close and kissed her, she felt her resistance crumble. Her heart and body began to respond and she gave in to his desire.

A few weeks later, Susan came to Arthur and said fearfully, "Arthur, I have to tell you something."

Arthur could see it in her eyes. "You're pregnant, aren't you?"

Susan nodded her head in shame. Arthur exploded. "Why didn't you protect yourself? I assumed you were on the pill!"

"It wasn't my fault, Arthur. I hadn't planned on us . . . you know. I asked you to stop." She paused, waiting for him to agree, but he just stood there. "What are we going to do?"

" *We?* There is nothing *we* are going to do. But there is something *you* are going to do. You are going to have an abortion and quick!"

"Oh, no, Arthur! I can't. How can we kill our child?"

"It's not a child yet, Susan. It's a fetus—just some tissue. Listen to me," he said in a desperate tone of voice she had never heard from him. "We both have many years of school ahead of us. We can't afford to have our plans messed up now with a baby."

Susan began to shake as she tried to hold her tears inside. She turned away so Arthur couldn't see. She longed for him to gently put her arms around her and tell her of his continued love, but he just stood there looking at the floor. He finally raised his head. "What are you going to do, Susan?"

"I don't know, Arthur," she said coldly. "But you don't have to worry yourself about me any longer." She suddenly started to walk away. Arthur reached out and grabbed her arm.

"Susan, wait! Let's talk this out."

She looked up at him with deep hurt and anger in her eyes. "I thought you loved me, but you're just like all the other men. You use a woman and blame her for the problem that comes. Don't worry, Arthur. You can go ahead with your studies and your career. Don't worry about me or the baby." She jerked her arm away, turned, and walked out of the room.

She fought back her tears, set her lips hard, and walked away toward her dorm, not daring to look anyone in the face. When she got to her room, she shut the door and threw herself on the bed with a groan of anguish. Her entire body convulsed with sobs. The awful nightmare of two previous abortions her father had forced her to undergo rushed into her mind.

The desire to end it all flooded her being and she staggered into the bathroom and opened the medicine cabinet. There on the shelf were the pills her psychiatrist had prescribed for anxiety. She opened the bottle and dumped all of them into her hand. Quickly, she swallowed every pill and washed them down with large gulps of water. Then she walked slowly back to her bed, lay down, and waited for the darkness.

About twenty minutes later, Melissa came back from class. She saw Susan stretched out on the bed, looking deathly pale. "Susan?" Susan didn't move. "Susan!" Melissa rushed to her side and took Susan's cold hand. "Oh! Susan! Wake up!"

Melissa ran out of the room, down the hall to the pay phone, forgetting to bring any coins. Halfway to the phone, she stopped, ran back, and grabbed her purse. She dumped its contents on her bed, rummaged through everything and found some change.

Just then Barbara Alpert walked by. "Hi, Melissa! Hi, Susan!" she shouted merrily.

"Barbara!" Melissa screamed. "Call an ambulance! Something's wrong with Susan! I can't wake her!"

. . .

Susan awoke in the hospital. She had the worst headache of her life, but she was alive. She groaned softly. Melissa was dozing in the chair by the bed. "Melissa?" Susan said sleepily.

"Susan!" Melissa grabbed her hand with a smile of relief. "Thank God, Susan! I was so afraid."

Dr. Samuel Jenson came in a few minutes later. "So you're finally awake, Sleeping Beauty!" he joked. He stood beside Susan, across from Melissa. "You had a close call, young lady. Fortunately, we got your stomach pumped in time. What could make a wonderful young woman like you try to take her own life?"

Susan turned away from him. Her eyes were swollen nearly shut and her eyelids and cheeks were a dark purplish brown.

"Don't want to talk about it, huh?" he said softly. "Well, we need to keep you here for a couple of days to see that there aren't any further complications." He looked at Melissa and nodded toward the door. "I need to talk with her alone for a minute." Melissa left the room and Dr. Jenson closed the door.

He scratched his chin and cleared his throat. "Look at me, Susan." She turned reluctantly. "You were bleeding pretty heavily when you came in. You miscarried. I'm sorry."

Susan stared at the ceiling without speaking. Tears welled up in her eyes then slid silently down and dropped onto the bed. "Is there anyone we should call? Your parents?"

"No. Don't call anyone. I'll be fine." The doctor left and Melissa returned and sat beside Susan.

"Want me to call Arthur?"

"No!" Susan snapped as she looked at Melissa angrily.

"For goodness sakes, Susan, don't yell at me. I'm just trying to help."

"I'm sorry, Melissa. But no. Don't call Arthur. It's over with us."

"Over? I thought you were going to marry him. What happened?"

"It's just over, that's all."

. . .

Arthur didn't find out that Susan was in the hospital until the next day when he called the dorm to talk with her.

"May I speak with Susan Aldrich, please?" he asked the operator at the main desk.

"I'm sorry, she's not in."

"Do you know when she'll be back?"

"I can't give out that information. I'm sorry."

"Come on, Janet. This is Arthur. Where is she?"

"I'm not supposed to say," she whispered as she looked around. "She's at the hospital."

"The hospital? What happened to her?"

"I don't really know. The rumor is she took some pills, but I don't know."

"Thanks, Janet!" He hung up the phone, grabbed his jacket, and rushed out.

At the hospital information desk, he asked which room Susan was in. "She's on the fourth floor, but you'll need to stop at the nurses' station first."

Arthur waited impatiently by the elevators. "Come on . . . come on," he urged the elevators to move, but they all seemed nonfunctioning. While looking around he spotted the stairway, went through the door, and rushed up three flights, two stairs at a time. When he got to the fourth floor, he walked quickly down the hallway to the nurses' station.

"I want to see Susan Aldrich, please."

"Are you a relative?"

"Well, no. Not exactly. I'm her boyfriend."

"I'm sorry. The doctor said no visitors today," the nurse said firmly.

"Can you at least tell me how she's doing?"

The nurse looked irritated. "She's stable. That's all I can tell you," she said as she picked up a chart and walked away.

Arthur ran his hand through his hair in frustration. Just then he saw Melissa get off the elevator. He waved at her and she nodded back with tight lips.

"Melissa! Tell me . . . what happened to Susan?" Arthur pled as she walked past him.

"I can't say, Arthur. She won't tell me. All I know is, she took an overdose and we barely got her here in time to save her life."

Shocked speechless, Arthur slumped against the wall.

Now it was Melissa's turn to ask questions. "What happened between you two, Arthur? I thought you were in love."

"I do love her, Melissa. It's just . . . " He stopped. "You'll have to ask Susan."

He looked up and down the hallway. "I've got to see her. Which room is she in?"

"You aren't allowed in," Melissa whispered.

"Please, Melissa. Tell me. I've got to talk with her."

"All right, but if you get in trouble, don't involve me."

"I won't. Which room?"

"She's in 403. And make it quick. The nurse comes by every fifteen or twenty minutes."

"Thanks, Melissa." Arthur patted Melissa's arm and snuck into room 403. Susan was asleep in her bed. "Susan?" he spoke her name gently. She stirred and opened her eyes a little.

"What do you want?" she mumbled.

"Susan, darling," He took her hand. "I just wanted to . . . ."

She pulled her hand away and said, "I don't want you here. It's over, Arthur. You made that plain enough. And you don't have to worry about the baby! That's over, too! Now get out of my life!" She closed her eyes and turned away.

Arthur stood there in shock. Just then, the nurse Arthur had seen at the desk walked in. "I thought I told you no visitors!"

"I'm just on my way out!" Arthur said bitterly as he left.

. . .

Arthur and Susan didn't date each other again that year, nor the next. Both dated other students, but nothing serious developed. Susan was afraid to get close to another man. *Each time I do, I get hurt,* she thought.

Arthur concentrated on his studies and tried to put Susan out of his mind. He had to maintain good grades to keep his scholarships active. Occasionally, Arthur would see Susan walking across the campus, but she never acted as if she noticed him.

One day in their senior year Arthur saw Susan walking out of the library. She was still the most beautiful woman he had ever seen. She looked especially beautiful this day, dressed casually in a plaid skirt and a wine-colored shell. Her shining blond hair was pulled back the way he liked it. His heart seemed to rise into his throat as she made her way down the sidewalk.

Arthur knew that he still loved Susan and felt that he just had to talk with her. He hurried up behind her. "Hi, stranger," he said as casually as possible. Susan turned and looked at him with mixed emotions.

"Hello, Arthur," she said tightly as she kept walking.

"Susan, please stop. I want to talk with you for a minute." Susan stopped, but did not turn to face him. "Look at me, Susan, will you?"

She slowly turned and faced him. "What do you want?" she said wearily.

"I want to see you again. I miss you more than I can say. I . . . I still love you. I want you to forgive me. Please, Susan." She looked up into his eyes and saw love, and for the first time in nearly three years, her dead heart began to beat again with hope.

"Do you mean it, Arthur?"

Arthur took her hands, his voice quivering. "Oh, Susan. I've never meant anything so much in my life. I can't think of living without you."

He took her in his arms and kissed her so hard it took her breath away. He felt her body relax against his and thought he would explode with happiness.

"I have missed you so much, Susan," he said as she lay her head against his shoulder.

. . .

A bolt of lightning flashed outside and thunder shook the house. Dr. Wilson's mind returned to the present in Bethesda. He missed Susan now like he had back in college. How he longed to see her, to hold her, and tell her how sorry he was.

. . .

Dr. Wilson got up early Monday morning, showered, shaved, and got dressed for work. He looked over at Susan's picture on the bureau. He wondered where she was and hoped he could keep his mind busy at work, but there was a tension inside he couldn't make go away.

He drove the few miles to the National Cancer Institute, parked his car, and went inside. He walked through the entrance and turned down the corridor toward the cafeteria. He wanted breakfast.

The cafeteria was already crowded but he found an empty table by the back wall where he could read *The Washington Post* in relative quiet.

He tried to put Susan out of his mind, but even in a crowded cafeteria, he felt terribly alone. *I've got to talk to someone,* he thought. But he didn't know anyone he trusted to help with personal problems. *Science, yes, but marriage? No way.*

Arthur briefly considered calling Susan's pastor, but shook his head in anger at himself for his weakness. He finished his coffee, picked up his briefcase and paper, and walked to his office.

. . .

Susan sat in her car listening to the gentle morning rain. She prayed quietly. *Dear Lord, I need help. Our marriage is almost over. Arthur hates me and I've lost nearly every shred of love I had for him. Please give Dr. Miller wisdom to guide me.*

Just before nine, the church secretary, Marianne Dunbar, drove up and parked her car. She noticed Susan sitting in her car and walked over. "Susan! I thought that was you. What are you doing here sitting in the rain?"

Susan rolled down the window. "Hello, Marianne. I was hoping I could see Dr. Miller for a few minutes. I am so confused," Susan stammered as she began to cry.

"Oh, Susan," Marianne sympathized, gently touching her arm. "Come inside with me. Let me fix you a hot cup of coffee."

The church office was attractively furnished. It showed good taste, without gaudiness. Marianne invited Susan to sit in her office while she made the coffee. Other staff began to arrive and greeted one another cheerfully in the foyer. Susan was glad she could sit in the privacy of Marianne's office. She didn't want anyone else to see her crying. Soon Marianne returned with the coffee and sat down.

"What's happening, Susan? Is there anything you can tell me about until Pastor comes?"

"Thanks, Marianne. I need to talk to someone. Ever since I started attending church here I have been learning so much about spiritual things. But it seems that the closer I get to God, the further my husband and I drift apart." She sipped her coffee as Marianne waited for her to continue.

"Pastor Miller makes it so easy to understand spiritual things that I thought Arthur would surely want Christ in his life, too. Instead, he told me that he is an atheist. Marianne, he really hates God, and he hates me, too."

Marianne heard Pastor Miller's private door open. "I think Pastor Miller is here, Susan. I'll go see if he can meet with you." She walked out and shut the door. Susan could hear her footsteps as Marianne walked down the hall to the pastor's office and knocked.

"Come in," Pastor Miller invited cheerfully. Marianne went in and shut the door behind her. "Good morning, Marianne!" Dr. Miller's voice boomed. "What a wonderful rainy day!"

"Hi, Pastor. Do you remember Susan Wilson? She's one of our newer members."

"Of course I remember Mrs. Wilson! She accepted Christ a little while back. What's up?"

"She's in my office, and seems terribly upset. She and her husband must have had a terrible fight. She wonders if you could take time to see her. I know you prefer it if people have appointments, but she seems so distressed."

Pastor Miller sighed, looked at his watch, and nodded. "I have a little time before my first appointment. Show her in."

"Thanks, Pastor," Marianne smiled and went to get Susan.

A few moments later, Susan entered Dr. Miller's office timidly. "Come in, Susan," he greeted her with a hearty smile. "Have a chair and tell me what's troubling you."

"I hardly know where to begin," Susan said nervously as she sat down in the chair opposite Dr. Miller's desk.

"Just tell me what happened to make you drive over here on such a rainy day," he chuckled pleasantly, helping to put Susan at ease.

"You've never met my husband, Pastor. He's a brilliant doctor and researcher with the National Cancer Institute. He's been antagonistic to religion since he was a child, but recently, when I told him of my decision to follow Christ, he openly declared that he is an atheist. He has become so hostile and cruel to me that I can't take much more. I packed my suitcase this morning to leave him. It's sitting out there in my car. I love Arthur and I don't really want to leave him, but I just don't think I can take his anger much longer."

Dr. Miller sat quietly, listening to every word. He paused before answering, then said, "Let me be sure I understand the situation. Your husband—Arthur?—says he is an atheist. Do you really think he is?"

"I don't know, Pastor. He certainly acts like it."

"I've known many people who declared that they were atheists," he said with a smile, "but I'm not sure I've ever met one. I believe that there are agnostics, but I honestly don't believe there is such a thing as an atheist."

Susan looked confused as the pastor continued. "What I mean, Susan, is that an agnostic is one who says he doesn't know whether or not there is a God. An atheist says he *knows* there is no God. A man may be intellectually honest to state that he does not know if God exists, but to categorically state that one knows that there is no such being as God goes beyond what science and logic can demonstrate.

"In fact, it is my opinion that the most vocal opponents of belief in God are desperately aware of His existence. In many ways, I would rather deal with someone who calls himself an atheist than an agnostic, because an atheist always cares, while an agnostic may or may not care at all." Susan sat fascinated as Dr. Miller talked.

"I want to encourage you, first of all, that your Arthur probably cares very much about the existence of God. My guess is that he has experienced some bitter disappointments or tragedies along the way to make him so angry toward God. Am I right?"

"Yes, you are," Susan said with mild amazement. She was impressed with Dr. Miller's insight.

"Can you tell me any specific incidents that may have triggered his passionate hatred of God?"

"Well, I think it began in high school. He had a biology teacher who influenced his thinking toward humanism. He helped Arthur get a full scholarship to Georgetown in medicine. They still stay in touch."

"That may explain some of his disdain for God, Susan, but it hardly explains his deep anger." Pastor Miller shifted in his chair and adjusted his glasses.

Susan leaned forward and said, "I think his deep anger began when his father died of cancer and it deepened when our son Jimmy was killed by a hit-and-run driver. Arthur and Jimmy were tossing a ball back and forth out in the yard as it began to rain one evening. Arthur threw the ball to Jimmy, and he missed it. The ball rolled out into the street, and Jimmy ran out before

Arthur could stop him. I don't think the driver ever saw Jimmy, but after the impact, the car never stopped." Susan's voice quivered and her eyes grew red and moist.

"I'm so sorry, Susan." Pastor Miller shook his head in deep sympathy for her sorrow. "I know how much pain we can experience through our children. How long ago did that happen?"

"Five years ago this month." She dabbed her eyes with a tissue.

"I can see how that could make Arthur bitter toward God."

"But he keeps telling me the issue is evolution. He says that science has proven there is no God and only fools still believe in religion."

Pastor Miller smiled sadly. "Many have been confused by the belief that science and Christianity are mutually exclusive. The fact is, extremists on both sides of the debate have done a great disservice to both religion and science. Those who call themselves scientific creationists insist on a young earth and dispute clear evidences for limited evolutionary processes, while those on the other extreme deny the very existence of God. They seem to feel that acknowledging God is intellectual suicide. Perhaps your husband is struggling with that."

Susan began to feel a confidence developing for this man of God. He was wise, well-read, sensitive, and appeared to be intellectually capable of discussing science with Arthur. "Would you be willing to talk with my husband, Dr. Miller?"

"Of course, Susan. If he is willing. I have found it fruitless to debate a person's belief system until he is ready to look at every issue honestly and with full integrity. When he's ready, I'll be happy to meet with him."

Susan sat quietly for a moment. She wanted to speak to him about her painful secrets. She was confident he would understand and would be able to help her find lasting peace through biblical counsel.

"Is there something else, Susan?" Dr. Miller asked, sensing her hesitation.

"Yes," she paused. "There are some deep and awful secrets in my past that continue to cause me incredible pain and shame.

I . . . I sometimes have horrible nightmares," Susan said, looking down at her hands. "When I was fourteen, my father . . . uh . . ." she stammered in deep embarrassment and swallowed hard before she could continue. "Well . . . he did some terrible things to me. And . . . and . . . these things have affected our marriage, even in our physical relationship," Susan confessed as her normally white complexion turned a bright red.

For the first time, Susan detected an uncomfortable reaction in Dr. Miller. He cleared his throat nervously. "Have you sought professional counsel for these deep inner problems?" he asked.

"Yes, I have," she replied softly. "I was under psychiatric care for more than two years, but I don't think it really helped. I never found inner peace. I never felt clean until finding Christ."

"Well, I'm not surprised. Secular psychiatrists often create more confusion than they cure. I would, however, recommend a *Christian* psychiatrist or psychologist for deep personal emotional problems, Susan."

"You mean, you don't counsel problems like mine?" Susan was stunned.

"No, my dear," Dr. Miller laughed gently. "One thing I learned in seminary was the limitation of pastoral ability and training. My degree is in theology. If your problem were spiritual, I could help you. But it seems to me that you're talking about deep psychological problems, sexual dysfunctions, and troubled family systems. For those kinds of problems, you need a professional counselor."

"I suppose you're right, Dr. Miller," Susan replied sadly. "Do you have someone you can refer me to?"

"By all means! A good friend of mine works at a nearby Christian clinic. I'm sure he will know how to help you." He wrote a man's name and number on a slip of paper and handed it to her. "I wish I could do more," he said as he stood to his feet, indicating that he had to move on to the next appointment.

"Could you pray with me, Pastor Miller?" Susan asked, almost plaintively.

"Oh. Of course," he said as he bowed his head. Dr. Miller prayed, but Susan sensed a formality and stiffness in his words.

Susan Wilson walked from the church office to her car with a measure of disappointment. *How could a godly pastor like Dr. Miller have such a thorough grasp of the Scriptures and still not have the confidence to counsel people with real problems?* She shook her head in disappointment. She looked at the paper he had given her with the name of a Christian psychiatrist, Dr. William Dewey.

Susan sat in her car thinking. *I don't want to go home. I'm tired of Arthur's tirades and tantrums. I've got to have a break.* She decided to go to her office to call the psychiatrist and to make arrangements for a couple of weeks away from Arthur.

Susan was a rising star at DoubleSoft, a computer software company that specialized in programs which allowed IBM computers to communicate with other platforms. She didn't know much about programming software, but she was a whiz in business management. William Costas, the owner of the company, was only thirty-six and well on his way to multimillionaire status. Everyone called him Billy.

When Susan walked down the hallway toward her office, Billy was just coming out of the executive suite. "Susan!" he shouted down the corridor. "Where have you been, love? We have all kinds of decisions to make and our main woman is gone!"

"I'm sorry, Billy," Susan smiled. "I called in to say I had to take care of some personal matters."

"I know, I know," Billy laughed. "I'm just harassing you. To tell you the truth, I miss you when you aren't here. If you weren't already married . . ." he said as he looked her up and down and raised his eyebrows like Groucho Marx and knocked the ashes off an imaginary cigar.

"That's enough, Billy," Susan said as she made a face and turned to walk to her office. "I'm too old for you."

"I like vintage wine, Susan," he called as she went into her office.

She hated to admit it, but she enjoyed his attention. At least he seemed to feel that she was still attractive. *If only Arthur could appreciate me a little.*

. . .

Arthur's secretary, Jenny Pfister, was hard at work sorting papers when Arthur arrived at his office. When he walked in, Jenny smiled and greeted him. She handed him his mail and phone slips and asked, "Are you feeling better, Dr. Wilson?" referring to the attack that had put him in the hospital overnight.

"Yes, Jenny," Arthur said as he looked through the mail. "I'm just fine."

"Is there anything I can do for you, Dr. Wilson? Do you want some coffee or something?"

"No, Jenny," Arthur said as he stared blankly at his file cabinets. "Thanks, anyway. Wait . . . would you get Larry Eisley on the phone for me?" The phone intercom beeped a few seconds later and Jenny said, "Dr. Wilson, I have Mr. Eisley on the phone for you."

"Thanks, Jenny. Larry, how are you?" he said trying to sound as natural as possible. "Jenny said you called about the fundraiser banquet for the Humanists. Is there a preference on my topic?"

"That's what I called about, Arthur. I have an interesting idea I want to run by you."

"Go ahead," Arthur said.

"Well, since the courts ruled against the creationists in Louisiana, we thought that public education was finally safe. But there is still a great deal of grassroots support for creationist positions."

"I know it. Did you see that survey of biology teachers across the nation? A large percentage still believe in a divine cause for the universe. I'm absolutely appalled by the ignorance of some of our public school teachers," Arthur said.

"I agree. That leads to my idea: Let's have a debate with a creationist, right at the banquet. I think it would sell, especially with you on the evolutionary side. What do you think?" Eisley asked.

"Hmm. I don't know. I've heard that debates with creationists get kind of messy. The average person is so easily confused by a few scientific-sounding words, and there is a certain emotional appeal to their religious point of view."

"That's true, but remember, most of the folks coming to our banquet are committed to humanistic values and ideas."

"Do you have someone in mind for me to debate?" Arthur asked.

"Yes, as a matter of fact, I do. There's an old guy from Baltimore who lectures on creationism. I saw him on a PBS report. He has a doctorate in biology, so it could be interesting."

"What's his name?"

"Arnold. Dr. Benjamin Arnold."

"Dr. Arnold!"

"You know him?"

"Why, he's one of the reasons I went into science. I heard him speak when I was in high school, and he made me so mad I decided to prove him wrong," Arthur laughed. "I bet he's eighty years old by now."

"Well, he is in his seventies, I think," Eisley said. "What do you say, Arthur? Will you debate him?"

"I wouldn't miss it! What is the premise of the debate?"

"Resolved: that there is no scientific basis for creationism."

"Good enough. That's on August 21, right? At the Washington Hilton? Seven thirty? I'll be there." He hung up the phone. As long as Susan was gone, he figured he may as well make good use of his time alone. *At least I'll have time to do my homework. Dr. Arnold will have done his, I'm sure. Where should I start?*

He had an idea. "Jenny," he said into the intercom, "would you get me Michael Rollins at the Smithsonian?"

"I will just as soon as you finish this call. Your wife is on line one." Arthur eagerly picked up the phone, took a deep breath, and pushed line one.

Susan had called Arthur's office to leave a message with his secretary, but Jenny put her on hold. She was surprised when Arthur came on the line.

"Oh! Arthur," she stuttered. "I . . . I didn't mean to disturb you."

"Where are you, Susan?" he said with genuine concern. "I've been going crazy wondering if you were all right. I called your office, and they said they didn't know where your were, just that you were out attending to some private business."

"Well, that was true. They didn't know where I was."

"When are you coming home, Susan?" *Tell me you're coming home, please,* he thought to himself.

Susan thought he sounded like he missed her. *Good!* she thought. "I don't know, Arthur. I've decided that I need some time away from you. I'm tired of all our arguing. I'm tired of being put down and sneered at. I'm tired of your making fun of my faith."

"Look, Susan . . ." Arthur began. *I've got to tell her how sorry I am for being such a jerk!*

"No, Arthur," she interrupted. "*You* look! It's time for you to take a good look at yourself, at me, at our marriage, and whether you want it to survive. I'm going to be away from home for a couple of weeks at least. I'm trying to get help with some of my problems. I suggest you find someone you can talk with, because you need help as badly as I do!"

Arthur was unprepared for Susan's assertiveness. "Well, where will you be?"

"I don't know yet, Arthur. I'll check in with you at your office from time to time."

"Well, all right, Susan, if that's the way you want it," Arthur said with his jaw clenched.

"It's not what I *want*. It's what I *need* right now, Arthur."

"Susan?" *I need to tell her how much I love her.*

"Yes, Arthur?"

"I want you to know . . . that . . . I . . ." *Just say it, you fool!* he thought.

Say it, Arthur, Susan thought. *For our marriage's sake, say it!*

"I miss you."

"Yeah. I love you, too, Arthur," she said dryly and hung up. Susan sat down at her desk, shaking with anger. *He can't even say he loves me. He just can't get those words out anymore!*

. . .

Arthur's intercom beeped again. "Michael Rollins, Dr. Wilson."

"Thanks, Jenny," he said. He pushed the button on the phone. "Michael? This is Arthur Wilson over at NCI. You may not remember me, but I met you several months ago at a social function your church sponsored. I came with my wife, Susan."

"Sure, Arthur, I remember. Your specialty is genetics, if I recall."

"That's right. Listen, Michael, I wonder if I could set an appointment to talk with you. I overheard you mention that you seriously question the Darwinian theory of evolution. Is that right?"

"Well, yes, that's correct. Why?"

"I want to know why a trained geologist such as yourself would have any doubts. You see, I'm scheduled to debate a biologist on the issue of creationism in a few months, and I would like to prepare, but I'm not sure where to start."

"I'd be glad to talk with you. When's convenient?" Rollins asked.

"Any time at all. But I'd like to get started as soon as possible," Arthur said.

"I'm free for lunch today, Arthur. Can you meet me here at about 11:30?"

Arthur looked at his watch. "I can just make it if I leave right now, Michael. Where will I meet you?"

"At the brontosaurus display."

Arthur carefully locked his office and walked past Jenny's desk on his way to the main corridor. "Jenny, I'll be out of the office for a couple of hours. You can reach me on my cellular if you need me. Thanks for your help."

"No problem, Dr. Wilson. Is there anything you want me to do while you're gone?"

"Yes, there is. I need you to go to the library and get me some books on evolution."

"Evolution?" she asked.

"That's what I said," Arthur replied with a tinge of irritation in his voice.

"All right," Jenny said. "Have a nice lunch." Then she added, "God bless you, Dr. Wilson."

He nodded and walked out. *Right. God bless us every one.*

Arthur drove toward the Smithsonian. When he arrived, he pulled into the special parking area for the employees and showed his NCI identification card. "I have an appointment with Dr. Rollins," he said to the attendant, who waved him through.

He walked quickly into the building and toward the large dinosaur display in the main hall. His watch read 11:25 as he turned the corner. Rollins was already there. He didn't see Arthur coming because he was facing the display, deep in thought.

"Michael," Arthur called out, his voice echoing in the cavernous hall along with those of many others who were talking loudly. There was an large group of elementary school children gazing up at the brontosaurus in awe. Rollins turned toward Arthur with a warm smile and extended his hand in greeting.

"Arthur, it's good to see you again. I'm glad you called. Let's go where it's a bit quieter so we can talk. There's a neat little restaurant a few blocks away. We can walk, if you don't mind."

"I don't mind," Arthur laughed. "I need the exercise."

When they got outside and began walking, Michael said, "Tell me more about this debate you're going to have, Arthur. It sounds interesting."

"Well, it is sponsored by the local chapter of the American Humanists. Lawrence Eisley is the area coordinator. Do you know him?"

"I've heard his name, but I can't say that I really know him."

"His main field is biology, but he spends most of his time trying to defeat the creationists in the educational system."

"He sounds like a crusader," Rollins said. "What is he like as a person?"

"What do you mean, Michael?" Arthur asked.

"I mean, is he happy? Is he intellectually honest? What is he like on the inside?"

"I never gave it much thought," Arthur said uncomfortably. "Why do you ask?"

"Because I have found that a driven man is often intellectually dishonest with himself. And, frankly, I have found many fellow scientists to be less than objective when it comes to the area of origins."

"I suppose there are some like that, but I would like to believe that most scientists believe in evolution because of the overwhelming evidence, and not merely because of emotional preference," Arthur said. "How about you, Michael? What made you begin to doubt evolution?"

"It was when I was on the geology staff at the American Museum of Natural History in New York. We had a guest lecturer, a British paleontologist, Colin Patterson, who asked us a question I simply couldn't answer, and neither could anyone else in the room." They stopped at the corner, waiting for the light to change.

"Well, what was his question?" A taxi honked loudly, causing Arthur to jump. The light changed and they crossed with the crowd of pedestrians.

"He looked us right in the eyes and asked us to tell him just one thing we actually *knew* about evolution. No one answered a word. I later read an article in which Patterson said that he had always assumed that evolution was true—that it was a sort of revealed truth. He later came to realize that he believed in evolution not on the basis of knowledge, but on the basis of faith."

"Faith?" Arthur asked incredulously. "Then Patterson is a creationist?"

"Not really," Rollins replied. "He still claims to be an evolutionist, but he is honest enough to admit that both evolution and
creation are equally based on faith. Many other scientists are
coming to the same conclusion." He stopped in front of a quaint
little building. "Here's the restaurant."

They walked into a small Italian restaurant and sat at a table
near the front window. Arthur asked Rollins to be more specific.
"How can you say evolution is based on faith when you are
surrounded every day by the bones and rocks which prove
evolution?"

"Those very bones and rocks are testimony to creation,
Arthur. Patterson had to come to a point in his life when he
admitted to himself that there are no transitional forms anywhere
in the fossil record. There are no in-between forms. I came to
that same conclusion soon after hearing Patterson."

"Is that when you started going to church?" Arthur asked
tightly.

"Well, not right away, I didn't. I had denied the very existence of God for so long I could hardly force myself to attend a
church. I felt it would be hypocritical. But the more I thought
through the implications of Patterson's admission of faith in evolution, the more I realized that I was being intellectually dishonest. I thought that perhaps I should at least look at the evidence
from the other side."

A waitress stood patiently, waiting for a break in their conversation. When Michael paused, she broke in, "Have you decided
what you want?"

"Oh, sorry," Michael said with an apologetic smile. "What'll
you have, Arthur? It's on me."

"What do you recommend?"

"I like their canolis."

"What's a canoli?"

"It's like a pizza, folded in half and sealed around the edges.
It's stuffed with meatballs, sausage, cheese, or whatever. Then
they put a thick Italian sauce over it." Michael kissed his fingers
like an Italian chef and said, "Itsa wonnaful!"

"I'll try one," Arthur said with a smile.

"Anything to drink?" the waitress asked.

Arthur wanted something strong, but waited for Michael. "I'll have a coke with lemon in it," Michael said.

"Lemon?" Arthur made a face.

"Yeah. It gives it a bite," Michael laughed.

"Make that two," Arthur said. As the waitress walked away, he asked, "Now where were we before we were so viciously interrupted?"

"I was just saying that there aren't any transitional forms in the fossil record."

"But geology and paleontology are just part of the evidence for evolution," Arthur objected. "What about the chemical evidence for biogenesis?"

"I have a book I want you to read, Arthur. It is written by three men who have doctorates in chemistry, materials science, and geochemistry. It's titled *The Mystery of Life's Origin: Reassessing Current Theories*. It is one of the most influential books in recent years. Each of the authors was an evolutionist at one time. But through their studies, they concluded that it was impossible for life to have started by chance."

"But as creationists, surely they have lost credibility in the scientific community," Arthur said.

"Actually, the amazing thing is that evolutionists have praised the book for its scholarship. Dean Kenyon of San Francisco State University is a committed evolutionist. In fact, he wrote the book *Biochemical Predestination*, which is considered by many to be a key work on the evolutionary origin of the first cell. Yet he wrote the foreword to *The Mystery of Life's Origin*.

"You're kidding!"

"No, really. After we eat, let's go back to my office and I'll give you the book."

The food came, and Arthur found himself enjoying Michael Rollins's company. He liked his sense of humor and the fact that he wasn't preaching about his faith. The waitress came with the check.

"Here, let me get the check, Michael. It's the least I can do. After all, I called you."

"All right, but next time it's on me."

Arthur noticed a spot of spaghetti sauce on Michael's shirt. "Next time, nothing. It's on you right now!" They both laughed.

When they got back to Rollins's office, Michael pulled the promised book out of the shelf behind his desk. "It's a little worn, Arthur. I have read it several times." Turning to the foreword of the book, Rollins said, "Listen to this, Arthur. '*The Mystery of Life's Origin* presents an extraordinary new analysis of an age-old question: How did life start on earth? The authors deal forthrightly and brilliantly with the major problems confronting scientists today in their search for life's origins.' Later on, the book discusses the question of the origin of genetic information in biopolymers. That's right down your alley, Arthur."

Arthur stood looking at the book in silence. Finally he looked up and said to Rollins, "Michael, how can you continue to work here at the Smithsonian if you are a creationist?"

"It isn't easy, Arthur. I have to walk a very fine line. But I honestly believe that I can have a greater impact from within the system than I could if I resigned. I respect others' rights to believe in evolution, and I'm trying to earn their respect for my convictions as well."

"Well, Michael, you have my respect, even if I don't agree with you. Thank you for taking time to meet with me." Arthur turned to leave.

"Arthur, would you mind if I attend the debate?"

"Why, no, Michael. I'd consider it an honor if you would be my guest. I'll call you and pick you up."

Arthur walked down the marble stairs and went to the bookstore near the front entrance. There he found several volumes that would provide him with information about evolution—information that he would need for the debate.

· · ·

Susan drove to Dr. William Dewey's office. Pastor Miller had assured her that he was a Christian psychiatrist, so she had a measure of hope that he would be able to help her sort out the painful memories from her past and help her to move on with her life.

As she sat in the waiting room, filling out the intake form, she sensed a painful familiarity in the process. The questions on the form were much the same as those she had answered countless times before with other therapists. *I suppose they need this kind of information*, she thought, *but where does God fit into all of this?* She looked around the room for a sign that this clinic was a Christian counseling service, but nothing—neither the pictures on the wall, the music being played, nor the literature and brochures in the rack—even hinted that Christ was the central focus.

She completed the form and took it to the receptionist. "Excuse me," she said, "I was told that this is a Christian clinic. Is that true?"

The receptionist looked a bit surprised and looked at Susan for a moment, as though trying to determine what answer she was looking for. "Well . . . yes," she finally said. "Our clinic is Christian, for the most part. Of course, we have clients that do not share our faith and we are careful not to try to force our convictions on them. Dr. Taykhem, however, is Muslim, but again, his counseling is on a purely professional basis."

"Oh," Susan said, truly surprised. "But Dr. Dewey is a Christian, isn't he? He's the one I'm seeing."

The receptionist nodded and smiled, "Of course Dr. Dewey is a Christian. I know you'll like him. Just have a seat and he'll be with you in a few minutes.

About fifteen minutes later, a kind-looking man in his late fifties walked into the waiting room. He was dignified in his bearing and sported a neatly trimmed beard. His round gold-rimmed glasses and thinning white hair gave him a grandfatherly appearance. He smiled warmly as he held out his hand to Susan. "Mrs. Wilson? Come on back to my office." He led her down the hallway to his office, held the door open for her, followed her in, and closed the door.

"I think you'll find that chair the most comfortable," he said as he pointed to a deeply padded chair that matched the sofa on the other side of a beveled-glass end table. He took a chair opposite her near his desk and sat down. He glanced at her counseling form for a few moments, made a couple of notations on it, then looked up and said, "Now tell me what's going on in your marriage."

Experienced in therapy, Susan quickly outlined her story. "And then I became a Christian," she told Dr. Dewey, "and things got even worse. I am so terribly unhappy and so is Arthur. What can we do?"

Dr. Dewey nodded as he wrote on his pad. He took off his glasses, looked at his watch, looked up and asked, "What do you think you should do?"

"I just don't know anymore, Doctor. Some days I think I still love Arthur and then there are times I'd like to kill him! Well, not really, of course, but he makes me so angry I just want to get away from him completely."

"Do you think your marriage is worth saving?" Dr. Dewey asked.

"Yes, I think so, but I don't want to keep feeling this awful pain all the time."

"I can understand that, my dear," he said gently. "No one should have to go through what you have endured. And the good news is, you *don't* have to."

Susan leaned forward. "What do you mean?"

"I mean just what I said. You don't have to go on being beaten down, taking abuse from one male after another. It is time you learned how to set some boundaries. You see, Mrs. Wilson, all the pain you have experienced—from the time your father abused you to the verbal and sexual abuse you experienced from your husband—must come to an end."

Susan sat back in the chair and listened with a renewed sense of hope. Maybe Dr. Dewey really could help her.

He continued, "I want to teach you how to assert yourself, how to put an end to abusive conversations, how to demand your rights. Unless you learn these important skills, you are going to be a victim for the rest of your life."

He took some books from his desk and handed them to Susan. "I want you to read these books before we get back together. They will help you to understand the entire abuse dynamic and how some men hate women and get their sense of masculinity from dominating and controlling their wives. It sounds to me like your husband is one of those men, and it also seems to me that you were set up for that kind of relationship by what your father did to you. Now it is time to turn things around, don't you agree?"

"Yes," Susan said as she stood to her feet. "I do think I need to learn how to stop the abuse. But Arthur needs counseling, too, don't you think?"

"Oh, absolutely, Mrs. Wilson! But he's not going to come in unless he's forced to. He is going to resist the changes you are going to bring into your home. Frankly, I doubt that he will respond favorably. The sad truth is, you may have to end this marriage and start over again. But as you learn how to set the boundaries you need to survive, you will never again be the victim."

"That sounds good to me, Dr. Dewey," Susan said with a smile. "Something has to change, that's for sure!"

. . .

On Thursday, as Arthur was studying for the debate, Lawrence Eisley called. "Arthur, there's been a slight change in our plans for the debate."

"What kind of change, Larry?"

"Well, Dr. Arnold has agreed to the debate, but on one condition."

"And what's his condition?" Arthur said with a chuckle.

"That we change the topic a bit."

"Change the topic?"

"Yeah. He said he would debate if the topic is 'Resolved: Evolution Is a Religion and Not a Science.'"

"Hm!" Arthur grunted. "I wonder what that old fox is up to?" He tapped his pencil on the desk as he thought. Finally he said, "I guess we could agree to that, Larry. What do you think?"

"Personally, I don't like it, but time is growing short and I don't know who else we could get at this late date. You can handle the old guy, can't you?"

Arthur forced a laugh and said, "No problem."

"Good! I'll tell him it's on!"

Arthur studied the arguments for several hours over the next few days. It wasn't just the upcoming debate; it was a personal search. Michael Rollins had planted some serious doubts in Arthur's mind for the first time since his college days.

As he sat at his desk at home, he thought back to a guest lecture given by Stephen Gould from Harvard University when he explained his theory called *punctuated equilibrium*. Gould taught that individual species remained unchanged during long evolutionary periods which were "punctuated" by the sudden arising of new species. This theory had become necessary because of the imperfection in the fossil record.

He remembered a fellow student laughing after the lecture and saying, "The fossil record doesn't show enough transitional forms to support Darwinian theory, so Gould has made up a new one. Oh, I just love it! There aren't really any transitional fossils between reptiles and birds, so—correct me if I'm wrong, Arthur—one day a reptile egg hatches, and out comes a bird? Right! And they laugh at creationists!"

Arthur remembered how angry he was at that student. *Maybe I was mad because I thought he had a point. It is a stupid theory. But, then, so is all this stuff about a God.* It all came back. He had made a conscious decision to not believe in God. Time and again, he had been confronted by people who believed in God—his mom and dad, friends in school, and Susan! His lips drew tight as he thought about her. He deeply resented the fact that Susan had resisted his every romantic advance for the past several months. *If that's what Christianity does to a marriage, I don't want any part of it!* he thought. *I could never believe in a God like Susan's. Never!*

He slammed his fist to the desk and returned to the present. Susan's face faded from his mind as he focused again on the book in front of him. Pages of handwritten notes were stacked to the side. Now it was time to organize them.

One book in particular had fascinated him. It was a volume listing many of the discrepancies in the Bible. He began to write out a list of problem passages to introduce into the debate. *If I can show how flawed the Bible is, I can rip Dr. Arnold to shreds!*

He was surprised to find several creationist books that actually argued for a form of evolution. The authors seemed to want to integrate evolutionary theory with the Bible by calling their concept "theistic evolution." As he understood their argument, they agreed with real scientists that the universe is billions of years old. But they still wanted to find a place for God in their system, so they argued that God started the whole thing rolling, and then kind of stepped back and allowed evolutionary processes to direct biological development.

That's even more ridiculous than pure creationism! Arthur thought. If God were involved, why would He resort to evolutionary process?

He worked late into the night at his computer entering his notes. There was a bitter satisfaction knowing that he might be able to free someone else from the bondage of guilt caused by believing in God. He looked up suddenly.

That's it! he thought. *Belief in God is a personal bondage. It has caused more sorrow, more wars, more guilt than anything else. If we could erase the terror of God from the human heart, we could set millions free! What did belief in God get Mom and Dad? Poverty and ignorance, that's all! What did Susan's belief in God do for us? It destroyed our marriage! I'll do whatever I can to destroy the divine superstition. If I can free someone like Michael Rollins, it would be worth it all.*

Now Arthur Wilson had a mission.

FAITH FOR
OUR HOMES

4

Faith for Healing a Marriage

FAITH CAN BE DAMAGED in many ways, as we have already seen from Paul's list of the fruit of sinful living in Galatians 5. He reminds Titus that many people "claim to know God, but by their actions they deny him" (Titus 1:16).

It is not only our personal lives that are affected when our faith becomes weak. Our closest relationships also suffer when we act as practical atheists. This is especially true in the home.

WEAK FAITH, WEAK MARRIAGES

A couple with six children came to me for marriage counseling. The husband was a hard worker, providing marginally for their needs. He insisted that his wife remain at home with the children so she could school them. In her frustration at being "cooped up" all day long with children, she often complained to him that she needed help. Instead of giving her a sympathetic hearing, he belittled her concerns and suggested she was becoming emotionally unstable. She in turn became increasingly bitter toward her husband, and he reacted with sharp-edged sarcasm, putting her down at every opportunity. Though both were sincere believers in Christ, their relationship was growing more and more hostile by the day.

I worked with them for weeks, showing them the principles of a healthy marriage as found in the Scriptures, but each determined to wait for the other to make the first move. Neither had the faith to trust God to work in the other's heart if each would choose to be the first to submit to His Word. As far as I know, they are still in turmoil and misery because their continued actions deny God.

Their case is not unusual. Over the years, we have ministered to hundreds of couples whose marriages seemed to have great potential, but instead became powerful arguments for remaining single. How do Christian marriages get so messed up? Let's quickly look at seven major causes of unhappy marriages.

WRONG BEGINNINGS

Physical Attractions

Many marriages are troubled before they even begin. Young couples accept the cultural notion that engaging in sex before marriage is acceptable and inevitable. They misunderstand the very purpose and foundation of marriage—a commitment of companionship. This concept is outlined in Genesis 2:18,23-24, which says, "It is not good for the man to be alone. I will make a helper suitable for him . . . She shall be called 'woman,' for she was taken out of man. For this reason a man will leave his father and mother and be united to his wife, and they will become one flesh."

The biblical emphasis in marriage is upon becoming closely united in every way—spiritually, mentally, socially, and physically. In too many cases, however, Christian men and women are drawn into marriage for the same reason unbelievers are—physical attraction. It's not that physical attraction is wrong in and of itself. God has designed us in such a way that we are normally drawn to the opposite sex and we find certain physical attributes pleasing and attractive. This is clearly illustrated in the Song of

Solomon. But if sexual desire is the primary motivation for a marriage, the couple is headed for serious problems.

Mixed Marriage

Another cause of marriage difficulties is mixed marriage. By mixed marriage, I am not referring to interracial unions, but to those who come together from different faiths. Marriage can be difficult under the best of circumstances, but when a couple adds the difference in strong religious convictions, they are asking for trouble.

I once had a Catholic woman and a Mormon man ask me to officiate their wedding. Our policy is that we do not perform marriages for couples not attending our church, but I agreed to counsel them. When they arrived, I asked them why they were not being married in one of their own churches, and they replied that their own priests would not permit it. In addition, their parents strongly opposed their marriage.

"And you think I would go against your parents' wishes?" I asked. I explained to them the likely consequences of marrying someone who does not share the same faith: inability to worship together, to pray together, to raise their children in the same faith, or to settle problems within the context of the same religious framework.

I asked them to think about it for a few days before they made a final decision. A short time later, the young woman called me to say that she had broken the engagement. But it rarely works this way. Normally, the couple has already decided they are going to marry no matter what anyone says. And they end up paying the consequences for years to come.

Unrealistic Expectations

It is not unusual for couples to enter marriage with unrealistic expectations of perpetual bliss. The young woman is convinced that she will be able to change her fiancé into something nearly human once they are married, and the young man has the mistaken idea that his wife will be dedicated to fulfilling his every fantasy and desire. She thinks he will grow up and become responsible. He thinks she will retain her youthful figure. She thinks he will be charming and attentive to her every mood. He thinks she will understand his need to join a ball league. She thinks he will continue to look into her eyes and listen to every thought which spills from her lips. He thinks she will appreciate his wisdom and hard work. Too late, they discover that they have each married a sinner more focused on self than the needs of the other.

A teenage couple sat before me asking if I would marry them. Neither had completed high school. He was working in a low-skilled, low-paying job with little prospect for advancement. She was planning on subsidizing their income by babysitting. They had virtually no concept of how expensive it is to set up housekeeping, yet they were convinced they could overcome the odds and make a success of their marriage. One of her motives, however, was to get away from her mother and stepfather, whom she despised. She thought her young man was the way to accomplish this goal, but it would have been a wrong beginning. After I discussed the issue with his parents, it was clear that marriage was out of the question for the present time and the wedding was called off.

PREVIEW OF HEAVEN
OR FORETASTE OF HELL?

As I inevitably state when performing a wedding, marriage is intended to be a preview of heaven, but in far too many homes, it is instead a foretaste of hell. Rather than providing love and romance, comfort and companionship, and joy and satisfaction, for many, marriage is a disappointment too great for words.

What is surprising to some and a shame to all believers is that this heartbreaking disillusionment appears in Christian homes as well as pagan. Practical atheism emerges from its dark and gloomy den, casting an evil shadow of hopelessness upon husbands and wives alike, convincing them their marriages cannot be saved, even by God Himself.

I know a pastor whose wife suddenly decided she no longer wanted to be married. She was tired of the demands of ministry and motherhood and felt she had lost all love for her husband. She walked away from a weeping husband and two beautiful children into a life of immorality and loneliness. When the divorce was finalized, she literally strode out of the courthouse waving her fist over her head in triumph.

A former missionary from Hong Kong wrote me that he and his wife had returned to America due to his wife's health and an emotional breakdown. She was so depressed that she ended up in a Christian mental health hospital where she was diagnosed as having a "uni-polar mood disorder." After nearly $100,000 spent for therapy in seven series of treatments, she finally separated from her husband on the grounds of incompatibility because he didn't agree that psychological counseling was helping her get better and he wanted her to follow biblical counseling instead. He wrote me,

> I am sure this story is not the first such story that you have heard, but I just wanted to thank you for your book on why we should not trust Christian psychology. What I have found out over the last few years of my life has certainly turned my heart even more toward the fact that God's Word holds the answers to our deepest sorrows. I pray that ministries like the one the Lord has given you will continue to inform the Christian community of the fallacies behind a bankrupt system like psychology.
>
> Pastor Bulkley, I want you to know that my church has stood behind me throughout this whole ordeal. From the very beginning, our church has not only provided a loving atmosphere to grow spiritually, but it also has an excellent pastor who is committed to the Word of God. He has tried to help us in our situation, but due to what

has happened, our church had to write a letter to my wife because of her refusal to come back to the home. The pastor and our elders are all aware of the situation and the efforts that I have personally made toward reconciliation. I am not sure at this point if our marriage will ever be reconciled, but I do know that by not taking a godly and biblical stand there is no hope for any kind of reconciliation.

A veteran missionary wife with more than twenty years of service in Europe was now back in America and was tired of financially supporting her husband, who had proven himself incapable of providing for his wife and children. She had prayed for him and pleaded with him over the years, to no avail, as he led them further and further into debt. In desperation and too ashamed to expose the matter to her pastor, she turned to a Christian psychologist for advice and was told that there was no hope for her marriage and that her best course of action was to divorce her husband. Though there was never any sexual unfaithfulness and no biblical grounds for a divorce, she was so full of despair that she finally divorced her husband.

Across the nation, regardless of economic status, church affiliation, educational achievement, ethnic background, or geographic location, Christian marriages are being torn apart by unbelief. That's right—unbelief! Christians no longer believe that God is able to heal their wounded hearts, restore their broken relationships, rekindle their love, or rebuild their homes.

But God *is* able. Let me tell you how.

BRINGING GOD INTO A MARRIAGE

Both Must Commit to Obeying God's Word No Matter What the Mate Does

One of the first questions I ask couples who come to me for counsel is this: "If I can show you from the Bible what God wants you to do, will you each commit right now to do it?" The question is like a hand grenade blowing off the battle armor as it explodes in the warring couple's faces. The initial reaction I normally see is fear and reluctance to make such a sweeping commitment, but as I explain it further, they begin to relax, realizing that each is protected by the balanced instructions in God's Word.

I point out that both must make the commitment individually regardless of what the other does. When they ask, "But what about her?" or "What about him?" I am reminded of Peter when he was confronted by Jesus with the overwhelming commission to feed Christ's sheep. Peter looked around and saw John a little way off and asked, "Lord, what about him?" Do you remember what Jesus replied? He said, "What is that to you? You must follow me" (John 21:22).

The first step is this: You must decide that you are going to humbly follow after Christ no matter what your mate does. Your job is not to change your mate, but to obey the Lord. The moment you make that commitment, healing has begun.

Divorce Must Not Be an Option

If you want the Lord to rebuild your marriage you must put the option of divorce out of your mind. Remember that God Himself said, "I hate divorce . . . and I hate a man's covering himself with violence as well as with his garment. . . . So guard yourself in your spirit, and do not break faith" (Malachi 2:16).

If God hates divorce so much, why was it permitted even in Israel? That is the precise question Jesus was asked in Matthew 19:7: "Why then . . . did Moses command that a man give his wife a certificate of divorce and send her away?" Jesus answered, "Moses permitted you to divorce your wives because your hearts were hard. But it was not this way from the beginning. I tell you that anyone who divorces his wife, except for marital unfaithfulness, and marries another woman commits adultery" (Matthew 19.8-9).

Note that Jesus did recognize a biblical cause for divorce: infidelity. But short of that, He said God never intends for a marriage to end in divorce.

For some people, that is just too rigid a position. Even Jesus' own disciples objected and said, "If this is the situation between a husband and wife, it is better not to marry" (Matthew 19:10).

Did you catch what Jesus described as the primary cause of divorce? "Because your hearts were hard." When angry couples come into my office, the hardness of their hearts is written plainly on their faces. But I have watched hard hearts melt when both husband and wife submitted their hurt feelings to the Lord and rejected divorce as an option. It was their next step in the healing process.

Each Must Examine His or Her Own Heart

For healing to continue, both partners must examine their own hearts before God to see how they have contributed to the failure with their own sinful attitudes and actions. It's the Matthew 7 "Get-the-Log-Out-of-Your-Own-Eye" Principle. Read this passage carefully and meditate on it for a moment:

> Do not judge, or you too will be judged. For in the same way you judge others, you will be judged, and with the measure you use, it will be measured to you.
>
> Why do you look at the speck of sawdust in your brother's eye and pay no attention to the plank in your own eye? How can you say to your brother, "Let me take the speck out of your eye," when all the time there is a plank in your own eye? You hypocrite, first take the plank out of your own eye, and then you will see clearly to remove the speck from your brother's eye (Matthew 7:1-5).

Since in God's plan our mates are also our spiritual brothers and sisters, it would be perfectly appropriate to read the above passage with the word *husband* or *wife* in place of "brother." Go back and try it, and see what happens.

You see, our natural tendency is to see the faults in others while we ignore or excuse our own failings. This is especially true in marriage, in which we have unlimited opportunity to observe the character flaws and irritating habits of our mates.

Don't make the mistake of casually looking inward to see if any minor flaws float to the top of your consciousness. Our consciences are not well equipped to detect sin unless they have been calibrated and sensitized by the Scriptures. That's why Jeremiah writes, "The heart is deceitful above all things and beyond cure. Who can understand it?" (Jeremiah 17:9). Here is a key principle if you are going to find real peace in your own life: *Don't allow anyone to teach you to trust your heart!* It will always lead you astray. If a counselor or psychologist tells you to trust your heart, get up and leave his office. He's leading you down a false path.

So how can you examine your heart? Through Jeremiah, God said, "I the LORD search the heart and examine the mind, to reward a man according to his conduct, according to what his deeds deserve" (Jeremiah 17:10). Along the same line, David writes, "Search me, O God, and know my heart; test me and know my anxious thoughts" (Psalm 139:23).

Let me ask you, dear reader, how has your mate sinned against you? What has he or she done that has caused you so much pain, anger, and bitterness that you wish you could end your marriage?

I hope you replied, "That's not important anymore. What I must concentrate on now is what *I* have done that has damaged our marriage." If you said that, bless your heart; you are already on your way toward healing.

When we stop looking for the sin in our mate and allow the Lord to show us our own sins, then humility, gentleness, and mercy develop, which can result in genuine forgiveness. Paul tells us, "Be kind and compassionate to one another, forgiving each other, just as in Christ God forgave you" (Ephesians 4:32). There are perhaps no more powerfully healing words than these: "I was so very wrong. Will you forgive me?" No longer demanding an apology from the other, each confesses his or her own sin to the Lord and to the mate, asking for forgiveness. Oh, dear child of God, wonderful restoration of peace and joy is just around the corner!

Each Must Repent of His or Her Sin

It is not enough to know where we have sinned. We must now turn from it and allow the Lord to change our behavior and thoughts. Do you understand that true repentance involves sorrow for past behavior? Isaiah writes, "The Lord, the LORD Almighty, called you on that day to weep and to wail, to tear out your hair and put on sackcloth" (Isaiah 22:12). God emphasized this aspect of repentance when He said, "Return to me with all your heart, with fasting and weeping and mourning" (Joel 2:12). It isn't that God gets pleasure out of our misery; the reason Scripture calls for genuine remorse is that "godly sorrow brings repentance that leads to salvation and leaves no regret" (2 Corinthians 7:10).

Genuine repentance results in radical changes of behavior. As Daniel advised his king, "Renounce your sins by doing what is right" (Daniel 4:27). God is not impressed by verbal repentance unless it is validated by deeds. That is exactly what James was getting at when he wrote, "Show me your faith without deeds, and I will show you my faith by what I do" (James 2:18). Paul said that wherever he went, no matter who he was addressing, "I preached that they should repent and turn to God and prove their repentance by their deeds" (Acts 26:20).

Countless husbands have sat in counseling offices shaking their heads in frustration as they say, "I don't get it! I told her I was sorry. What more does she want?" Dear friend, what your wife wants is to *see* by your consistent actions that your life is really *changed*. She has heard your weak apologies too many times to count. She is tired of your broken promises that it will never happen again. Like James, she is saying, "Don't tell me. *Show* me!"

It will take time to rebuild the trust, but when proper actions and attitudes are consistently evident in your life, a new joy and peace will appear that would have seemed impossible just a short time ago. Peter preached this to his countrymen when he said, "Repent, then, and turn to God, so that your sins may be wiped out, that times of refreshing may come from the Lord" (Acts 9:19).

Do you want to restore a lightness of spirit, a sense of joy, a depth of peace in your heart once again? Then turn toward God in wholehearted repentance, and you will find a refreshment you could only dream of before.

Each Must Change His or Her Thought Patterns

After you have invited the Lord to expose the sin in your own life and have genuinely repented of it, you must allow the Lord to change the very way you think about handling problems of living. If the Bible is true, then Christians have resources for healing that the world cannot begin to match. That's why serious medical researchers are beginning to examine the effects of prayer and faith on the healing process.

Ironically, twelve-step support groups flourish in churches that have more confidence in psychological techniques than in the Word of God. Pastors refer their parishioners with "serious problems" to "mind experts" because they believe the Bible by itself is insufficient to produce wholeness.

That Paul would disagree strongly is evident in his statement that our weapons "have divine power to demolish strongholds" (2 Corinthians 10:4). He would be horrified to see how low a view today's church has of the Scriptures and how high a view people have of the world's methods of change. He wrote that it's necessary for us to "demolish arguments and every pretension that sets itself up against the knowledge of God, and . . . take captive every thought to make it obedient to Christ" (2 Corinthians 10:5).

Take a closer look at that last thought: We "take captive every thought to make it obedient to Christ." Left to ourselves, we will think the way the world thinks—in rebellion against God. To take our thoughts captive for Christ, we must make a concerted, willful, conscious effort to submit our minds to the control of the Holy Spirit.

Perhaps turning your mind over to God is a frightening thought for you, but consider this: "The mind of sinful man is death, but the mind controlled by the Spirit is life and peace" (Romans 8:6). Do you understand what the Scriptures are saying? Thinking the world's way ultimately ends in misery and destruction, whereas training our minds to think God's way produces genuine peace of heart and mind. That is why Paul counseled us, "Do not conform any longer to the pattern of this world, but be transformed by the renewing of your mind. Then you will be able to test and approve what God's will is—his good, pleasing and perfect will" (Romans 12:2).

Because I have dealt at length in another book[27] with the subject of changing the way we think, I will touch only briefly on the process of renewing our minds as explained in Ephesians 4, Romans 12, and 2 Timothy 3.

Taking every thought captive for Christ is described in Ephesians 4:22-24 as putting "off your old self," being "made new in the attitude of your minds," and putting "on the new self, created to be like God in true righteousness and holiness."

In Romans 12:1-2 we are told to offer our "bodies as living sacrifices, holy and pleasing to God." In contrast, we must "not conform any longer to the pattern of this world, but be transformed by the renewing of your mind."

How do we accomplish this daunting task? Paul lays out four biblical steps in 2 Timothy 3:16-17:

> All Scripture is God-breathed and is useful for [1] teaching, [2] rebuking, [3] correcting and [4] training in righteousness, so that the man of God may be thoroughly equipped for every good work.

1. *We Must Learn Correct Doctrine.* Believe it or not, the health of your marriage depends upon your obedience to the principles and commands of God's Word. To do that, you must know what those principles and commands are. There is no shortcut to biblical knowledge; you must read, study, meditate, and obey the Bible over and over, day after day, week after week,

year after year. It is one of the most important disciplines we could ever acquire.

2. *We Must Courageously Confront Our Own Sin.* That's what rebuking is—an exposure of sin. Unless we are willing to see our sin as the awful rebellion against God that it truly is, we will desperately cling to it. Think about this: The reason most people remain captive to their sin is *they love their sin more than they love God.* I can tell you categorically, I have never yet met an addict who loved Jesus more than his drug. I have never met an adulterer who loved Jesus more than his immorality. And I have never met a person who loves Jesus with all his heart who has remained a helpless captive to his sin. Do you want to be free? Then call your destructive behavior what it is: *sin.*

3. *We Must Correct Our Thoughts and Behavior.* The Greek term for "correcting," *epanorthosis,* literally means "to make upright again." Simply put, correction means *stopping the wrong and doing the right.* It is not enough to know what God expects and to know how short we have fallen from His standards. Now we must *do* something about it. This is where most people fail in the process of change. I know of a man who has suffered for years with obsessive behaviors and talked to psychologists, psychiatrists, medical doctors, counselors, and pastors in hopes of finding a magical way out of his bondage. He wanted to use the "dry cleaner approach" for his healing: "Here's my dysfunction, preacher. I'll stop by on Friday when it's fixed!" That is, he wanted to drop off his problems at my office for me to cure, and he didn't want to do any of the work himself.

Correction demands 1) a firm decision to change (Joshua 24:15); 2) confession to others (James 5:16); 3) prayer support (Ephesians 6:18); 4) consistent Bible study (Psalm 119:9-11); 5) fellowship, encouragement, and accountability (Hebrews 10:23-25); and 6) determined actions of obedience (James 1:22). Correction is putting off wrong patterns of thinking and acting and replacing them with those which are pleasing to God.

4. *We Must Maintain Our Walk with God.* To be changed is an ongoing battle to build up the new nature by training ourselves in

righteousness. *Practice, practice, practice!* As Paul wrote, "What-ever you have learned or received or heard from me, or seen in me—put it into practice. And the God of peace will be with you" (Philippians 4:9).

Each Must Learn to Love by Faith

We have already touched upon obedience as it relates to changing the way we think, but the point is worth repeating here. Obedient action is far more important than subjective emotions. Too many couples mistakenly believe that the *feeling* of love must be present before the marriage can survive.

"We just don't love each other anymore!" is a phrase every experienced biblical counselor has heard in one form or another. And the proper response is, "So?"

I mean it! The issue at this point is not emotion, but obedience to the Lord. Do you want to please Him or not? If so, the question is not, "Do I *feel* love for this person?" but, "Am I willing to *be* loving in obedience to my Lord?"

As one master counselor is fond of asking, "Is your mate your enemy?" Many, thinking the counselor will finally see just how hopeless the situation actually is, eagerly respond, "Absolutely!"

"And what does the Bible say we are to do with our enemies?"

Some may not know, or may choose not to reply, but the answer is found in Matthew 5:44: "I tell you: Love your enemies and pray for those who persecute you." Jesus' command is not to feel a fuzzy emotion, but to care for the other person with Christlike compassion and gentleness. It is the *agapé* love you have heard about—Christ's unselfish love. It is a love that puts others ahead of our own desires. It is the decision to love unselfishly, which must precede the fluctuating emotions so often identified as love.

One of our married couples recently shared their testimony in our new members class. They had been separated for more than five years and had fallen hopelessly out of love. During the separation, the husband had accepted Christ as Savior. The wife told us, "I knew divorce was not pleasing to the Lord, but I just didn't love my husband any longer. I finally prayed, 'Lord, if you want us together, you're going to have to change my heart.' And He did!" When she softened her heart before the Lord and was willing for Him to create His love, it happened. They are back together, with a glow on their faces, two more children around their table, and another one on the way.

The Character of Christ Must Be Developed in Both Mates

What qualities were you looking for in a mate before you got married? Some years back, I wrote my daughters the following letter as they began searching for God's choice of a partner for their lives:

> Counseling is starting to pile up again—lots of marriage problems. That's why I'm so very concerned that you find the man God has chosen for you. Be sure whoever you commit your heart to is genuinely in love with the Lord and has a happy family background. So many young men come from messed-up homes and they have no idea what it is to be a husband and father. They are not usually thinking of lifelong companionship unless they have seen their parents genuinely in love. Not just romantic love, mind you, but love that grows from absolute commitment to the marriage, whatever comes. I say "grows" intentionally, because the love you experience early in marriage is nothing compared to what it can become as both put the other ahead of their own desires.
>
> Your mother has been that sort of wife. Her unselfishness and sense of humor help make our home a joyful refuge from the harshness of the world. We have found such peace and contentment in and with each other as we both seek to obey the Lord individually and together. She amazes me with all she does, and she keeps such a sweet—and mischievous—attitude through it all. She has been the model daughter-in-law

to Gramma. No one has been more helpful to her than Marlowe. I am so very thankful for her and I bless the moment I first saw her walk into chorale rehearsal. I had no idea how blessed I was that she would fall in love with me. I had no idea how very capable she was in so many areas. Not only does she plan the music for the church, but now she is also growing in her ability as a Bible teacher. The women love her so very much and they enjoy her sense of humor and the fact that she doesn't take herself too seriously. No pastor could ask for a more wonderful partner in the ministry.

That is what I want for you. I want you to marry a husband that you can respect for his wisdom and knowledge, his humility and desire to listen to others, his diligence and patience, his vision and courage, his seriousness and good humor. I want someone who will laugh with you and cry with you. Someone who takes his job, but not himself, seriously. Someone who will comfort you when you're lonely and fearful and will protect you from a wicked world. Someone who will cuddle children in his strong arms and get misty-eyed when they go off to kindergarten.

Someone who is thankful for everything, realizing how blessed he is for health, family, friends, and the free gift of salvation. Someone who is thoughtful of others and polite, but is not easily intimidated or impressed. Someone who will open the door for you and walk on the outside protecting you from passing cars. Someone who can deny himself and his own desires, able to control his spending. Someone who has learned the joy of giving to the Lord and to those in need. Someone who is balanced, not given to extremes of mood, opinion, or doctrine, yet someone who is fanatical about the absolute authority of the Scriptures.

Someone who will guide you and your children with the principles of the Scripture and will be an example because he obeys the Word himself. Someone who is humble enough to know how very little he knows and is always willing to learn.

Someone who says yes as often as possible, but knows when to say no and has the courage to say it. Someone who is not afraid of hard work, and knows how to play. Someone who is competitive, but enjoys the game, even if he loses. Someone who has a desire to understand life, people, tools, projects, children, marriage, the Scriptures, and how to walk with God.

Someone who is more concerned with your inner spirit than outer beauty. Someone who is organized enough to get a job done, but relaxed enough that he won't lose his sanctification when the house is cluttered and needs dusting. Someone who can present himself with dignity at the right time, but who can be silly when it's called for. Someone who can eat as happily with paper plates and plastic ware as with fine china and silver. Someone who likes healthy food and french fries.

Someone who enjoys people. Someone secure enough to ask for advice from a variety of people. Someone who will listen . . . to me. But someone who knows where God is leading him and his family and has the determination to see it through. Someone I can respect and love as another son. Someone I can thank God for bringing into our lives. Someone I can be proud of as the father of my grandchildren. Someone who will lead his family and friends closer to the Lord by the way he conducts his life. Someone who knows he isn't perfect, but is trying to be holy as our Lord is holy. Someone who apologizes and asks for forgiveness when he has wronged someone. Someone who can look into his child's wide eyes and say, "I'm sorry. I was wrong."

When you find someone like that, your mother and I will lift our hearts toward heaven and say, "Thank you, dear Lord, for answering our prayers of more than twenty years." I want to remind you that no one you meet will fulfill all those qualifications immediately. It takes time to grow as a husband and father. The main things you need to look for now are: a genuine walk with the Lord, good family back-ground, intelligence, spontaneous sense of humor, gentle-ness, humility, and a willingness to grow in the fruit of the Spirit toward maturity in Christ. The rest will come.

Love from your sentimental ol' Daddy!

What matters in a marriage is not physical beauty, but depth of character. For a marriage to be fully restored, both the husband and wife must individually develop the character of Christ in their own inner lives. Paul describes these qualities in Galatians 5, where he writes, "The fruit of the Spirit is love, joy, peace, patience, kindness, goodness, faithfulness, gentleness and self-control" (Galatians 5:22-23). Peter lists these qualities: faith, goodness, knowledge, self-control, perseverance, godli-ness, brotherly kindness and love (2 Peter 1:5-7), and says that we must "make every effort" to develop them in our lives.

Space does not allow me to develop each of these character traits for our current study, but it would be well worth your time to do a word study on each of the qualities God says we are to develop. As you meditate on them, you will begin to see the holi-ness and purity of Christ, the only One who has ever fit the description.

Your marriage will grow stronger and sweeter in direct pro-portion to the development of these spiritual characteristics in both husband and wife.

Marriage Must Be Maintained and Nurtured Continually

As your marriage is restored through obedience and the choice of love, it must be consciously maintained and nurtured. According to the dictionary, the word *maintain* has at least five shades of meaning:

1. To continue; carry on: maintain good relations.
2. To preserve or keep in a given existing condition, as of efficiency or repair.

3. a. To provide for: maintain a family.
   b. To keep in existence; sustain: food to maintain life.
4. To defend, as against danger or attack.
5. To declare to be true; affirm.[28]

Each of these definitions apply to marriage, and you will note that maintenance requires deliberate effort and is best done *before* serious damage occurs. That's the difference between maintenance and repair. To be sure, maintenance is hard work, but it is normally easier and less costly than repair. It is amazing to me that there are many husbands who will spend countless hours maintaining their cars or computers, but will not invest even a few moments per day to strengthen their own marriages.

A major component in marriage maintenance is nourishing the relationship, and that takes time. To nourish means to feed, to help to grow, to develop or cultivate. The term *nourish* comes from the Latin *nutrire*, which meant "to suckle." It is the ultimate picture of a mother's tender care for her child who is deeply loved. It is that sort of tenderness that Paul instructs husbands about when he writes, "Husbands ought to love their wives as their own bodies. He who loves his wife loves himself. After all, no one ever hated his own body, but he feeds and *cares* for it, just as Christ does the church" (Ephesians 5:28-29, emphasis added).

May I ask you right now—especially if you are a husband—what are you doing to maintain and nourish your marriage? Are you spending time with your mate, learning to understand one another's language, sharing moments of joy and pain, understanding and making room for each other's weaknesses while encouraging growth?

In all fairness, wives are normally much better at marriage maintenance and nurturing than husbands are. I have known exceptions, but this sort of thing often comes more naturally for women than men. This means that we men must work much harder to develop relational skills if we are going to meet our wife's needs.

There are, however, some women who take their husband's love for granted. I have a friend who over the years has consistently written cards and notes to his wife, and to my surprise she has not responded in the way I would have expected. Though her husband has carefully taken time away from his work to share vacations and retreats with her, she has spurned his love and walked away. I'm not sure I'll ever understand it. For whatever reason, she chose not to maintain and nurture her marriage, and her whole family suffers for it. She has become a practical atheist so far as her marriage is concerned, not trusting and obeying God so that He can bring total restoration.

As I examine my own marriage of nearly thirty years, I must confess that I still have a lot of growing to do in the nurturing department. I find it hard to understand why my wife would actually *want* to be alone with me for an afternoon or evening "date." Receiving flowers and cards mean little to me personally, and I have to consciously remind myself that they can be important to my darling wife. Even as I write this I am convicted about how long it has been since I have just spontaneously written her a love note.

Excuse me for a few minutes while I take care of that . . . .

I'm back.

A little love note—such a minor thing, but so very important. It's a part of maintenance and nurture that takes so little time, yet can mean so very much. I encourage you to take a few moments to write your mate a love note, expressing specifically what you appreciate about his or her character, actions, personality, and life.

Determine that so far as it depends upon you, your marriage is going to be a preview of heaven—a place of comfort, courage, and cheer!

———

A Widening Gulf

Susan felt a bit betrayed by Pastor Miller's unwillingness to counsel her. *He was actually scared to hear my story!* she thought bitterly. *Maybe he thinks he's too good to deal with damaged goods!*

She hadn't returned to church since the day he had referred her to a psychiatrist.

She sat at her desk, staring blankly at her computer, confused by her swirling emotions of anger, bitterness, hurt, and loneliness. She hated to admit it, but she actually missed Arthur. She hadn't seen him now for nearly a month but she was determined she would not call him again. *If he wants to talk with me, let him call me for a change!*

"Hi, beautiful!" a cheery voice called out.

Susan jumped, startled at the sudden intrusion into her thoughts. She turned to see Billy Costas, her boss, standing at the door. Billy was single, having been divorced three years before, but due to his financial success, his charm, and good looks, he was considered by some of the women in the company to be very desirable.

"How about lunch?" he asked.

"How many are going?" Susan replied.

"Oh, I thought maybe just the two of us today," Billy said, almost shyly.

Susan blushed slightly and turned back to her desk, pretending to look for a file. "I . . . I don't know, Billy," she stammered "I have a lot of work to do."

Billy walked to her desk, pulled up a chair and sat down across from her. He looked her straight in the eyes, smiled, and said with a little grin, "Oh, come on, Susan. You need to get out of here for an hour or so." He nodded his head mischievously and said, "I'm buying. You can't pass up a deal like that."

Susan smiled in spite of herself. She felt a surge of warmth flow through her chest up into her throat as she looked at Billy. Though he was several years younger than Susan, there had always been a chemistry between them which she had resisted. His boyish eyes, dark flowing hair, and perfect mouth made up for his stature, nearly an inch shorter than Susan.

She tilted her head in indecision. Billy reached across the desk and touched her hand gently with his finger. He smiled again and said, "Come on, Susan, it's just a friendly lunch."

Out of the corner of her eye, Susan noticed Melissa Johnson pause for a moment in the hallway as she looked into Susan's office, then she quickly walked away.

Susan wasn't sure of what to say. She was still uncomfortable with the idea of going out with another man. But then her lips tightened slightly and she nodded her head as she stood up. "Okay, Billy. Where do you want to go?"

"You name it. It's your choice."

She got her jacket and purse and walked out of the office with Billy Costas close behind. Susan could feel the curious stares of other workers as she and Billy walked down the hallway, out the door, and toward his car. Her heart beat with a mixture of shame and a sense of naughty anticipation. Still, she dreaded the gossip which by now was already spreading in the lunchroom.

As Billy backed the car out of his parking space, Susan noticed Melissa Johnson looking out a second-floor window, talking to someone out of view. They drove off in Billy's silver Mercedes and headed toward a restaurant overlooking the Potomac. Susan looked out the window as Billy drove, angry with herself that even now she was thinking about Arthur.

"How come you're so quiet?" Billy asked as he reached over and patted her hand.

Susan stiffened momentarily, then relaxed and breathed out slowly. "Oh, nothing, really," she lied. "I was just enjoying the drive."

"You're not a very good liar, are you?" Billy laughed easily. "Come on, Susan, relax. We're just friends going for lunch, okay?"

She flashed a quick smile and nodded, "Okay."

When they entered the restaurant, the hostess led them through the main dining area back to a booth with a flowing canopy. Susan slid in to one side while Billy sat across the table from her.

They ordered their meal, and as they talked, Susan began to enjoy their time together. It had been a long time since she had been to a restaurant with anyone, let alone a man who seemed attracted to her. She couldn't help but feel a measure of warmth and pleasure as she looked at Billy.

"How is it going with you and your husband?" Billy asked as they ate.

Susan tried to answer nonchalantly as she raised her eyebrows in seeming unconcern. "I really don't know, Billy. I haven't talked to him now for several weeks."

"Do you think you'll be getting back together?"

She looked down at her plate, hesitated for a moment, and then looked up and replied, "I honestly don't know. I'm beginning to doubt it, quite frankly."

"Do you want to get back with him?" Billy asked softly. His eyes glistened as he looked at Susan. He swallowed involuntarily as he took in her beauty. He had been with many women since his divorce, but no one had attracted him like Susan. There was something elegant about her, unapproachable, yet with a tender vulnerability.

Susan didn't answer at first. She sensed Billy's attraction and felt a response growing in her heart. She knew it was wrong, but the anger and loneliness she felt because of Arthur's coldness began to overcome her sense of loyalty to her husband.

"I'm not sure, Billy," she finally said as she reached out her hand to take his. "I'm not sure what I want anymore."

"Maybe I can help you make up your mind," he said almost whispering.

Susan looked down momentarily and then back up, straight into Billy's eyes. "Maybe so, Billy. Maybe it's time."

. . .

Dr. Arthur Wilson was seething with anger. Susan hadn't called him except that one time when she told him she wasn't coming home. He wanted desperately to talk to someone, to express his frustration and anger, but since Susan had left, Arthur had avoided social interaction with people.

He picked up the phone, started to dial, then stopped and hung up. A few minutes later, he repeated the sequence. After a few moments, he said out loud, "I've got to talk to somebody!" He dialed Michael Rollins's number.

Soon, Michael's pleasant voice came on the line. "Arthur! How are you?"

"Well, to be frank with you, Michael, things are not going very well."

"I'm sorry to hear that, Arthur. Do you want to talk about it?"

"That's why I called you, Michael. I know we don't agree on some issues, like evolution, but ever since our last conversation, I've felt that you are a person I could talk with." Arthur paused with embarrassment, then said, "Michael, my wife has left me."

"Oh, I'm sorry to hear that, Arthur. I didn't know." Again, there was an awkward pause. Then Michael said, "Say, would you be interested in a good home-cooked meal? You remember meeting my wife, Ellen, don't you?"

"Sure I do. But I really don't want to be a bother. I know both of you are so busy."

"Nonsense! She would be upset at me if I didn't invite you over. We live over in Alexandria, but it would be worth your drive. How does tomorrow night sound?"

"Well, if you're sure Ellen won't mind . . ."

"I'll call her right now. If there's a problem, I'll call you back. Otherwise, it's our house at seven. Okay?"

"Okay, Michael. Thanks."

"No problem, Arthur. Let me give you our address." Michael gave Arthur the directions to their home on the other side of Washington.

Arthur left early the following evening to take a leisurely drive to the Rollins's house. It had been a long time since he had driven a scenic route. The trees hung densely over the winding side streets he chose. He noticed children playing in a yard. A few houses down, a barbeque was in progress. As car after car passed him, going the opposite direction, he noticed that many of them held families, and a sense of loneliness filled his chest.

The sun was beginning to set in shades of orange and pink. It was an unusually brilliant sunset and Arthur seemed to hear his father's voice in the back of his memory. When Arthur was ten, he and his dad had taken a hike one afternoon. His father had pointed at the sky and said, "See that sunset, Arthur? That's God's way of saying 'Good night, my child. Sleep well.'"

The sunset faded and Arthur realized that tears were running down his face. He sniffed and rubbed the tears away with embarrassment. *Oh, Dad*, he thought, *if only I could believe.*

He followed Michael's directions and arrived at the Rollins's home a few minutes early. He sat in the car, not wanting to rush them. He shifted uncomfortably in the bucket seat, dreading the conversation before him, yet longing to share his hurt with someone.

Michael looked out the front door and saw Arthur sitting in his car. He walked out, waved at Arthur and said, "Come on in, stranger! Supper is getting cold!"

"I just didn't want to hurry Ellen," Arthur said almost timidly.

"No problem! Ellen isn't working outside the home right now, so she had plenty of time. In fact, she's already fed our children, and they're down in the recreation room watching a Bible video. I thought it would be less confusing if we weren't interrupted."

"Thanks, Michael," Arthur said as they stepped inside. "How many children do you have?"

"Four. And every one a blessing! Ellen homeschools them, and they consistently test above their public school grade level. We're really proud of them."

"I'll bet you are," Arthur agreed with a tinge of pain.

As they stood in the front hallway, Arthur sensed a warmth, an almost tangible joy in the home. Family pictures decorated every wall in sight. Ellen came out of the kitchen, still wearing her apron.

"Hello, Arthur," she said with a smile. "Welcome to our home."

"Thank you, Ellen. I really appreciate your letting me come on such short notice."

"Don't you say another word about it. You come in to the dining room and sit down with Michael. I'll bring everything right out." Ellen's ease made Arthur comfortable. He followed Michael into the dining room and sat at the table. Ellen brought in a platter of fried chicken and a bowl of mashed potatoes. She returned to the kitchen and came back with vegetables and rolls.

"Good grief, Ellen," Arthur exclaimed, "I told Michael not to put you to any trouble. This looks like Thanksgiving!"

"Well, Arthur, I must confess," Ellen said, looking at her husband, who was smiling wryly, "I didn't have to do much work. Michael stopped by the store and picked up a bucket of chicken. I hope you don't mind."

"I don't mind at all," Arthur laughed. "To tell you the truth, I just needed the company."

Michael looked at Ellen, who had taken her seat. Then he said, "Our custom is to give thanks for our meals, Arthur. I hope you don't mind."

"Oh . . . not really. Go right ahead," Arthur said with bit of embarrassment.

Michael and Ellen bowed their heads. Arthur looked down at his plate, but kept his eyes open. Michael said, "Heavenly Father, we thank You tonight for this food. Thank You for the health and strength You have given us. And thank You for bringing Arthur tonight to share his time with us. We pray this in Jesus' name, amen."

Arthur's eyes were moist when they looked up. "That reminded me of the prayers my father used to say when I was a boy," he said.

"Tell me about your childhood, Arthur," Michael said.

"Oh, there's nothing very dramatic, Michael. I grew up northwest of Baltimore in a little town called Winfield. My parents were devout Baptists. I had a very normal and happy childhood. I went to Georgetown University in pre-med and continued my studies later in genetics. I've been working at NCI for about twelve years. That's about all there is to my life story. Boring, huh?"

Ellen began passing the food. "Michael tells me that you consider yourself an atheist, Arthur. Tell me what happened. I mean, your folks were real believers, weren't they?" Ellen asked.

"Yes, they really were. And I do respect their sincerity. There just came a time when I could no longer believe in their God. I didn't have a traumatic experience which caused me to turn away in anger, except when my dad died, I guess. I just gradually realized I didn't believe. And the more I studied about religion in the light of modern science, the less I could believe. To tell you the truth, Ellen, I wish I *could* believe. But I don't," Arthur said with a sad smile.

"Tell Ellen about the debate," Michael said.

"I'm debating on the unscientific nature of creationism. The ironic thing is the man I'm to debate is the very man I heard speak in Mom and Dad's church when I was a teenager. In some ways, I'm where I am today because of him," Arthur chuckled.

"What do you mean?" Michael asked.

"He was the one who actually caused me to examine the conflict between science and creationism. In so doing, I became convinced by the overwhelming evidence for evolution."

"Has your faith in evolution made you happy, Arthur?" Ellen asked quietly.

He looked down at his plate, sighed quietly, than looked at Ellen. "No, Ellen, it hasn't. But simply claiming to believe in God wouldn't make me happy either. Either he exists or he doesn't. And what I believe or what you believe will not change the fact or the fiction of that existence."

"I agree with you, Arthur," Michael said with a smile. "Simply believing something does not make it true. There needs to be a rational basis for faith. But every philosophical, religious, and scientific system has a foundation of assumptions. Wouldn't you agree?"

"Well, I'm not sure I would put assumptions in the same category as faith," Arthur replied.

"How do they differ?"

"I think that assumptions in science are based upon logic, reason, and observation, whereas, in religion, assumptions are based on blind faith."

"Let's examine that for a moment, Arthur," Michael said. "Science is based on several unprovable assumptions. We assume, for instance, that present processes, the known laws of physics, were the same in the past and will be the same in the future. We assume that physical laws are the same in all parts of the universe. We assume that the laws of the universe are consistent with our own minds' understanding of physical lawfulness. We assume that the universe is knowable. These assumptions are logical. They make sense to me and I accept them. But, I can't prove them scientifically. So tell me, Arthur, how are these assumptions different from faith?"

Arthur rested his elbow on the table with his hand supporting his head in deep thought. After a few moments he looked at Michael and said, "The primary difference I see is that scientific assumptions are rational and conform to the trends of scientific laws, whereas religious faith is based upon wishful thinking, with no supporting evidence."

"And your definitions are, in themselves, assumptions, based not on actual evidence but pseudoscientific prejudice," Michael said without raising his voice. "What I hear you saying is that an assumption is allowable unless it deals with a Creator. Then it becomes faith."

"Oh, come now, Michael," Arthur said, putting his fork down. "You're beginning to take this personally."

"Not at all. I'm merely pointing out that faith in a Creator is no less scientific than the assumption of cosmic knowability. The ordered nature of the universe is excellent supporting evidence for a Creator. Kepler put it this way: 'Geometry is one and eternal, a reflection out of the mind of God. That mankind shares in it is one reason to call man an image of God.'

"If we deny that man can make sense of the universe we join Carl Sagan's twisted musings found in his book *Cosmos*. Let me get my copy, Arthur," Michael said, getting up and walking toward his study. He returned in a few moments with several books.

"Listen to this: 'We can imagine . . . wormholes as tubes running through the fourth physical dimension. We do not know that such wormholes exist. But if they do, must they always hook up with another place in our universe? Or is it possible that wormholes connect with other universes?'

"'What would those other universes be like? Would they be built on different laws of physics?'" Michael handed the book to Arthur. "Look at what he is saying, Arthur. He is suggesting that nothing is really knowable. And yet Sagan is considered by many to be one of our top scientists!"

Arthur looked at the page and said nothing. Michael pulled out another book, turned to a marked page and said, "Listen to what Isaac Asimov suggested in an article in *Science Digest:* 'We don't know all the kinds of things that are happening in the universe. The changes we do observe are all in the direction of increasing entropy. Somewhere, though, there may be changes under unusual conditions that we can't as yet study which are in the direction of decreasing entropy.' Do you catch what he is saying, Arthur?"

Ellen leaned forward with a little smile and said, "Well, *I* sure don't. Could you explain it to me?"

Arthur shifted uneasily in his chair and said, "Asimov is basically saying that maybe there are places in the universe where things don't run down."

"So?"

"Well, according to standard physical law, all of the observable universe is tending toward decay and disorder, which could be used as an argument against evolution," Arthur said reluctantly. "Asimov's argument is silly, at best. You have to remember that he is primarily a science fiction writer. However, creationists forget to take into account the possibility of a closed system on our planet, which may have led toward the beginning of life."

"But, Arthur," said Ellen. "Isn't that another assumption?"

Arthur smiled slowly, nodded, and said, "Yep. But it makes more sense to me than any other alternative." He pushed back from the table and said, "Ellen, that was a fine meal. I really enjoyed it."

"Oh, Arthur, I'm sorry," Michael said. "I forgot that you came here to talk about your home situation. Don't hurry off. Besides, you haven't had dessert yet."

"Why don't you two move into the family room? I'll bring dessert in there," said Ellen.

Michael and Arthur went into the family room and sat in the comfortable easy chairs. "So, Arthur, fill me in on what's happening at home," Michael said.

Arthur sighed deeply and said, "I hardly know where to begin, Michael."

"Just tell me what's happening, Arthur," Michael said gently.

"Well, as I told you, Susan has left me."

"Uh huh."

"I figured you probably already knew since you go to the same church."

"Well, our church is fairly large, and we don't see everyone every week. In fact, now that you mention it, I haven't seen Susan at church for some time now."

Arthur was a bit surprised. "She hasn't been at church? I thought she attended every Sunday."

"Maybe she has, Arthur. I just haven't seen her."

"I don't know what to do. Our marriage has been pretty shaky for several years, but I thought we could work our way through it. Then Susan got into this Christianity-thing and everything kind of went downhill. That's why I called you. I just needed someone to talk to."

"Why me?" Michael asked.

"Because I think I can trust you. I know we don't agree on religion, but I do think you're a person of integrity."

Michael nodded, a bit embarrassed, but pleased that Arthur felt he could confide in him. "How can I help, Arthur?"

"I guess I just need a sounding board. And maybe you can help me think of some way to turn the situation around."

They sat silently for a few moments. Then Michael said, "I'll do whatever I can, Arthur. But right now, I don't know what to tell you." He reached across the coffee table and patted Arthur's knee. With a twinkle in his eye he said, "If you weren't such a pagan, I'd offer to pray with you right now for God to give you wisdom. But I won't."

"Thanks," Arthur chuckled good-naturedly. Just then Ellen walked in with coffee and apple turnovers.

"But we will be praying for you, Arthur, on our own time," Ellen said with a smile.

"Okay, Ellen. You do just that. I need all the help I can get."

Later, as he drove home, Arthur thought about Ellen's promise to pray for him. *Wouldn't it be wonderful if a person really could talk with a god somewhere and get results?* He remembered seeing his dad praying early one morning when Arthur was a child. Arthur had awakened earlier than usual and tiptoed down the stairs to get something to eat. He heard a soft voice coming from the living room. He walked to the door and peeked in. There was his father, kneeling in front of his chair, with his head resting on his folded hands. Arthur listened as his father said, ". . . and Lord, watch over my little Arthur. He's a good boy and I love him. Please protect him, and help him to grow up to be a godly man, a man we can be proud of." Arthur sensed the holiness of the moment and stole away quietly.

A godly man, Arthur thought as the memory faded. *Dad was a godly man. And I bet he prayed for me every day until he died.* The pain was still sharp in Arthur's heart as he recalled his father's physical suffering and sudden painful death from cancer. *Dad never even smoked!* he thought angrily. *How could a loving God allow a good man like Dad to die such a miserable death? I'll never pray to a God like that! If God is so loving, why has He allowed all this to happen to me? Why couldn't He keep Susan and me together? Why couldn't He protect my son? No! There is no God!*

When he got home, Arthur resumed his preparation for the debate with renewed determination.

5

Faith for
Marital Purity

BIBLICAL FAITH IS A vital part of satisfying sex. I know that sounds strange coming from a conservative biblicist, but it is absolutely true. When a couple comes to my office declaring that they have a sexual dysfunction, I ask if there has been a medical confirmation of a physical disorder. It is rarely the case. Usually, the "dysfunction" they describe is the direct result of deep resentment and anger between the partners.

Many people have the mistaken notion that the Bible does not deal with sexual issues, but it does. And the world believes that the Bible condemns sexual desire and expression, but it doesn't. In fact, if people would take the time to carefully study what the Bible teaches about human sexuality, they would discover that God gives the gift of sex as a reflection of His own creative power, and sex in its proper context is pure, joyful, and holy. It is only when it is distorted by Satan's twisted schemes that it becomes perverted and vile. Let's look briefly, therefore, at what the Bible teaches about Christian sexuality.

SEX AND GOD'S
CREATIVE POWER

Why does Satan seem to have a fascination with sex? It is because sex carries with it the power to create—something Satan has always coveted. You see, Satan wanted to be God. It was his plan to overthrow the Almighty and to assume God's position in the universe. This is related to us in Isaiah 14:

> You said in your heart, "I will ascend to heaven; I will raise my throne above the stars of God; I will sit enthroned on the mount of assembly, on the utmost heights of the sacred mountain.
>
> I will ascend above the tops of the clouds; I will make myself like the Most High" (verses 13-14).

In his pride, Satan believed he could actually become God. He would not accept the fact that he was a created being immeasurably below God in strength and nature, and he determined to wrest the throne from God. Too late he discovered God's infinite power and because of his rebellion, Satan was cast out of heaven. Reporting on this event, God said about Satan,

> I drove you in disgrace from the mount of God, and I expelled you, O guardian cherub, from among the fiery stones. Your heart became proud on account of your beauty, and you corrupted your wisdom because of your splendor. So I threw you to the earth (Ezekiel 28:16-17).

Jesus himself declared, "I saw Satan fall like lightning from heaven" (Luke 10:18). Since that time, Satan has done everything in his wicked but limited power to counter God's plans for His creation. I believe his motive for this is sheer fury that he cannot create anything except destruction.

Think about it for a moment. Only God is able to create something out of nothing. All of the universe—the vastness of space, the incalculable number of stars, the glowing dust of His heaven—was created by His will alone. He merely spoke and the universe appeared. The psalmist wrote, "By the word of the LORD were the heavens made, their starry host by the breath of his mouth" (Psalm 33:6).

Nehemiah worshipped the Lord and His creative power when he wrote, "You alone are the LORD. You made the heavens, even the highest heavens, and all their starry host, the earth and all that is on it, the seas and all that is in them. You give life to everything, and the multitudes of heaven worship you" (Nehemiah 9:6).

God did not even need a supply of raw materials to accomplish creation. He created the universe *ex nihilo*—out of nothing. "By faith we understand that the universe was formed at God's command, so that what is seen was not made out of what was visible" (Hebrews 11:3).

The closest reflection of God's creative power is found in human sexual union, for in this act humans are able to cooperate with God in the creation of other eternal souls. Even the holy angels of God cannot create spiritual beings that will live forever. Much less could the fallen angels of hell.

Satan's insane jealousy of God causes him to "oppose and . . . exalt himself over everything that is called God or is worshiped" (2 Thessalonians 2:4). It is because sexual union comes closest to the power Satan desires—the ability to create as only God can do—that he has determined to distort and pervert human sexuality in every possible way.

PREOCCUPATION WITH SEX

One way Satan distorts the purity of the sexual gift is through people's fascination with sex itself. It is, of course, one of the most powerful drives known to human beings. It involves virtually every physical sense and it normally provides an explosive moment of pleasure that can blank out all other thoughts and concerns. When you couple this level of sensual pleasure with the mystical emotions that accompany "love," the appeal of sexual release can become an all-consuming preoccupation.

Our culture fosters sexual desire in every possible way from the earliest age. We need not linger over the sexually implicit or explicit images that bombard us daily from television, radio, books, magazines, billboards, music, catalogs, clothing styles, entertainment, fitness clubs, cosmetic advertisements, and other imaginations that stimulate lustful thinking and behavior. You know exactly what I'm talking about.

Both males and females can be seduced by the allure of a sensual touch, a scent of romance, and an enticing look. Part of the problem is that humans have been designed to respond to the opposite sex physically, mentally, and emotionally. That is how God intended it to be, and the attraction is normal. Males are naturally drawn to the female body and are fascinated with feminine softness and form. Women have been designed to respond to the attention of men and respond to a gentle but masculine touch. But remember, Satan desires to corrupt anything natural, good, and of God, and one of his primary tools of corruption is imbalance.

Anything taken to excess can become sinful. The natural appetite for food can become gluttony. The need for rest can be extended into lethargy, laziness, and waste. The natural desire to avoid pain can grow into cowardice and deceit. And the normal and God-given interest in sex can become a perverted obsession whenever a person becomes preoccupied with lustful thoughts.

When God is left out, sex is an appetite which is never satisfied. Paul writes, "Having lost all sensitivity, they have given themselves over to sensuality so as to indulge in every kind of impurity, with a continual lust for more" (Ephesians 4:19).

SEXUAL PERVERSION

Why has sex become such a source of disappointment, sorrow, and pain in a society obsessed with lust? Because most people ignore the spiritual component, which is essential for human sexuality to be truly satisfying. The sexual act, after all, is as spiritual as it is physical because it truly affects the inner being. Humans know this instinctively and seek a measure of spiritual fulfillment in sex, but are disappointed when casual sex leaves an emptiness too deep for words.

Have you ever noticed that Romans 1 connects atheism with sexual perversion? Starting in verse 18, Paul warns us of the consequences of pushing God out of our minds. Read this passage carefully:

> The wrath of God is being revealed from heaven against all the godlessness and wickedness of men who suppress the truth by their wickedness, since what may be known about God is plain to them, because God has made it plain to them. For since the creation of the world God's invisible qualities—his eternal power and divine nature—have been clearly seen, being understood from what has been made, so that men are without excuse.
>
> For although they knew God, they neither glorified him as God nor gave thanks to him, but their thinking became futile and their foolish hearts were darkened. Although they claimed to be wise, they became fools and exchanged the glory of the immortal God for images made to look like mortal man and birds and animals and reptiles.
>
> Therefore God gave them over in the sinful desires of their hearts to sexual impurity for the degrading of their bodies with one another (Romans 1:18-24).

Note the word "therefore" in the last verse above. It refers back to the willful rejection of God, even though our world knows full well that He exists. Four of the most frightening words in the Scriptures follow: "God gave them over." In other words, God says to our unbelieving world, "Have it your own way. Do what you want and see where it leads." Then He tells us that the fruit of rebellion is abject degradation, where human beings engage in activities so disgustingly vile and putrid that they lose all respect for one another. They willingly use and abuse one another's bodies as they burn with unrestrained desire. Natural sexual relations no longer satisfy and they feel compelled to sink ever deeper into perversion. Homosexuality and lesbianism are the result of sexual atheism.

> Because of this, God gave them over to shameful lusts. Even their women exchanged natural relations for

unnatural ones. In the same way the men also abandoned natural relations with women and were inflamed with lust for one another. Men committed indecent acts with other men, and received in themselves the due penalty for their perversion (Romans 1:26-27).

Though society has come to consider homosexuality as an acceptable lifestyle, the truth remains that it is clearly forbidden by Scripture. Leviticus 18:22 says, "Do not lie with a man as one lies with a woman; that is detestable." What could be clearer? But there are some who call themselves Christians who believe that a person can be a practicing homosexual and a Spirit-filled Christian at the same time.[29]

Here is the problem: Once we remove God and His Word from our sexual lives, anything becomes acceptable. San Francisco has moved to license sex clubs where people can pay a fee to view or engage in group sex. Homosexuals are lobbying for the right to marry—which if it has not already been granted by the time of this printing, it soon will be. If society sanctions homosexual marriages, why stop there? Who is to say polygamy is wrong? Why not allow two men to marry one woman? Or a father to marry his daughter? Or a woman to marry an animal? God warns that people will sink to such levels when he says, "Do not have sexual relations with an animal and defile yourself with it. A woman must not present herself to an animal to have sexual relations with it; that is a perversion" (Leviticus 18:23).

UNFAITHFULNESS IN MARRIAGE

One of the most basic concepts in human society is that marriage is the legal and binding union between one man and one woman. That was God's original intent as described in Genesis 2:24: "For this reason a man will leave his father and mother and be united to his wife, and they will become one flesh." There are several vital points that are taught in this verse: 1) marriage involves the formation of a new home in a covenant of companionship; 2) a person's first loyalty must be to his or her mate; 3) God intended the relationship to be monogamous; 4) under those parameters, sexual expression is holy and pure.

Outside of marriage, sexual activity is forbidden. Exodus 20:14 says, "You shall not commit adultery." This prohibition, by the way, was not God's way of ruining our "innocent" fun. He gave this command to protect us from our own lustful desires, because unrestrained sex defiles body and soul, destroys marital trust, transmits a host of diseases, and places a barrier between us and God.

What is adultery? It is when a married person engages in voluntary sexual intercourse with a person other than his mate. Our English word *adultery* comes from the Latin *adulter,* which means "one who approaches another (unlawfully)."[30] We get the word *adulterate*—or *pollute*—from the same root. The essence of this action is the betrayal of the most intimate trust contracted between two human beings.

Adultery is such a serious violation that God will not stand for it. Listen to what He says in Malachi chapter 2:

> Another thing you do: You flood the LORD's altar with tears. You weep and wail because he no longer pays attention to your offerings or accepts them with pleasure from your hands. You ask, "Why?" It is because the LORD is acting as the witness between you and the wife of your youth, because you have broken faith with her, though she is your partner, the wife of your marriage covenant.
>
> Has not the LORD made them one? In flesh and spirit they are his. And why one? Because he was seeking godly offspring. So guard yourself in your spirit, and do not break faith with the wife of your youth.
>
> "I hate divorce," says the LORD God of Israel, "and I hate a man's covering himself with violence as well as with his garment," says the LORD Almighty (Malachi 2:13-16).

Do you see the consequences of sexual unfaithfulness? God ignores the adulterer's prayers, no matter how desperately or sincerely they may be uttered (verses 12 and 13) because He takes the side of the innocent party (verse 14). According to verse 15, God sees a married couple's sexual union as a deeply spiritual covenant from which He desires little believers to come. Note how strongly God states His aversion to divorce (verse 16) and to the husband's physical violence that so often drives a woman to seek it.

Never mistake God's hatred of adultery as a disgust with sexual intercourse itself. We are told, "Marriage should be honored by all, and the marriage bed kept pure, for God will judge the adulterer and all the sexually immoral" (Hebrews 13:4). No, sex within marriage is holy and right if we bring our faith into the relationship.

UNMARRIED SEXUALITY

Someone might be saying, "Adultery is sexual unfaithfulness involving *married* people. I'm still single, so I'm not betraying a mate. No one can expect a healthy young adult to remain a virgin in this modern day of contraception and safe sex. When I get married, then I'll reserve myself for my mate, but until then, it's no sin to be sexually active."

If that's what you're thinking, you are sadly mistaken. Not only is premarital sex sinful, it is harmful and you will pay a terrible price. Since sexual intercourse is such a spiritual act, no one can engage in it without spiritual consequences, and contrary to popular thought, sex is not a recreational sport. It was created for the purpose of procreation and the most intimate form of communication between husband and wife. That is why the Scriptures forbid fornication: "Flee from sexual immorality ['fornication,' KJV]. All other sins a man commits are outside his body, but he who sins sexually sins against his own body" (1 Corinthians 6:18).

Paul wrote, "To avoid fornication, let every man have his own wife, and let every woman have her own husband" (1 Corinthians

7:2 KJV). Are you a single believer in Christ wanting to please your Lord? Then read carefully what Paul wrote to the Thessalonians: "This is the will of God, even your sanctification, that ye should abstain from fornication" (1 Thessalonians 4:3 KJV).

The term "fornication" or *porneia* in the Greek text, includes *all* sexual sin, so it includes but is not exclusive to the sexually active unmarried.

SPIRITUAL SEX

A recent study about sexual satisfaction stated that married couples had more frequent and satisfying sex than single people, though the media tries to convince our society that marriage is boring and single swingers have all the fun. The facts prove that the opposite is true.

Still, many married couples do have a miserable sex life because their personal walk with God is so weak and their focus on self is so strong. They have never learned that satisfying sex cannot be achieved by technique or therapy, but is a by-product of unselfish love for one's mate.

Our society has accepted the playboy philosophy which glamorizes casual sex and contemptuously discards the commitment of marriage. The result is emptiness, disappointment, and spiritual defeat.

How can a married couple make their sexual life as spiritual as any other part of their Christian walk? There are at least six aspects of sexuality in marriage that need to be considered:

- The Covenant of Marriage
- The Commitment to Obedience
- The Practice of Godliness
- The Act of Forgiveness
- Understanding One Another (Wisdom)
- Fulfilling One's Marital Duties

The Covenant of Marriage

For sex to be truly satisfying, it must be entered into voluntarily, but there also needs to be a safeguard against the exploitation of the other person for one's own selfish gratification. That is the covenant of companionship taught in Genesis 2:24, which we looked at earlier.

The marriage covenant is a contract of protection which states that the husband and wife will be there for one another regardless of the circumstances which life brings about: "I am yours and you are mine." There is a security in this most important of all agreements which allows a couple to relax in each other's arms.

Without this covenant, sexual encounters are nothing more than the physical release of hormonal drives. Ask the thousands of now-aging single women who once thought that the marriage covenant was old-fashioned and outdated and that casual sex was a benign form of entertainment. Ask them now, as they raise their children alone, if they wish they had found one man of integrity who was willing to join her in a permanent covenant of companionship.

Ask the men and women who have been abandoned by heartless and selfish mates about their sense of total betrayal when their life-long covenant was broken by their partners' unfaithfulness. The marriage covenant was given for our mutual protection, and God expects us to honor the agreement.

The Commitment to Obedience

This commitment is not primarily to obey one another, but to submit our beliefs and actions to the Lord as He reveals His will through His written Word. As I mentioned earlier, when a troubled couple comes to me for counseling, one of the first questions I ask is, "If I can show you from the Bible what God wants you to do, will you agree right now to do it?" If they sincerely agree to this requirement before we begin the counseling process, I know their marriage is going to be healed. I have never—and I do mean *never*—seen a couple fail to restore their marriage when they both were seeking to obey the Lord.

One of our faithful listeners of *Return to the Word* called in to share three questions he asks when people come to him for help with their marriage: 1) What does God's Word say? 2) What would Jesus do? 3) What will bring God the most glory? If Christians would examine their situation with these diagnostic tools, they would quickly find solutions for their problems.

Let's apply those questions for a moment to the issue of sex within marriage. First, what does God's Word say? The Bible tells us that sexual union is natural, pure, and without shame (Genesis 2:24-25). In God's eyes, romance and sexual desire for one's mate is encouraged (*see* the Song of Solomon). The marriage bed is to be honored and kept undefiled. Sex is not to be used as a tool to get one's own way and is to be engaged in regularly and according to the needs of both mates (1 Corinthians 7:3-6). Of course, the Bible says far more about sex, but for our present purposes, this explains the point.

The second question one needs to ask is, What would Jesus do? This may seem an odd question to ask because Jesus was never married and never involved Himself sexually with anyone. But the answer is so very clear: He would have done whatever was holy and unselfish. That is the secret to spirituality, even in marital sexuality—unselfishness, seeking to please God.

Have you ever wondered if God has given us a checklist of spiritual traits? He has indeed. You can find His list in Galatians 5:22-23, where we read that "the fruit of the Spirit is love, joy, peace, patience, kindness, goodness, faithfulness, gentleness and self-control."

Do these characteristics describe your sexual experience? Is it an expression of genuine love for one another or is it merely a momentary release of lust? Is sex with your mate joyful or is it boring or even emotionally painful? Do you experience a blessed peace of heart as you lie in bed with your mate, or is there a nagging heartache and emptiness? Are you patient with your mate in the area of sexual expression or do you demand your way on your terms and timing?

Are both of you kind toward one another in your sexuality or do cutting remarks about the other's body and performance taint the moments which should have been such a positive time together? Is there a deep confidence in each other's moral purity and goodness or are there nagging doubts about one another's faithfulness? Are you both people of your word who fulfill your promises or have you betrayed one another with lies and excuses? Is there a gentleness in words and touch that allow you to relax and enjoy each other or is there a harshness that dilutes the joy? Is there enough self-control over your desires to keep you from demanding your own way when your mate doesn't feel well or if the timing is wrong? All these characteristics answer the question, What would Jesus do?

The third question we need to ask to examine the spiritual level of our sexual lives is, What will bring God the most glory? Paul says in 1 Corinthians 10:31, "Whatever you do, do it all for the glory of God." Had you ever realized that the "whatever you do" includes your sex life? Well, it does.

Perhaps you are wondering how sexual activity has anything to do with glorifying the Lord. Think about it for a moment. Sexual arousal ordinarily involves intense mental images. For many these images include immoral fantasies of sex with a person other than one's mate, and we must ask ourselves: Does this glorify the Lord? Or perhaps we enter into a sexual encounter with resentment, selfishness, harshness, or any number of sinful attitudes. Again, are we glorifying the Lord at that moment?

There is hardly anything we do with our bodies with more spiritual overtones than sexual intercourse. This passage, then, is important to consider: "Do you not know that your body is a temple of the Holy Spirit, who is in you, whom you have received from God? You are not your own; you were bought at a price. Therefore honor God with your body" (1 Corinthians 6:19-20). Do you doubt that this applies to sex? Then you will want to look at the verses which precede the ones quoted, for they specifically address sexual issues.

The Practice of Godliness

There is nothing that will protect your marriage like the practice of godliness. This is a concept totally foreign to our modern age but it is one written about frequently in the Bible. To practice godliness means to honor God with our entire being—physically, mentally, socially, spiritually.

It is amazing to me the fascination people have with the perfect body. There are health clubs across America where people come to sweat and lift and stretch and row and cycle so that they can have "hard bodies." Advertisements promise if you buy the latest exercise machine you too can have the body of an Amazon—lean, trim, and sexy. Can you believe that the Bible even speaks to this? Paul writes, "Physical training is of some value, but godliness has value for all things, holding promise for both the present life and the life to come" (1 Timothy 4:8).

The New Testament term "godliness," *eusebeia,* comes from two Greeks words, *eu,* which means "good," and *sebomai,* "to worship devoutly or to adore." It literally means "good worship." Put another way, godliness is the consistent practice of righteousness motivated by a heart that truly desires to please God.

Scripture teaches that godliness pays wonderful dividends now and throughout eternity. This is true even in the area of sexuality. One who is godly in his sex life does not fear contracting a sexually transmitted disease. He does not wonder if he is going to be caught in an immoral act or if someone will see him come out of the prostitute's apartment. As the Bible says, "The righteousness of the upright delivers them, but the unfaithful are trapped by evil desires" (Proverbs 11:6).

A godly man does not purchase pornography or watch immoral videos. He doesn't tell dirty stories or gaze long at an attractive woman. He does not trust himself with unnecessary temptation, but he purposely avoids such things. He takes Paul's advice seriously: "Flee the evil desires of youth, and pursue righteousness, faith, love and peace, along with those who call on the Lord out of a pure heart" (2 Timothy 2:22). If a movie suddenly assaults him with scenes of immorality, he will get up and leave, even if it is embarrassing to do so. You see, a godly man takes his moral purity seriously. He does not want to have to confess to his wife that he has allowed his mind to become sexually polluted, so he strives to keep his "conscience clear before God and man" (Acts 24:16).

Titus writes about moral dichotomy in the verse preceding our key passage:

> To the pure, all things are pure, but to those who are corrupted and do not believe, nothing is pure. In fact, both their minds and consciences are corrupted. They claim to know God, but by their actions they deny him. They are detestable, disobedient and unfit for doing anything good (Titus 1:15-16).

Godliness is a choice each person must make for himself. As someone has said, a person really is what he does when no one is looking. Daniel is a powerful example of godliness in private. As a young man, he was taken captive in Israel and carried off to Babylon. There, away from his family and the façade of his religious culture, Daniel was faced with the huge temptation to compromise his convictions just a little in order to advance his career a lot. But, we are told, "Daniel purposed in his heart that he would not defile himself" (Daniel 1:8 KJV). If you read his exciting biography, you will see how God blessed Daniel because of his personal godliness.

Years later, Daniel was tested again:

> Daniel so distinguished himself among the administrators and the satraps by his exceptional qualities that the king planned to set him over the whole kingdom. At this, the administrators and the satraps tried to find grounds for charges against Daniel in his conduct of government affairs, but they were unable to do so. They could find no corruption in him, because he was trustworthy and neither corrupt nor negligent. Finally these men said, "We will never find any basis for charges against this man

Daniel unless it has something to do with the law of his God" (Daniel 6:3-5).

This story of political intrigue rivals that of modern-day Washington D.C., as Daniel's enemies plotted his ruin. They convinced the king to issue an edict that no one could pray to any god or man for thirty days, except to the king, on penalty of death.

Instead of compromising by praying in secret, Daniel continued his normal practice of worship: "Now when Daniel learned that the decree had been published, he went home to his upstairs room where the windows opened toward Jerusalem. Three times a day he got down on his knees and prayed, giving thanks to his God, just as he had done before" (Daniel 6:10). In response to Daniel's righteousness, God delivered him again from death. It is such a glorious story that you just have to read it!

The point is, real godliness is not sporadic; it is a daily walk with God. This kind of personal integrity is part of the plan of salvation which "teaches us to say 'No' to ungodliness and worldly passions, and to live self-controlled, upright and godly lives in this present age" (Titus 2:12). Keep in mind that Paul was writing this to the young pastor he had appointed to minister on the island of Crete. The Roman culture practiced unrestrained sexual immorality and depravity, just as people do in our own day. Yet Paul expected God's people to practice godliness in a pagan world, and God still expects it of His children today.

The Act of Forgiveness

It is almost unbelievable to me what passes for biblical doctrine in our day. A local television call-in program in Denver features a man who claims to be a Christian counselor. One evening he boasted on his program that he hadn't spoken to his sister for more than two years after she had offended him one day. He said he had told her that until she was ready to talk with him on his terms, she was no longer welcome to communicate with him. He told his viewers that they needed to learn this skill and that they should order his book on "boundaries."

Where in God's Word do you find the concept of setting boundaries where you will not converse with someone who disagrees with you? Nowhere! Yet across our land, men and women are being instructed by false teachers in the hideous doctrine of boundaries.

Wives are leaving their husbands by the thousands, unwilling to discuss their offenses in a biblical fashion. Adult women in repressed memory therapies cut themselves off from their elderly parents, believing they were abused as children. They are taught to interrupt anyone who "crosses their boundaries"—whatever that means. And what it *does* mean is if they don't get their way, you have violated their boundaries.

Under this ungodly teaching, those who have set their boundaries are free to scream obscenities, throw objects and smash things in anger, and hang up the phone when confronted or disagreed with. Of course, those on the other side of the boundary markers are expected to meekly accept these childish tantrums because the victim's inner child must be validated.

What does God say?

> Do not let any unwholesome talk come out of your mouths, but only what is helpful for building others up according to their needs, that it may benefit those who listen. And do not grieve the Holy Spirit of God, with whom you were sealed for the day of redemption. Get rid of all bitterness, rage and anger, brawling and slander, along with every form of malice. Be kind and compassionate to one another, forgiving each other, just as in Christ God forgave you (Ephesians 4:29-32).

One boundary-believer demands that her husband—whom she has abandoned—accommodate her schedule for child visitation, which he has tried to do. She feels free to change the arrangements at her discretion, but if he asks her to reciprocate and to work with his schedule, she adamantly refuses, demanding that he stick to the schedule which she feels free to violate.

I contacted her pastor, asking that he arrange a meeting between the woman, her husband, her pastor and myself to mediate the dispute. She refused to meet, out of "fear of her controlling husband." The pastor weakly stepped back, not willing to challenge or discipline his church member over her ungodly attitudes and actions because he had to honor her boundaries.

Where is the forgiveness which God expects His children to extend to one another—especially in marriage? We are told to "bear with each other and forgive whatever grievances you may have against one another. Forgive as the Lord forgave you" (Colossians 3:13). Furthermore, we are warned, "When you stand praying, forgive, if you have anything against anyone; so that your Father also who is in heaven may forgive you your transgressions. But if you do not forgive, neither will your Father who is in heaven forgive your transgressions" (Mark 11:25-26 NASB).

Is it any wonder that those who have accepted the boundaries heresy fall into deep sin and depression? If we refuse to forgive others, we are living in daily guilt, not forgiven of our sins. But the moment we forgive, the burden begins to lift and we can learn to love once again.

Understanding One Another

The issue is not that men are from Mars and women are from Venus. God's rules are the same for both genders and sexual confusion can be removed as we learn to obey God in the ways we think and behave toward one another.

Peter writes about this issue in his epistle to the church. He addresses the fearful matter of wives submitting to their husbands and then turns to the men and says, "Husbands, in the same way be considerate as you live with your wives, and treat them with respect as the weaker partner and as heirs with you of the gracious gift of life, so that nothing will hinder your prayers" (1 Peter 3:7). The King James Version translates this "dwell with them according to knowledge." In other words, *wise up!* The New American Standard Bible says, "live with your wives in an understanding way."

While God does not tell the wives to understand their husbands, He does insist that all Christians, including husbands and wives, "live in harmony with one another; be sympathetic, love as brothers, be compassionate and humble. Do not repay evil with evil or insult with insult, but with blessing, because to this you were called so that you may inherit a blessing" (1 Peter 3:8-9). Living in harmony, showing true sympathy, loving unselfishly, demonstrating compassion in a humble way, not getting back at one another or calling each other names, but speaking gently— these are the things that show spiritual maturity in dealing with the opposite sex.

Living in an understanding way does not mean that we comprehend the full range of emotions and mental processes of our mates. I doubt that will happen in this life, because men and women are so very different. Just accept the fact that it is part of the curse. Nonetheless, though we may not mentally understand one another fully, we are to live in such a godly way that it doesn't really matter.

Fulfilling One's Marital Duties

One final thought on solving sexual confusion is God's expectation for husbands and wives to meet one another's sexual needs. Paul puts it this way:

> Since there is so much immorality, each man should have his own wife, and each woman her own husband. The husband should fulfill his marital duty to his wife, and likewise the wife to her husband. The wife's body does not belong to her alone but also to her husband. In the same way, the husband's body does not belong to him alone but also to his wife. Do not deprive each other except by mutual consent and for a time, so that you may

devote yourselves to prayer. Then come together again so that Satan will not tempt you because of your lack of self-control (1 Corinthians 7:2-5).

Let's look briefly at the principles involved. First, sexual release is one of the legitimate purposes of marriage and it is to be exercised in a monogamous male/female relationship. Nowhere in the Bible is there even the slightest hint that God permits homosexual marriages.

Second, when we marry, our mates are given joint title to our bodies. The modern pro-abortion argument that a woman's body is solely her own is a hideous error; her body also belongs to her husband. In the same way, the husband's body belongs to his wife.

Third, neither is to deprive the other of sexual release unless they have mutually agreed to this and for only one reason—to give increased time for prayer. I have yet to meet the couple who have decided to become celibate in order to improve their devotional life, yet theoretically it is possible. Even then, however, this abstinence is to be temporary, so that Satan cannot use their pent-up sexual drives as a temptation for immorality.

Dear reader, God has given us the principles to remove sexual atheism from our lives. But we must personally determine that we are going to obey His Word. When we do, His blessings follow.

Death of a Fantasy

It was Susan's birthday and Billy Costas ordered her a dozen long-stem red roses. Several women in the office turned with raised eyebrows as the delivery man brought the bouquet down the hallway to her office.

Susan smiled as she opened the card. It read, "I have enjoyed these past few weeks more than any time in my whole life! You are the most exciting woman I have ever known. Billy."

Susan swallowed with pleasure and blushed slightly. She had enjoyed the attention Billy showed her and his gentle touch and warm embrace caused her heart to pound with excitement. How long she had needed to be desired!

Still, whenever she took time to read her Bible, she felt a depth of guilt, knowing that her unfaithfulness to Arthur was a sin. She argued with herself that Arthur deserved the betrayal for all that he had done to her over the years. *Surely God would not want me to stay miserable the rest of my life!* she reasoned. She was comforted as she read the story of King David's adultery and of God's continued blessing upon his life. *If God could forgive David, He can certainly forgive me!*

Strangely, her worst moments of guilt came when she thought of her son. She pictured him often, with deep pangs of sorrow, especially when she saw other children who were about the age he would have been had he lived. *What would he think of me if he knew his mother was sleeping with her boss?* she thought. Most of the time, however, she pushed the troubling guilt out of her mind.

One evening as she was driving home to her apartment, she saw some teens silhouetted against a light-colored fence, running down the street laughing as they looked back down the alley. At the corner, they split up, leaving in different directions. One of the boys started across the street before noticing Susan's car, then stopped momentarily as Susan skidded to a stop, his face lit brightly by her headlights, then he continued on and disappeared into the darkness.

Susan shook her head in surprise and whispered, "That was Jason, the pastor's son!" She quickly glanced down the alley to her right. There, under a dim street light, lying unconscious against a garbage can was an elderly man, bleeding from the head. Susan gasped, her eyes wide with fear and anger. She checked to see that her car was locked, then grabbed her cellular phone and dialed 911.

The police arrived in moments, followed by an ambulance. As the emergency crew worked on the injured man, the police questioned Susan to see if she could identify any of the youths.

"How old were they?" one officer asked.

"I'm not sure," Susan replied, still shaking. "They looked to be about 14 to 16 years old."

"How many were there?"

"I think there were five or six. It . . . it was dark and I didn't have time to count."

"If you saw them again, would you be able to identify them?"

"I'm not sure," she said as she shook her head, "I . . . I don't think I would."

The police took down her name, address, and other information and told her they would call her if they needed anything more. With that, they allowed her to leave.

The next day, as she read the newspaper, she was sickened to discover that the old man had died of his injuries an hour after arriving at the hospital. Evidently, the teens had followed him down the alley after they saw him cash his Social Security check. They had hit him in the head with a pipe and had taken his money, throwing his wallet into a trash container a block away.

When she arrived at her office, she was still trembling. She got a cup of coffee and walked to Billy's office and knocked.

"Come in!" Billy said cheerfully.

Susan walked in with a troubled look on her face.

"What's wrong, love?" Billy asked.

She handed him the newspaper and said, "Did you see this?"

"Yeah. That's really sad, but why are you so upset? Did you know the old guy?"

"No, Billy, but I'm the one who called the police. I saw the kids running down the street," she said as she closed his door.

"And . . .?"

"And Billy, I recognized one of the kids," Susan said softly, her voice shaking. "It was Pastor Miller's boy!"

"Who?"

"My pastor's son. I've seen him in church. I don't understand it. He seemed like such a nice kid."

"Did you tell the police?"

"No, Billy," she said almost desperately, "I didn't!"

"Why *not*, Susan?" Billy asked incredulously as he stood to his feet. "You could be in real trouble!"

"I . . . I . . . didn't think the man was going to die. I didn't want to get the boy in trouble with the law. I figured maybe I could talk to the pastor privately and he could get help for his son. Kids do make mistakes, you know!"

"*Mistakes?* Susan, for the love of—" Billy stopped and shook his head. "Listen! You've got to call the police!"

Susan sat down in the deep-padded chair, nearly in shock. Finally, she nodded her head in agreement. "I know. I know. Will you go with me?"

Billy sat down in his chair and bit the inside of his lip in deep thought.

"Billy?"

He looked at her with a coldness she hadn't seen before. Slowly he shook his head and said, "I can't, Susan. I can't jeopardize my future and the future of this entire company by becoming involved in any way. The publicity could really hurt us badly."

"But, I—"

"Now, Susan," Billy said softly, but with distance still in his eyes, "you need to call them right away. Take the day off. In fact, you can take the rest of the week off, so you can get this thing resolved." He stood to his feet again as though finishing an interview with a rejected applicant. "Call me as soon as you find out . . . ."

"Find out what, Billy?" Susan asked, her desperation turning into a deep and familiar disappointment. "Find out if I'm going to jail?" She turned angrily to open the door and leave. At the door, she looked back over her shoulder at the man she thought she loved and realized she hadn't known him at all. With her lips white with tension and bitterness she said, "You're just like the rest, Billy. Get what you can and move on to the next conquest. How could I have been such a fool?" She shook her head in deep embarrassment and walked out.

. . .

Arthur Wilson sat alone in his den that same evening thinking about Susan and her precious faith. *Maybe I should call her pastor,* he thought. *Maybe he can talk some sense with Susan.*

The next morning, Arthur called Pastor Dave Miller to set an appointment with him. Late that afternoon, he drove to the church where Susan had attended. The secretary led him back to the pastor's office. Pastor Miller got up with a smile and extended his hand across the desk.

"Thanks for seeing me on such short notice, Pastor Miller," Arthur said stiffly. "I know it's late in the day, too."

"I'm glad you called," Pastor Miller said with a smile. "But please, call me Dave. I've wanted to meet you ever since your wife began attending our church. One of our members, Michael Rollins, tells me you do medical research at the National Institutes of Health."

"That's right. Actually, it's the National Cancer Institute," Arthur answered but volunteered nothing else.

"That sounds interesting. Exactly what sort of research are you involved with?" Dave continued. One skill he had developed in his ministry was drawing reluctant people into conversation. He knew that if he could get a man talking about his work, he could establish a measure of rapport.

"It involves genetics and cancer. I'm involved in the genetic mapping project at NCI and we're beginning to find some of the genetic triggers for certain types of tumors."

"Wow! That must be exciting!" Dave said with enthusiasm. "I've always been interested in medicine. It seems like it would be so fulfilling to be able to help people overcome their physical illnesses."

"Well, I don't actually practice medicine in the generic sense," Arthur explained. "I am working more in the theoretical realm, attempting to discover *why* cancers develop. If we can figure out the exact mechanisms that make tissues grow abnormally and spread to surrounding areas, we can devise cures for those specific cancers using surgery, chemotherapy, radiation, or a combination."

Arthur sat forward in his chair, now feeling more at ease as they discussed his area of expertise. "In addition to genetic predisposition, cancers may be caused by environmental factors, such as smoking, pollution, and exposure to occupational chemicals, and other hazards. Some cancers are generated by viruses, such as Burkitt's lymphoma. Others, such as some breast cancers, can be caused by abnormal hormone levels."

Arthur continued as Dave showed genuine interest. "Given enough time and funding, I believe that we truly will conquer cancer in the years to come."

"I certainly hope so," Dave said. "Is it possible for a person to worry himself into cancer? I mean, I've read about people generating their own illnesses psychologically."

"I suppose it is possible, though we haven't been able to prove a specific cancer has been caused by an individual's psychological condition. It is important, however, to differentiate between psychosomatic illnesses and somatopsychology."

Dave smiled at Arthur and said, "I'd like to know the difference. I've never even heard of soma . . . somato—whatever."

"Somatopsychology," Arthur pronounced again. "That's the study of how diseases, disabilities, or disfigurements affect a person's mental stability and behavior. It's a psychological specialty that endeavors to rehabilitate cancer victims, crime and accident victims, and those who are blind or otherwise disabled." Arthur felt drawn to the pastor and he appreciated Dave's refreshing curiosity.

An idea flashed into the pastor's mind. He leaned forward and said to Arthur, "I've been doing a personal study in psychological counseling systems, and I'd love to have your perspective on it."

"Oh, no!" Arthur laughed in mock terror. "Don't get me started on psychology, Dave! We'll be here all day!"

Dave looked at his watch and saw that it was indeed getting late. "I'm sorry!" he apologized. "I didn't realize what time it is. What was it that brought you here to see me?"

Arthur sat back in his chair uncomfortably. He hated talking about his own personal issues, especially with a pastor. He sighed and said, "Maybe Susan has told you about our marriage."

"Well, she did come in several weeks ago for some advice," Dr. Miller said guardedly.

Arthur cocked his head a little to the left and asked, "Did you suggest that she leave me?"

Dave Miller sat back in his chair and shook his head. "No, Arthur, I had no idea that she left you. When did that happen?"

"A few weeks back. I've talked with her a couple of times on the phone, but that's about all the communication we have had."

"I'm sorry to hear that, Arthur," the pastor said genuinely as he leaned forward again. "How can I be of help?"

"I was thinking that maybe you could talk with her and help her to see things more clearly. There is simply no reason for her to walk out on me."

"Maybe the reason she left has nothing to do with you," Dave suggested. "She did tell me about some serious issues in her own life and asked me to refer her to a counseling professional, which I did."

Arthur sat back in shock. "You sent her to a *psychologist?*"

"Well, not exactly. I did give her the name of a friend of mine who practices psychotherapy nearby. That seems to bother you. Can I ask you why?"

"Because I have seen the damage done by psychology and psychiatry, that's why!" Arthur replied hotly. "I'll put it quite bluntly, Dave. Psychology has achieved one of the greatest con-jobs ever to deceive the modern mind. As a roadblock to the development of full human potential, psychology is second only to religion! Actually, in a very real sense, it *is* a religion. Psychology has its own prophets and messiahs, its organized rituals, its holy writings, its official priesthood, and its paying congregations.

"Psychologists have begun to recognize the symbiosis—the mutual advantage—that exists between psychology and religion," Arthur continued as Dr. Dave Miller sat back in his chair, tight-lipped. "It is the joining of two parasitical systems. What churches fail to see, Dave, is that psychology will one day replace the church altogether. Psychology was first an *ecto*symbiont—an organism living *on* its host; it is fast becoming an *endo*symbiont— an organism that lives *within* its host. As such, it will eat away at the church from the inside out!"

Hardly pausing for breath, Arthur concluded, "And the sooner that happens, the better! When the church is gone, science will be able to demonstrate that psychology is as void of scientific merit as religion, and people will turn to the only rational solutions for their problems: man's own creative mind and talents coupled with true science."

Dave sat back, stunned at Arthur's impassioned attacks on religion and the church. "I can understand your concern about the validity of psychology, Arthur, but I'm not sure I follow your reasoning in connecting it to religion."

Arthur detected the change of tone in Dave's voice. "Did I hit a nerve somewhere, Dave?"

"Not really," Dave responded with seeming unconcern. "I did my undergraduate degree in psychology, but I'll admit that I have some concerns about some forms of psychology, too. Still, it seems that we're talking about two separate issues simultaneously: science and religion. I'd like to discuss both topics, but one at a time."

Pastor Miller stood to his feet and looked out his office window. "If you'd like, we could take a walk over in the park while we talk, Arthur. It looks like a nice evening out."

Arthur pulled a pipe and tobacco pouch out of his jacket pocket. "Susan doesn't like for me to smoke in the house. Do you mind?"

"It won't bother me, Arthur, once we get outside," Dave said, leading Arthur down the hall. The pastor stopped at the front desk and told his secretary that he wouldn't be back. "Would you mind having Al lock up tonight, Marianne? I'm going to take a walk in the park with Dr. Wilson."

When they got outside the church, Dave Miller looked at Arthur and said, "I'm a bit surprised that a cancer researcher and medical doctor would smoke, considering all the evidence that smoking causes lung cancer."

Arthur laughed as he stuck the pipe in his mouth and held a lighter over the bowl. The flickering light of the flame dimly illuminated Arthur's face in the twilight as he sucked air through the pipe, lighting the tobacco. He drew hard for several puffs and blew out the smoke. "We all have our inconsistencies, don't we?"

Dave straightened reflexively and swallowed hard, and then realized that Arthur was just admitting that his smoking was indefensible.

They walked across the street to a small city park. It was a warm and beautiful spring evening with a full moon that cast deep shadows under the trees that were now in full leaf. The pale pink blossoms on the crabapple trees gave off a gentle perfume, and fireflies flew drunkenly in all directions blinking their greetings to one another.

Arthur continued the discussion as though they had never paused. "The scientific and religious questions that arise in psychology are not two separate issues, Dave. They are intimately connected."

"How so?" Dave asked as he swatted a mosquito that nipped at his neck.

"Because if psychology is not an actual scientific discipline," Arthur explained as he blew a smoke ring out and up, "then its findings, theories, methods, and therapies are based on faith, making it a religion, not a medical practice."

David Miller scratched his head. "Explain to me why you feel psychology is not a true science."

Arthur led Dave over to a park bench that sat in the shadow of a large oak tree. Crickets chirped and whirred lazily and behind them a half-acre pond was alive with the croaking of frogs. "Psychology has been striving for scientific status since man began to think of the mind as an entity distinct from the body. Even an unschooled layman can readily see the categorical difference between psychology and true sciences such as mathematics, chemistry, biology, and medicine. That's the reason psychologists came up with the term 'social-behavioral science' to describe their trade." Arthur sniffed his nose loudly. "Excuse me. I've got allergies and this park is full of pollen!"

"Do you want to go back to the church?" Dave asked.

"No, I'll be fine, if you can stand my sniffing."

"No problem," Dave replied. "Arthur, explain to me how you can insist that psychology is not scientific? I've read many of the studies that psychologists do on the brain, the nervous system, and human behaviors."

"Don't make the mistake of confusing physiological psychology with behavioral or counseling psychology, Dave," Arthur warned. "They are two separate fields. Physiological psychology can indeed be scientific if the researchers follow scientific methods carefully. I'm not disputing that bio-psychologists can examine the brain for disease and lesions. Unfortunately, because both fields use the term *psychology* people easily transfer the scientific label from physiological psychology to behavioral or counseling psychology."

"You've used the adjectives *behavioral* and *counseling* as though they are the same," Dave observed.

"Well, you're correct in pointing that out. They are not exactly the same. Behavioral psychology attempts to use scientific methods to explain why people behave in certain ways under given conditions, while counseling psychology attempts to devise therapies to help people change from negative behaviors to positive. You might say that behavioral psychology tries to *define* normal and abnormal behavior while counseling psychology is concerned with the application of *cures* for abnormal behavior. It's a fine line that is frequently blurred."

"Okay, but you still haven't explained why you say that psychology is not scientific," Dave pressed.

"True. Let me see if I can make it clear," Arthur said as he took his pipe and tapped it against his heel, knocking out the ashes. "Science tries to accomplish three things: It observes raw data as accurately and objectively as possible. Then it tries to organize the information it collects into meaningful theories or generalizations; and lastly, science tests and verifies general theories by rigidly controlled experiments. For any discipline to qualify as a science, it must follow scientific method with rational impartiality, accuracy, and controlled verifiable experiments. Except for the physiological aspect, it is impossible for psychology to fulfill such qualifications."

"Why is it impossible?" Dave challenged.

"Because with the human mind it is *impossible* to prove a clear cause-and-effect relationship. Even psychologists and psychiatrists are finally admitting this. I read a report that was published by the Social Science Research Council that admitted that psychoanalysis depends upon techniques that—how did they put it?—'techniques that do not admit to the repetition of observation, have no self-evident validity, and are colored by the observer's own suggestions' or something along that line."

Arthur uncrossed his legs, turned to Dave, and said, "The point is, psychotherapies simply *can't* qualify as science because human beings are unique, their circumstances and experiences are unique and each therapist's observations are tainted by his own experiences, biases, and preconceived ideas."

Dave nodded. "I think I understand where you're going with this: Human beings do not react consistently like chemicals do. For instance, if you mix certain chemicals in precise amounts, you should get the same reaction every time."

"Exactly!" Arthur replied. "And humans cannot be scientifically categorized with that same precision. A psychiatrist friend of mine, Fuller Torrey, has written extensively on this very topic. He says that psychologists and psychiatrists arbitrarily assign labels to human behaviors not because of empirical evidence, but to provide the scientific appearance of classification."

"I've seen him on TV, and I have his book," Dave interjected. It's called *The Death of Psychiatry*. And you say you know him?"

"Well, we're not buddy-buddy, but I've met him. We both lectured at a conference in San Francisco.

Dave stood and pointed toward the pond. "Let's walk around the lake over there."

"What lake?" Arthur said sincerely.

"That one!" Dave responded, wondering if Arthur was blind.

"You call that a lake?" Arthur said, laughing. "Where I come from we call those puddles."

Dave smiled and said, "Well, I grew up out West where any pool of standing water classifies as a lake! Come on, let's walk."

Arthur refilled his pipe and lit it again as they walked. Dave breathed the night air deeply, enjoying the mixture of sounds and fragrances.

"Tell me, Arthur, how has psychology been able to convince everybody that it is a genuine science?"

"Several ways. One of the first is the use of scientific rhetoric. Psychology uses scientific-sounding terms like *controlled studies, clinical research,* and *statistical indications* to connect with science in general. Then they add terms such as *diagnosis, patients, therapy, treatment,* and *cure* to link psychology with medicine. Because psychiatrists are also medical doctors, people assume that what they do is scientific.

"Having convinced people that they are scientific and medical, the psychotherapeutic industry creates new technical terms, designed mostly to confuse and intimidate. They talk about *identity crisis, self-actualization, complexes, paranoia, schizophrenia, transference, sublimation, obsessions, dysfunctions,* and a bunch of other labels designed to impress and confuse the layman."

Arthur stopped, bent over to pick up a stone, and skipped it across the little pond. He hadn't done that since he was a kid back in Winfield.

"Not bad, Arthur," Dave said, picking up a flat rock of his own. "Four skips. What'll you give me if I beat you?"

"I'll tell you some more of the reasons people accept psychology as science," Arthur said as he puffed his pipe.

"Fair enough!" Dave said as he drew upon his rusty athletic skills and flung the rock at the precise angle needed. "One, two, three, four, five, six!" he said triumphantly. Arthur rolled his eyes upward in the darkness and let out a large puff of smoke in Dave's direction.

"Okay, professor," Dave said, "carry on!"

Arthur smiled and shook his head good-naturedly. "Another major reason the general public believes psychology is a legitimate science is that the media pours out an endless stream of propaganda. They use the terms *truth* and *findings* interchangeably. They publicize thousands of 'studies' on sex, dysfunctions,

personality theories, mental health, how to raise children, learning theories, and so on, and people are led to believe that these
psychological 'studies' are the same as 'scientific evidence.'"

"Well, you do have a point there," Dave agreed. "You can't
pick up a newspaper or magazine or watch television without
some sort of new psychological finding or study being reported.
And it sometimes seems that the findings that come out one day
are contradicted by the next day's findings."

"Absolutely!" Arthur said, feeling more comfortable with
Dave after their rock-throwing contest. "Clever use of statistics is
another tactic used to convince the public. Another professional
acquaintance of mine, Dr. Robert Taylor, wrote an article in
Reader's Digest a while ago entitled, 'Beware the Health Hype.'
In the article he said that 'the media often trumpet questionable
research findings as major medical breakthroughs.' They do this,
he said, 'through the magic of statistics.' They make sweeping
generalizations based on limited studies and promote some
sort of treatment that's currently popular, regardless of scientific
merit."

"You know," Dave said, "I've often wondered about the statistical pronouncements psychologists make. For instance, when
they say that eighty percent of our thoughts, feelings, and motives
are in our subconscious, how do they arrive at that figure?"

"They simply make up such mathematical figures!" Arthur
said flatly. "No one can accurately measure thoughts or feelings.
For that matter, science cannot truly be applied to even verify the
existence of the subconscious, though I believe that it exists."

They rounded the pond and headed back toward the church.
Dave looked at the medical researcher and said, "I can understand
your doubts about psychology being a true science, Arthur, but it
seems almost personal. Why do you react to it so negatively?"

Arthur's mouth tightened as he replied, "I guess I'm sick of
seeing people ripped off by pretenders. Psychologists are more
like sideshow palm-readers at the carnival than real scientists.
And to tell you the truth, Dave, I'm surprised that you, as a religious leader, aren't concerned about the fact that psychology is

making the church obsolete. Instead, you actually refer people out to your own competitor."

Dave breathed in sharply, trying to think of a clever reply, but shook his head instead and softly said, "I guess I just don't see psychology the same way you do, Arthur."

"No, Dave," Arthur replied with some satisfaction as he sensed Dr. Miller's uncomfortable attitude, "I guess you don't. But if I claimed to believe that God exists and can give humans eternal life in the future, I would be embarrassed to admit that I didn't think He has power to deal with their psychological problems in the here and now."

He paused for a moment, and then asked, "How big *is* your God?"

Pastor Miller stopped in his tracks and opened his mouth to reply, but instead he looked down at his feet, realizing how pathetic his faith must look to this avowed atheist.

Arthur sighed deeply and started back across the street to the church parking lot as Dave Miller followed. When they got to Arthur's car, he turned to Pastor Miller and asked, "Why should I believe your God could bring my marriage back together?"

Without waiting for an answer, he got into his car and drove off as Pastor Miller stood and watched the taillights fade into the distance.

Slowly, Dave walked back to the church to see why the lights were still on in the secretary's office. As he walked through the door, his secretary called out in a concerned voice, "Pastor Miller, is that you?"

"Yes, Marianne, what's wrong?"

"Your wife called while you were out with Dr. Wilson. She said that it's urgent that you call her right away. She said . . ." the secretary hesitated.

"Yes? What did she say?"

"She said to tell you it's your son again."

Dave Miller's shoulders slumped noticeably as though he'd been hit in the stomach. He shook his head in disgust and said, "Oh, Jason! Not again! I wonder what it is this time?"

CHAPTER
6

Faith for Raising Godly Children

THE TROUBLING FRUIT OF practical atheism may be seen most clearly in the condition of our youth. Violent crime committed by juveniles is on the increase as a generation of children have grown up in homes filled with unbelief. Having been taught that man is the end result of billions of years of evolution, young people logically question the sanctity of life. Couple that with the political victories of the abortion lobby and the growing acceptance of euthanasia, and we have the makings of a terrifying future.

In the past decade, the filing of criminal charges against juveniles has more than doubled in Colorado. "The bottom line is that juvenile crime is mushrooming faster than youth prisons can be built, prosecutors say."[31]

Civil authorities are seeking an explanation for the explosion in juvenile crime. Karen Steinhauser, chief deputy Denver district attorney, says, "It has to come somewhere, from the family. In so many of these families, we're dealing with a history of abuse and neglect. Drug use by parents, parents in prison, parents who disappeared and left them. There are a lot of awful things that are happening to young kids."[32]

Why are children age eleven, ten, and six committing violent crimes of assault and murder? Steinhauser believes that kids are becoming hard and cold. "There's a total lack of empathy for victims and it's very scary."[33]

Regis Groff, who heads Colorado's youth corrections sys-tem, "thinks the rise in youthful criminals can be blamed on the breakdown of the family, compounded by easy access to guns."[34]

He believes the violence can be explained, to some extent, by the images and sounds offered by the media industry. "There's so much violence in movies, TV, music—they're sur-rounded by nothing but."[35]

Another reason suggested for the rise in juvenile crime is that young criminals know they have a good chance of being released without doing time in prison. "Judges will sternly tell youths that they belong at [a] detention facility . . . then, they'll reluctantly send them home. The reason: overcrowding."[36]

In addition to a general contempt for the justice system, some juveniles engage in crime because they have no fear of authority. They have been taught by the public school system and social workers that they do not have to obey their parents. Television programs regularly mock parents as ignorant buf-foons whose only function is to provide materially for their chil-dren's every wish.

Others have found the public schools to be such dangerous places that to protect themselves, they have joined gangs. "When the family isn't strong, they get involved in gangs, in drugs, terri-torial squabbles and ritual violence."[37] Desiring to be accepted and safe, they fall under the influence of an evil crowd since they fear their peers more than the authorities.

THE BATTLE PARENTS FACE

Child psychologists insist that the average parent is ill equipped to successfully raise his children and that we need professional help to do the job. Politicians believe that they are in the best position to raise our children and they resist any attempt to cod-ify parental rights.

A recent battle in Colorado over the Parental Rights Amend-ment illustrates the governmental arrogance which insists that it knows best what children need. Banding with the ACLU, the library association, the video rental industry, the Education Association, and other extremist liberal groups, the governor of Colorado brazenly labeled supporters of the Parental Rights Amendment as members of the "religious right" who were trying to undermine the security of the state. Opponents of the amendment succeeded in convincing the voters that parents have no fundamental right to oversee the upbringing of their own children.

Thoroughly intimidated by governmental authorities and psychological professionals, parents have lost confidence in their ability to raise their own children. Average citizens have come to believe that there are experts who know far more than they do about everything, including their own children's needs. A generation ago, many turned to Dr. Benjamin Spock for guidance in raising their children, and the results were disastrous. Today, there is a never-ending stream of books from psychologists flowing into the hands of trembling parents, giving conflicting and erroneous advice with absolute confidence and destructive results.

Even worse is that there's a growing ignorance of the biblical principles that have guided parents down through the centuries in the upbringing of their children. This is true even in Christian homes, and it is amazing that the one source of proven authority for the successful raising of children—the Bible—is almost universally forgotten.

THE BIBLE AND PARENTS

What *does* the Bible teach about raising children? In this and the next chapter, we will look at seven foundational truths that will help us to understand the role of Christian parents in an unbelieving generation.

Children Are a Gift from God

The first step in raising believing children in a pagan world is to appreciate them as gifts from God. I have been blessed to be present at the birth of each of my children (and coincidentally, so has my wife!). God has graciously entrusted us with three beautiful daughters and one delightful son, and they are, without question, the most valuable gifts we have ever received outside of salvation itself.

I find it almost impossible to comprehend the fact that some parents actually resent their children and can hardly wait until they are old enough to move out on their own. I can honestly tell you that my wife, Marlowe, and I have enjoyed every stage our children have moved through in their development and growth.

I have photographed and videotaped them from their first breath, capturing a variety of precious moments as they slept in their cribs, smeared their faces with pabulum when learning to eat, played on the floor with their little toys, and took their first uncertain steps. We were faithful to tape their events at field days, their performances at recitals and concerts, and we followed them like a television news crew as they moved from preschool through elementary, junior high, senior high, and college. We filmed vacations and cross-country drives in our old Dodge van and we have sat together and laughed in great delight as we looked back on the joyful years we have shared. I can tell you with all my heart that some of the best investments we ever made have been in cameras and film.

Our children are our very best friends and we enjoy them more than words can fully express. We talk together, laugh together, and sometimes cry together. Marlowe and I have benefited from their counsel, encouragement, and love, and we look forward to the years ahead as they marry and produce a new generation of children to love.

God wants us to realize that our children are gifts from His hand. The following passages underline the attitude God desires parents to have toward their children:

> They are the children God has graciously given your servant (Genesis 33:5).

> He settles the barren woman in her home as a happy mother of children. Praise the LORD (Psalm 113:9).

Sons are a heritage from the LORD, children a reward from him. Like arrows in the hands of a warrior are sons born in one's youth. Blessed is the man whose quiver is full of them. They will not be put to shame when they contend with their enemies in the gate (Psalm 127:3-5).

Children's children are a crown to the aged, and parents are the pride of their children (Proverbs 17:6).

Jesus said, "Let the little children come to me, and do not hinder them, for the kingdom of heaven belongs to such as these" (Matthew 19:14).

We Are to Love Our Children

A second foundational truth for raising godly children is that we are called to love our children. In earlier and more innocent days, this would have seemed too obvious to mention, but Jesus warned us that in the last days "because of the increase of wickedness, the love of most will grow cold" (Matthew 24:12). We are in that generation.

Newsweek magazine reported that "now it's kids, seemingly good ones, charged with murder."[38] In horror, the magazine reported the case of two college freshmen who were indicted "on charges that they crushed their newborn son's skull and left him in a dumpster behind the Delaware hotel where [the young woman] gave birth."[39]

With gross intellectual and spiritual hypocrisy, newspapers report the arrests of young parents for discarding their newborn infants in the trash while supporting the right of medical doctors to murder full-term babies with the barbaric practice of partial-birth abortions. In the hospital, it's legal to kill the child so long as the doctor prevents the baby's head from emerging, but it's a crime if the mother ends the child's life seconds after birth. The only difference is a few inches of the birth canal. The selfishness of our modern age has produced the rationale for this legal yet murderous procedure. Is it any wonder that love has grown cold?

Further evidence for coldness of heart is seen in television reports about parents in Asia who sell their children into forced labor and prostitution, fully realizing that they are condemning them to a life of pain, disease, and terror. Other parents simply kill their female babies when they are born because they believe girls to be an unbearable economic and social burden.

In God's plan, women are to rejoice when a child is born. "A woman giving birth to a child has pain because her time has come; but when her baby is born she forgets the anguish because of her joy that a child is born into the world" (John 16:21). Her love overcomes the agony of birth and gives her an unshakable determination to protect her helpless infant.

God has given us vivid illustrations of parental love in the animal kingdom. Perhaps nothing pictures this better than the fierce devotion of a mother bear for her cubs. When I was a child our family visited Yellowstone National Park, and back then bears were a common sight. At one location, we were excited to see a mother bear with twin cubs begging for handouts from the tourists and we hurried out of the car to capture the moment on film.

Just as my uncle checked his light meter to adjust the camera aperture, one of the cubs squealed with outrage as his brother stole a morsel right from under his nose. The mother bear thought her cub was being threatened, and charged the crowd with a roar. Everyone ran for their cars in terror—except for my uncle. Totally absorbed with photographic technicalities, he was oblivious to the danger and remained blissfully unaware of his impending doom as the bear bore down on him at full speed. The only thing that saved him was that he remained motionless and the mother bear slammed on her brakes just yards from his tripod. She retrieved her cubs and sauntered away, her dignity fully intact.

The Bible pictures the similar love of devoted parents. The courage of the Israelite women who protected their newborns is told in Exodus chapters 1 and 2. They risked their lives by defying Pharaoh's edict to destroy all newborn males because "the midwives . . . feared God and did not do what the king of Egypt had told them to do; they let the boys live" (Exodus 1:17).

Moses' mother hid him from the authorities as long as possible (Exodus 2:3), but she finally was forced to part with him. We can only imagine the anguish she experienced as she placed him in his little basket, hoping and praying he would be discovered and protected by a benevolent Egyptian.

Hannah longed to become a mother (1 Samuel 1:10-11) and God eventually answered her prayers, "because I asked the LORD for him" (1 Samuel 1:20). She had promised the Lord that she would dedicate the child to His service, and true to her word, she gave him to the Lord (1 Samuel 1:27-28). She was able to see her boy only once a year after that as she and her husband came to perform the annual sacrifice. The Bible tells us that she brought Samuel a little robe each year (1 Samuel 2:19) as a token of her heartfelt love.

In 1 Kings 3 we find a moving story of two women who illustrate true parental love and love grown cold. Both had newborn infants, but one had died when his mother accidentally lay on him during the night. She took the dead child and placed him beside the other woman as she slept, and took the living child, pretending it was her own. Now they stood before King Solomon, each claiming the surviving child.

Because both the women claimed the baby, Solomon ordered that the child be cut in half.

> The woman whose son was alive was filled with compassion for her son and said to the king, "Please, my lord, give her the living baby! Don't kill him!"
>
> But the other said, "Neither I nor you shall have him. Cut him in two!"
>
> Then the king gave his ruling: "Give the living baby to the first woman. Do not kill him; she is his mother" (1 Kings 3:26-27).

What kind of evil could have possessed the woman who wanted the helpless little child to die? The same kind that causes abortionists in our day to snuff out the lives of millions of innocent babies. It is the result of love grown cold. Isaiah may have anticipated such heartless people when he wrote, "Can a mother forget the baby at her breast and have no compassion on the child she has borne? Though she may forget, I [the Lord] will not forget you!" (Isaiah 49:15).

We see several poignant examples of the love of fathers in the Bible. Jacob loved his son Joseph so much that it nearly killed him when he thought his favorite child was dead. "All his sons and daughters came to comfort him, but he refused to be comforted. 'No,' he said, 'in mourning will I go down to the grave to my son.' So his father wept for him" (Genesis 37:35).

David prayed desperately as his and Bathsheba's baby lay dying (2 Samuel 12:16) and he grieved inconsolably when Absalom was executed during his attempt to take over Israel (2 Samuel 18:33). David was not a wise father, but he did love his children.

In the New Testament, deep parental love is seen in Jairus, a ruler of a synagogue, who humbled himself by falling at Jesus' feet to plead with the Lord to heal his little girl (Mark 5:21-43). As you read the story, you can almost feel his loving desperation as he begged for his daughter's life.

This came home to me recently when Kendra, the daughter of our associate pastor, was in a tragic automobile accident. As she drove along the freeway, she somehow lost control of the car, which flipped violently across the highway again and again, finally landing on its roof. Though Kendra wore her seat belt, the force of the impact broke her neck in two places, and for weeks she lay in a coma.

Her parents have hardly left her side since they rushed to the hospital. In their depth of love for her, they talk to her as they rub her arms and feet and they pray continually, asking the Lord to preserve her life and to raise her to health once again.

Kendra's parents now understand more than ever that children are a gift from God and we are to love them while we may. In this modern day when love seems less instinctual, we must apply Titus 2:4 aggressively: "Train the younger women to love their husbands and children."

Love Is More Than a Feeling Loving our children is more than having deep parental emotion. It means we care for them enough to invest our lives into them, to pass on the heritage of godliness. No Christian parent can rest satisfied until he knows that his children possess a fervent personal faith in Christ and are ready to pass it on to the next generation.

Think about this for a moment: We would never consider depriving our children of necessary food, clothing, and shelter. We understand the importance of education and are willing to spend multiplied thousands of dollars to see that our children get a marketable degree. We work hard to train the next generation in essential domestic skills. Yet, when it comes to the information that matters the most—how to move from this world into eternal life—most parents barely discuss it with their children.

It is amazing to me how quickly faith can depart from a family; it takes only one generation that fails to pass eternal truth on to the next for Christianity to disappear. I see it happening every Sunday as parents attend church alone because their children have walked away from Christianity, believing it to be a meaningless relic of the past. These, by the way, are often good and decent Christian parents who—for whatever reason—have lost their children to the world.

The Elements of Parental Love God defines parental love with several primary responsibilities. One of the most essential is *to teach basic Bible history* to our children. This is illustrated in Deuteronomy 6, where the Israelites are told:

> In the future, when your son asks you, "What is the meaning of the stipulations, decrees and laws the LORD our God has commanded you?" tell him: "We were slaves of Pharaoh in Egypt, but the LORD brought us out of Egypt

with a mighty hand. Before our eyes the LORD sent miraculous signs and wonders—great and terrible—upon Egypt and Pharaoh and his whole household. But he brought us out from there to bring us in and give us the land that he promised on oath to our forefathers. The LORD commanded us to obey all these decrees and to fear the LORD our God, so that we might always prosper and be kept alive, as is the case today. And if we are careful to obey all this law before the LORD our God, as he has commanded us, that will be our righteousness" (Deuteronomy 6:20-25).

Bible history is not to be taught as a painful duty, but to deeply impress our children with the power and loving character of our heavenly Father. As Isaiah wrote, fathers who follow the Lord "tell their children about [God's] faithfulness" (Isaiah 38:19).

As a part of parental love, *we are to mold our children by careful supervision and instruction.* Paul tells us to "bring [our children] up in the training and instruction of the Lord" (Ephesians 6:4). The results are well worth the effort, as we are told in Proverbs 22:6: "Train a child in the way he should go, and when he is old he will not turn from it."

There are many helpful illustrations of this principle in nature. Those who train wild beasts for the circus find it easiest to gain control when the animals are young. A topiary bush must be bent while it is pliable and green. Those who would form concrete must do so while it is newly mixed and soft. And a child's character must be molded while it is still tender and innocent.

Another essential element of parental love is to *pray faithfully for the safety and spiritual health of our children.* Scripture says that we are to "arise, cry out in the night, as the watches of the night begin; pour out your heart like water in the presence of the Lord. Lift up your hands to him for the lives of your children" (Lamentations 2:19).

Dear Christian parent, when was the last time you prayed desperately for your child's salvation? How badly do you really want to see them in heaven throughout all eternity? Then pray without ceasing for the Lord to turn their hearts. You may be all that is standing between your child and eternal hell.

A loving parent will take the next duty to heart: *We are to teach our children responsible financial stewardship.* Of course, we all want our children to have enough of the basic necessities so that they will not needlessly suffer. But our goal should not be for our children to amass a great financial fortune. We should teach our children this prayer: "Give me neither poverty nor riches, but give me only my daily bread. Otherwise, I may have too much and disown you and say, 'Who is the LORD?' Or I may become poor and steal, and so dishonor the name of my God" (Proverbs 30:8-9).

Instead of making riches the goal, we should be teaching our children the godly character traits of diligence and faithfulness in labor. If we do that, prosperity is a natural result. "Lazy hands make a man poor, but diligent hands bring wealth" (Proverbs 10:4).

We need to warn our children about the dangers of greed. Solomon, one of the wealthiest men who ever lived, wrote, "Whoever loves money never has money enough; whoever loves wealth is never satisfied with his income" (Ecclesiastes 5:10). Paul expanded the warning when he said that "people who want to get rich fall into temptation and a trap and into many foolish and harmful desires that plunge men into ruin and destruction" (1 Timothy 6:9).

Rather than focusing on how much our children can acquire, a loving parent should teach that real success is measured in how much of what God has entrusted we are able to give away. If we care about their future prosperity, we should teach our children the discipline of the regular and sacrificial gift (2 Corinthians 9).

Another important part of parenting is to *encourage our children to fully develop their talents, skills, and gifts for the glory of God.* Successful parents of well-adjusted children seem to have the wonderful ability to draw out the best from their children. A homely and awkward little girl can be brought to genuine beauty by a father who convinces her that, in his eyes, she is stunningly gorgeous. A weak-eyed little boy who peers out at his world through huge eyeglasses can believe he is capable of great achievement by the example of his parents who see him as an inevitable success in progress.

On the other hand, parents who try to motivate their children by sarcasm, belittling, criticism, and other negative forms of communication will often produce twisted adults who find it difficult to enjoy success regardless of how much they achieve. That's why Paul wrote, "Fathers, do not embitter your children, or they will become discouraged" (Colossians 3:21).

How much better it is to teach our children that, with God's help, they can achieve almost any dream if they are willing to invest the necessary time and work. I recall a young man who auditioned for a special youth ensemble I directed many years ago. He presented himself as a tall gawky monotone barely able to look me in the eye, but his voice was deeper than any other boy in our church, so I let him join.

To my surprise, he began to match notes with others in the group and then moved on to singing harmony on the bass parts. When he graduated from high school, he enrolled in the music department at a Christian university. Years later, he showed up in my office with record albums and tapes he had produced as a soloist in Europe!

Our minister of music, Les Gilmer, is also our television producer, who does outstanding work shooting and editing video, though he has had minimal professional television training. Our facilities are extremely humble and our equipment was actually designed for home and semi-professional use. Nonetheless, he turns out programs which are seen across the nation. He recorded in the balcony of our church a wonderful audio CD that is as good as those produced in professional studios.

When I asked him how he is able to produce such outstanding results with substandard equipment and facilities, he replied, "Our advantage is that we don't know what can't be done." His parents instilled in him a confidence in God and the gifts God has given him that enables him to accomplish what others merely dream about.

Parents, we must never discourage our children by stunting their dreams. Rather, we must encourage them by helping them to believe in a great God who will help them to accomplish great things. I do not recall my parents ever telling me, "You could never do that, Ed! Wake up! Be realistic!" Instead, they exuded a quiet confidence that if I really wanted to accomplish something, I probably could.

When I graduated from Moody Bible Institute, I was approached by the largest Baptist church in Denver, asking if I would consider coming on staff as the minister of music. Little did they know that I had never directed a full choir rehearsal. My responsibilities would include directing and overseeing five choirs, producing the weekly television broadcast, and heading up the junior high Sunday school department.

My wife knew that I was completely inexperienced and privately told me that she questioned the wisdom of accepting the position. Looking back on it now, I understand her hesitation, but at the time, I was surprised that she could doubt my abilities. With a confidence born of ignorance, I said to her, "Just watch me!" I accepted the job and was soon directing choirs at the church and on television. My primary asset was—as Les says so well—not knowing what couldn't be done.

I was blessed with a group of musicians who rallied around me—I suspect more from pity than admiration—and determined that I would succeed. One of our businessmen sent Marlowe and me—all expenses paid—to spend a week at a large church in California which had an outstanding music program. "Just follow the director around like a puppy," he told me, "and learn everything you can." We came back with an exciting new vision of what could be accomplished, and our choirs grew.

The years Marlowe and I spent in that first ministry were a joyful learning experience, and our five choirs grew to 22 choirs and ensembles, 3 record albums, tours, radio, and television. I will never forget the kindness of those dear church members who encouraged me to produce far more than I was capable of, and of the senior pastor, who put up with my youthful enthusiasm and inexperience.

In addition to encouraging our children, we as loving parents have the heavy responsibility of controlling them. We will deal with this subject in greater detail later, but Scripture clearly tells us that in a spiritual home children will be respectful and obedient. Paul wrote that an elder "must manage his own family well and see that his children obey him with proper respect" (1 Timothy 3:4).

I am astounded at how little control many Christian parents exercise over their children. I am not talking about becoming a stereotypical "controlling parent" as parents who discipline are alarmingly described by child psychologists. Of course, we need to give children a measure of freedom commensurate with their age and level of maturity. To do otherwise creates frustration, anger, and exasperation. Nonetheless, balanced parenting requires a level of control over our children's attitudes and actions.

The reason this is important is not to create mindless robots who obey without thought. On the contrary, it is to help our children to develop thoughtful self-control, an essential element of godly character. Undisciplined children are an embarrassment to the church, and *should* be an embarrassment to parents, but too often, parents of misbehaving children are oblivious to the irritation their children produce in those around them.

Many young parents today have no concept of appropriate public behavior, allowing their children to disturb others at ball games, theaters, and even at worship services. During one holiday service I attended, a mother thought it would be adorable to have little bells tied around her daughter's ankles so that she jingled with every step she took. While that might have been appropriate on a dance floor or at a hockey match, it was evidence of incredible thoughtlessness during a quiet and meditative worship service. Imagine the distraction the little darling produced as she jingled her way to the drinking fountain, restroom, and back.

I have watched the enemy of our souls create monumental distractions during the very moment the pastor calls unbelievers to the altar. Babies begin to cry, children start to wiggle, wriggle, and giggle, causing others to turn and shake their heads with frustration because thoughtless parents were unwilling to control their children's behavior. As a pastor, I am embarrassed for our guests when this happens at our church.

Perhaps you have never considered the following passage in connection with church manners, but I challenge you to do so: "Each of you should learn to control his own body in a way that is holy and honorable" (1 Thessalonians 4:4). Now, I realize Paul was not writing about going to the restroom during church. Rather, he was talking about controlling our sexual desires. The principle is, however, that to please the Lord, we must learn to discipline our physical bodies. I am convinced that children who are out of control in the relatively minor areas of their lives can succumb to the danger of translating that lack of discipline into the major issues of immorality and impurity.

Such ongoing lack of self-control can devastate people's lives, destroying careers, friendships, marriages, and sometimes life itself. Proverbs 29:11 says, "A wise man keeps himself under control," and a wise parent is one who will instill self-discipline in the character of his or her child.

A well-behaved child is a delight and is welcome in almost any setting, but a child out of control is a plague to his own parents and to all those around him. Do your friends, yourself, and your children a favor: get them under control, and the sooner, the better. Well-behaved children are so unusual you will find people coming up to you in restaurants, on airplanes, and at church congratulating you on your expertise as a parent, and they will want their kids to play with yours!

When we continue our study, we will look at some preventive measures parents can take to head off rebellion and to keep practical atheism out of the home. Our children's lives depend upon it!

Fateful Choices

Dr. David Miller drove home, dreading to hear the latest report about Jason's rebellion. Ever since they had moved to Bethesda, it seemed as though the family had grown further and further apart. They had all been happy back in Colorado, where David had served as pastor of a small church, but when the opportunity came for them to move to a larger congregation near the center of American political power, David had jumped at the chance.

His wife, Darla, had been reluctant to leave the church they had served for nearly eight years, but supported David's decision, even through her tears, as they drove away. She found herself looking back every few minutes to watch the Rocky Mountains sink ever lower on the horizon until they disappeared from view.

The children were even more affected by the move. Faith, then age 9, cried for days, missing her schoolmates and the house she had known most of her life. Jason, 11 years old when they moved, had become angry and distant. He resented the move deeply and felt totally out of place among the kids at school, who all seemed rich and self-assured. The only ones who accepted him were "losers" who deliberately wore torn and baggy clothes and sported weird hairstyles designed to make a statement.

Jason, who had made outstanding grades before the move, brought home failing marks, and to David Miller's frustration and shame, Jason seemed totally unconcerned. Worse than that, however, was Jason's total disinterest in the church. He went with the family on Sundays, of course, but only because his father insisted.

Now, some three years after the move, Jason had become even harder. There was little positive communication between Dr. Miller and his son as the wall of mutual resentment grew ever higher. Their arguments became more frequent and increased in hostility and they avoided each other more as each week passed.

Darla had remarked one evening to David, "Have you noticed that Jason seems to get angrier when he listens to that heavy metal rock music?"

David paused for a moment to think, then nodded as he replied, "Now that you mention it, I think you're right. He tells me that the music is put out by a Christian group, but I sure can't tell by listening. I can barely make out a word. When I tell him I don't like it, he just looks at me, shakes his head in disgust, and shuts his door. At least now he listens with earphones so we don't have to hear it."

"But, David, he hardly comes out of his room anymore. When he isn't listening to his music, he plays with that video machine hour after hour. I happened to see the box one of the cartridges came in. Here, look at this, David!" Darla held up a box which had a nearly pornographic picture of sex and violence on the front.

"And that's not all, David. I found this under his bed when I was cleaning his room today." She handed David a copy of *Playboy* magazine.

David felt sick to his stomach as he realized the images his son was feeding his mind on. "I'll go have a talk with him right now."

He went up to Jason's room, knocked on the door and turned the knob, but the door was locked. "Jason, open up," he said, trying to control his anger.

"I'm busy! Go away!"

"I said open the door!"

"Leave me alone."

"Jason, if you don't open the door, I'm going to break it down!"

"Right! Go ahead," Jason said without a shred of fear.

David thought seriously about doing just that, but decided against it since the church owned the parsonage, and he didn't want to have to explain any damage to the trustees. He stood outside Jason's door for a minute with his hands on his hips, then he turned, shaking his head, and walked back downstairs.

From that time on, Jason's contempt for his father had become even more obvious as he drifted further and further from the family. Now the urgent call from Darla indicated that a real crisis was at hand.

As David drove down his street to their attractive parsonage, he couldn't help but think back to happier days in Colorado when his family had been close and full of love. They had often driven into the high mountains just west of town to view the majestic scenery and to hike alongside cascading streams. Now, however, David had become too busy with his ministry to spend much time with the family.

As he walked into the house, Darla was sitting in the front room crying. Faith sat next to her mother trying to comfort her.

"What's wrong, Darla?" David asked as he hurried to her side.

"Jason's gone, Dave!" she cried out. "And I found these out in the trash," she said as she held up Jason's jeans. "Look at them!"

At first glance, David didn't see what Darla was trying to show him, but then he saw blood smeared on the thighs of the jeans. He sat, speechless as he looked first at Darla, and then at the jeans. "What happened? Is he hurt? What's going on?"

"I don't know, David," she said as tears filled her eyes. She looked down at the floor blankly. Finally, she looked up. "I'm afraid something is terribly wrong. David, what are we going to do?"

He looked at his wife and suddenly felt totally exhausted. "I don't know, Darla," he said. "I just don't know."

· · ·

Susan Wilson sat in her apartment looking out her window with a deep sense of hopelessness and foreboding. Her emotions ranged from bitter anger to deep humiliation as she realized that Billy had merely found her a convenient and temporary distraction from his one true love—success—and the power, pleasure, and prestige it offered.

Tears of silent rage trickled slowly down her face, leaving streaks in her makeup. An observation she had denied for years began to emerge in her mind: *All men are hypocritical liars who look upon women as something to use for their own selfish pleasure and to discard when it suits them.* Every man she had ever known had deceived and abused her—her father, high school and college boyfriends, Arthur, and now Billy. She shook her head and smiled bitterly as she realized that her own pastor must be living a double life just like other men if his own son were so twisted and brutal to have attacked an old man, leaving him for dead in an alley.

Billy was right about one thing, however. She had to call the police and right away. She had devised a plan since leaving the office that would keep her out of trouble. Wearily, she picked up the phone and dialed the police.

Less than an hour later, she drove to the police station and went inside. She was led back to an office where two detectives, a man and a woman, waited, seated behind a table. "Come in, Mrs. Wilson," the male officer said as he stood and pointed to a chair across from him. "Have a seat." He switched on a tape recorder which lay on the table. "I'm George Gustafson and this is Patricia Aker. We're investigating the Czezak slaying."

Susan smiled weakly and sat down.

"According to your call, you have additional information regarding this crime?"

"Yes, I think so," Susan replied as she swallowed involuntarily.

"You were the person who called the police initially, weren't you, Mrs. Wilson?" Patricia Aker asked as she wrote on a legal pad. She sucked on a long cigarette and smoke began to fill the room.

"Yes."

"And have you remembered something else that you didn't report at the time?" the woman asked as she blew smoke up and away in Susan's direction.

"Well, yes, I have," Susan said as she cleared her throat. "You see, I didn't think I actually saw any of the kids clearly enough to identify them, but later, after I calmed down, I realized that one of the boys looked familiar. At first I thought perhaps I was just imagining it, but the more I thought about it, I finally realized I could identify him."

"You know the boy personally?" Detective Gustafson asked.

"Well, I can't say that I know him well," Susan said as she twisted her ring finger, missing her wedding band. "But I know who he is."

Both detectives waited as Susan paused. Finally Detective Aker said, "So . . . who is the boy, Mrs. Wilson?"

Susan looked down for a moment, hating to accuse her pastor's son, but when she remembered the old man lying in the alley, she looked up with determination and said, "It was Jason Miller."

"And how do you know this Jason Miller?" Patricia Aker asked as she wrote on her pad and coughed with a metallic smoker's rattle.

"He's my pastor's son." Her eyes began to water from the cigarette smoke as she stifled a cough.

The detectives looked at one another, then back at Susan. "And you just suddenly realized you recognized him?" Detective Aker said in a tone that dripped with accusation.

Susan's heart beat rapidly as she lied to the officers and her face grew red. "Well . . . yes. Surely, you can understand how confusing it was at the time. It all happened so quickly. Besides, I don't know Jason all that well. I've just passed him in church a few times, so it shouldn't seem so strange that I didn't recognize him immediately."

"Of course. Still, it does seem strange that you would conveniently fail to recognize a kid from your own church, doesn't it?"

"I . . . I suppose it looks odd, but that's how it happened," Susan said, trying to sound as confident as possible.

"And you are absolutely positive now that he was one of the kids at the crime scene?" Gustafson asked.

Susan nodded as her head began to pound with one of her migraine attacks.

"And you'd swear to that in court?" Patricia Aker asked.

"Yes," Susan said as she broke into a cold sweat in reaction to her pain. "Now, please, can I go? I feel a migraine headache coming on and I'm beginning to get nauseous."

Aker and Gustafson looked at one another and nodded. "I guess that's all we need for now, Mrs. Wilson," Gustafson said. "We'll have to have your signature on the report when we get it typed up. Later you'll have to identify the boy here at the station."

"I understand," Susan said, standing to her feet. She turned to leave the room.

"Oh—and Mrs. Wilson," Detective Aker said as she stubbed out her cigarette into a dirty silver tray filled with ashes and cigarette butts. Susan turned back to face the woman detective as she blew a final puff of smoke. "You don't lie very well."

Susan straightened her back and started to reply, but turned indignantly and walked out.

. . .

Arthur Wilson decided to call Susan to tell her of his discussion with her pastor. He could hardly wait to tell her what a hypocrite Dr. Miller was. He walked around the family room with a smirk on his face as he held the cordless phone to his ear.

A secretary answered, "Thank you for calling DoubleSoft. Melissa Johnson speaking. May I help you?"

"Put me through to Susan Wilson, please," Arthur replied. "This is her husband."

"I'm sorry, Mr. Wilson, but Susan probably won't be in this week."

"Why not? Is she sick?"

Melissa Johnson hesitated. "Well, I'm not really sure that I should say anything. . . ."

"Why not? I'm her husband! What's going on?"

"Well, I thought you and Susan were separated."

"We are, at least temporarily. So what?"

"Well, I just assumed—since she's been seeing Mr. Costas . . . ."

"She's *what?*"

"Oh, I'm *sorry!*" Melissa said, sounding as though she suddenly realized she had mistakenly passed on sensitive information. "I thought you knew!"

Arthur felt as though he had been punched in the stomach. He sat down hard in his chair and swallowed, trying to get control of his emotions. "How long has this been going on?" he finally asked in a subdued tone.

"Oh, Mr. Wilson, please don't ask me any more questions. I'll get in trouble for what I've already said. Please don't tell them how you found out!"

"Don't worry," he said, having already forgotten the secretary's name. "It's not your fault." He pushed the "off" button and set the phone down on the end table. He sat in silence, stunned. Even through all of their problems, it had never occurred to Arthur that Susan might become unfaithful to him.

His emotions moved from deep pain, to intense anger, to bitterness, then hopelessness. *I guess it's really over,* he thought. He stood to his feet and went to the liquor cabinet and poured himself a scotch. He downed it in one gulp, then poured another. Taking the bottle, he walked back to the chair and flopped down. "I know how to forget that filthy little tramp!" he said as he gulped down the second shot and poured another.

"Some Christian!" he laughed bitterly. "Right, Susan! And you were praying for your pagan husband, weren't you! Well who's the pagan now? You're no better than I am! Never have been!"

As his mind began to dull with alcohol, his anger turned to tears. "Oh, Susan!" he cried out in loneliness and a despair deeper than he had ever experienced.

Then he thought about Billy Costas. "I never did trust that rich little bum!" he said as he drank straight from the bottle. "He finally got to her with hizzmmmoney," he stammered as his tongue became thick with drunkenness. "I don't need her! I don't need anybody!" he said as his hand dropped to the side of the chair, slowly releasing the bottle, which spilled the alcohol onto the hardwood floor, gradually forming a puddle.

. . .

Susan arrived at her office about 10:30 that morning, wondering how many women in the office knew Billy had turned his back on her. Her humiliation hurt as deeply as the rejection itself. She had taken additional time to fix her makeup and hair perfectly, and wore a stunning black-and-white business dress and jacket she had been saving for a special occasion. She completed the effect with dark hose, black heels, and elegant gold earrings.

She tightened her jaw, got out of the car, walked into the building and took the elevator to the second floor. When she opened the oak-and-brass door of DoubleSoft Corporation, the person she most dreaded seeing—Melissa Johnson—sat at the reception desk.

"Why, Susan, how nice to see you," Melissa purred with a smile playing at the corner of her lips. "Oh, my dear, you look absolutely stunning! Nice outfit! Special occasion?"

Susan's face flushed with embarrassment and anger. "Not really, Melissa. It's just something I already had," she said as she hurried on down the hallway toward her office. She had to pass Billy's office on the way and was careful not to even glance into his office as she walked by.

Hearing female footsteps in the hallway, Billy looked up from his computer just as Susan passed. She was even more beautiful than he had remembered, and he stood involuntarily as she disappeared into her office and shut her door. He looked down at his desk and breathed deeply. He sat down and waited a few minutes, then buzzed Susan's office.

"Yes?"

"Susan, it's Billy. Can you come in for a minute?"

There was a long silence. "What is it, Mr. Costas? What do you want now?"

"I need to talk with you. Please come."

"I'll be there in a few minutes." Susan replied coldly. Her nostrils flared in anger strangely mixed with hope and desire. She sat down behind her desk and looked at the pile of mail and began to sort it. *He can wait a while!* she thought as her lips tightened. She flipped advertisements, letters, orders, and bills into separate piles and finally stood to her feet. Taking a deep breath, she opened her door and walked toward Billy's office. When she got there, she paused and knocked on the door frame.

Billy looked up and smiled easily. "Come in, Susan," he said warmly as he stood and walked to the door to greet her. "Here, give Billy a hug!" he said, arms outstretched.

"I don't think so, Mr. Costas," she said as she tipped her head to one side and brushed past him and took a seat in front of his desk. "You wanted to see me about something?"

Billy, still facing the doorway, dropped his arms awkwardly, closed the door, turned, and went back to his chair behind the desk. "Oh, come on, Susan," he said softly. "Don't be mad at me. I've thought it all through and realize I really let you down. Please . . ." he said leaning forward, "please forgive me, Susan."

She hadn't heard those words since Arthur had asked her forgiveness when they were in college. Her anger began to melt, and her resolve as well, so she swallowed hard and sat straight, looking Billy squarely in the eyes. "I'm through being used, Billy!" she said firmly.

"I understand, Susan," he said in a sincere tone as he ran his fingers through his perfectly styled hair. "I know I didn't support you when you needed me, and I can't tell you how sorry I am."

Susan's face softened for a moment and Billy smiled gently as he reached across his desk to hold out his hand. He tilted his head in request and looked at her. Slowly, she reached out and touched his hand, shaking with intense feelings.

"Never again, Billy," she whispered. "Never let me down again!"

"I promise, beautiful!" he said as his eyes glistened, already thinking of the evenings he would spend with her. He came around the desk as she stood slowly to her feet, and they embraced passionately.

. . .

The call Dr. Miller and his wife, Darla, dreaded came that afternoon.

"It's the police," Darla whispered as she covered the mouthpiece of the phone.

David's hand shook as he took the phone. "This is Dr. Miller."

"Yes, Mr. Miller, this is Detective George Gustafson at the police station. I'm afraid I have some bad news for you."

David's heart sank and he closed his eyes, trying to prepare himself for the worst. "Is it my son?"

"Yes, Mr. Miller, I'm afraid so. You see—"

"Has he been hurt, officer?" David interrupted.

"No, Mr. Miller, he's fine. but—"

David pulled the receiver from his ear for a moment and breathed deeply as he said, "Oh, thank God!" He looked at Darla and said, "Jason's all right."

Darla broke down in tears of relief as she slumped into a chair at the table.

"Mr. Miller?" the detective said, realizing he had been speaking without being heard. Again he called out, this time louder, "Mr. Miller!"

David heard Gustafson's voice and held the receiver to his ear again. "Oh, I'm sorry, officer! I was just telling my wife that Jason wasn't injured." He paused for a moment and then asked, "But why is he at the police station?"

"That's what I've been trying to tell you. He's been arrested."

"On what charges, officer?" David asked almost indignantly as he looked at his wife.

"I'd rather talk with you when you come in, Mr. Miller," the officer replied.

"No, officer, I want to know now. What has he done?" David swallowed hard as Darla stood, eyes wide with fear.

"We've booked your son for murder."

Dr. David Miller gasped and nearly dropped the phone. His face turned pale as he said, "We'll be right down."

He hung up the phone and stood there blinking as though in a trance. He didn't even hear Darla when she called his name. Then through the fog, he finally heard, "David! What did the officer say?"

He slowly turned his eyes toward Darla and said in disbelief, "He said Jason has been charged with murder."

"Oh, no!" Darla said as she leaned on the counter to catch her balance. "It can't be! There has to be some mistake!"

"I know, I know," David said as he pulled on his jacket. "We've got to get down there." He stopped. "First, I'll call Robert Everett. Jason's going to need a lawyer."

As soon as he finished talking with the attorney who attended their church, they got into their car. They drove as fast as traffic would allow and arrived at the police station within minutes. They hurried inside and were introduce to Detective George Gustafson. He took them to his office and invited them to sit down.

"Officer, there has to be some mistake," Dr. Miller said. "Our son couldn't possibly have harmed anyone."

"I wish that were true, Mr. Miller," Gustafson said, "but we have an eyewitness who puts your son at the crime scene and we found the victim's credit card in your son's possession." He opened a file folder and looked at a report as he adjusted his glasses. "Oh, there's one more thing," he said as he looked up.

"What's that, officer?" David said in a raspy voice as grief nearly overwhelmed him.

"Your son confessed."

When their attorney arrived, the officer led them to the juvenile section of the jail. There in a glassed consultation cell, they waited at a table until Jason was escorted into the room. When Darla saw him, she burst into tears and stood to embrace her son. Jason couldn't hug her and she stepped back, suddenly aware of the handcuffs that he wore. "Oh, Jason," she cried softly as she touched his hands tenderly.

Jason began to cry and as Darla pulled him close, his body shook with sobs of terror and remorse. After a long awkward period of tears and whispers which echoed off the hard concrete walls and wire-meshed windows, they all sat down at the table as the guard stepped outside, keeping them all in his view.

"Jason, just tell me one thing," his father said intently as he looked into the boy's eyes. "Did you do it?"

Robert Everett raised his hand to stop Jason from answering and said, "I don't think you should ask your son that, Pastor." He looked around the room with a sigh. "You never know who's listening."

Jason looked down at the handcuffs on his hands, thinking, then he looked up at his father. He shook his head as tears began streaming down his face. "I wasn't the one who hit the old man. I was just there with them, Dad, but I didn't do it! I swear, I didn't do it!"

"Who were you with, Jason?" the attorney asked.

"I can't tell you! They'll kill me!"

"Jason," Robert said in a soft and patient tone, "if you don't cooperate with me, I won't be able to help you."

Jason shook his head as beads of sweat appeared on his forehead. "No! No . . . I can't!"

David Miller exploded with frustration and pent-up emotions. "Jason! Tell Mr. Everett what he wants to know! *Now!* Who were you with?"

Jason swallowed hard and shook with terror. "Dad, if I tell you—if I tell anybody—they promised they'd kill me and our whole family!"

Robert Everett leaned forward and touched Jason on the arm. Jason flinched as he looked at the attorney. Robert smiled gently and asked, "Is it a gang, Jason?"

Jason nodded as he hung his head. His shoulders slumped as he thought about the threats. The gang wasn't kidding, and Jason knew it.

"What gang, Jason?" David Miller asked. He hadn't been aware that a gang even existed in their quiet suburb. He could understand if it had been downtown D.C., but out here? He repeated his question, "What gang, Jason?"

"I can't tell you, Dad!" Jason almost shouted. "Don't you understand? They'll kill you and Mom and Faith! Then they'll kill me! They mean it, Dad!"

David sat back in his chair in disbelief. He looked away from Jason and then at Darla, who was dabbing at her eyes with a tissue. "Did you know Jason was in a gang, Darla?" he asked in an almost accusing tone of voice.

Darla shook her head in surprise. "Of course not, David! How would I have known? And do you think I'd keep it a secret from you?"

David looked down as he shook his head. "No, of course not," he said softly.

He looked back at Jason. "How long have you been in this gang, son?"

"Only a few weeks, Dad. I joined it only because I was afraid at school. I was threatened several times by different gangs, and I figured I'd better join one if I didn't want to get killed."

"Why didn't you tell me?"

"I *tried* to, Dad," Jason said, his lips stiffly curled with emotion as he tried to keep from crying. "But you never listen to me. If you're ever home, you're watching the news or talking to someone on the phone! I did try to tell you—and you shushed me up and told me to go do my homework."

"So you're blaming me for all this?" David said defensively.

"No, Dad! See? You *still* aren't listening! I'm just trying to tell you how I got hooked up with a gang."

"But that's not my fault, Jason!"

"I know, Dad! I didn't say it was your fault!" Jason said in exasperation. "Oh, what's the use?" He looked down at his feet as his lips tightened with anger.

There was an awkward pause and then Robert Everett asked Jason, "Is it true that you confessed to killing the victim?"

Jason looked up in surprise. "No! I never touched the old guy! And I never confessed! All I told them was that I was there!"

Robert sat back and sighed deeply. "As far as the police are concerned, Jason, that *was* a confession. If you were part of the group that committed the crime, the law says you are just as guilty as the one who crushed his skull."

"But I didn't do it!"

Robert continued to probe Jason to get as much information as possible. "How many kids were there with you?"

"I can't tell you that."

"Did you see who actually hit the man?"

Jason shook his head and looked down. He began to cry again as he relived those terrifying moments.

"Jason!" his father said sternly, "you've got to tell us so we can help you!"

Jason looked up and shook his head again. "I didn't see who did it! I was at the back. I didn't even want to be there, but they told me if I wanted to be part of the gang, I had to pass the initiation. I was supposed to be the one to whack him, but at the last minute, I just couldn't do it. So Brandon did it—" He gasped, realizing he had broken the gang's code of silence.

"Brandon *who?*" David asked.

"Don't ask, Dad! I can't tell you!"

Mrs. Miller was finally composed enough to ask, "Jason, what happened to you? How could you have gotten caught up with such a terrible gang? Didn't we teach you anything?"

Jason began to explain to his mother his feelings of loneliness after their move to Maryland. He talked for some time about his anger over leaving his friends in Colorado, having to attend a new school and prove himself to the other kids. "I wanted to fit in, Mom. I was tired of being made fun of for not having the right shoes and for you driving me to school and for not smoking or cussing. They invited me to parties to see pornographic videos and I turned them down several times. But, I finally decided I wanted to be like the rest of the kids, so I went—I hated it! But, I figured if I was just as tough as the other guys, maybe they'd leave me alone. But, Mom, I never thought it would go this far! You've got to believe me, I never hit that man!"

Darla Miller smiled sadly through her tears and said, "I do believe you, Jason."

She turned to Robert Everett and asked, "What do we do now, Robert?"

The attorney scratched his head, looked at David, then Jason, then Darla and said, "I'm not sure, Mrs. Miller. But I can tell you this: It isn't good! If the court decides to try Jason as an adult, he could face life imprisonment. On the other hand, if they try him as a minor—and I think that's a possibility because this is his first offense—he may spend only a year or two at a juvenile facility. His only chance is for him to identify the rest of the gang. Hopefully, the police can isolate each one, interrogate them, and find out who actually killed the man. But it starts here with Jason," he said as he looked Jason directly in the eyes.

"I can't, Mr. Everett! I just can't!"

Robert stood to his feet. "Then, son, you'd better get ready to spend the rest of your life in prison. Those are your only two choices right now. Until you're ready to cooperate, I can't be of much help." He waved to the guard, who returned to the room.

Darla hugged Jason desperately, not wanting to let him go. She finally held him at arms length, looked into his eyes, and said, "Jason, remember, God still loves you. You've got to learn how to trust Him like you used to."

Jason looked at her, then at his dad. "It's because you were so involved in serving God that I'm in here! So where is God now?"

The guard said, "Come on. It's time to go," and led him towards the door.

Jason turned back and looked sadly at his father and said, "Huh, Dad? Where is God now?"

7

Faith for When Children Rebel

LET'S CONTINUE OUR STUDY in raising godly children in a pagan world. In the last chapter, we looked at two important principles for preventing practical atheism from damaging our children as we try to guide them through this dark and confusing world into God's glorious kingdom: 1) children are a gift from God, and 2) we are to love our children. Now let's look at five more principles.

Children Are Natural Rebels

A third key principle for understanding how to raise godly children in a pagan world is to realize that children are natural rebels. I do not mean to imply, however, that rebellion is inevitable or that it is to be excused. I'm simply pointing out that parents pass on the sin nature to their children, and your children and mine are no exception.

Sociologists and psychologists are fond of teaching our culture that children are merely the product of their environment. While it is true that our homes and families color and mold our characters, evil behavior is not solely the result of what children see and imitate. Sin is deeply ingrained in the very essence of what it means to be human.

Perhaps you may feel that is an overstatement, but if Scripture is true, I have actually understated our natural inclination to disobey authority. Paul writes, "There is no one righteous, not even one; there is no one who understands, no one who seeks God. All have turned away, they have together become worthless; there is no one who does good, not even one" (Romans 3:10-12).

It is as natural for us to rebel as it is to breathe. Genesis 6:5 says that "every inclination of the thoughts of [man's] heart was only evil all the time." Look at the superlatives in that verse: "*every* inclination . . . *only* evil . . . *all* the time." Humans are so perverse that we "love evil rather than good, falsehood rather than speaking the truth" (Psalm 52:3). I have known people like that—people who will lie even when it is in their best interest to tell the truth. Lying is a way of life for them and they "delight in doing wrong and rejoice in the perverseness of evil" (Proverbs 2:14).

If you are going to understand your children, you must come to grips with this fundamental truth: Left to themselves, little humans are rotten to the core. I do not say that sarcastically or in a mean-spirited way, but as a simple statement of fact. As someone has well said, "We are not sinners because we sin; we sin because we are sinners." You will never have to teach your children to tell a lie, steal a cookie, cheat on a test, or disobey the law. Without firm parental direction, they will do those things because it is their very nature to do so. With that in mind, we are told, "Discipline your son, for in that there is hope; do not be a willing party to his death" (Proverbs 19:18). That leads us to the next important principle.

Children Are to Be Brought Under Control

We discussed this briefly in the last chapter, but this principle is so important that I want to mention it again. A fourth key point for successful parenting is to understand that parents are charged with the duty of bringing their children under control. God makes a seemingly outdated statement in Proverbs 13:24:

"He who spares the rod hates his son, but he who loves him is careful to discipline him." Our culture has come to believe that corporal punishment is cruel abuse and that those who spank their children are unfit to be parents.

As a result, many parents are so afraid that they will be reported to the authorities by neighbors or teachers if they spank their children that they shy away from all forms of discipline. We see the tragic result of such foolishness in the growing problem of juvenile crime. Children are growing up without respect for their parents or fear of authority. Little children stand defiantly in their yards making obscene gestures at passersby without fear of rebuke or punishment. They throw tantrums and scream until they get their way as helpless parents shrug their shoulders as if to say, "What can I do?"

A recent "20/20" television broadcast featured a story about profanity and how common it is in our culture. They showed a little boy who cursed with foul obscenities while his parents giggled nearby because they thought he was so cute.

The telecast also showed teens from average middle-class homes walking through school hallways using curse words as a major part of their vocabulary. Girls and boys alike punctuated their minimal thoughts with words so foul the producers had to bleep the words again and again.

It all begins with parents who use vulgar language themselves and who tolerate such communication in their homes. Unbelievably, this is even true in homes that claim to be Christian. James tells us that "if anyone considers himself religious and yet does not keep a tight rein on his tongue, he deceives himself and his religion is worthless" (James 1:26).

I recall hearing my father utter a curse word only once in my life, and he was as shocked as I was when the word popped out before he realized it. We were in our old garage and Dad must have hit his hand with a tool and reacted in a totally uncharacteristic way. What I recall about that event was not the word he spoke, but that he called me to his side and earnestly asked me to forgive him. "Oh, Ed, I am so sorry!" he said as he put his hand on my shoulder. "I heard that word so many times with the men I used to work with at the factory that it came out before I even thought about it."

I was impressed with his genuine sorrow and that he had the humility to ask his son's forgiveness. He taught me at that very moment that cursing and Christianity are not compatible, and as I watched him through the years, I observed a consistently self-controlled life.

It was his integrity of living that made it easier for me to accept the discipline he administered when I needed it. My parents were gentle and loving, but when correction was needed, they were not hesitant to apply it. One of the few sermons I recall my father preaching was taken from Proverbs 23:13: "Withhold not correction from the child: for if thou beatest him with the rod, he shall not die" (KJV).

I want to make it clear that I am not in favor of brutality in the correction of children, and neither was my father. The fact is, since he was confident in his role as a parent and I knew he would punish me if necessary, I was determined to make it as unnecessary as possible.

I will explain the process of control in the following section on discipline and training. Read it carefully and thoughtfully, for it is an essential element in overcoming practical atheism in our children's hearts.

Parents Are Charged with Discipline and Training

Another foundational truth for raising children involves control and training. We live in a generation of parents who are too terrified to discipline their children for fear they will be reported to Social Services and their children might well be taken away. Hardly a week goes by without news stories of government officials intruding into homes, ignoring due process as traumatized children are snatched away from caring parents who dared to discipline. Then society stands amazed at the lawlessness of our youth who respect no one. Paul predicted such a day when he wrote, "People will be lovers of themselves, lovers of money, boastful, proud, abusive, disobedient to their parents, ungrateful, unholy" (2 Timothy 3:2).

In contrast, Paul writes that an elder must have "children [who] believe and are not open to the charge of being wild and disobedient" (Titus 1:6). While this is especially important for leaders in the church, it is the standard God would have all homes to follow. You see, if a child does not learn submission to authority while in his home, he will have to learn it in a more painful environment later on—either at work, in the military, or in prison.

Solomon wrote, "Folly is bound up in the heart of a child, but the rod of discipline will drive it far from him" (Proverbs 22:15). If you are a young parent, may I give you some helpful advice? Begin the discipline of your children early. Don't wait until your child is in his teens to try to teach him to obey; it will be too late. Don't even wait until he is eight or ten years old. Don't wait until he is four or five. Bring your child under control *immediately*, as soon as you bring your baby home from the hospital. It is important for the tranquillity of your household that you establish who is in control. As Hebrews 12:11 says, discipline "produces a harvest of righteousness and peace for those who have been trained by it."

Your child can learn within a few days or weeks, and certainly within a few months that you mean it when you say, "No." Psychologists will try to tell you that you will warp your child's self-image and creativity if you use a word as negative as *no*, but they are wrong. "No" is a powerful tool when coupled with the appropriate use of "Yes" and "I love you."

Part of the art of parenting is in knowing when to say, "Yes" and when to say, "No." It's all in the timing, as we are told in Proverbs: "A man finds joy in giving an apt reply—and how good is a timely word!" (Proverbs 15:23).

You do not have to say, "No" in an ugly or angry way. You can say it softly and with a smile. But you must mean it when you say it, and you must enforce it consistently and firmly so that your child knows that your "yes" means yes and your "no" means no (*see* James 5:12). Children become frustrated, confused, and ultimately lose respect when parents apply rules inconsistently and do not back up their orders. For the home to be an island of peace in a world of confusion, children must be brought under control—and that is a job God has given to parents.

For discipline to be successful it must be *loving, firm, and consistent.* These three elements are essential and must be carefully balanced if your goal is to produce happy and balanced maturity in your children as they grow into adulthood. Paul writes about these essential characteristics of godly discipline in Ephesians 6:4: "Fathers, do not exasperate your children; instead, bring them up in the training and instruction of the Lord." Let's take a closer look at these three essential elements of successful discipline.

Biblical discipline is to be motivated by love, not frustration, anger, or pride. "Fathers, do not exasperate your children." That is precisely what happens when discipline is not first tempered with love. Over the years, in dealing with hundreds of families, I have never seen angry rebellious children come from homes where love was the foundation of all discipline. But it is equally important to understand that real love requires a parent to faithfully correct his children. That's what the Bible means when it says, "He who spares the rod hates his son, but he who loves him is careful to discipline him" (Proverbs 13:24). Furthermore, it says, "Discipline your son, for in that there is hope; do not be a willing party to his death" (Proverbs 19:18). The point is that if you really love your children, you will discipline them, for their own sake, so they will learn how to live productive lives in a twisted world of sinful rebellion.

Parents must have a sound understanding of the Scriptures to know right from wrong so that they will not be confused and swayed by contemporary social trends. Many parents today simply have no idea what to tell their children when a crisis arises because they don't know God's Word. But those who have a solid foundation of biblical truth find it much easier to decide what to do when a problem comes up.

The connection between love and discipline is clearly taught in Hebrews 12:6: "The Lord disciplines those he loves." This passage is important because it connects love with discipline, and for discipline to be biblical, it must also be firm. Firmness in discipline means that parents enforce what is right and are not intimidated when their children whine, pout, cry, or try to manipulate with statements like, "All the other kids get to do it!" Firmness gives parents the courage to apply strong discipline when it is required, even though our culture has come to believe that any corporal punishment is cruel and unusual.

Firmness, however, must never become harshness. It is tragic that so few parents apply Proverbs 15:1 to the raising of their children: "A gentle answer turns away wrath, but a harsh word stirs up anger." An angry tone of voice or belittling, embarrassing, and demeaning words have a way of creating lifelong barriers between parents and children. When discipline is applied in an unfairly harsh manner, children become exasperated, frustrated, and intensely angry.

Biblical discipline must be firm but based scrupulously upon truth and not mere accusation. Nothing exasperates a child more than being punished for something he did not do, so parents must ask intelligent questions and take the time to discover where the guilt lies before executing judgment. And when punishment is finally meted out, it must be done with consistency.

The reason consistency in discipline is so important is that it provides a framework of clear expectation and consequence for failure. What is confusing to a child is to be excused one day for a rebellious act only to be harshly punished the next day for the same deed. It is like the cartoon grandmother who sees her daughter being manipulated by a whining child. Turning to her daughter, she says, "You are so inconsistent with your discipline." The daughter replies, "Sometimes I am, and sometimes I'm not." Exactly.

Even more exasperating to a child is to see rules applied differently to various children within the home. Favoritism toward one child over another can create deep-seated hostility and bitterness that may take decades to overcome. Parents must examine themselves constantly to see that they are evenhanded in the treatment of their children.

Finally, an ultimate source of rage for a child is to see his parents violate the very rules he is forced to follow. Children abhor hypocrisy in their parents, whether it be financial, moral, ethical, or religious. Only in eternity will we know how many children have turned away from God because they saw personal inconsistency in their parents' lives.

Instead, the Bible tells parents that we must bring our children "up in the training and instruction of the Lord" (Ephesians 6:4). That is the positive side of discipline. It is the "word of encouragement" spoken of in Hebrews 12:5. Pause with me for a moment and examine this passage on discipline:

> You have forgotten that word of encouragement that addresses you as sons: "My son, do not make light of the Lord's discipline, and do not lose heart when he rebukes you, because the Lord disciplines those he loves, and he punishes everyone he accepts as a son."
>
> Endure hardship as discipline; God is treating you as sons. For what son is not disciplined by his father? If you are not disciplined (and everyone undergoes discipline), then you are illegitimate children and not true sons. Moreover, we have all had human fathers who disciplined us and we respected them for it. How much more should we submit to the Father of our spirits and live! Our fathers disciplined us for a little while as they thought best; but God disciplines us for our good, that we may share in his holiness. No discipline seems pleasant at the time, but painful. Later on, however, it produces a harvest of righteousness and peace for those who have been trained by it (Hebrews 12:5-11).

Discipline is not fun for children or their parents, but it is an essential part of overcoming practical atheism in our homes, and produces a wonderful island of peace in the midst of a world of chaos and rebellion.

Training Needs to Take Place in Real-Life Situations

It is important to understand that in raising godly children the best training occurs in real-life situations. I did not learn much about raising children from a parenting class or from a book or video. The most important things I learned were passed on to me by my parents in our day-to-day lives. The lessons were taught around the dinner table or in the old station wagon as we traveled together on vacations. The important principles of living were taught as Dad, my brother, and I hunted in the woods on cold snowy days or when Dad insisted that I complete my paper route, with his help, even though I was coming down with the flu. Lessons of integrity were taught at the grocery store when mother handed back the money she so desperately needed when the clerk gave too much change.

That's what the Bible means when it says, "These commandments that I give you today are to be upon your hearts. Impress them on your children. Talk about them when you sit at home and when you walk along the road, when you lie down and when you get up" (Deuteronomy 6:6-7). Practical theology is best taught at home by godly parents. God's commands and principles of living are to be discussed with our children in real-life situations so that his precepts become a part of their very character.

The reason this is seldom done in our day is that parents invest a diminishing amount of time with their children. Instead, we spend our time working so we can buy more things, and as a result we have limited time and energy for the little lives God has entrusted into our care. And even when we are all finally at home, we sit entranced before the television, effectively silenced by the tyranny of the tube.

God tells us to impress His commands on our children by talking with them when we sit at home, or when we walk along the way. When was the last time you took a walk with your child? Some of the best conversations my son Dan and I have enjoyed have taken place as we walked along our favorite path near our home. We have gazed in awe at our snow-covered mountains as they stand proudly to the west, showing the creative power of God. We have watched with delight as a green-headed mallard and his mate paddled peacefully alongside as we walked beside the irrigation canal. We have run together to the dirt hills and stood quietly in worship in the glow of a fiery sunset. Rarely have we returned home without talking about the Lord and His glorious creation. Dan has often said, "I can't understand how anyone can look at what God has made and not believe in Him."

God says that we are to teach our children when we lie down at night to rest. Some of my most treasured childhood memories center on family devotions when, night after night, my father would call our family together for a short time of Bible reading and prayer. I do not remember the doctrinal content of many of those gatherings, but I do remember the lifelong habit of pausing each evening to thank the Lord for His provision and protection. We would pray around the circle, beginning with me, the youngest, and ending with Dad praying around the world as he mentioned by name every missionary he had ever met. Then as I was almost asleep, I would hear the family quote in unison Psalm 19:14: "Let the words of my mouth, and the meditation of my heart, be acceptable in thy sight, O LORD, my strength, and my redeemer."

Night after night, hundreds of times a year, thousands of times during my childhood, our family would read the Bible, pray, and close with Psalm 19:14. In this day with few meaningful traditions, it was an anchor for my soul, and it is a habit I have passed on to my children as well.

Deuteronomy 6 goes on to say that we are to teach our children in the morning. While we may be more rushed in the morning as we all hurry to get ready for school or work, it is important that we pause to prepare our hearts before we venture out into a hostile world. It takes only a few moments to read a passage of Scripture and to pray for God's protection, and it makes a powerful impression on children. Even now, as nearly all our children are grown, we gather in a group hug with those still home and bow our heads together in prayer asking the Lord to use each of us in His service that day.

The most profound training of our children—for good or for evil—does not happen at school or at church, but in the home.

The Most Important Legacy Is Eternal Life

Perhaps the most significant and vital principle for raising godly children in a pagan and unbelieving world is to give them eternal vision. Just as a kitten comes into the world with its eyes tightly closed, we humans are born spiritually blind. Isaiah describes our plight this way: "Like the blind we grope along the wall, feeling our way like men without eyes. At midday we stumble as if it were twilight" (Isaiah 59:10).

Have you ever stopped to think how difficult it is to communicate visual ideas to a person who has never seen? How would you explain colors to a man blind from birth? You might tell him that red is the color of an apple, but would he then understand what red looks like? You might try to explain red in terms of its wavelength in the visible light spectrum, but it would always remain a mystery to the one who cannot see.

In the same way, spiritual concepts are foreign to our impaired human minds. Spiritually speaking, we are in a total blackout. Jesus said, "If your eyes are bad, your whole body will be full of darkness. If then the light within you is darkness, how great is that darkness!" (Matthew 6:23).

We live in a generation that demands physical evidence to prove something exists, yet we realize there are many real things which cannot be seen, heard, felt, or measured scientifically. We cannot, for instance, use MRI technology to detect the presence and quantity of love, yet we know it exists and that it produces what is best in mankind. We can plainly perceive the presence of life in plants, animals, and humans, but we cannot see *life* itself. We can tell when it has left an organism, for its physical body ceases to function, yet we have no instrument to see, feel, or measure that force we call life.

Without the aid of electronic and optical instruments, we are extremely limited in what our senses can discern. Our eyes are sensitive to only a small portion of the electromagnetic spectrum, yet we know more exists outside what we can see. The spiritual world is like that. While our bodies are now limited to the three dimensions of space and the element of time, there is another dimension in God's universe that we cannot presently view with our eyes—even when aided by the most sophisticated scientific instruments. It is *eternity*—where God dwells—and it encompasses our physical cosmos.

We are given a brief glimpse into the spiritual world in 2 Kings 6 when Elisha was surrounded by a hostile army determined to capture him:

> When the servant of the man of God got up and went out early the next morning, an army with horses and chariots had surrounded the city. "Oh, my lord, what shall we do?" the servant asked.
>
> "Don't be afraid," the prophet answered. "Those who are with us are more than those who are with them."
>
> And Elisha prayed, "O LORD, open his eyes so he may see." Then the LORD opened the servant's eyes, and he looked and saw the hills full of horses and chariots of fire all around Elisha (verses 15-17).

Until God gave Elisha's servant supernatural eyesight, he was unable to see the spiritual forces that protected them. Though at the present we cannot see into the spiritual realm, it exists in reality even more than our physical world. Presently, our only access to the spiritual world is through faith. We are told that "without faith it is impossible to please God, because anyone who comes to him must believe that he exists and that he rewards those who earnestly seek him" (Hebrews 11:6).

Faith that leads our hearts and minds into the spiritual dimension can be developed only as we allow God to communicate His thoughts to us. He has chosen to do this in two ways: through His written Word, the Bible, and the Living Word, the Lord Jesus.

In the past God spoke to our forefathers through the prophets at many times and in various ways, but in these last days he has spoken to us by his Son, whom he appointed heir of all things, and through whom he made the universe (Hebrews 1:1-2).

The reason God gave us His Word in hard copy was because we are so incredibly dense when it comes to spiritual things. We need something we can go back to again and again to study, meditate on, and understand, rather than to rely upon subjective inner revelations that are so prone to error and misinterpretation. The reason God gave us His Son was to reveal in flesh and blood the loving character of God to a cynical and suspicious world.

Both forms of God's Word were essential to open the spiritual realm to us. The written Word was necessary because "faith comes from hearing the message, and the message is heard through the word of Christ" (Romans 10:17). The Living Word was needed because He shows us the way to heaven: "Let us fix our eyes on Jesus, the author and perfecter of our faith, who for the joy set before him endured the cross, scorning its shame, and sat down at the right hand of the throne of God" (Hebrews 12:2).

Albert Einstein longed to understand the relationships between space, energy, matter, time, and eternity. He worked many years with his mathematical theories to make sense of our existence, yet with all of his intellectual power, he was unable to explain the connection between material and spiritual realities. No wonder, then, that many parents feel inadequate to explain eternal matters to their children. Yet, it is so simple.

In order to help our children develop spiritual vision, we must teach them to look beyond *time, circumstances,* and the *physical world*. Though these subjects are immeasurably profound, we do not have to become deeply philosophical to understand all that is necessary to move from the natural world to the supernatural, from mortality to immortality, or from time to eternity. Let's look ever so briefly at these realities we all experience to see how we can expand the vision of our children.

Volumes have been written to explain the concept of *time*, an entity we can measure but not see or feel. We do not need to understand the Theory of Relativity to experience the effects of time, nor to reach beyond it. We simply need to understand that our time in this life is limited. The psalmist wrote, "The length of our days is seventy years—or eighty, if we have the strength; yet their span is but trouble and sorrow, for they quickly pass, and we fly away" (Psalm 90:10). We need to teach our children that life is brief and eternity is just around the corner. As David prayed, "Show me, O LORD, my life's end and the number of my days; let me know how fleeting is my life" (Psalm 39:4) and, "Teach us to number our days aright, that we may gain a heart of wisdom" (Psalm 90:12).

Regardless of what man does in medical research, transplant technology, bionics, or cryogenics, the Bible says, "Man's days are determined; you have decreed the number of his months and have set limits he cannot exceed" (Job 14:5). For children of God, however, this is not bad news, for we know that when we are "absent from the body" we are "present with the Lord" (2 Corinthians 5:8 KJV).

Everything in our lives is affected by our view of eternity. It determines our philosophy of life, our values, how we do business, our personal goals, our marriages, how we raise our children, the way we face illness and death—*everything*. Teach a child that this life is merely the beginning of an eternal adventure, and he will view setbacks, disappointments, circumstances, and suffering in an entirely different way from one who believes this mortal life is all there is and that we must grab all the gusto we can while there is still time.

Most who do not have a clear view of eternity have difficulty accepting their circumstances, which can lead a person to frustration, anger, and bitterness. But when a child is taught early that those who know Christ as Savior have an unlimited future to enjoy all that God provides, he can say with Paul, "I have learned to be content whatever the circumstances" (Philippians 4:11). You see, it is all in how we look at life. That's what Jesus was teaching when He said, "Do not store up for yourselves treasures on earth, where moth and rust destroy, and where thieves break in and steal. But store up for yourselves treasures in heaven, where moth and rust do not destroy, and where thieves do not break in and steal. For where your treasure is, there your heart will be also" (Matthew 6:19-21).

When my father was a little boy growing up on a homestead in the high mountains of Colorado, he and his father stood out under a velvet-black sky one night watching the shimmering diamond-like stars as they glistened overhead. "Son," his father said, pointing to a particularly bright star above, "do you see that star? Someday, I'm going to be in charge of that." His point was that in eternity, God has promised responsibility and reward for those who have proven themselves to be trustworthy. It was a defining moment in my father's life which helped move him beyond time and space in his thinking.

Spiritual thinking includes not only our view of time and circumstances, but our understanding of the physical world as well. If we see the cosmos only as the random interaction of molecules and energy, it makes no sense whatsoever. That's why evolutionism is such a meaningless and hopeless philosophy. It reflects Solomon's view of life in his latter years when he became careless toward God and in his depression he wrote, "When I surveyed all that my hands had done and what I had toiled to achieve, everything was meaningless, a chasing after the wind; nothing was gained under the sun" (Ecclesiastes 2:11).

In direct contrast, one who sees the physical universe as clear evidence of the hand of God finds it full of meaning, purpose, and order. After spending many nights of his youth tending sheep while looking up into the sky brilliantly flecked with galaxies of stars, David wrote, "The heavens declare the glory of God; the skies proclaim the work of his hands" (Psalm 19:1).

Paul stated that God "has not left himself without testimony" (Acts 14:17) and expanded on this thought in Romans 1:20: "Since the creation of the world God's invisible qualities—his eternal power and divine nature—have been clearly seen, being understood from what has been made, so that men are without excuse."

Paul, in addressing the Greeks at Athens, said,

> The God who made the world and everything in it is the Lord of heaven and earth and does not live in temples built by hands. And he is not served by human hands, as if he needed anything, because he himself gives all men life and breath and everything else. From one man he made every nation of men, that they should inhabit the whole earth; and he determined the times set for them and the exact places where they should live. God did this so that men would seek him and perhaps reach out for him and find him, though he is not far from each one of us. For in him we live and move and have our being (Acts 17:24-28).

We must teach our children early in their lives that everything in the physical realm is the work of God's hands so they can understand the origin of all life including mankind, our purpose for existing, and the destiny God has prepared for those who love Him.

Proper spiritual understanding of time, circumstances, and physical reality will help to prepare our children for life in an age of relativism, confusion, and uncertainty. It is an awesome and daunting task, but absolutely necessary if we are to guide them through the portals of time into eternity.

Conviction and Choices

Dr. Arthur Wilson was devastated by the discovery that his wife Susan was having an affair with her boss, Billy Costas. He tried to put her out of his mind by focusing on his research at the National Cancer Institute, but he found that his mind often drifted from the genetic experiments to Susan and he realized, now that she was gone, that he longed for her more than he thought possible.

He often attempted to dull his pain with alcohol, but even in a drunken fog, he dreamed of her face turning slowly away from him with a sadness too deep for words.

One evening, as he sat alone in the den reading the newspaper, his phone rang. He reclined in his chair, not reacting as the phone rang again. Finally, he reached out and picked up the phone. "Hello?"

"Arthur?"

"Yes."

"It's Michael Rollins. I hadn't heard from you in a while and just thought I'd call and see how you're doing."

Normally Arthur would have been irritated by a call in the evening, but this time, he found himself strangely grateful. "Well, hello, Michael," he said in an almost-friendly tone. "I'm doing fine. It's been a while since we've talked."

"I know. I was wondering how it was going between you and Susan. We haven't seen her in church for quite some time."

"Well, I'm not surprised, Michael," Arthur said, his tone changing. "From her lifestyle I would say she doesn't belong in church."

Michael paused, then asked, "What do you mean, 'she doesn't belong'?"

"I mean she's having an affair with her boss, Michael! She's supposed to be a Christian, right? But it doesn't seem to have made much difference. She's just like everybody else—and let me tell you something else," Arthur said loudly as he stood to his feet. "I am so fed up with the hypocrisy of you Christians! You look down on the rest of us pagans and think you're so holy, but you're no different. Take your pastor, for instance!"

Michael sat stunned as Arthur raged against Christianity. "What about my pastor, Arthur?" he said, trying to control his temper.

"He's as phony as they come, Michael! On the one hand he says he believes in God and in Jesus and that they can give immortality to humans, yet on the other hand, he believes that God is too weak to give people help in this life without the aid of psychology—a pseudoscience if there ever was one. I don't see much difference between his view of God and mine, except I'm more honest about my atheism than he is."

Michael paused a moment to collect his thoughts, then said, "I can't defend his view on psychology, Arthur. I have serious concerns about its scientific validity, let alone its potential for spiritual deception, but I can't agree that Dr. Miller is an atheist. That's simply untrue."

"Is it really, Michael?" Arthur pressed. "What's the difference between saying there is no God and saying that God is too weak to heal a person's twisted psyche? What kind of God would be able to save a person's soul for eternity but unable to give him peace of mind in this life? Why should anyone believe in a God like that?"

"I see your point, Arthur, but you're going too far when you say Dr. Miller is an atheist. I know he truly believes in the existence of God and in the power of Jesus Christ to save our souls. I might concede that he has bought into a false philosophy which weakens the church, but I can't equate philosophical confusion with atheism."

"So correct doctrine doesn't really count, is that it?" Arthur said sarcastically. "If that's true, then a committed evolutionist can also be a Christian."

Again Michael paused, feeling as though he were defending heresy. "Well . . . I suppose an evolutionist could be a Christian, though he could not fully understand the implications of both worldviews and hold to both simultaneously, since they are actually oppositional."

"So, in other words, an evolutionist could be a Christian so long as he didn't fully understand evolution or biblical doctrine?"

"Well, yes, I guess that's one way of putting it," Michael admitted reluctantly.

"But the more this person learns about evolution and/or the Bible, he would have to eventually make a decision and turn from one or the other?"

"I think that's true as well."

"So what about the 'theistic evolutionist'?" Arthur asked. "What about those so-called scientists who want to believe in God but say that the way God created the universe was through evolutionary processes? It seems to me that they want to believe in a spiritual reality that transcends the physical world, yet they are anxious to move into the scientific mainstream by accepting the scientific evidences for evolution."

Michael was impressed that Arthur was grasping the finer nuances of the evolution/creation debate. "Again, I would have to say that I disagree with their position, but I am not prepared to say that theistic evolutionists are atheists."

"But what's the difference, Michael?" Arthur said, his voice rising with excitement. "Either way, the god they believe in is not the God described in the Bible. Their god is a weak and limited being, not the omnipotent Creator the Bible portrays. No, I can't agree with you, Michael, as much as I respect you. You can't have it both ways. Either God is God, or He isn't! Either the Bible is true or it's false! Either He created the universe instantaneously out of nothing, by His own will, or He doesn't exist at all. Whether you want to admit it or not, they *are* atheists. They just don't realize it."

Michael was silent. Finally he said, "Arthur, you've given me a lot to think about. Before I let you go, tell me what happened with Susan."

"I don't know, Michael," Arthur replied. "We've been having some problems, as you already know. I thought we'd work them out if she got some counseling. She went to your pastor, and he sent her to a Christian psychiatrist. Before I knew what happened, she decided she had to leave me for a while. Then I found out she's been having an affair. I tell you, Michael, if I had been tempted to become a Christian—and I was, after talking with you and your wife—now I'm not interested. Being a Christian didn't make much difference in her life, did it?"

Michael shook his head with embarrassment. "I can't argue with you about Susan's decisions. If it's true, she's made a serious mistake. But I can tell you that God still loves her, just like He loves you, Arthur, and that He can forgive her. The question is, can you?"

It was Arthur's turn to pause in silence. He sighed deeply, then said, "To be honest with you, Michael, I don't know if I can."

. . .

Susan began to feel more complete again now that she and Billy had made up. There was a nagging hint of emptiness, however, and an uncomfortable sensation deep within her chest whenever she saw her Bible. She stumbled across a troubling passage one day as she read in 1 Corinthians 6:9-10, "Do you not know that the wicked will not inherit the kingdom of God? Do not be deceived: Neither the sexually immoral nor idolaters nor adulterers nor male prostitutes nor homosexual offenders nor thieves nor the greedy nor drunkards nor slanderers nor swindlers will inherit the kingdom of God."

She closed the Bible angrily, walked to her closet, and put it away. *I don't have to listen to that kind of stuff!* she thought. But she felt a deep spiritual loss as conviction swept over her heart and she willfully pushed it aside.

Over the next few weeks, she tried to deal with her growing sense of guilt by visiting different churches. She knew she couldn't return to Pastor Miller's church since she was the one who had turned Jason Miller in to the police. The strange thing was, it seemed that no matter which church she attended, the message was always the same—the need to protect the sanctity of marriage. It was as though each pastor realized she—an adulteress—was in attendance and was preaching directly to her and, as soon as she left the service, the pastor called the next church to tell the next pastor to speak on that topic during her visit.

Even the visitors' card reminded her of her guilt when she saw the boxes to check her address and marital status: married or single. *Where's the box for adulteress?* she wondered as she shook her head and tucked the card in her purse.

She began to think that if Billy attended church with her, perhaps he might become a Christian, and then God would understand and forgive her. She asked him to visit a church with her, but he wasn't interested.

"Why would you want to go to church, Susan?" he asked in all seriousness. "All they want is your money, and all they do is lay a guilt trip on you."

Her longing for peace of heart and mind grew daily as the excitement of her affair with Billy began to wane. And she had noticed Billy glancing longingly at some of the younger women at the office. Though she fought against it, the old depression began to settle over her once again, and as it did, her face aged noticeably and her work began to suffer.

She visited the psychiatrist she had been referred to months before, Dr. William Dewey, and he listened to her symptoms of growing anxiety and depression. After a short interview, he prescribed Prozac for her, assuring her that it was non-addictive and quite safe. "I think this will help put you back into balance," he said, having never discovered that she was having an adulterous affair.

But the relief never came. Though she felt less anxious, the guilt she experienced continued as a gigantic weight on her heart and an almost tangible barrier between her and God. She longed for the joy she had known when she first committed her heart to Christ, but she didn't know how to find it once again.

Then she remembered a friend she had met at the church—Ellen Rollins. She and her husband Michael had been so warm and helpful to her and she felt as though Ellen was someone she could talk with. She looked in her file drawer at her apartment and found an old church directory with Ellen's phone number. Shaking with anxiety, she dialed the number.

"Rollins's residence."

Susan recognized Ellen's voice right away. "Ellen?"

"Yes?"

"This is Susan Wilson. You might not remember me. I used to attend your church."

"Of course I remember you, Susan! It's so nice to hear your voice!"

"Thank you, Ellen. I . . . I need someone to talk with. Do you have a few minutes?"

"Yes, of course, dear. What's the problem?"

"Well," Susan began hesitantly, "I suppose you knew that Arthur and I are separated."

"Yes, I'd heard that. Actually, Arthur was our dinner guest a few months back, and he told us. I'm so sorry. Is there anything I can do to help?"

"Well, not with our marriage, I'm afraid," Susan said, feeling a deep resistance to restoring her broken marriage. "That's over. But I do need help getting my life back together with God."

"I'll help any way I can, Susan. Would you like to get together?"

Susan paused for a moment, then replied, "Yes, Ellen, I'd like that."

They agreed to meet the next day in a quaint little French restaurant near Susan's apartment. Susan was waiting at the table when Ellen arrived.

Ellen couldn't help but notice how much older Susan looked than when she had last seen her. Wrinkles of anxiety strained at her eyes and she looked weary. She had lost some weight and her face was drawn.

Ellen sat down and said, "It is so good to see you, Susan! I'm glad you called me."

"Thank you for seeing me," Susan said with genuine gratitude. "I just feel so empty and alone."

Ellen leaned forward and said, "Just relax and tell me what's going on in your life."

As they ate, Susan told her the story of Arthur's coldness toward her and how she had finally left him. She sighed deeply when she got to the part about her affair with Billy. "And then . . . I got involved with my boss. I'm ashamed to admit it, Ellen, but I'm still involved with him." She waited for Ellen to sit back in horror and then to condemn her for her adultery, but Ellen just waited quietly for Susan to continue.

"It's not like I've taken him away from anyone, Ellen. He's divorced, and Arthur and I are separated and I'm sure we'll be getting a divorce soon."

"Have you done anything officially to divorce Arthur?" Ellen asked.

"No. I just haven't had the energy to pursue any legal action. I kind of hoped Arthur would take care of it, but as far as I know, he hasn't done anything about it either. We're still legally married, but we haven't seen each other in months."

"So what's your question, Susan?"

"I want to know how to get my relationship with God back the way it was. It's the only time in my whole life that I've felt any relief from anxiety and depression."

"What do you think you should do?"

"I've tried to read my Bible, but it just isn't like it used to be. I dread opening it now. I guess I need to get back into church, but even that seems empty now."

"Let me ask the question another way, then. What do you think God would have you to do?"

Susan looked down at her plate, shook her head, and looked back up at Ellen. "I'm not sure. That's what I'm asking you."

"And if I can show you what God wants, are you willing to do it?"

"What do you mean?"

"I mean if I can show you from the Bible what God wants you to do, will you obey Him?"

Susan swallowed nervously. "I . . . I don't know."

Ellen smiled sadly and said, "Then we don't need to go any further."

"Why not?"

"Susan, the problem isn't information. The problem is your will. Until you are willing to obey the Lord, regardless of what He says to do, you will never find the peace you once had. No Christian can be happy and disobedient at the same moment."

Susan's head began to throb with pain as a migraine took hold. She looked Ellen in the eyes and said tightly, "If you're going to tell me that I have to go back to Arthur, forget it. I want the peace and joy I had, but I can't believe God would want me to go back into a marriage that's so unloving. Doesn't the Bible say that God wants us to be happy?"

"I believe God wants us to be full of joy, Susan," Ellen replied gently, "but His Word says real joy only happens when we do things God's way."

Susan leaned forward, cupping her forehead in her hands as she began to weep quietly. "I can't do it, Ellen. I just can't do it! I can't go back to Arthur. I don't love him anymore. I think I actually hate him! Please don't tell me God wants me to live with Arthur! I just can't do it!"

"I never said you have to go back to Arthur, Susan. You are the one who brought him up in our conversation. But let me ask you a tough question. Is it that you *can't* go back to Arthur, or that you *won't?*"

Susan looked up at Ellen as she rubbed her neck, trying to find relief from the pain. Through her tears she finally answered, "I guess the only honest answer is I *won't.*"

"At least you're being truthful about it. You see, God never asks us to do something we *can't* do. And if He wants you to return to your marriage, He will give you the strength to do it."

"Is that what you think I should do? Go back to Arthur?"

"I'm not going to tell you what to do, Susan. I'd rather you asked the Lord to show you in His Word. Would you do this for me? I want you to read 1 Corinthians this week and then let's meet again next week and you tell me if the Lord has given you an answer. Is it a deal?"

Susan nodded reluctantly. "It's a deal. But I'm telling you right now, I'm *not* going back to Arthur!"

. . .

Dr. David Miller sat at his desk, trying to prepare his sermon. The words of Arthur Wilson often rang in his mind: *How big is your God?* He recognized the truth of Arthur's accusation and his heart was cut deeply with conviction. Now, however, the trauma of his son's impending trial weighed heavily on his heart. The newspapers had not released Jason's name because he was a minor, but if the judge decided to try him as an adult, the news would make it impossible to continue the ministry in Bethesda.

He and his wife had wept countless times in an agony too great to communicate. Jason still refused to cooperate with the authorities and David simply didn't know where to turn for advice. He had called Dr. Dewey and was told that Jason might be able to plead temporary insanity as a defense. Yet David knew that was simply untrue.

David tried to pray for wisdom, but each time he did, Arthur Wilson's face appeared in his mind with the accusation, "Why should I believe in your God?"

"Indeed, why should *anyone* believe in my God," David said out loud as he slammed his fist down onto his desk in anger.

"Are you all right, Pastor?" his secretary's voice came over the intercom.

"Uh, yes, Marianne," he said sheepishly. He got up from his desk quietly and shut his office door. He sat back down and suddenly remembered a man he had met while pastoring in Colorado—a counselor by the name of John Kryer.[40] Dr. Kryer had appeared on a Christian television station arguing that the Bible alone was sufficient to deal with the deepest problems of mankind. Even back then David's heart had resonated with Dr. Kryer's message, but he was so impressed by a national Christian psychological clinic that he decided Dr. Kryer was a bit too radical and had dismissed any interaction with him. Now he wondered.

David tried to remember how to contact Dr. Kryer. Then it dawned on him to call the television station that had carried the program. He called information, and quickly located the station. At first the station could not recall Dr. Kryer, but when David explained how important it was that he locate the counselor, the secretary put him on hold and asked others at the station if they had any record of Dr. Kryer's number. Finally, a producer who had been at the station for several years located Dr. Kryer's office number and the secretary relayed it to David.

He dialed the number immediately and was soon connected with Dr. John Kryer. "How can I help you, Dr. Miller?" John said warmly.

David quickly related his story to John Kryer. "I've called to ask you what I should do," he concluded.

"First, let me ask you, why are you calling me? Surely you have a godly elder or member in your church you can turn to."

"I . . . I guess I'm just too embarrassed to tell this to my church. Frankly, I'm not sure how they'll handle it. I could well lose my job, and I can't say that I'd blame them."

"But they will find out sometime, won't they?" John asked gently.

David sighed and agreed, "I'm sure they will." He paused a moment, then said, "I think you're right. I need to talk with someone here. But as long as I have you on the phone, would you mind telling me what you would advise?"

John thought for a moment, then said, "I believe the Lord would have your son tell the truth. I don't know what sentence the judge will give, but the Word tells us that we are to be people of the truth."

"But Jason won't squeal on his gang, Dr. Kryer. He's afraid they will kill us if he does."

"Do you think they are a danger to you?"

"Yes, from what my son has told us, I do."

"And if he refuses to cooperate with the authorities what are the consequences?"

"He could be tried as an adult and spend his entire life in prison."

"And you're sure he didn't actually commit the crime?"

"I'm absolutely certain of it. But that won't matter if he refuses to cooperate. They'll still convict him."

"Then I suggest you continue to plead with him to tell the truth, no matter what," John said gently. "As far as your safety goes, you've got to trust the Lord, don't you?"

"Yes, Dr. Kryer," David said after a short pause, "that's exactly what we have to do."

"And can you help your son to trust God for your safety?"

"I don't know. But I will try."

"You know, David, it is at times like this when a person's faith is revealed. Either God works in our day-to-day lives or He doesn't. If our religion is only theoretical, it doesn't mean much, but if it is true, it will touch every part of our lives. If God *is* God, then He is as practical in the jail cell and courtroom as He is in the church."

FAITH AND THE
WORLD AROUND US

8

Why Faith Is Needed in Education, Philosophy, and Religion

I WAS INVITED TO SPEAK for the Student Forum at a world-renowned Bible institute about the subject of why Christians can't trust psychology.[41] I shared my conviction that God has provided everything the believer needs for mental and emotional health through the knowledge of Jesus Christ (*see* 2 Peter 1:3) and found the students to be generally receptive to my arguments. Some of the professors, however, sat sullenly in the back of the room. At one point I remarked, "When I was a student here some twenty-five years ago, I never dreamed I would some-day stand here, defending the sufficiency of the Bible, and be viewed as a radical."

I am still a bit amazed that some within the administration and faculty of the school not only resist the doctrine of biblical sufficiency, but are openly antagonistic to it, believing that psychological training is necessary to minister to wounded hearts in our "dysfunctional" age. I am convinced that the schools' founder would weep. Even so, I am equally convinced that there are many sincere Christian leaders and instructors at the school who still cling stubbornly to biblical truth.

I do not point out the problems at this flagship institution with anger or bitterness, but with sadness and love. This historic Bible institute has sent thousands of pastors, missionaries, and evangelists throughout the world who have led countless souls to Jesus Christ. I have listened to impassioned sermons by its leadership, calling Christians to holiness and commitment, and I commend the messages of racial harmony and social involvement. Yet when it comes to the personal application of the Scriptures to individual problems of living, there is growing doubt about the power of God to transform lives without the aid of psychological therapies.

EDUCATIONAL ATHEISM

This problem is not limited to one famous Bible institute, however. I have spoken with pastors, elders, lay people, seminary and college presidents and professors across the nation who have reported similar problems in virtually every denomination in the American church.

A licensed psychologist in Georgia called my office after hearing our radio broadcast and told me his tragic story. "I have practiced psychotherapy now for several years," he told me, "and have come to the conclusion that it does not work. I now believe that true inner healing is available only through the truths of the Scriptures. Here's my problem: though I spent 12 years studying in Southern Baptist institutions, I have absolutely no idea how to use the Bible to help people find healing in their lives." When he asked me for information about instruction in genuine biblical counseling, I told him that formal counselor training is not required, but a thorough knowledge of the Bible is. In order to warn others, he agreed to be a guest on our radio broadcast[42] and encourage people to find answers to problems of living in the Word of God.

Having served as a Southern Baptist minister years ago, I was grieved to hear the psychologist's report. Many Southern Baptists have welcomed psychology into their churches with open arms. In a highly-successful marketing concept, *Rapha* counseling centers have sprung up in thousands of churches across the country, teaching psychological heresies to unsuspecting parishioners who are referred by their pastors.

You might assume that pentecostal Christians who claim to believe in the power of the Holy Spirit would not be seduced by psychological doctrines which depreciate the Counselor from heaven. But that's not the case. I discovered this when I was in Springfield, Missouri, recording some television interviews with Assembly of God minister Tom Rutherford, his wife Joyce, and their three daughters.[43] Tom's oldest daughter, Beth, had been led into false memories of childhood sexual abuse by a therapist— her pastor's wife—a counselor highly regarded by the national leadership of the Assembly of God churches. Beth accused her father of impregnating her and forcing her to abort the babies with the full knowledge and complicity of her mother, Joyce.

Tom was soon fired from his job at the national headquarters of the Assemblies of God on the basis of the unsubstantiated accusations by Beth's therapist. Tom was reduced to odd jobs and janitorial labor to survive.

After two horrible pain-filled years, Beth realized that none of the events she had "remembered" had ever taken place. A subsequent investigation revealed that Beth was still a virgin and that Tom had undergone a vasectomy when Beth was only 4 years old.

The therapist's insurance company settled for $1 million and Tom was rehired by the Assemblies of God, though denominational officials still doubt his innocence and the therapist still insists that Tom is guilty.

While I was there in Springfield, I was invited to speak to the students in the counseling class at the Assembly of God seminary. I shared my philosophy of biblical counseling and led the class through a quick survey of Scriptures dealing with the sufficiency of the Word of God. The professor was cordial and polite, but as the class drew to a close, he remarked that my position was "extreme."

I asked, "What's extreme about believing that God's Word provides everything we need for life and godliness, as it says in 2 Peter 1:3? Either the Bible is true or it isn't. Either it is sufficient or it's not." I then asked the professor my standard question, "If psychology is essential for the healing of the inner man, what did the saints of God do from the time of Jesus until the time of Freud?"

He responded, "Well, I guess they just got along." Ironically, a few years before, I had debated another Assembly of God psychologist and had asked him the same question. His reply had been, "I guess they just hurt a lot!" I am continually amazed at the professional arrogance these statements reveal. The saints of God just *hurt a lot* or they just *got along*? Doesn't it seem strange to you that there was not a hint in these statements that God's people in earlier generations may have experienced victorious joy through faith and obedience to God's Word? And isn't it equally revealing that with an ever-growing supply of Christian therapists, modern-day believers are becoming more and more "dysfunctional"?

As I sat in my motel room in Springfield, I spoke by phone with a former professor from Central Bible College, an Assembly of God institution. In great sorrow, she told me that "psychology has taken over the Assembly of God."[44]

I'm not sure I will ever fully comprehend how a denomination which claims to preach Holy Spirit revival and power has lost confidence in His ability to comfort and counsel those with "disorders" and "dysfunctions" as they turn to His Word.

In all fairness, however, this same problem is repeated across the nation regardless of denominational affiliation. I sat in the Florida office of a national television personality who asked me, "You know that I'm a clinical psychologist, don't you?" I admitted that I was aware of his background. He then said with sadness, "I used to teach psychology at a seminary in Maine. We taught the students how to counsel, but we never taught them how to open God's Word. Your message of biblical sufficiency *must* go out across the nation!" He has dedicated his life to opening the simple truths of the Bible to all who will hear.

I could relate story after story of conversations with people from Nazarene, Presbyterian, Evangelical Free, Conservative Baptist, Baptist General Conference, Lutheran, Catholic—churches of all denominations and traditions—who testify that psychology has infiltrated and weakened their denominations.

Students from Southwestern Seminary, Trinity Divinity School, Columbia International University, Wheaton College, Fuller Seminary, Biola, Moody Bible Institute, Colorado Christian University, Denver Seminary, Dallas Seminary, Bob Jones University, Liberty University, Taylor, Cedarville—and on and on—report that their schools are thoroughly committed to psychological philosophies and doctrines.

PHILOSOPHICAL INTIMIDATION

What has happened to the schools that once held forth the Scriptures with confidence and appropriate pride in God's power? How is it that they have more certainty in the unbiblical and unscientific therapies of the world than they have in the simple truths of the Word of God? The problem is intellectual intimidation and accommodation.

A pastor in Connecticut called me with an urgent request for help. He told me that a professor of psychology from a major ivy-league university had begun attending his church and had come to him for counseling, saying that "psychology has no power to transform lives."

"I have to admit," this dear pastor said, "his scholastic credentials intimidate me."

"But you have the Bible," I reminded him. "You have no reason to be intimidated." He received the encouragement gladly and determined to minister to his hurting parishioner from the only source that really does have the power to transform lives—the living Word of God.

In 1 Corinthians 1:17, Paul wrote that Christ sent him "to preach the gospel—not with words of human wisdom, lest the cross of Christ be emptied of its power." You see, whenever we try to integrate the questionable and transient "findings" of psychological "research" with the eternal truths of God's Word, we empty the gospel of its power.

The administrations and faculties of Christian educational institutions, however, are terrified that they might be viewed with contempt by their secular peers if they hold to the simplicity of the Scriptures. They are unable to say with conviction, "I am not ashamed of the gospel, because it is the power of God for the salvation of everyone who believes" (Romans 1:16), because in truth, they *are* ashamed of the gospel.

Paul wrote:

> The message of the cross is foolishness to those who are perishing, but to us who are being saved it is the power of God. For it is written: "I will destroy the wisdom of the wise; the intelligence of the intelligent I will frustrate."
>
> Where is the wise man? Where is the scholar? Where is the philosopher of this age? Has not God made foolish the wisdom of the world? For since in the wisdom of God the world through its wisdom did not know him, God was pleased through the foolishness of what was preached to save those who believe. Jews demand miraculous signs and Greeks look for wisdom, but we preach Christ crucified: a stumbling block to Jews and foolishness to Gentiles, but to those whom God has called, both Jews and Greeks, Christ the power of God and the wisdom of God. For the foolishness of God is wiser than man's wisdom, and the weakness of God is stronger than man's strength.
>
> Brothers, think of what you were when you were called. Not many of you were wise by human standards; not many were influential; not many were of noble birth. But God chose the foolish things of the world to shame the wise; God chose the weak things of the world to shame the strong. He chose the lowly things of this world and the despised things—and the things that are not—to nullify the things that are, so that no one may boast before him. It is because of him that you are in Christ Jesus, who has become for us wisdom from God—that is, our righteousness, holiness

and redemption. Therefore, as it is written: "Let him who boasts boast in the Lord" (1 Corinthians 1:18-31).

Regardless of how cleverly it is packaged or labeled, those who believe that we must drink from the polluted cisterns of psychology in order to achieve spiritual wholeness have accommodated their system of faith to the philosophies of the world.

That is precisely what Paul was warning against in Colossians 2:8, when he writes, "See to it that no one takes you captive through hollow and deceptive philosophy, which depends on human tradition and the basic principles of this world rather than on Christ."

In the passage leading up to this warning, Paul says that it is in Christ we may find "all the treasures of wisdom and knowledge" (Colossians 2:3). To emphasize the point, he says, "I tell you this so that no one may deceive you by fine-sounding arguments" (Colossians 2:4).

We can pay lip service to the sufficiency of Scripture, but if we believe it is necessary to integrate psychological principles into our counseling to produce inner healing, we are denying the power of the Word to produce sanctification. And when Christian scholars imply that the Bible is sufficient for salvation but not for sanctification or spiritual growth, they are sadly mistaken.

Paul wrote, "Just as you received Christ Jesus as Lord, continue to live in him, rooted and built up in him, strengthened in the faith as you were taught, and overflowing with thankfulness" (Colossians 2:6-7). The point is, the same Lord who promises eternal life through our trust in Christ also provides the power to live a joy-filled holy life in this evil and dysfunctional world on that *very same basis*—faith in our Lord Jesus!

RELIGIOUS IMPOVERISHMENT

Since a growing number of Christian institutes, colleges, universities, and seminaries have lost their confidence in the Scriptures, it is little wonder that many of the pastors they graduate have a weakened view of biblical sufficiency as well. Now, instead of finding peace of heart and mind through discipleship and careful instruction in the Word, modern-day church members are being directed into twelve-step group therapy sessions with the staff psychologist.

Call it what you will—we are seeing an ever-growing wave of practical atheism in the evangelical church. This is true even in many conservative "fundamentalist" groups who pride themselves on their doctrinal distinctives of short hair and dark suits with red ties.

Desperately hurting people come to church, hoping to find healing through God's gentle touch, only to be told that their problems are unique, profoundly serious, and beyond spiritual solution. As a television pastor recently said on the air, "If you come to us with a deep inner need, all we can do is pray. But we can refer you to a psychological professional who can give you real solutions for your problems."

Mission boards now routinely screen their applicants using psychological tests to see if they are fit for missionary service. Religious leaders in third-world countries flock to America to receive psychological training, believing it provides the healing people so desperately seek and which, they are told, the Bible lacks.

What has happened to Christianity? As one secular psychologist has warned, Christians have sold their spiritual birthright for a mess of psychological pottage. Though we still mouth words of faith, few really believe God can deliver wounded hearts from the pains and dysfunctions of their troubled lives. We have become practical atheists of the worst kind. And with unbelief comes deep confusion about the circumstances and problems of living in a cursed world.

Like Gideon, God's people are distressed about their condition, and they ask the same question he did: "If the LORD is with us, why has all this happened to us? Where are all his wonders that our fathers told us about?" (Judges 6:13). In other words, where *is* God, anyway? They do not realize that it is their own unbelief that has cut them off from the fellowship and healing power of God.

Our therapeutically anesthetized churches have produced people who are described in Ezekiel 33:31-32: "With their mouths they express devotion, but their hearts are greedy for unjust gain. Indeed, to them you are nothing more than one who sings love songs with a beautiful voice and plays an instrument well, for they hear your words but do not put them into practice." I do not say this angrily, but with deep sorrow for the weakened condition of our modern-day church.

You may believe that the position of biblical sufficiency is simplistic and extreme, but I appeal to you to consider Jesus' question in Luke 6:46: "Why do you call me, 'Lord, Lord,' and do not do what I say?" If we truly believe that Jesus can transform mortal humans into immortal beings who will live forever with Him in heaven, why can't we believe that He is also able to provide complete inner peace and wholeness in this life? Why don't we act like it? Why don't we do what He says?

Paul writes to Titus that there are many who "claim to know God, but by their actions they deny him. They are detestable, disobedient and unfit for doing anything good" (Titus 1:16). As a result, unbelievers have every right to ask us, "How big is your God?"

Instead of enjoying the riches of our spiritual inheritance (Colossians 1:12), we are living in a day of spiritual poverty. While megachurches proclaim that we are in the midst of a national revival, the truth is, there is a famine in the land, "not a famine of food or a thirst for water, but a famine of hearing the words of the LORD" (Amos 8:11).

The situation is serious, dear friend, but not yet hopeless. There is a ground swell of reaction to intellectual, philosophical, and religious atheism as many Christians around the world are beginning to reclaim their birthright. Don't despair. We are going to look at some strategies for rebuilding our faith in the chapters ahead, so stay with me.

The Debate

Dr. Arthur Wilson had looked forward to this day for months. Ever since Susan left him, he had had a burning desire to prove that her belief in God was superstitious nonsense. Now he finally had that chance in a debate with a creationist about the facts of evolution.

He was uncomfortable that Dr. Arnold had changed the topic for the debate to "Resolved: Evolution Is a Religion and Not a Science," and even more so because his research had raised some uncomfortable questions in his own mind. He had amassed a huge file of scientific articles that discussed the theories of origins, and some of the statements troubled him.

One old chemical journal said, "Scientific theories can be useful devices . . . to help order our thinking [and to] measure and evaluate apparent reality. . . . But let's not forget that they are indeed just theories. . . . Completely captive to your theories, you cannot be open minded . . . ."[45]

Arthur flattered himself that he was completely objective as a scientist, but in his more honest moments, he knew he was as biased as those he criticized. The fact was, he had consciously ignored certain data that appeared to contradict evolutionary theory by clinging to assumptions he knew could not be proved but which fit his desired conclusions.

He was particularly disturbed by a book called *Darwin's Black Box*, written by Michael J. Behe,[46] and it galled Arthur to realize that much of Behe's research had been funded by the National Institutes of Health. Behe's work seemed almost treasonous. Arthur only hoped that Dr. Arnold, his debate opponent, had not stumbled across the volume.

He was more nervous than he thought he would be and a bit disgusted with himself for worrying about a debate with a creationist—an old man at that!

A good offense is the best defense, he thought to himself. *I'll just show how contradictory the Bible is and how unscientific the creationist position is. Old Dr. Arnold will be so confused and defensive, he'll forget evolution altogether!*

Arthur phoned Michael Rollins to make arrangements to pick him up for the debate. In all honesty, Arthur had mixed emotions about bringing Michael, who considered himself both a scientist and a Christian. Still, he had invited Michael, and to back out now would surely reveal the cowardice he was beginning to feel.

"I'll pick you up at 6:00 o'clock at the Smithsonian, if that's okay with you," he told Rollins. "The debate is just a few blocks away at the Hilton."

"That will be fine, Arthur," Michael said. "I have some sorting to do. Call me when you're about five minutes away and I'll meet you curbside in front of the main building."

Precisely at 6:00, Arthur pulled to the curb in front of the Natural History museum of the Smithsonian and picked up Michael Rollins.

"Arthur!" Michael said cheerfully, "I'm looking forward to this!"

Arthur was not as enthusiastic. He mumbled, "Why is that?"

"Because I want to see whether or not you can be scientifically accurate while trying to defend evolution. I've never seen it done."

"And I suppose your creationist friends maintain a truly scientific stance when debating origins?" Arthur said somewhat defensively.

"I can't say all of them have, quite frankly, and I've been disappointed in them. I hope this Dr. Arnold won't let me down."

"We'll see," Arthur said as he signaled and switched lanes, and that ended the conversation until they arrived at the hotel.

They parked the car and Arthur got his briefcase out from the trunk and they went inside. A sign in the main lobby pointed them to the banquet room where the debate would take place. It had Arthur's photo facing off against a picture of Dr. Benjamin Arnold. It was headlined, "Is Evolution a Religion?"

As they walked into the room, a voiced called out, "Arthur! You had me worried!" It was Lawrence Eisley, the program chairman, and he looked a bit irritated. "Come on, it's time to start!"

"Good grief, Lawrence!" Arthur replied, "Why are you worried? I got here right when I said I would." He turned to Michael and said, "I've got to talk with Lawrence a few minutes, Michael. Do you mind?"

"Not a bit, Arthur. Take your time."

Michael was surprised to see the number of people who had come to support the American Humanists organization at the fund-raising banquet. Across the large room he spotted several friends and co-workers as they chatted in small groups.

Off to one side at the front of the room an elderly man with thinning white hair was seated at a table by himself, reading some notes. From the picture on the sign in the lobby, Michael recognized Dr. Arnold. He wanted to go introduce himself, but was concerned that Arthur might see them and think he was coaching Dr. Arnold for the debate. Still, he was determined to talk with him before the evening was over.

Soon, Lawrence Eisley stood at the podium and announced that dinner was about to be served and everyone should find their places, which were marked with name cards. Michael saw Arthur walking toward him and was delighted when he said, "Michael, that's our table up at the front. We're eating with Dr. Arnold."

"Wonderful!" Michael replied. "I'm anxious to meet him."

Lawrence met them at the table and introduced them all around. Smiling at Dr. Arnold, he said, "You'll be pleased, no doubt, to know you are not the only creationist at this gathering."

"Really?" Dr. Arnold replied, "and who else has the courage to admit such heresy among these world-renowned scientists?"

"I think he means me, Dr. Arnold," Michael laughed as he shook hands with the old man.

"And you are . . . ?"

"I'm Michael Rollins, an archaeologist with the Smithsonian."

Dr. Arnold raised his eyebrows in surprise. "Well, I am pleased to meet you Mr. Rollins. Indeed, I do not feel quite so alone as I did just a few moments ago."

Lawrence Eisley laughed nervously and said, "Have you met your opponent yet, Dr. Arnold? This is Dr. Arthur Wilson."

"No, I don't think I've had that pleasure," Dr. Arnold said with a twinkle in his eyes.

Arthur shook hands with Dr. Arnold and was a bit disappointed to find the old man's grip firm and warm.

"Actually, we have met before, Dr. Arnold," Arthur said.

"Really? I rarely forget someone so distinguished as yourself. When did we meet?"

"Well, I'm not surprised you don't remember," Arthur said with a half-smile. "It was nearly thirty years ago when you lectured in my little home town of Winfield. Do you remember? You were speaking in the Baptist church."

Dr. Arnold thought for a moment. "Winfield. Of course! Pastor Jim Stewart invited me to speak, as I recall. And you say you were there?"

"Well, yes. In fact, I challenged you about some of your statements following a lecture."

Dr. Arnold nodded as he cocked his head a bit to one side as though suddenly remembering something. "Even then we were debating, eh, Dr. Wilson? How ironic! And tonight, we meet again. I hope this time you won't walk out on me before you've heard my full argument."

Arthur's mouth opened slightly in surprise. "I . . . uh . . . I won't," he stammered as his face flushed red. He felt like a little child being scolded for misbehavior. Inside, Arthur was seething at himself. He realized he had underestimated his opponent and was suddenly on the defensive before the debate ever began.

To Arthur's immense relief, Dr. Arnold turned to Lawrence Eisley and engaged him in conversation. Arthur suddenly found himself without an appetite. Visions of humiliation swept over him as he imagined himself on the platform, stammering ridiculous answers to Dr. Arnold's challenges. He felt as uncertain as he had thirty years before in the little Baptist church in Winfield. He tried to calm himself and mentally organize his arguments as he took a drink of water.

Michael noticed that Arthur's hand was trembling as he raised the glass to his mouth. "Are you all right, Arthur?" he whispered.

"Yes! I'm fine!" Arthur snapped back in a whisper. Now he looked a bit pale. He stood to his feet, looked at Lawrence Eisley, and said, "I need some air. I'll be back in a few minutes."

"Well, don't be gone long, Arthur. The debate begins in about twenty minutes."

Arthur nodded. "I'll be back."

"Do you want me to go with you?" Michael offered.

"No, Michael," Arthur said tightly. "I just need some air. It's really stuffy in here." He turned and walked out the nearest door and into the hallway.

Dr. Arnold turned to Michael. "Arthur seems a bit uptight, doesn't he? Bless his heart, he doesn't know what he's in for tonight."

Now it was Lawrence Eisley who looked troubled. "What do you mean by that?"

"Oh, nothing," Dr. Arnold replied with a soft smile. "It's just that when you have no evidence it is very hard to prove something scientifically."

Eisley shook his head in disgust at the old man's cocky ignorance and hurried out the door after Arthur. He looked to the left and down the hall just in time to see Arthur entering the men's room. He walked quickly to the rest room and found Arthur at the sink, washing his face in cold water.

"What is *wrong* with you?" he demanded.

Arthur looked up at him, in exhaustion. "It's like a time warp, Lawrence! Talking with Dr. Arnold made me feel like I was back in eleventh grade. I just needed to clear my head for a moment. I'll be fine."

"Are you sure?"

"I said I'll be fine, Lawrence! Okay?"

Lawrence stepped back, startled by Arthur's flash of anger. "Hey, don't yell at me, Arthur. You told me you could take Dr. Arnold, no problem. Remember? So get your act together and quick! You don't want to look like a fool and let Dr. Arnold get the best of you."

Arthur sighed deeply and nodded. "You're right, Lawrence. I'm sorry I flared. Just give me a few minutes. I'll be fine. Really I will."

"For your sake, I hope so!" Eisley said as he left the room.

Arthur sat down on a padded bench under a large mirror. He closed his eyes, trying to mentally calm himself. *Picture yourself speaking with confidence!* he thought to himself. *Most of the people in that room are on your side. Dr. Arnold is an old man. Just get him a bit confused and you've got him. Remember the contradictions in the Bible.*

Still, his heart beat rapidly from nervousness and he found himself—for just a moment—praying for help. *Oh God, help me not to make a fool of myself out there!* Then he realized what he was doing and he stood to his feet and laughed out loud.

The humor of the moment seemed to break the spell of gloom which had descended over Arthur. He took a deep breath, squared his shoulders, and walked back down the hallway to the banquet room. He felt his confidence growing with each step and he was ready—no! he was anxious—to get the debate underway.

. . .

The stage was now set with three podiums—one for the moderator and two for the debaters. Lawrence Eisley went to his podium to introduce the speakers. "I almost feel as though we are in Madison Square Garden tonight, ladies and gentlemen," he said with a gesture toward the speakers' podiums. "I should probably introduce our guests by saying, 'And in this corner . . .'" The crowd joined him in laughter.

"But seriously," he continued as the crowd quieted, "we have the opportunity tonight to examine a question that has divided entire communities. We thought the issue had been settled after the Scopes Trial, but to the dismay of many, the argument between scientists and creationists continues to this very day.

"We are fortunate to have with us tonight two men exceptionally qualified to discuss the issue of creation versus evolution. Dr. Arthur Wilson, a medical scientist studying genetics as it relates to cancer, is a highly-respected researcher at the National Cancer Institute. His profound understanding of the complexity of cell structure gives him a unique platform from which to discuss the chemistry of life, and we are honored to have him as an esteemed member of the American Humanists organization. Please welcome Dr. Arthur Wilson as he comes to the platform."

The crowd broke into enthusiastic applause as Arthur strode to his podium and nodded his greeting.

Eisley continued, "And to speak for the creationist side, we have invited Dr. Benjamin Arnold, a biologist who has written numerous articles on the impossibility of macro-evolution and has lectured on the subject from coast to coast. Please welcome Dr. Arnold."

The audience politely applauded as Dr. Arnold walked to the platform and took his place behind his podium. Though he was in his late seventies, his step was steady and he carried himself with dignity and confidence.

Both men sat in the chairs behind their podiums as Eisley explained the format. "Our topic for debate is unusual, for it seems to put evolution on the defensive. It is entitled, 'Resolved: Evolution Is a Religion and Not a Science.' While this may seem to be an absurd statement, in the honored tradition of the American Humanists, we are willing to examine it honestly and openly. Our only interest is truth, wherever it may be found, for as many believers are fond of saying, 'All truth is God's truth.'"

The crowd laughed at the irony of the statement.

"Since the topic itself is an attack on evolutionary fact, we will ask Dr. Arnold to begin the discussion. Rather than follow a stiff format of statement and response, we plan to allow for a genuine exchange of ideas, with both men standing at their podiums. As moderator, my main function will be to guarantee equal time to both individuals. I'm sure, considering the sophistication, integrity, and breeding of this audience, I will not need to ask you to be polite. We will not permit booing, hissing, or other infantile responses."

The audience applauded the civility of the ground rules.

"With that," Eisley said, "let us begin."

Dr. Arnold and Dr. Wilson rose and took their positions. "It is my intent," said Dr. Arnold, "to demonstrate to any open mind the truth of the statement that evolution is a religion and not a science. I do not say this with anger toward genuine science, for I have the greatest respect for scientific method and the scientists who employ it. I share your enthusiasm for scientific research and for rigorous standards of investigation. That is why I find it curious that in the foundational question of origins many lay aside scientific method for religious faith without examining the evidences. First, however, let me acknowledge that my position of creationism *is* built on faith."

There was a stir in the audience and a few snickers of delight at Dr. Arnold's admission.

"Wait," he said firmly, "before you double up in laughter, let me remind you that evolutionism is built on a system of assumptions that require an even greater leap of faith than does creationism. The only difference is, creationists are willing to admit their faith, while evolutionists deny theirs with an intellectual arrogance that borders on dishonesty. As the great evolutionist Sir Arthur Keith admitted, 'Evolution is unproved and unprovable. We believe it because the only alternative is special creation, and that is unthinkable.'

"Aldous Huxley, grandson of the famous evolutionist Thomas Huxley, explains in his book *Confessions of a Professed Atheist* why belief in a Creator is so unthinkable: 'I had motives for not wanting the world to have meaning . . . . For myself . . . the philosophy of meaninglessness was essentially an instrument of liberation . . . from a certain system of morality. We objected to morality because it interfered with our sexual freedom.'"

Dr. Arnold paused and looked up at the crowd with a twinkle in his eye. "Huxley's reasons for denying the possibility of a creator had nothing to do with scientific objectivity, did they?"

The audience stirred uncomfortably under Dr. Arnold's confident and penetrating gaze. "The problem is this, folks. When we remove the disciplines of scientific method from our consideration of origins, we fall into incredible foolishness. Take for instance George Wald, who was professor of biology at Harvard University. He admitted in *Scientific American* that 'the only alternative to some form of spontaneous generation is a belief in a supernatural creation.' Yet, he confesses that 'the spontaneous generation of a living organism is impossible.' Nonetheless, Wald says, 'Here we are—as a result, I believe, of spontaneous generation.'

"According to Wald, spontaneous generation is the only alternative to believing in supernatural creation, yet he says that since most modern biologists are unwilling to accept such a possibility, they are left with nothing. It's kind of embarrassing, isn't it?"

Nodding toward Arthur, Dr. Arnold said, "I am thankful that my esteemed opponent is an expert in molecular mechanisms, for it is at that very level that evolutionism begins to fall apart."

He turned to Lawrence Eisley and said, "That sets the stage for my side of the discussion, Mr. Moderator."

Eisley nodded. "Thank you, Dr. Arnold. That was succinct and to the point. Were you able to teach our politicians your style, our country would owe you a great debt of gratitude."

The audience laughed and applauded.

"And now, Dr. Wilson, your response."

Arthur had been writing notes as Dr. Arnold made his opening remarks. Now he began. "Dr. Arnold is my senior by many years, and with respect due to my elders, I must say that I disagree with his view that evolution is a religion. This, of course, was settled following the Scopes Trial, as Mr. Eisley mentioned earlier. The courts have ruled again and again that creationism is a religious point of view while evolution is scientific. Creationists are determined to impose their narrow religious view upon our public school system even though it is devoid of all scientific content.

"Tonight, in this debate, I will prove to you that the Bible is not only unscientific, but that it is full of contradictions that undermine its claim to accuracy."

He looked to Lawrence Eisley to indicate that his opening remarks were finished.

"My, gentlemen!" Eisley said with a huge smile, "both of you are keeping your statements to digestible size, and for that we all thank you."

Again, the audience applauded.

"Now, gentlemen, I invite you to parry and joust at will. I will interfere only if one or the other begins to dominate and refuses to allow the other to reply. Fair enough?"

Both men nodded their agreement.

Dr. Arnold began. "Dr. Wilson, am I correct in understanding that this debate is about whether evolution is a religion or a science?"

"Yes, of course," Arthur replied.

"Then, how is it that you have introduced the topic of the Bible? You will notice that I do not have one with me, yet I see a Bible on your podium. I have come to discuss science, not the Bible. I will not quote a single verse in this entire discussion. Since I have already admitted that my view is based on faith, I have nothing to defend. The question tonight is not whether the Bible is accurate, but whether evolution is a religious faith and a scientific pretender."

Dr. Arthur Wilson stood at his podium, his eyes fixed on his useless notes, his mouth dry. He suddenly realized that he had spent months preparing for the wrong topic. A sense of rage grew in his heart and his eyes were hard as he glared at Dr. Arnold, who looked back with calm serenity.

"That's unfair, Dr. Arnold, and you know it!" he finally sputtered.

Dr. Arnold looked at the moderator and then at the crowd. "But that is what we agreed to debate, is it not?"

Lawrence Eisley did not reply at first. He looked at the crowd and saw that several were nodding their heads in agreement with Dr. Arnold. Eisley finally said, "As I understand the topic, Dr. Wilson, it appears that Dr. Arnold has a point. Knowing your depth of knowledge on this subject, however, I am confident that you can address the issue adequately."

Arthur sighed deeply and nodded in agreement. "I am more than willing to discuss the issue of evolutionary science, but I do want to point out what the Bible says about the origin of life."

Dr. Arnold smiled and replied, "That is certainly an interesting subject and one which we all could benefit from, I'm sure, Dr. Wilson, but tonight it has no bearing on our topic. It simply doesn't matter what the Bible says about the origin of life. That proves nothing scientifically about evolution, and I find it ironic that as an evolutionist, you continue to introduce the Bible, while I, a creationist, must insist that we leave the Bible out of the discussion altogether. I have already conceded that creationism is based on faith. It is you who must show that evolution is scientific—something I contend will be impossible for you to accomplish. Nonetheless, I await your attempt."

There was an awkward pause as Arthur Wilson tried to formulate an apologetic for evolution. Suddenly he understood why evolutionists routinely refuse to debate this issue with creationists, but it was too late for him to back out.

"Since you have removed the Bible from our discussion, I . . . I hardly know where to begin," Arthur said lamely.

"May I suggest," said Dr. Arnold, "that we start at the most logical point—the beginning of life itself. Perhaps I can lead our discussion by asking you some questions. First, Dr. Wilson, since evolutionism states that all matter and energy are the result of natural processes, let me ask you, where did life itself come from?"

Arthur breathed a sigh of relief. Here was an area he was intimately familiar with. "Modern science," he said, "has determined that—no matter how you define it—life is a molecular phenomenon. Biochemistry has identified the molecular basis for life itself and research has pushed forward our understanding of just how the chemistry of life actually works."

"Is life merely a molecular phenomenon, the end result of billions of years of random chemical reactions?" Dr. Arnold asked.

"I believe that has been demonstrated again and again," Arthur replied.

"Really? It has certainly been theorized again and again, but it has never been demonstrated. Never yet—not even once—has a scientist, under the most carefully controlled environment, been able to create the most simple form of life, even when combining carefully measured chemicals and applying an external energy source. Am I right?"

"No, you are not right!" Arthur snapped. "Even you must know of Stanley Lloyd Miller's experiments, in which amino acids were formed from a chemical solution to which an electrical charge was applied."

"I know the intimate details of Harold Urey and Stanley Miller's work, Dr. Wilson, and I wish we had time to discuss them. As you recall, in the experiment that Miller conducted in 1953, he attempted to replicate the conditions that might—and I emphasize the word *might*—have been present in the primordial Earth, because no one actually knows. As you no doubt recall, he mixed hydrogen, water, methane, and ammonia in a flask, and subjected this primordial soup to an electrical charge for a full week. Miller declared that the procedure had produced significant amounts of organic compounds like hydroxy acids, urea, aliphatic acids, and eight of the twenty amino acids which occur in nature."

Leaning his elbow on the podium, Dr. Arnold looked at Arthur with a smile. "May I ask you, Dr. Wilson, as a biochemist, a medical doctor, and a genetic researcher, do you confuse a few amino acids with life itself?"

"Of course not, but amino acids are the building blocks of life."

"So, I would assume, if you saw a pile of bricks, you would call them a completed house?"

Arthur sighed with deepening frustration. "No, I'm simply stating that we have demonstrated how the essential chemicals came into being through natural processes."

"I see," Dr. Arnold said, clearly enjoying himself. "Assuming that to be true—which in and of itself is a step of faith—I must ask you a question: Where did the original chemicals for that primordial soup on earth come from?"

"Well, it must be obvious that they condensed from the huge ball of gases that formed our earth," Arthur stated with the uncomfortable feeling that he was being backed into a corner.

"And where, Dr. Wilson, did the assumed ball of gas come from?"

"It came from the same place all of the stars, planets, and galaxies came from—the Big Bang."

"And where did this 'Big Bang' come from?"

"Of course, we all know that it came from an infinitely dense point of matter and energy that suddenly exploded into the universe."

"You were there when this happened?"

Some in the crowd shifted uncomfortably as a few snickered at the implication of Dr. Arnold's question.

Lawrence Eisley intervened. "Don't be ridiculous or condescending, Dr. Arnold. I must insist that you deal with scientific evidences, not philosophical nonsense."

"That is precisely what I am asking Dr. Wilson to adhere to—scientific evidence, yet he continues to introduce assumptions, guesses, and unprovable assertions. My point is, no one was there to observe this so-called 'Big Bang.' We can only look at the motion of universal matter and interpret the information. We cannot apply the scientific method to past events because they cannot be repeated or tested. Can you dispute that?"

Eisley remained silent.

"Let me continue my questioning, then," Dr. Arnold said as he turned back to Arthur Wilson. "Where did this assumed point of infinitely dense matter come from?"

Arthur Wilson sighed into the microphone as though to say, "Do I have to answer this stupid question?" but the crowd waited for his reply. He finally looked at Dr. Arnold and said, "It just always existed."

"Can you prove that statement scientifically?"

Arthur hesitated, for he knew the game was at checkmate. Finally he replied, "No, I can't prove it. I just believe it."

"Exactly!" Dr. Arnold said. "You just believe it. And you have every right to do so. Just don't call that science. It is not. What you have stated is faith. Your entire evolutionary doctrine is built upon a religious belief and I will tell you without hesitation that my understanding of reality, though it is also based on faith, has far more evidence which is supported by scientific method than does your evolutionary religion."

Arthur Wilson knew that he had lost the debate. No matter what evidence he might have suggested, the reality of evolutionary faith was no longer in question. The rest of the discussion became a blur of meaningless statistics and unrelated data.

When the ballots were passed out to the audience to see who had supported his argument more convincingly, there was little doubt as to the outcome. The ballots were counted as the audience stood to mingle and get their drinks from the bar.

Dr. Wilson and Dr. Arnold left the platform and returned to their table. Arthur tried to maintain his composure and made small talk with Michael Rollins as time slowly dragged by.

After a break of about fifteen minutes, Lawrence Eisley came to the podium and cleared his throat. "Uh, ladies and gentlemen, the vote is in. It is obvious that you were impressed with the sincere performance of Dr. Arnold, for you voted him the winner, 115 to 17.

"While even I am surprised at the margin, it must also be obvious to each of us that there is a visceral appeal to a religious understanding of the universe, while a mechanistic view seems a bit cold and clinical. Yet, continued scientific studies clearly show that evolution is the only rational way of making sense of our physical reality."

Nodding to the old creationist, Eisley concluded, "Dr. Arnold, while we disagree with your concept of creation, we appreciate your willingness to come and discuss the issue. Perhaps the next time, we will be wise enough to formulate the topic more carefully."

The audience laughed and applauded as Dr. Arnold stood to his feet and bowed.

Dr. Wilson joined in the applause, but even as he forced a smile, he had never known a deeper sense of humiliation than at that moment.

As he drove Michael Rollins back to the Smithsonian Institute, he was silent. Michael was wise enough not to force a conversation. When they pulled up to the curb, Michael turned to Arthur and said, "Thanks for inviting me, Arthur. I hope you won't let this get you down too much."

Arthur looked over at Michael with intense embarrassment. "I am ruined as a scientist, Michael. I will be the laughingstock of every serious researcher in the world. And do you know what's the worst of it?"

"No, Arthur," Michael said gently. "What?"

"The worst part is, I think Dr. Arnold actually convinced me tonight. As I stood there listening to him, I suddenly realized how ridiculous my beliefs are. I haven't been following genuine science at all. In my hatred for God, I pretended that I was an objective scientist, but actually, I was just an accomplished liar."

Michael Rollins smiled broadly, reached over and grabbed Arthur's arm and said, "Then what happened to you tonight is the best thing that could ever have taken place, Arthur!"

"But, don't you see, Michael? I'm done as a researcher. Some of my fellow scientists from NCI were there tonight. They saw what a fool I made of myself. This is the end for me!"

"No, Arthur," Michael said with deep conviction. "Tonight was just the beginning!"

9

Why Faith Is Needed in Science, Medicine, and Business

IN THE EVOLUTION-CREATION debate, Christians have been on the intellectual defensive for generations not because of hard scientific evidence that validates evolutionary theory, but because of an intense campaign of pseudoscientific propaganda jointly promulgated by an arrogant scientific community and a willing accomplice of the mass media.

The United States government has provided large financial grants to produce high school textbooks that are saturated with evolutionary doctrine.[47] The Time-Life organization has produced beautifully and imaginatively illustrated books on evolution that have influenced a credulous public to accept humanistic philosophy as hard science.

In 1959, Sir Julian Huxley addressed the Darwinian Centennial Convention at the University of Chicago, where he stated:

> In the evolutionary system of thought there is no longer need or room for the supernatural. The earth was not created; it evolved. So did all the animals and plants that inhabit it, including our human selves, mind and soul, as well as brain and body. So did religion.

Evolutionary man can no longer take refuge from his loneliness by creeping for shelter into the arms of a divinized father figure whom he himself has created.[48]

Huxley's overtly atheistic comments, which reek of unscientific dogma, represent the views of many who have uncritically accepted the pronouncements of science fiction writers such as Carl Sagan.

ACQUIESCING TO SCIENCE'S THEORIES

What is more disheartening, however, are not the arrogant assertions by secular humanists, but the attempts of professing Christians to accommodate the immutable Scriptures to the latest theories of science, which shift with each passing hour.

Dr. James Beck, dean of the counseling department at Denver Seminary, wrote an article in the *Journal of Psychology and Theology* entitled, "Christian Anti-Psychology Sentiment: Hints of a Historical Analogue," in which he compares the evolutionist-creationist controversy to the current division over psychology. He laments the fact that "the evolutional centrist position was taken over by those opposed to the harmonization of Christianity and evolution. Can the same thing happen to today's psychological centrist position?"[49]

He condescendingly states that "anti-evolutionists share with those in the anti-psychology movement a general distrust of science and an inability to distinguish benign scientific contributions from more antithetical findings."[50] He appears to find it shocking that "both groups have the deep conviction that science and religion must go hand in hand."[51]

Dr. Beck seems to feel it unfair that biblicists have "a decided advantage in taking their case to the general public: intuitive appeal. It makes a lot of sense to many people that God created the world in six literal days at the command of his voice. Scientists who are aware of other data have a more perplexing task. . . . Likewise, psychotherapy is a mysterious and somewhat baffling phenomenon in the eyes of the general public. The ideas of an unconscious or multipli-determined behavior makes less sense to a layperson than does the idea that God can help us with our problems as we pray and study the Bible."[52]

Accepting such arrogant pronouncements by the self-protecting intellectual establishment, many Christians have become "theistic evolutionists" who say they believe there is a God who created the universe, but He did so through evolutionary processes. They do not seem to understand that they have repudiated the first eleven chapters of Genesis as historic biblical truth and in so doing have eliminated the need of a Savior.

You see, dear reader, it all holds together or falls together. Either there was an actual first human called Adam whose sin plunged us all into the curse, or he was a mere metaphor of human deficiency. If Adam did not exist in time and space, then the fall of man into sin is nonsense and there is no universal need for a redeemer. Jesus' coming, His mission, His death, and His resurrection become meaningless except for sentimental symbolism.

In effect, then, theistic evolution is another name for practical atheism. Call it what you will, defend it however you may, theistic evolution presents a god of man's own imagination, not the omnipotent God of special revelation whose existence, character, plan, and power are revealed in the pages of Scripture.

The tragic result of "Christian evolutionism" is increasing doubt in the message, authority, and power of the Scriptures, which leads to spiritual despair. You see, if the Bible is wrong about creation, why should we have confidence that it is accurate regarding man's salvation? And because we doubt God's creative power, we begin to doubt His regenerative power as well.

Even though there is a built-in hunger to know and fellowship with God, many Christians have been led into a spiritual desert by Christian evolutionists. Study with me for a moment Psalm 42, for it relates powerfully to this problem. Read it slowly enough to meditate deeply about the truths God wants us to know and apply. I have left the verse numbers in the passage intentionally so we can examine the thoughts more easily.

> [1] As the deer pants for streams of water, so my soul pants for you, O God. [2] My soul thirsts for God, for the living God. When can I go and meet with God? [3] My tears have been my food day and night, while men say to me all day long, "Where is your God?" [4] These things I remember as I pour out my soul: how I used to go with the multitude, leading the procession to the house of God, with shouts of joy and thanksgiving among the festive throng. [5] Why are you downcast, O my soul? Why so disturbed within me? Put your hope in God, for I will yet praise him, my Savior and [6] my God. My soul is downcast within me; therefore I will remember you from the land of the Jordan, the heights of Hermon—from Mount Mizar. [7] Deep calls to deep in the roar of your waterfalls; all your waves and breakers have swept over me. [8] By day the LORD directs his love, at night his song is with me—a prayer to the God of my life. [9] I say to God my Rock, "Why have you forgotten me? Why must I go about mourning, oppressed by the enemy?" [10] My bones suffer mortal agony as my foes taunt me, saying to me all day long, "Where is your God?" [11] Why are you downcast, O my soul? Why so disturbed within me? Put your hope in God, for I will yet praise him, my Savior and my God.

Verses 1 and 2 powerfully describe the spiritual thirst so many are experiencing in this day of practical unbelief. The psalmist asks the question, "When can I go and meet with God?" Many heartsick Christians today are asking the same question of their pastors and churches. They long for a genuine touch of healing from the Master and to be fed from His Word, but instead are offered irrelevant and even irreverent music and drama programs, sessions of forced and unholy laughter, unbiblical mass babblings falsely described as tongues, and spiritual pabulum seasoned with an occasional verse of Scripture.

Crying out for help, the majority of God's people are offered therapy, twelve-step programs, support groups, psychoactive medication, and dream interpretation rather than biblical discipleship, prayer, and ministry. With this kind of spiritual diet, is it any wonder that so many starving Christians are "dysfunctional" and depressed?

David speaks for many when he asks, "Why are you downcast, O my soul? Why so disturbed within me?" (verse 5). The answer is, of course, that people who have lost confidence in the Scriptures and the power of God to deliver the disturbed from their "dysfunctions" have lost hope. As Jesus said, "You are in error because you do not know the Scriptures or the power of God" (Matthew 22:29).

The solution for deep spiritual depression is found in the psalmist's next phrase: "Put your hope in God, for I will yet praise him, my Savior and my God. My soul is downcast within me; therefore I will remember you" (verses 5-6). Of course, if you doubt the very existence of God, His power to create in an instant, or His ability to heal your inner being, you will have no one in whom to place your hope.

David describes this feeling of despair as the drowning sensation a person would experience when struggling for life, flailing exhausted at the foot of a powerful waterfall which sucks its victim back again and again into its dark vacuum of death (verse 7). It is the false sense of abandonment that cries out, "Why have you forgotten me? Why must I go about mourning, oppressed by the enemy?" (verse 9). In addition to intense spiritual suffering, there is genuine physical pain that accompanies such depression. "My bones suffer mortal agony," David writes (verse 10).

Even worse, when professing Christians exhibit such despair and hopelessness, unbelievers inevitably—and with some justification ask—"Where is your God?" (verse 10).

This question seems to jolt David back into reality and he counsels his own soul with these powerful words: "Why are you downcast, O my soul? Why so disturbed within me? Put your

hope in God, for I will yet praise him, my Savior and my God."
There is more healing in that phrase than in all the humanistic
psychological therapies in the world. *Put your hope in God.*

MEDICAL DOCTORS AND FAITH

In a surprising report published in *Parade* magazine, we are
told that medical doctors have begun to recognize the power of
prayer:

> In a recent survey of 269 doctors, a remarkable 99%
> said they were convinced that religious belief can heal. In
> fact, that's 20% higher than the figure for the general
> public.
>
> Why do doctors feel this way? "Because we've seen the
> power of belief," said Dr. Herbert Benson, author of
> *Timeless Healing*, which offers scientific evidence that
> faith has helped to cure medical conditions. "We've seen
> that belief is powerful in conditions including angina
> pectoris, asthma, duodenal ulcers, congestive heart fail-
> ure, diabetes, all forms of pain. We see it all the time, and
> we can't deny it."

According to the article, 75 percent of the doctors surveyed believe that a patient can heal more rapidly as others pray
for him.

> Physicians recognize the limitations of drugs and
> surgery, noted Dr. Benson, who added: "The real break-
> through is the acceptance of these approaches by mod-
> ern medicine."
>
> "We have scientific data showing that people who use
> self-help—relaxation, nutrition, exercise and belief—
> reduce their visits to doctors by 30% to 60%," said Benson.
> "In a prepaid system, that's money in the bank."[53]

Isn't it amazing that the world sees the value of faith at the
very time that Christians seem to be losing it? Paul writes,

"Though we live in the world, we do not wage war as the world does. The weapons we fight with are not the weapons of the world" (2 Corinthians 10:3-4). Nonetheless, Christians flock to psychological clinics and psychiatric hospitals to be chemically treated for their despondencies, depressions, and dysfunctions.

UNBELIEF IN THE
BUSINESS WORLD

Some believers have wondered if it is possible to live a consistent Christian life and to succeed in business at the same time. There is ample evidence in the lives of J.C. Penney, R.G. LeTourneau, and other successful business people to show that it is more than possible and that a consistent Christian testimony has rewards not only in eternity, but also provides a wonderful return on investment in this life.

Jesus makes an almost incredible promise in Matthew 6 when He tells us not to worry about accumulating possessions. "The pagans run after all these things, and your heavenly Father knows that you need them. But seek first his kingdom and his righteousness, and all these things will be given to you as well" (Matthew 6:32-33).

I have seen this promise fulfilled in the lives of countless believers. Though they did not set out to become wealthy, by following biblical business principles, they succeeded beyond their wildest dreams.

This was true in my own parents' lives. Dad and Mom served in the pastorate for some 30 years before Dad suffered a heart attack that forced him out of the ministry. They had never ministered in large churches and their salary had always been humble at best. Dad had inherited a little shack of a house in Grand Junction, Colorado, which he traded for an even seedier cottage in a Denver suburb that had been built out of old army surplus ammo boxes. He worked hard to repair it as well as he could and then rented it out.

With the small income and equity from the first building, he bought a second, and fixed it up and rented it out. He continued this pattern for several years and was amazed one day when he realized that his net worth was greater than he had imagined possible. The income from the rental units was more than he had ever received as a pastor, and to his and Mother's great delight, they were able to support missionaries and Christian organizations all over the world. They even put up their properties as security for the purchase of the land where our church now stands.

Though they lived modestly the rest of their lives, they were continually astonished at God's rich blessings upon their lives of simple faithfulness. A few years before he went to be with the Lord, Dad shook his head, almost in unbelief, and remarked to me as we sat in their beautiful home, "What am I doing, living in a place like this?" By the world's standards, they were never extremely wealthy, but for a couple who had gone through the depression and had scrimped their entire lives to save a few dollars, it was remarkable.

Note that we are not promised inordinate wealth in Matthew 6, but the things that we need. In fact, we are warned in the Scriptures about the perils of wealth. Paul wrote to Timothy,

> Godliness with contentment is great gain. For we brought nothing into the world, and we can take nothing out of it. But if we have food and clothing, we will be content with that. People who want to get rich fall into temptation and a trap and into many foolish and harmful desires that plunge men into ruin and destruction. For the love of money is a root of all kinds of evil. Some people, eager for money, have wandered from the faith and pierced themselves with many griefs. But you, man of God, flee from all this, and pursue righteousness, godliness, faith, love, endurance and gentleness (1 Timothy 6:6-11).

Verse 10, of course, is one of the most misquoted passages in the Bible. It is not *money* which is at the root of a great variety of evil, but the *love* of money. Money, in and of itself, is morally neutral. But the love of money is an incredibly cruel master.

It is a rare man who is not spoiled by wealth. In Proverbs, there is a remarkable prayer of wisdom that reflects this problem: "Give me neither poverty nor riches, but give me only my daily bread. Otherwise, I may have too much and disown you and say, 'Who is the LORD?' Or I may become poor and steal, and so dishonor the name of my God" (Proverbs 30:8-9).

A practical atheist will not believe Matthew 6:33. He will be tempted to cheat in business, but God's Word gives timeless principles for business success:

1. Hard work brings its own reward (Proverbs 10:4; 12:11; 13:4).

2. Honesty will bring recognition (Genesis 39:6; Deuteronomy 25:15; 2 Kings 12:15; Nehemiah 13:13; Proverbs 11:1; Daniel 6:4).

3. Faithfulness is a requirement for God's blessing (1 Corinthians 4:2).

4. Integrity is important for the sake of testimony (Romans 12:17; 2 Corinthians 8:21; 2 Corinthians 7:2).

5. Dishonest money will not endure (Proverbs 13:11).

6. Integrity is in a person's own best interest (Proverbs 11:3).

7. A righteous man will leave a great heritage for his children (Proverbs 20:7).

Business done in God's way will be rewarded, usually in this life as well as in eternity. But even if it were only in eternity, it would still be worth obeying God.

In science, medicine, and business, unbelief has had devastating results in our society. In our final chapter of laying out the problem, we will look at how practical atheism has affected essential elements of the church, with suggestions for how we can make changes that can restore faith and vitality to our local congregations. I'll see you on the other side of the story.

Breaking the Bondage

After her meeting with Ellen Rollins, Susan was more depressed than ever. She increased her dosage of Prozac, but it only seemed to fog her mind. Her guilt, however, loomed larger day by day. She found it difficult to concentrate at work and she wondered if Billy would fire her like he had so many others. *If he dares to get rid of me,* she thought, *I'll file a sexual harassment suit on him so quick it will make his head spin!*

Susan and Billy were not seeing each other as frequently now. At first, it was due to her migraine headaches and she had felt so foolish each time she had said, "Not tonight, Billy. I have a headache." But it was the truth.

To her dismay, Billy didn't seem too upset one afternoon when she said she wasn't feeling well enough to be with him that evening. "That's all right, Susan," he had said. "I have a client I need to take out. You just get some rest so you can work tomorrow."

Susan's anger had flared immediately. "So I can *work* tomorrow? That's why you want me to rest? So I'll be more productive at the office? Has my work been substandard, Billy?"

Billy's eyes grew wide with surprise as he eased back in his desk chair. "Why . . . no, Susan. I just meant that with your headaches, you need to get some rest, that's all." He tilted his head to the side as he looked at her quizzically. "What's the matter with you, Susan?"

"Nothing's the matter with me!" she snapped. "I'll be just fine if I can find some stronger medicine."

Billy had to go out of town on business for a couple of weeks, and Susan found herself strangely relieved that she didn't have to see him. Still, as she sat in her apartment that Saturday evening, a sense of loneliness swept over her and she began to cry. As she did, her headache began to pound again and a wave of nausea swept over her body.

"Oh, God," she wept, "where are You? Please help me. I don't know what to do!"

Inside, she sensed a quiet voice saying, *Open My Word, Susan.* Her heart resisted for a moment, but her anguish was so intense she got up, went to her dresser, and pulled open the top right-hand drawer. Inside was her Bible, where she had hidden it from view. She took it with her to the front room and sat on the couch.

She hesitated for a moment, then remembering Ellen Rollins's suggestion that she read 1 Corinthians, she flipped the pages to the middle of the New Testament and found the book Paul had written to a congregation that was very similar to a modern American church.

As she began to read, she sensed the presence of God and a calm came over her she had not felt in months. The Holy Spirit began to gently apply God's truth to her heart as pertinent phrases seemed to leap off the pages with living energy. "The message of the cross is foolishness to those who are perishing, but to us who are being saved it is the power of God," she read out loud as she nodded in agreement.

She read on and from time to time, she would pause and repeat a passage in an attempt to fully comprehend what God was saying. "God was pleased through the foolishness of what was preached to save those who believe. . . . We preach Christ crucified. . . . Christ the power of God and the wisdom of God. . . . Christ Jesus . . . our righteousness, holiness, and redemption."

Tears began to fill Susan's eyes and she dabbed them away with a tissue and kept on reading. "We . . . speak a message of wisdom among the mature. . . . God's secret wisdom. . . . God has revealed it to us by his Spirit." How she longed for God's wisdom to flood her heart! All her life she had known pain and betrayal, depression and despair. Now she sensed a flicker of hope as she moved from verse to verse.

"I gave you milk, not solid food, for . . . you are still worldly . . . there is jealousy and quarreling among you. . . . Are you not acting like mere men?" A stab of guilt pricked Susan and she felt an almost physical pain in her heart as she nodded in agreement. *Yes, Lord, I have been acting like everyone else in the world,* she thought.

"Don't you know that you yourselves are God's temple and that God's Spirit lives in you?" Susan sat up straight as she read the verse and then read it again. *I'm the temple of God? The Holy Spirit lives inside me? Then what I am doing is dishonoring Him!*

For a moment she realized she would have to break off her relationship with Billy Costas, but she stiffened as she thought, *It's Arthur's fault! If he had been even a little loving, I'd still be with him.*

She read on. "My conscience is clear, but that does not make me innocent. It is the Lord who judges me. . . . He will bring to light what is hidden in darkness and will expose the motives of men's hearts." Susan sat back and sighed deeply. *I guess I can't blame Arthur for my own sin,* she thought, and was surprised that with that admission she felt a lightness in her heart rather than the depression she expected.

"It is actually reported that there is sexual immorality among you." Again, Susan sighed as God's conviction swept over her heart with renewed force. When she came to 1 Corinthians chapter 6, a sense of dread fell over her as she read, "Do you not know that the wicked will not inherit the kingdom of God? Do not be deceived: Neither the sexually immoral nor idolaters nor adulterers nor male prostitutes nor homosexual offenders nor thieves nor the greedy nor drunkards nor slanderers nor swindlers will inherit the kingdom of God."

She looked up in anger and said out loud, "Can you believe that God classifies me with those kinds of people?" She slammed the Bible shut, put it on the coffee table, stood up, and walked into the kitchen. As she did, her head began to pound furiously once again and she stumbled with dizziness. She barely made it to her table before nausea swept over her in waves of pain.

"Oh, God!" she cried out, "Help me!" She stood up in a panic and rushed to the sink just in time to vomit. Her head felt as though someone had plunged a spike into her skull, and with shaking hands, she grabbed the prescription her doctor had given her for just such an emergency. In desperation, she doubled the dose and washed the pills down with gulps of cold water. She shuffled back to the couch and collapsed with her left arm outstretched over the Bible.

. . .

It was Sunday morning at Community Bible Church and Dr. David Miller sat in his office, dreading the moment he would step into the pulpit. The joy had long since gone out of the ministry for him, especially now that his son Jason was in prison awaiting trial. He had to tell the congregation today before they learned about the charges from the news media. The state attorney had decided to try Jason as an adult because he refused to identify the others who had participated in the murder of Mr. Czezak.

David Miller had not dared to tell anyone in the church except for the lawyer, Robert Everett. Not even Michael Rollins or the rest of the elders were aware of the tragedy about to unfold.

The time came for the service to begin. David forced himself to his feet, opened the door to the platform, walked to his ornately carved chair at the center of the stage, and sat down. The organist played a majestic anthem, but to David it seemed more like a funeral dirge than a composition designed to prepare the heart for worship.

David's wife, Darla, had stayed home with their daughter, Faith, too ashamed to face the church. The choir filed in and sang the call to worship in the same way they had sung it a hundred times before—almost mechanically—and David resented it. In fact, as he looked out over the congregation that morning, anger boiled up in his heart. *Where were you when we needed you?* he thought as he clenched his jaw tightly. *Why can our church be a refuge for so many others and not for my own family?*

As the announcements were read by the assistant pastor, David thought back on his life before they had moved to this city. He hated this wicked place which had destroyed the ones he loved the most and now would end his ministry as well.

After what seemed an interminable delay, Dr. Miller was standing behind the pulpit to deliver the message. His heart pounded heavily as he began. "What is the church?" he asked. "What is its purpose and why is it failing to meet the needs of our nation?"

The congregation looked up in surprise. This was different from Dr. Miller's normal style of speaking.

"Please turn with me today to Ephesians 2 as we consider how God has charged us to meet the needs of others."

As the congregation turned to the passage, David took a drink of water to moisten his throat.

"I direct your attention to verse 19, where we read, 'You are no longer foreigners and aliens, but fellow citizens with God's people and members of God's household.'

"The problem is, many who visit a church in today's selfish generation do not find a welcome into a family of believers, but are left on the outside, longing to be accepted, to be loved, to be cared for.

"I believe this is true of our own church as well, and I must shoulder the greater responsibility for our failure. I have not taught you well, and frankly, I have been intimidated by the wealth, power, and influence of some of our members."

By now, the congregation was sitting alert, listening to every syllable David uttered. Some sat red-faced with teeth clenched, while others nodded sadly.

"I know that you must have sensed that something has been wrong in my life in recent weeks," Dr. Miller continued. "I was too ashamed and fearful to tell you, but today I have come to deliver my last message here at Community Bible Church."

Now there was a stir among the congregation as the shock of Dr. Miller's resignation swept across the church.

"You will, no doubt, read about it in the news tomorrow and I felt you should hear it from me first. Our son Jason was arrested recently and is in jail."

There was a gasp of surprise as the news hit home. Some people displayed expressions of compassion for their pastor.

Others looked embarrassed, while still others were obviously indignant that such disgrace had been visited upon the church.

With tears in his eyes, David continued. "Let me quickly tell you what has happened, and then I'll be done. Jason got involved in a gang at school because he was threatened and was afraid. As part of the initiation, he had to go along with several members who attacked the old man you read about in the papers. As you recall, Mr. Czezak died. Jason was identified, and though he never actually touched the man, he is the only one arrested so far. He's afraid to tell the police who else was involved for fear that the rest of our family will be harmed.

"I'm asking you to pray for us, and to forgive us for the shame we have brought on this church. I am tendering my resignation as of today."

Tears were running down the faces of some of the people, while others stared at the floor embarrassed for the pastor, the church, and themselves.

"Before I close, let me share one last thing," Dr. Miller said softly. "My greatest regret is that I never led this church to experience the joy and love of truly being a family of believers. I didn't feel that I could come to you to share our struggle. I was afraid you would fire me, and I hoped something would happen to free Jason before the scandal broke in the media. I am so sorry and so ashamed," he said with lips so tight they were colorless. "Please remember us in prayer."

He called for Michael Rollins, the chairman of the elders, to close the service in prayer and hurried from the platform through the stage door and went directly to his office. He slumped into his chair and began to sob.

Nearly half an hour later, there was a knock at the door. "Pastor?"

David didn't answer, but blew his nose and wiped his eyes on a tissue.

Again there was a knock. "Pastor? It's Michael Rollins. May I come in?"

David sighed deeply, then answered, "Come in, Michael. The door's unlocked."

Michael opened the door and stepped in. "Pastor, would you come with me, please? We have something to say to you."

"Oh, please, Michael! Can't you see that I'm in no shape to meet with anyone? Have a heart, man! I've already resigned. What more do you want?"

Michael smiled gently and said, "Please, David. As a friend, I'm asking you to trust me, and come."

David struggled to his feet. He was exhausted by the intensity of his grief, but he managed to walk the short distance from his office to the church platform. To his surprise, most of the congregation was still seated, and when he walked through the door, they stood and greeted him with applause.

He looked at Michael and said, "I don't understand."

"You will in a few minutes, David. Here, take a seat and listen to what your friends have to say."

Michael motioned for the congregation to be seated and then turned to Dr. Miller. "David, we were all shocked to hear of the tragedy that has fallen on your house and we grieve with you. But as you pointed out, we are members of God's household together, and we want to stand with you during this terrible trial."

In the back, David saw Darla walk quietly into the auditorium with their daughter Faith, led by Ellen Rollins.

Michael continued, "We understand that in obedience to 1 Timothy 3:4-5 there is a need for you to temporarily step aside as the pastor and to focus on your family. But there is no need for you do this all alone. We're asking you to stay on with us as a member of our church so that we can help you with encouragement, prayer, and financial support. I believe I am speaking for the entire church when I say this. Am I right?" he asked as he looked to the congregation.

Again, the people stood and applauded as they smiled and cried together. Ellen led Darla and Faith to the front of the church to join David as the organist began to play. One by one the people of Community Bible Church came by the Millers to embrace them, share their sorrow, and pledge their support.

Even in their pain, David, Darla, and Faith Miller began to sense the love of their church and felt less alone than they had since their nightmare began.

. . .

The newspapers carried the story of Jason's arrest the next morning along with his picture. Several stories emphasized that Jason was the son of an evangelical Christian pastor. One editorial stated,

> Though violent criminals often find religion behind bars and claim to be "born again," it is not unreasonable for law-abiding citizens to question the sincerity of their sudden conversions. Now we find a case where a supposedly "born again" Christian—and the son of a prominent local pastor— is part of a vicious gang that murdered a helpless old man. We think it's time that people stop hiding behind religious labels and pay the price for their crimes. While we are not indicting all religious conversions as an attempt to manipulate the justice system for a lighter sentence, we think many "born again" experiences are just that.
>
> The only way to know whether a person is sincere in his newfound faith is to see whether it makes a permanent change in his life, regardless of a prolonged prison sentence or parole.
>
> Jason Miller's unwillingness to cooperate with the police seems to us a clear indication of how meaningless his faith really is. Yes, he's young, and frightened, but the sad truth is, in this modern day, whether one is a member of a church or not seems to have little bearing on his behavior. The "old-time" religion is dead and gone, and we are the poorer for it.

David Miller read the editorial and wept with bitter shame. He clipped it from the paper and put it in his jacket to show to the lawyer, Robert Everett.

As he drove to the attorney's office, David thanked the Lord for the church's understanding and support. He was heartbroken, of course, to step down from his role as pastor, but he agreed with the elders' decision. And he was grateful that the church not only wanted the Millers to stay in the parsonage, but that they would continue to pay their salary for several months or until a permanent decision could be made. It took a lot of the pressure off and gave him time to concentrate on helping Jason, Faith, and Darla.

The editorial nagged at David's mind. "The 'old-time' religion is dead and gone, and we are the poorer for it." Though he hated to admit it, he knew that it was largely true. Even as an atheist, Dr. Arthur Wilson had pointed that fact out to him in their confrontation a few months back.

What has happened to Christianity? David thought as he slowed and pulled to a stop at a traffic light. *Why are we just as messed up as everybody else? If God is God, why don't we have more power over sin? Why are Christians just as likely as atheists to need a psychotherapist? Arthur Wilson saw the irony in that!*

David arrived at the lawyer's office and went inside. "Hi, Robert," he said glumly as he took a chair across from the lawyer. "You said you had some news for me."

"Yes, Dr. Miller, and it could be good or bad, depending upon Jason's reaction."

"What is it, Robert?"

"The prosecutor has offered to reduce Jason's indictment to accessory to a violent crime if Jason will identify the person or persons who actually beat Mr. Czezak to death. He might actually get off with probation, Dr. Miller, but Jason has got to cooperate!"

"Then let's go talk with him, Robert," David said with the first sense of hope he had experienced in weeks.

As they drove to the jail, David read the news editorial to Robert Everett. "That's what the world thinks of us, Robert," he said, shaking his head. "And who can blame them? We sit in church on Sunday telling people God can save them, give them peace of heart and mind, and heal their homes, yet all the time we're no different from unbelievers."

Robert nodded in agreement as he signaled to turn into the secured parking area at the jail. "I can't blame my unbelieving friends, David. The attorneys in my office are a generally pagan group, but they don't see anything appealing about Christianity. They have even had to arbitrate between professing Christians in divorce cases and I've heard them say more than once that Christians are just hypocrites."

"And this situation with Jason hasn't helped either, has it, Robert?"

"No, David, I have to admit, it has made it a lot harder to witness at the office."

They walked inside and after a short delay, were led back to a meeting room. Jason was ushered in a few minutes later.

He looked tired and older than his years. "Hi, Dad," he said, trying to appear calm and assured.

"Hi, son," David said awkwardly. "How are you doing?"

"Okay, I guess," Jason said, looking down quickly, trying to maintain control of his emotions.

"Are you sure?"

Jason looked up with tears in his eyes and his face slowly revealed the pain and terror he was going through. He tried to hold back his tears, but he suddenly began to cry.

David also began to cry, and for a moment they stood looking into each other's eyes. Then David reached out and pulled his son into his arms and held him in a tight hug as they both wept.

"Oh, Jason, my little boy!" David whispered as he held his son's head to his own shoulder and rocked him from side to side as he had done when Jason was an infant. "I love you. I always will!"

Jason clung to his father, his body shaking with sobs. "I'm so sorry, Dad," he finally whispered in a raspy voice. "Can you ever forgive me?"

"Of course, Jason," he said tenderly, and then looking him straight in the eye, added, "But, son, you've got to cooperate with the court. You just *have* to!"

Jason looked down for a moment, sighed deeply, then looked back up and said, "Dad, I *want* to do that, more than anything! But you don't seem to understand. If I tell anyone about the gang, they said they will kill you and Mom and who knows what they'll do to Faith!"

"I know you're trying to protect us, Jason, and I appreciate it. But we can't let fear keep us from doing what's right. Look where fear has taken us already! We have to stand up to these people and trust the Lord to protect us. Now, I'm asking you again—for your sake and for ours—please tell the authorities who actually attacked Mr. Czezak. It can help end this nightmare!"

10

Why Faith Is Needed in the Church

HOW BIG IS GOD IN OUR PRAISE?

HAVE YOU EVER STOPPED to think about how many songs we would have to remove from our hymnals if we sang only the hymns we truly believe? If psychology is true, then many of the old songs are lies. Just flip through an old songbook and you'll see what I mean.

Here's an old one you probably haven't heard in church lately: "There's not a friend like the lowly Jesus, no, not one! No, not one! None else could heal all our soul's diseases, no, not one!, No, not one!" Yet, if our seminaries are right, Jesus is *not* able to heal our soul's diseases. We desperately need the psychologist to help us make sense of our inner world. We'd better rip that song out.

Here's another: "Calvary covers it all, my past with its sin and stain; my guilt and despair Jesus took on Him there, and Calvary covers it all." Wrong again! Now we're told that to be healed on the inside, we must return to the past and embrace our pain. We have to delve deep into our repressed memories so we can find healing from our guilt and despair. That song has got to go!

And all those gory hymns about Jesus' blood—they're so outdated! "What can wash away my sin? Nothing but the blood of Jesus. What can make me whole again? Nothing but the blood of Jesus. Oh! Precious is the flow that makes me white as snow; no other fount I know, nothing but the blood of Jesus. . . . This is all my hope and peace, Nothing but . . . ." No, that's too simplistic, believing that Jesus' sacrifice can produce wholeness, cleansing, hope, and peace. R-r-r-i-p!

"I Believe in a Hill Called Mount Calvary" dares to state that Christ "has the power to change lives today; for He changed me completely, a new life is mine, that is why by the cross I will stay." Ridiculous.

Why, there are dozens that will have to be removed! "A Mighty Fortress Is Our God," "Blessed Quietness," "Where the Spirit of the Lord Is," "Jesus, What a Friend for Sinners," "Down at the Cross," "Are You Washed in the Blood?" and "It Is Well with My Soul."

Again I am reminded of Ezekiel 33:32, where we read about the foolishness of singing songs that no one believes. "Indeed, to them you are nothing more than one who sings love songs with a beautiful voice and plays an instrument well, for they hear your words but do not put them into practice."

Keep in mind that I'm not arguing against singing in the church. I love music! I served as a minister of music for several years in a large metropolitan church. What I am trying to point out, however, is that for many Christians, the music of worship has become a sentimental journey with little content or conviction.

Some of the contemporary songs currently circulating are mindless ditties without a shred of doctrinal content. They are repeated over and over and over until the mind is numbed and the heart is dulled by artificial fervor in an attempt to work up an emotion often confused with worship. Some churches spend a large amount of time trying to generate an emotional spirituality with drums, swaying choirs, screaming and growling soloists, flashing lights, smoke machines and "dancing in the Spirit." If you examine many of the songs, you will find there is little biblical content.

On the opposite side of the worship spectrum is the emotionless singing of stiffly proper liturgical hymns with barely a hint of conviction that the messages are true or have deep significance for our personal walk with God. While the songs may have content, there is a coldness more suited for a walk-in freezer than a sanctuary of worship.

A balance in worship music would seem to be in order—a balance which provides both for content and conviction, meaning and emotion, truth and joy. Each church must allow for its own unique personality to emerge, yet the central focus of all our music, it would seem to me, must be on our Lord Jesus and what He has accomplished for us on the cross. We need to ask ourselves, "How big is God in our music?"

HOW BIG IS GOD IN OUR PREACHING?

When I was in seminary, a guest lecturer who pastored a prominent church in the Los Angeles area told us that he spent a minimum of 40 hours in preparation for his sermon each week, and we were duly impressed. I have since come to realize that he was speaking evangelistically. Nonetheless, I believe that when God's people come to church, they have a right to expect a clear message from His Word.

I am not particularly concerned with homiletical perfection composed of the required introduction, the correct number of outline points, humorous illustrations, a poem, and a compelling close. I am far more interested in hearing a clear and accurate exposition of the passage of Scripture. I want to know what God is saying to us and what He expects us to do as a result.

I do not enjoy listening to a screamer who rages and pounds the pulpit, believing that volume, red complexion, and perspiration are a substitute for meaningful content. On the other hand, I suppose I would prefer to sit under the preaching of a screamer than a sleeper. I once had a professor who nearly fell asleep during his own sermon—I'm not kidding!

What ministers to my heart is a pastor who preaches with power and deep personal conviction the life-changing truths of the Scriptures as he explains the intended meaning and presents an accurate application for our lives.

Unfortunately, there are many pastors who have lost their confidence in the soul-cleansing power of the Scriptures. They cannot preach with conviction because they no longer believe that God means what He says nor that He has the power to deliver souls from bondage to sin.

Only eternity will reveal how many practical atheists inhabit today's pulpits. In Matthew 7 there is a sobering passage regarding unbelieving ministers: "Many will say to me on that day, 'Lord, Lord, did we not prophesy in your name, and in your name drive out demons and perform many miracles?' Then I will tell them plainly, 'I never knew you. Away from me, you evildoers!'" (verses 22-23).

I wonder what the Lord will say to those who weaken the faith of their people by convincing them God is powerless to transform their lives and heal their souls. What of those nationally known radio teachers who tell their listeners that they must understand their dreams to experience inner healing? Moses writes that there are prophets and dreamers who have "tried to turn you from the way the LORD your God commanded you to follow" (Deuteronomy 13:5).

What's frightening is that the move from faith to unbelief can be so gradual and subtle we may not even notice when it happens. In Jeremiah, the Lord says, "What fault did your fathers find in me, that they strayed so far from me? They followed worthless idols and became worthless themselves. They did not ask, 'Where is the LORD?'" (2:5-6). The reason they didn't ask was they didn't know He was gone. The congregations of many churches could rightly ask their pastors, "Where is your God?"

HOW BIG IS GOD IN OUR PRAYERS?

We live in a day of increasing prayerlessness. Oh, there are many who pray, but not in the simple and powerful way the Lord taught us. In an admirable attempt to draw Christians' attention to prayer, some have devised "prayer concerts" and established prayer ministries. Numerous volumes have been written on prayer, and some, no doubt, are excellent. Nonetheless, it appears that prayer has been affected by our loss of confidence in God.

The disciples, seeing Jesus' power with God, asked Him to teach them about prayer (Luke 11:1). His extended reply is found in Matthew 6, where He first tells us what *not* to do in prayer. "When you pray, do not be like the hypocrites," who pray in order to impress others with their spirituality (Matthew 6:5-6). Second, we are not to think that longer prayers are more effective (verse 7). Then Jesus gives us a model prayer that takes all of 25 seconds to complete. Do you know why His prayer was so effective and sometimes ours are so powerless? Because He was walking moment by moment in obedience to the Father and oftentimes we are not.

I have seen people who prayed for hours at the Wailing Wall in Jerusalem, believing that God is present in the massive stones remaining from Herod's Temple, yet for all of their sincerity and fervor, God was not moved. Others painfully climb Roman cathedral stairs on their knees, hoping to get God's attention, yet the windows of heaven seem to remain closed.

If sincerity, desperation, and even pain would make prayer effective, then the prophets of Baal in 1 Kings 18 would have produced the most effective prayer meeting in history. We are told that they called on Baal from morning until evening, as Elijah, in effect, asked, "Where is your God?" They danced around their altar in growing desperation and shouted even louder until they finally began slashing themselves with their swords and spears, "but there was no response" (verse 29).

In contrast, Elijah merely prayed for approximately 20 seconds (verses 36-37) and "the fire of the LORD fell" (verse 38). Why such a different result? It wasn't the length or volume or passion of the prayer that made it effective; it was the One to whom Elijah prayed that made the difference.

If we do not have an intimate relationship with our heavenly Father, our prayers will have little more effect than those of the prophets of Baal. We can organize prayer breakfasts, prayer concerts, and national days of prayer, but unless we believe that God is still God, our prayers will be meaningless and futile.

Some people, however, do believe in God, and yet their prayers still seem to go unanswered. Why is that? So far as I understand, there are at least three causes for failure in prayer: sin, unbelief, and selfishness, which in effect are the same.

Sin simply short-circuits the prayer process. David wrote, "If I had cherished sin in my heart, the Lord would not have listened" (Psalm 66:18). Isaiah confirmed this truth when he wrote, "Your iniquities have separated you from your God; your sins have hidden his face from you, so that he will not hear" (Isaiah 59:2).

Unbelief, a root sin, also prevents successful prayer. James wrote, "When [a man] asks, he must believe and not doubt, because he who doubts is like a wave of the sea, blown and tossed by the wind. That man should not think he will receive anything from the Lord" (James 1:6-7). Unbelief in God's character and power are the primary cause for all spiritual failure. That is why modern-day prayer is so weak and miserable. We simply don't believe.

The third reason prayer fails is because we ask in a selfish manner. James explained, "When you ask, you do not receive, because you ask with wrong motives, that you may spend what you get on your pleasures" (James 4:3). God is not a magic genie that we can command and get what we want when we want it. Jesus made that quite clear when He said that we have to pray in His name (see John 16:23)—that is, we must have His authorization. In other words, He has to sign the request, and the only way He will do that is if our prayer is in agreement with His will (1 John 5:14).

Prayer is not as mysterious as some believe. It is the simple communication of heartfelt desires between a child and his father. What God requires is a genuine heart. "You will seek me and find me when you seek me with all your heart" (Jeremiah 29:13). The formulation of words, the verbal pattern, the tone of voice, and the posture of the body do not really matter. God hears the meaning of our hearts and He cannot be manipulated or deceived.

That's why He says, "If my people, who are called by my name, will humble themselves and pray and seek my face and turn from their wicked ways, then will I hear from heaven and will forgive their sin and will heal their land" (2 Chronicles 7:14). You see, "the prayer of a righteous man is powerful and effective" (James 5:16).

Do we want our prayers to be answered? Then we must turn from sin.

How Big Is God in Our Evangelism?

When we believe God's Word, we will seek to bring others to Christ—if not because of compassion for the lost, then as a result of a sincere desire to obey our Father. Hopefully, we will be motivated by both.

I am challenged by the burning motivation some people have to share Christ with the world and I admire missionaries who have devoted their entire lives to taking the gospel to other lands. What confuses me, however, is that some of the very groups that work so hard to translate the Scriptures into obscure dialects do not believe what the Bible says.

One major translation organization, for instance, has done a wonderful job of taking the Bible to the nations. Yet they have stated in writing that psychology lies at the very core of their ministry and they insist that their personnel receive psychological testing to determine emotional fitness for the mission field. We have letters from former missionaries from this organization who were forced to leave because of its stand on psychology.

One missionary with another organization told us that the people he worked with were hungry for spiritual encouragement and they asked the headquarters to send a Bible teacher to the field. Imagine their disappointment when a psychologist got off the plane to help them deal with their personal dysfunctions.

I have heard reports of a major "Christian" psychiatric clinic sending psychologists to the mission field, and we have been told by various missionaries that psychology is sweeping into third-world countries, weakening the infant church. Would you blame a native for doubting the missionary who tells him that God can give him eternal life when that very same missionary needs a psychologist to solve his own problems because he believes the Bible is not enough to heal his wounded heart? Wouldn't the native be justified in asking, "How big is your God?"

Aren't our neighbors, relatives, friends, and fellow workers also justified in wondering what Jesus has to offer them if He cannot give us peace of heart and mind without psychotherapy and drugs? Our unbelief has weakened our witness.

HOW BIG IS GOD
IN OUR FELLOWSHIP?

Practical atheism has emptied churches all across the land. Mainline Protestant churches are dying just as they did in England when formalism and unbelief spread across the island. When attendance at church is viewed as an inconvenient obligation rather than a joyful privilege, atheism has come home to roost.

Let me ask you—are you faithful in your church attendance? Do you go because you want to be with other believers, worship, and feed on God's Word, or do you go out of reluctant duty? Once again, it's all a matter of the heart, isn't it?

If we truly believe God is present when His people join together, and if we actually expect Him to speak to our hearts through His Word, and if we love Him with a depth too great for words, we will look forward to our time at church.

Perhaps the problem is that we aren't hearing His Word at the church we attend. Then maybe it is time to find a church where God's Word is faithfully delivered.

Or, maybe there is a coldness in the fellowship that repels you. Why not introduce a warm smile and loving handshake? Someone has to begin the warming trend, and it may as well be you.

When our family is away from our home church, on vacation or business, we make it a practice to be in attendance at church wherever we are. Worship is not an option for us; it is a consistent habit and pleasure. We have found warm fellowship regardless of the locale, because where Jesus is worshiped in spirit and in truth, there is an instant bond.

On our radio broadcast, callers will sometimes talk about their problems and say they just can't find a church that's warm and friendly. When I press for details, it often turns out that they have never settled in one church long enough for people to get to know them. Instead, they flit from one church to another like moths around street lights. After a while, they lose interest and stop attending altogether, blaming churches for being insensitive and uncaring.

This is, of course, another form of practical atheism. The habit of not attending church is blatant disobedience to the clear commands of Scripture. Hebrews 10:25 says, "Let us not give up meeting together, as some are in the habit of doing, but let us encourage one another—and all the more as you see the Day approaching."

There is simply no valid excuse for not being in regular attendance in church unless you are physically bedridden. The fact that there are hypocrites in the church is no excuse, either. Though there are hypocrites in every church, you will also find some sincere believers living consistent lives if you will just take the time to find them.

Perhaps you have gone to church and found the sermons to be boring and dry. God will not accept that as an excuse for dropping out of regular worship attendance, for if we go with a heart ready to receive from God's Word we will find food for the soul. If you are not stirred by the Word of God, I encourage you to examine your own heart to see if there is a root of bitterness or spirit of criticism coming between you and God's blessing. On the other hand, if you can honestly say that you are open to Scripture and are not looking for things to criticize, and you are still left spiritually empty, then perhaps it is time to find a different church where your soul's needs can be met.

Don't leave too quickly or make the mistake of expecting your church to be perfect. You will never find such a place this side of heaven. Be patient with your pastor and the people who attend your church, and do your part to help make it the best church it can possibly be. "Make every effort to keep the unity of the Spirit through the bond of peace" (Ephesians 4:3) so that the world will have no cause to ask, "How big is your God?"

HOW BIG IS GOD IN OUR STEWARDSHIP?

I've often heard that the *last* topic Christians want to hear about is giving, so I've placed this last on the list. Perhaps the most tangible sign of practical atheism is revealed by a person's checkbook. I'll be even more specific: Those who do not give generously to the Lord's work and to those in need do not trust God to supply. They prefer to trust in their own resources, and if that's the way they want it, God will step back, and they will be the poorer for it. Proverbs puts it this way: "One man gives freely, yet gains even more; another withholds unduly, but comes to poverty" (11:24).

God promises to bless those who are generous. "He who gives to the poor will lack nothing, but he who closes his eyes to them receives many curses" (Proverbs 28:27). And He warns that those who hoard will suffer loss: "I have seen a grievous evil under the sun: wealth hoarded to the harm of its owner" (Ecclesiastes 5:13).

Perhaps you are thinking, *I would like to give to the Lord and to others in need. I really would. But I can't afford it right now. In a year or so, I'll give, but not now.* Be honest with yourself: How many years have you been saying that?

I know a man who for more than twenty years has been promising himself that he would begin tithing as soon as things eased up a bit, and for that same length of time I have watched him suffer loss after loss. He has cheated himself and his family of years of God's blessing by his unbelief that God would meet their needs if he would only give generously to the Lord.

I believe there is a universal principle of stewardship: If we refuse to give God what He has asked, He will see to it that we do not have the money to spend on ourselves. It will be taken from us in medical bills, automobile repairs, or some other unexpected expense. On the other hand, if we give to God willingly from our hearts, He has made another promise: "I will prevent pests from devouring your crops, and the vines in your fields will not cast their fruit" (Malachi 3:11). God will stretch your resources in ways you have never known.

The purpose in our giving, you see, is not to meet God's needs. He already owns it all. The reason He has told us to give is to draw our hearts into the spiritual realm, "for where your treasure is, there your heart will be also" (Luke 12:34).

Do you *really* trust the Lord? Do you believe He can and will provide for your every need? Then put it to the test. That is the exact invitation He gives in Malachi 3:10: "Test me in this . . . and see if I will not throw open the floodgates of heaven and pour out so much blessing that you will not have room enough for it." Try it! Begin a systematic giving plan, even though it will hurt at first. You will be surprised how the Lord will stretch what you have left over so that every need is met.

One more point about biblical giving: We need to do it willingly. God will still bless, even if we obey Him reluctantly, but He much prefers that we give because we love Him. Read this passage carefully as you consider whether you are a practical atheist in your giving:

> Remember this: Whoever sows sparingly will also reap sparingly, and whoever sows generously will also reap generously. Each man should give what he has decided in

his heart to give, not reluctantly or under compulsion, for God loves a cheerful giver. And God is able to make all grace abound to you, so that in all things at all times, having all that you need, you will abound in every good work. As it is written: "He has scattered abroad his gifts to the poor; his righteousness endures forever." Now he who supplies seed to the sower and bread for food will also supply and increase your store of seed and will enlarge the harvest of your righteousness. You will be made rich in every way so that you can be generous on every occasion, and through us your generosity will result in thanksgiving to God.

This service that you perform is not only supplying the needs of God's people but is also overflowing in many expressions of thanks to God. Because of the service by which you have proved yourselves, men will praise God for the obedience that accompanies your confession of the gospel of Christ, and for your generosity in sharing with them and with everyone else (2 Corinthians 9:6-13).

Let's look at the passage carefully. First, another principle of stewardship: You reap in direct proportion to what you sow. Just as this is true in agriculture, so it is in the spiritual world. God has a way of returning our investment with interest if it is given unselfishly. Proverbs 19:17 says, "He who is kind to the poor lends to the LORD, and he will reward him for what he has done."

As in all other areas of our relationship with the Father, the motives of our heart are of vital concern to God. Paul writes, "Each man should give what he has decided in his heart to give, not reluctantly or under compulsion, for God loves a cheerful giver" (2 Corinthians 9:7). And, friend, it is not hard to be cheerful when we give if we truly love the Lord and believe that He will never remain our debtor.

The final principle in the above passage is that as we give in loving obedience, God will see to it that we have all we need and more so that we can give even more—to "enlarge the harvest of your righteousness." And look at this promise: "You will be made rich in every way so that you can be generous on every occasion."

Have you said, "Oh, I just wish I had more to give!"? Well, you *can* have more if you will begin giving from the little you have now. I am not preaching a prosperity gospel here, by the way. Our motive must not be to enrich ourselves, but to glorify the Lord and to minister to others.

It is amazing how few Christians ever learn this powerful principle of giving. Do you realize that if every believer supported his church faithfully with his tithes and offerings that every need would be met and there would be an abundance for missionary outreach as well?

But, Ed, you might be thinking, *we are living in the age of grace and are not under the Law, so we don't have to tithe.* I agree. God has never limited us to 10 percent. But I have never heard anyone use the "grace giving" argument to *increase* their giving, have you?

I'm not trying to tell you the amount you are to give, except that the Lord says we are to give to Him generously, willingly, obediently, and faithfully. What would your checkbook say about your pattern of giving?

In our praise, our preaching, our prayer, our passion to evangelize, our participation in attendance and fellowship, and our stewardship, much is revealed about the condition of our faith. And much is revealed about how big our God is.

Enough said about the problems. Now it's time to look into the biblical solutions for practical atheism. Move with me into the next section, and you will see how we can rebuild our personal faith for a joy-filled walk with our heavenly Father.

Time for Decisions

Arthur dreaded going back to work at the National Cancer Institute on the Monday after his humiliating debate with Dr. Arnold. Outsiders were generally unaware of the level of competition for research dollars and the petty infighting and gossip that swept through the Institute on a continual basis. Now, as he walked through the halls toward his office, he could sense the whispers and laughter of his colleagues.

"Hello, Dr. Wilson!" Gene Powell called out as he walked up with a bit of a smirk on his face. "How are you feeling after your debate?"

"I'm feeling just fine, Gene," Arthur said tightly. "Why do you ask?"

"Oh, I just thought you might be a bit bruised after the thrashing Dr. Arnold gave you. Hey! Don't feel so bad, old man! He set you up with that topic."

"Yeah? Well, how would you have handled the topic, Gene, since I obviously messed up so badly?"

Gene laughed as he clapped Arthur on the shoulder. "I would have been smarter than to accept the debate in the first place, Arthur!" He walked on down the hallway.

"That's a cowardly approach if I ever heard one!" Arthur called out after him.

Gene stopped and turned to face Arthur. "Maybe so," he replied, "But then I wouldn't have embarrassed myself in front of so many people, would I?"

Arthur turned and walked away, shaking his head in anger. He walked into his office and his secretary asked him, "How did the debate go, Dr. Wilson?"

He looked at her with cold fury and said, "Don't ask, Jenny! Just don't ask! And hold all my calls!" He went into his office and slammed the door as Jenny sat at her desk in stunned silence.

Arthur sat down trembling with emotion. Of all the things he feared, professional humiliation was the worst, and now he felt that his credibility was damaged beyond repair. There would be no more invitations to lecture at prestigious conferences around the world. No more offers to become a professor at a major university. No more government grants. All because he had been foolish enough to debate an old creationist. He shook his head in unbelief. "How could I have been so stupid?" he said to himself.

Jenny's voice came over the intercom, "Dr. Wilson? I know you said you weren't to be disturbed, but there's a friend here to see you. He says you'll want to talk with him."

Arthur sighed and hung his head wearily. He pushed the intercom button. "Who is it, Jenny?"

"Michael Rollins from the Smithsonian."

He paused for a moment, then replied, "Have him come on in."

Jenny opened the door and Michael Rollins came in with a warm smile and walked over to shake Arthur's hand. "How are you doing, Arthur?" he asked with genuine concern.

Arthur shook Michael's hand, swallowed hard to contain his emotions, pointed Michael to a chair and sat down behind his desk. Finally he replied, "I'm not doing so good, Michael. I don't remember ever being this discouraged." Then, in a near whisper, he confided, "They're all laughing at me out there!"

Michael's eyes softened with genuine compassion as he said, "I'm so sorry, Arthur. I was afraid this might happen, but I didn't know how to warn you. I wasn't sure you'd listen."

"I probably wouldn't have. I was so sure of myself—so cocky! I thought I would shred Dr. Arnold in a debate, but I feel like I went through a meat grinder myself," Arthur said with a half-smile.

"That's why I stopped by. I thought you might need to talk to a friend. I hope that's how you see me."

Arthur looked at Michael for a moment and then nodded. "I do see you as a friend, Michael. Maybe one of the only real friends I've had in some time. Even though you knew I totally disagreed with your beliefs, you never turned away from me. I'm grateful to you." Arthur's eyes misted and he looked down at the floor and cleared his throat.

Michael smiled and said, "You're more than welcome, Arthur. Your life is far from over, though. In fact, I think it may just be starting."

"What do you mean by that?"

"Well, Arthur, something you said the other night got me to thinking over the weekend. You said Dr. Arnold had almost made a believer out of you, or something along that line. Remember?"

Arthur nodded and chuckled as he said, "I do remember, and to tell you the truth, I think I meant it. Don't get me wrong, though, Michael. I'm not ready to join your church or anything like that. I just have to admit that I wasn't intellectually honest with myself as I prepared for this debate. I was more concerned with trashing the Bible than I was about an open-minded consideration of the evidences. All I can promise you for now is that I'm willing to look at the other side and to consider whether God really exists."

Michael smiled, slapped his own knee and said, "Arthur, that's the place to begin. Would you be open to studying the issue with me? I promise not to pressure you into making a commitment or going to church."

Arthur smiled in return and said, "It's a deal. When do we begin?"

"Why not right now?" Michael asked. "I've got a couple of hours before my next meeting. What's your schedule like?"

"Today I'd like nothing better than to hide here in my office!" Arthur said as he leaned back in his chair. "How do you want to go about this quest for God?"

"Well, first, let's look at the big picture. Isn't it *possible* that God exists? I mean, is there any actual scientific proof that there is no Master Designer?"

Arthur thought back through his many weeks of study in preparation for the debate. He had read numbers of books and articles from both sides. "No, Michael," he replied, "there is no proof that God does not exist. On the other hand, so far as I can determine, there is also no scientific proof that He does."

"But does that really surprise you, Arthur? If God is above and beyond His creation, if He is neither captive to time or space, is it inconceivable that He exists in a dimension that is not accessible to our physical instruments of observation?"

"No, Michael," Arthur answered firmly, "it is not inconceivable, nor does it violate any actual law of science."

Michael shifted in his chair. "Arthur, let me ask you a difficult question, and I'm not implying anything about you personally, but why are so many scientists almost religious in their commitment to evolutionary faith?"

Arthur thought for a moment, then replied, "Do you want my honest answer?"

"Of course I do."

"I think the real reason we evolutionists cling so emotionally to this theory is that we are rebels at heart."

"What do you mean by that?"

"I mean we don't want to give an account of our lives to a moral overlord. We like to think of ourselves as the highest form of life on the evolutionary scale—at least here on earth. We are willing to concede the possibility that higher life forms exist on other planets, but there is no moral accountability required toward other evolved beings. The more I think about it, Michael, the more I believe that independence is the primary issue."

Michael nodded, but didn't reply.

"Still," Arthur continued, "our reluctance to accept the existence of a cosmic lawgiver does not automatically prove that one exists, does it?"

"No, not by itself."

"So we are left with the uncomfortable possibility that God exists, but we are unable to prove His existence with scientific instruments or the scientific method. How then, can one be intellectually honest and also hold firmly to religious faith? It would seem to me that an agnostic position is more honest than either a firm evolutionary position or a committed creationist position. How do you deal with that, Michael?"

"The way I personally handled the question was to ask which position has the stronger evidence. Over a period of time, it became clear to me that there is no cogent scientific argument that explains the existence of the universe unless one postulates a first uncaused cause. There are only two options, ultimately: either matter and energy have always existed, or they haven't. Scientific theories and studies have demonstrated again and again that so far as we can prove, matter and energy do not spontaneously arise out of nothing, nor do they cease to exist. Rather, they merely change form. Am I right?"

Arthur nodded in agreement.

"And," Michael continued, "we must admit that the universe is not infinitely old but that it had a point of beginning."

"Why is that a necessary conclusion?" Arthur asked sincerely.

"Because we know from the Second Law of Thermodynamics that all things tend toward disorder—in other words, hot things eventually become cold, new objects oxidize and fall apart, our houses need constant repair. If the universe were infinitely old, there would be no suns still burning, for they would have burned out billions of years ago and we would not exist."

"I follow you," Arthur said as he stroked his chin in deep concentration. "Go on."

"Since we know the universe must have had a beginning—and fairly recently, from a cosmic point of view—we can no longer hide behind the argument of unlimited time for evolution to occur."

"I'll concede that point," Arthur agreed.

"Then we must deal with the question of whether there is any statistical support for the concept that, even given billions of years of time, random chance could ever account for the complexity of molecular chemistry, let alone life itself."

Arthur nodded, "I know. That is perhaps the greatest problem I encountered in my study. I was especially challenged by the book *The Mystery of Life's Origin*. As I recall, its primary argument is that DNA is an intelligent code and, as with any other form of communication, this implies an intelligent designer."

Michael nodded. "It's a strong argument. Philip Johnson makes a similar point in his books *Darwin on Trial* and *Reason in the Balance*."

"I'm not familiar with him," Arthur said.

"Johnson teaches at the Berkeley law school, and his focus is on the illogical and empty rhetoric used to support Darwinian evolution. I think his work shows that much of what passes for science is actually more religious and philosophical than scientific."

Arthur pursed his lips, but didn't reply.

Michael looked past Arthur to the bookshelf behind Arthur's desk and saw the book *Darwin's Black Box.* "I see you have Behe's book on this issue, Arthur. Did you read chapter nine?"

"Yes, but which part are you referring to?"

"May I borrow your copy for a moment?"

Arthur swiveled in his chair, found the book, and tossed it to Michael, who quickly turned to the passage he was seeking. "Here it is: 'The impotence of Darwinian theory in accounting for the molecular basis of life is evident not only from the analyses in this book, but also from the complete absence in the professional scientific literature of any detailed models by which complex biochemical systems could have been produced.'"

"In other words," Arthur said, "it could not have happened the way Darwin and evolutionists have claimed through the years."

"Exactly! But listen to Behe's next statement: 'No one at Harvard University, no one at the National Institutes of Health, no member of the National Academy of Sciences, no Nobel prize winner—no one at all can give a detailed account of how the cilium, or vision, or blood clotting, or any complex biochemical process might have developed in a Darwinian fashion. But we are here. Plants and animals are here. The complex systems are here. All things got here somehow—if not in a Darwinian fashion, then how?'"

Arthur shifted in his chair and began to smile slightly. "There is really only one other alternative, isn't there?"

"That's Behe's point exactly! He says: 'To a person who does not feel obliged to restrict his search to unintelligent causes, the straightforward conclusion is that many biochemical systems were designed. They were designed not by the laws of nature, not by chance and necessity; rather they were *planned*. The designer knew what the systems would look like when they were completed, then took steps to bring the systems about. Life on earth at its most fundamental level, in its most critical components, is the product of intelligent activity.'"

"Do you know what's most amazing to me about Behe?" Arthur asked.

"What?"

"Even though he wrote those words, so far as I know, he still is not a creationist."

"Why should that amaze you, Arthur?" Michael said quietly as he leaned forward. "As far as I can tell, neither are you."

. . .

When Susan awoke, she was groggy, but the pain in her head had eased somewhat. Her anger had cooled and she decided to continue her reading in 1 Corinthians so she could meet with Ellen Rollins again.

The moment she opened the Bible to the sixth chapter, her eyes fell onto verse thirteen: "The body is not meant for sexual immorality, but for the Lord." As she read further, another phrase seemed to burn into her heart: "Flee from sexual immorality."

Then the phrase that had moved her heart earlier jumped out again: "Do you not know that your body is a temple of the Holy Spirit, who is in you, whom you have received from God?"

Susan looked up, deep in thought, then back to the Bible. "You are not your own; you were bought at a price. Therefore honor God with your body." Tears formed in her eyes and began to trickle down her cheeks. At that moment, the path back to God was clearly revealed to her heart.

In anguish of soul, she fell to her knees, her head bowed onto the Bible, which lay open on the coffee table. "Oh, dear Lord," she prayed softly, "please forgive me! I have been so disobedient to You and I don't know how You could still love me. But somehow, I know You do. I want to come back home to You. I promise You this very moment that I will break off the affair with Billy. You are more important to me than anyone or anything else. I love you, Lord Jesus!"

For the first time in months, Susan felt a lightness in her soul that filled her very being. The burden that seemed to weigh heavily upon her heart was lifted the moment she decided to obey her Lord. Now tears of joy rolled down her face and she realized that the throbbing pain in her head was gone.

At that very moment, her phone rang. She blew her nose, wiped her eyes, and picked up the receiver. "Hello?" she said.

"Hey, beautiful!" Billy Costas said. "How's it going there in D.C.?"

"Uh . . . just fine, Billy," she said hesitantly.

"I miss you, Susan! I can hardly wait to get home!"

"Well, thank you, Billy. That's nice of you to say," she replied, almost formally.

"Are you okay, Susan?" Billy asked. "You sound like you've been crying."

Susan knew her moment of decision had come. Either she would follow through on her new commitment to Christ, or she would return to the world that had caused her so much pain yet held such attraction for her. The passion she and Billy shared flashed into her mind as well as the affluence he could offer. But the quiet peace she had just experienced alone with the Lord cleared her mind.

"I have been crying, Billy, but they were tears of joy. I found my dearest Friend once again, and I haven't been this happy in months."

"Well, that's great, Susan! Who is she? Have I met her?"

"I'm talking about Jesus, Billy. Ever since I walked away from Him when I left Arthur, I have felt so heavyhearted, but I couldn't figure out why. Now I realize that I have been so disobedient to Him that I couldn't really be happy."

"What are you *talking* about?" Billy asked with deepening concern. "You sound like some kind of religious fanatic, Susan. Snap out of it!"

"That's just what I've done, Billy. I've snapped out of a nightmare, and I'm seeing things clearly again."

Billy's voice grew cold. "Don't talk like that, Susan. Before you know it, you'll be telling me we have to break it off."

There was a long pause and finally Billy said, "Susan? Did you hear me?"

"Yes, Billy, I heard you, and you're right. We do have to break it off. In fact, I have to do that right now. We can't see each other again, not the way we have, at least. And I'll understand if I'm out of work."

"Well, good for you, Susan! I'm glad you'll understand!" Billy said bitterly. "You don't need to be at DoubleSoft when I return. I'll see that you get your check. Oh—and Susan. Did you really think I was all alone here in my hotel room? Well, I'm not! Good-bye, Susan! I hope your Jesus can keep you warm and satisfied." He slammed his phone down and the line went dead.

Susan sat on the couch, shaking with emotion, but she immediately sensed a release from her guilt and a new freedom to move on with her life. She was surprised that Billy's response hadn't devastated her, but instead, she felt true relief.

She picked up the phone and dialed Ellen Rollins. "Ellen? This is Susan Wilson. Do you have a moment to talk?"

"Of course, Susan! You won't believe this, but Michael and I were just praying for you not five minutes ago! I'm so glad you called. What can I do for you?"

"I'd like to get with you again just as soon as possible, Ellen. I've been reading through 1 Corinthians like you asked, and the Lord has been working overtime on me."

"Oh? Do you want to tell me about it now?"

"No, I'd rather talk face to face, if you don't mind. When would you have some time?"

"I can meet with you tomorrow for lunch, Susan. Do you want to meet at the same restaurant or somewhere else?"

"Do you mean at Chez Louise? That would be perfect."

"Chez Louise it is, then," Ellen said. "About 11:30?"

The next morning, Susan awoke early, with renewed energy. She drew back the curtains and let the sunlight flood in upon her face and she smiled in the sheer joy of knowing she was back on the right path.

After she dressed for her appointment with Ellen, she sat down in the front room and opened her Bible to 1 Corinthians chapter 7. She winced uneasily as she read about the sexual aspects of a godly marriage. Then she came to verse ten: "A wife must not separate from her husband. But if she does, she must remain unmarried or else be reconciled to her husband."

"Oh, Lord," she said out loud, "do You mean I have to go back to Arthur?" She was willing to break off the affair with Billy Costas, but the thought of returning to the turmoil and abuse she had experienced with Arthur was more than she could bear. She began crying and she shook her head. "No, Lord! You can't ask me to do that! I broke off with Billy. Isn't that enough?"

It was as though a cold blast of winter air had blown through the window and into her heart. Her neck tightened with tension and the joy she had experienced fled as quickly as it had come.

Wearily, Susan drove to the restaurant, less eager to talk with Ellen, yet anxious to recover the peace she had known the night before. The sunlight of the morning had faded into overcast skies, reflecting perfectly the mood of her heart.

She had taken her Bible with her and because she arrived early, she sat in her car and read again from 1 Corinthians chapter 7. Verse 13 seemed to describe her situation exactly: "If a woman has a husband who is not a believer and he is willing to live with her, she must not divorce him. For the unbelieving husband has been sanctified through his wife."

She rubbed her neck and thought, *No, Lord! Please, not that!*

It seemed as though the Lord was answering her in the quiet recesses of her heart. *No? . . . Lord? Those two words don't go together, Susan.*

"But I *can't* go back to Arthur, Lord!" she whispered almost angrily.

Again, she sensed the Lord's response. *You can't?*

Just as Ellen had challenged her the week before, the issue was very clear. It wasn't that Susan *couldn't* obey. She just didn't *want* to. It was now a matter of her choice.

For several moments, a battle raged within her heart. She tried to bargain with the Lord. *I'll do anything You say, Lord. I'll go anywhere to serve You. Just don't make me go back to Arthur.* But there was no response except the Scripture: "If a woman has a husband who is not a believer and he is willing to live with her, she must not divorce him."

Another thought emerged, almost hopeful: *Maybe Arthur won't want me back if he finds out about Billy.* Then shame pierced her heart as she thought about how foolish her faith would look to Arthur now. *Why would he ever want to be a Christian when he finds out how sinful I've been?* She was surprised to find that she was almost disappointed to think that Arthur might reject her.

Now a new question surfaced as she stared blankly at the restaurant, not seeing the people who came and went. *Do I want Arthur's salvation more than my own comfort?* This thought had never crossed her mind until that very moment. The question suddenly put everything into perspective. Jesus had died for her, she realized, and now she was being asked to sacrifice her own desires for Arthur's sake.

She bowed her head and quietly prayed, "For You, Lord Jesus, I am willing to go back to Arthur. Oh, I pray that You will bring him to salvation. Not just for my sake, dear Lord, but for his. You know I don't love Arthur, Lord, but because I love You, I will obey. Please give me the capacity to learn to love him again. I pray this in Your holy name, amen."

As Susan opened her eyes, sunlight broke through the clouds and a beam shined directly onto her car as though the Lord were smiling on her. Again, peace flowed into her heart and through her whole body and she smiled as she leaned back against the headrest.

Just then Ellen drove up and came over to Susan's car. She knocked on the window. "Are you ready to go in, Susan?" she asked.

"Hi, Ellen! Yes! Let's go!" she said with more enthusiasm than she had thought possible just moments before.

When they were seated inside, Susan related the events of the previous evening and the battle she had just won. "Oh, Ellen! Thank you for being here for me! Thank you for telling me where to find the answers I needed!"

Ellen's eyes were full of tears as she listened to Susan's story. She reached across the table and squeezed Susan's hands. "I am so happy for you!" she said. "I know it won't be easy, but you will look back on this morning as the turning point in your life. I'm sure of it."

"But I have to admit, Ellen—I'm afraid."

"Of what, dear?"

"I'm afraid of what Arthur will say when he finds out about the affair. I'm afraid he will be even more bitter than before and I'm afraid of the pain I will have to endure just living with him. He can be so cold and cruel."

"I know, Susan," Ellen said compassionately, "but the Lord will give you strength. And who knows? Maybe God will break through to Arthur's heart."

"Do you think so?" Susan said as she looked into Ellen's eyes.

"Well, I don't know for sure what Arthur will do, of course, because each of us has the freedom to choose or reject the Lord. But I think you should know that Michael and Arthur have developed a friendship, and Michael says that Arthur is actually examining the question of whether God exists. That's why Michael and I were praying for both of you last night."

Susan sat silent, almost unbelieving that Arthur would sincerely consider the existence of God. It was a long way from a personal decision for Christ, but it would be a start, at least. "Oh, Ellen," she finally said. "That's almost more than I can hope for."

"But it isn't more than you can pray for, is it?"

"No," Susan agreed. "At least I can pray for him."

Susan sat up as a new concern came to mind. "How will I approach Arthur, Ellen? He must hate me as much as I have hated him. Do I just call him and say, 'Let's do lunch?' I don't know where to start."

"What would you think if Michael and I invited both of you over to our house for dinner? I know Arthur trusts Michael, and it might be the perfect way to introduce the two of you again."

"Okay, Ellen, but I doubt Arthur will come. And I really can't blame him."

When they had finished eating, they went back out to Susan's car. "Would you like to pray before we go?" Ellen offered.

"I'd like that, Ellen. Thank you."

They got into Susan's car, shut the doors, and bowed their heads. "Lord Jesus," Ellen prayed, "Thank You for working so powerfully in Susan's life through Your Word. Now we pray that You will touch Arthur just as powerfully and bring him to Yourself. Prepare him, Lord, so that he will be open to meeting with Susan. Soften his heart and open his mind, dear Lord. Do a miracle, and heal their home. We pray this in Jesus' name, amen."

"Amen," Susan said through her tears.

Then they both looked up and laughed as they saw each other's streaked makeup. They hugged, and Ellen got out to hurry home, anxious to play the part of matchmaker.

. . .

Attorney Robert Everett asked Jason and David Miller to sit down to discuss the decision that had to be made. "Jason, the prosecutor has told me that this is your last opportunity for leniency. If you will cooperate with the police in the Czezak murder, he is prepared to reduce your charges. I don't know exactly what that will mean, but instead of life in prison, we're looking at a few years at most, and even the possibility of parole.

"I know you're worried about your family's safety and I explained that to the prosecutor. He has promised that the police will work with him to protect your mom, dad, and sister if you will cooperate. They really want to break this gang problem right now, Jason, and with your help, they think they can."

Jason stared at the floor, clasping and unclasping his hands with nervous energy. He looked up at his dad, then at Robert Everett. "I want to help, Mr. Everett. I don't want other kids to get trapped into the gangs like I did. But I don't know if I could go on living if anything ever happened to my family because of me!"

David Miller patted Jason on the knee and said, "Son, we have to do the right thing. There's more at stake here than just our family, but God will protect us. Please, Jason, tell Robert that you'll cooperate."

Jason's jaw firmed as he looked at his dad, and then with a bit of a smile, he said, "Okay, Dad. If that's what you really want, I will." Turning to Robert, Jason said, "Mr. Everett, you can tell the prosecutor that I'm ready to help in every way possible."

David sat back in his chair with a sigh of relief. "Thank God!" he said.

· · ·

That evening, Michael called Arthur at home. "Arthur! It's Michael! Are you free on Friday night for supper with Ellen and me?"

"I think I could arrange it, Michael," Arthur said in a friendly tone as he leaned back into his recliner. "What's the occasion?"

"I have someone I'd like you to meet."

"Really? And who might that be? Another creationist?" he said with a laugh. "I thought you said you wouldn't pressure me."

"No, Arthur, this is more of a social event. We've invited a beautiful lady to join us for supper and we want you to come as well."

Arthur shook his head and smiled slightly. He hadn't been out socially with a woman since Susan had left him. At first, he had thought it was just his preoccupation with the debate, but as time went along, he had to admit that he really missed his wife and wasn't ready to get involved with anyone else. Even now, though he was lonely, he wasn't interested in dating.

"I don't think so, Michael," he said. "Even though we're separated, I'm still not legally divorced from Susan. I guess I'm just not ready to try again with someone else."

"Do you mean you're still in love with Susan?" Michael said, enjoying his secret.

Arthur sat up in his chair, a bit irritated. "I guess you could say that, Michael. Why do you sound so surprised? I thought Christians believed in the sanctity of marriage."

"Oh, we do, Arthur. I can't think of anything I would rather see than you and Susan getting back together."

"Well, don't hold your breath, Michael," Arthur said bitterly. "Like I told you before, Susan's been having an affair with her boss."

"Hmm. That does complicate matters," Michael said. "But would you consider getting back together if she broke off with him?"

Arthur didn't answer for a moment, and he leaned back in his chair again. The thought hadn't occurred to him for some time that he and Susan might get together again someday. "You know, Michael, a few days ago, I don't think I would have even considered it, but now? Well, maybe I'm just getting old, but, I have to admit, I still love Susan. Yeah, if she were free again, I'd do whatever I could to try to rebuild our marriage."

"Are you serious?"

"Yes, Michael!" Arthur said, becoming irritated again. "Is it so strange that I still care for Susan?"

"No, Arthur, it isn't strange at all. To tell you the truth, it gives me a lot of hope for your future."

"Why do you say that?"

"Because, Arthur, the lady we invited for dinner is Susan. And she has agreed to come, knowing I'm inviting you."

Arthur sat upright in his recliner and swallowed with deep emotion. It took a moment or so for him to regain his composure.

His first reaction was to jump at the invitation, but then his old pride took hold and he didn't want to seem too eager.

A mixture of anger, hurt feelings, loneliness, humiliation, and pride surfaced, displacing his desire for reconciliation. On the one hand, he desperately wanted to accept Michael's invitation, but on the other, he found himself angrily wanting to hurt her for the pain she had caused him.

Now he was angry at Michael, too. "Why didn't you tell me about Susan before now? What's the idea of trying to manipulate my emotions? Good grief, Michael! I thought we were friends!" He slammed the phone down with a curse.

Michael hung his head with disappointment. Ellen saw his reaction and asked, "What did Arthur say, honey?"

"He cussed me out and hung up."

"Oh! I'm so sorry. He must be more bitter than we thought. We're going to have to pray even harder."

They bowed their heads and asked the Lord to soften Arthur's heart and to bring him to faith in Christ and restore the marriage between Susan and Arthur. "Lord Jesus," Michael said, "we know it will take a miracle to heal their home, but that's what we're asking. Please, Lord, help Arthur to change his mind and to come to our dinner with Susan on Friday."

. . .

Arthur sat in his recliner, still seething with anger at Michael Rollins for trying to trick him into meeting with Susan. What made matters even worse was that he desperately wanted to accept the invitation. He stood to his feet, walked to the window of the family room, and looked out, his mind in a turmoil. Inside, his emotions alternated between angry pride and the desire to rebuild his marriage.

His nostrils flared, and he swallowed deeply as he ran his hand over his thinning hairline. As he stared vacantly through the window, his mind went back to the moment he first saw Susan and then to the moment when he realized he loved her.

A longing so deep he could actually feel it suddenly filled his chest and he began to weep. All of his loneliness, frustration, anger, and pain seemed to flow from the very depths of his being as tears streamed down his face.

Even as he clung to his bitterness, a voice seemed to speak to his spirit, *How long, Arthur? How long will you continue to run from Me?*

"Oh, God!" he said out loud as he grabbed the windowsill and held on as though he was afraid he was about to fall. He breathed deeply as he became overwhelmed with emotion, and whispered again, "Oh, God, please. . . ." And for the first time in many years, Arthur did not feel foolish for praying.

REGAINING OUR
FAITH IN GOD

11

A Greater Knowledge of Our God

EVERY SYSTEM BEGINS WITH ASSUMPTIONS

EVERY SCIENTIFIC, PHILOSOPHICAL, and religious system begins with assumptions. There are no exceptions, since we are limited by time and space to what we can deduce from empirical evidence.

Scientists like to pretend that they are dispassionate, objective observers, analyzers, and reporters of physical truth, but the fact remains: they must begin with certain unproved and unprovable assumptions. Let's quickly look at a few.

ASSUMPTIONS OF SCIENCE

The impressive accomplishments of science are based on several basic assumptions, without which we would still be in the dark ages of ignorance. Evolutionism, however, ignores basic scientific method and rules of evidence in the transparent desire to remove God from our consciousness. The tragedy is, as researchers move further away from these foundational scientific precepts, mankind moves closer toward the occult and paranormal.

Christians have nothing to fear about *genuine* scientific research and discovery. So long as we hold scientists to rigid accountability and consistent submission to scientific method, biblical faith will always stand the test.

This discussion could easily fill an entire work, and indeed has inspired multiplied thousands of volumes. Limitation of space and time (and your interest span) force me to merely touch upon these basic principles.

Existence of the Cosmos

For us to make sense of the physical realm, we must first assume the *existence of the cosmos*—that matter and energy actually exist and are not imaginary. We cannot prove that because it is philosophically possible that nothing exists at all except in the mind of a superbeing. In that case, all our experimentation and accomplishments are also imaginary because there would be no stars, no galaxies, no electromagnetic spectrum, no life, no humans, no minds—nothing at all. Most people find this point of view patently ridiculous and move on toward reality.

Knowability of the Cosmos

The second assumption of genuine science is *knowability*—that is, the physical cosmos, within the limitations of time and our ability to travel, can be observed and examined by our physical senses and instruments which extend those senses.

Rationality of the Cosmos

The third foundation of genuine science rests on the assumption of *rationality*. This is the belief that there is order in the physical realm which governs all energy, matter, time, and motion. This is what the study of physics is all about—the attempt to discover and make sense of physical laws that are "universal"—that is, they are consistent and apply in all places and at all times, regardless of location in the cosmos or time of the event.

Carl Sagan, in his incredibly unscientific volume *The Cosmos*, argued that there might be other universes where the physical laws as we know them do not exist. While that makes for interesting science fiction, it escapes the notice of many that by definition, there is *only one universe*. Otherwise, we would have to redefine reality as a *"duo*verse*"* or even a *"poly*verse.*"* To do so, however, reduces all scientific inquiry to meaningless conjecture and philosophy, since we cannot observe or analyze other dimensions.

The word *cosmos* comes from the Greek language and means "order." The dictionary defines the term as "the universe regarded as an orderly, harmonious whole; an ordered, harmonious, and whole system; harmony and order as distinct from chaos."[54] Seeming to believe that there is no essential order in reality, Sagan should have titled his book *Chaos*, since his philosophy would render all organized understanding meaningless.

Deducibility of the Cosmos

A fourth essential assumption of genuine science is *deducability*. This means that we can draw a conclusion by logical reasoning. Deduction is actually a conjoined and dependent twin of *induction*, which moves from the specific to the general—that is, deriving general principles from particular facts. Having then inductively observed general behaviors and interactions of energy, matter, time, and motion, we are able to deductively infer specific truth from general observation.

Validity of the Cosmos

A final assumption of science is *validity*. This means that we are able to validate the conclusion we have arrived at by repeated experimentation.

None of the five assumptions of science can be proven scientifically. They are received by faith because they make sense and are the only way we can arrive at logical conclusions about our physical universe.

No doubt you have realized that these assumptions correspond to the *scientific method*, which is composed of the observation of phenomena (existence of the cosmos), collection of data (knowability), creation of a hypothesis (rationality and deducability), and testing of the hypothesis by repeated observation and controlled experimentation (validity).

ASSUMPTIONS OF BIBLICAL FAITH IN GOD

Perhaps by now you have slumped back in your chair and wondered why it's important to understand all this. If you stay with me, you'll come to see a very important point: faith in God is just as valid as scientific assumptions, and believers have no reason to be intimidated by the pretensions of scientific superiority.

The Existence of God

The first assumption of faith is similar to the assumption of knowability in science: *the existence of God*. We cannot prove His existence by scientific method, nor can we disprove it, because He stands above, around, and through all physical reality, yet He exists in a dimension that supersedes and encompasses the physical universe. The very existence of the cosmos is strong evidence, however, for the existence of God, since its vastness and orderliness imply the existence of an infinite mind. There is no contradiction between this assumption and that of science, since neither are exclusive of the other.

We find this first assumption in Genesis 1:1: "In the beginning God . . ." There is no attempt to prove God's existence, because the physical evidences are clearly apparent to any rational and open mind. In fact, it takes far more faith to believe that God does *not* exist than to believe that He does.

The Knowability of God

The second assumption of biblical faith is the *knowability of God*. This is another way of defining *general revelation*—that which may be known about God from His creation. Romans 1 puts it this way:

> What may be known about God is plain to [human beings], because God has made it plain to them. For since the creation of the world God's invisible qualities—his eternal power and divine nature—have been clearly seen, being understood from what has been made, so that men are without excuse (verses 19-20).

David wrote in Psalm 19:1, "The heavens declare the glory of God; the skies proclaim the work of his hands." You do not have to look beyond your own body to see the work of God. The intricacies of the human eye, the brain and nervous system, the delicate balance of flesh, chemicals, electricity, and spirit all point to a Divine Maker who can be known by His creatures.

The Revelation of God

The third foundation of faith in God is the *revelation of God*. Without *special revelation*, we would simply know of God's existence and certain aspects of His nature, but we would not know His name, the fullness of His character, or His unchangeable plan.

God revealed Himself first to Adam and Eve and spoke to them directly in Genesis 1:28: "Be fruitful and increase in number." Even after man rebelled against God, there was a general awareness of His existence and a remnant of believers (*see* Genesis 4–5), but as man became more evil, he willfully ignored God (Genesis 6:5; 2 Peter 3:5) and tried to put God out of his mind by elevating mankind to divine status (Genesis 11:4).

God continued to reveal Himself to receptive individuals such as Melchizedek (Genesis 14:18) and Abraham (Genesis 12:1; 15:1), but spiritual darkness spread across the world until God was all but forgotten, even among the Israelites. Then God appeared to Moses (Exodus 3:4), and through him, delivered Israel from slavery in Egypt. He revealed Himself in a special way to the descendants of Abraham. He said, "On the day I chose Israel, I swore with uplifted hand to the descendants of the house of Jacob and revealed myself to them in Egypt. With uplifted hand I said to them, 'I am the LORD your God'" (Ezekiel 20:5).

Through Moses and the prophets who followed, God continually revealed more of His character, purpose, and plan *in written form* so man could carefully examine and meditate on this special information we call Scripture, or "that which is written down." This process of giving more and more information as time went along is called *progressive revelation.*

This process of special revelation continued through the coming of Jesus Christ and the completion of the New Testament. As the writer of Hebrews says,

> God, after He spoke long ago to the fathers in the prophets in many portions and in many ways, in these last days has spoken to us in His Son, whom He appointed heir of all things, through whom also He made the world. And He is the radiance of His glory and the exact representation of His nature, and upholds all things by the word of His power (Hebrews 1:1-3 NASB).

Again, there is nothing scientifically invalid in the assumption that God has revealed Himself to mankind through Scripture. No proven law of physics or even the theory of relativity can disprove this assumption, nor, for that matter, can prove it. It is by definition an assumption or statement of faith.

The Rationality of God

The fourth assumption of Biblical faith is the *rationality of God.* It corresponds to the assumption of deducability in science and takes for granted that God is an intelligent Being who processes information in a reasonable fashion. This does not, however, negate the fact that an infinite God is so superior to man that His thoughts will not always make sense to man. That is the point of Isaiah 55:8-9:

> "My thoughts are not your thoughts, neither are your ways my ways," declares the LORD. As the heavens are higher than the earth, so are my ways higher than your ways and my thoughts than your thoughts.

The orderliness of the universe testifies to the rationality of God. Mathematical precision, the laws of physics, and logic itself all lend support to this foundational assumption, which can neither be proven true nor false.

The Character of God

The final assumption that lays the foundation for biblical faith and a consistent philosophy of life is the *character of God*, which includes God's loving nature, sovereignty (absolute control), immutability (unchangeableness), omniscience (knowing everything), omnipresence (in all places at all times), and omnipotence (power over all things). The assumption of God's character corresponds to the assumption of scientific validity, since it is what can be examined and verified by repeated interaction in the spiritual test tube of life experience.

UNASHAMED CONFIDENCE IN GOD

Paul's Great Confidence

Paul writes, "I am not ashamed of the gospel, because it is the power of God for the salvation of everyone who believes: first for the Jew, then for the Gentile" (Romans 1:16). Today, however, there are many professing Christian leaders who *are* ashamed of the Word of God and desperately desire the intellectual approval of their secular peers in education and science. John wrote this of the secretly believing Pharisees who would not openly identify with Christ: "They loved praise from men more than praise from God" (John 12:43).

Paul confronted the hideous error of compromising the truth for the sake of worldly approval when he said that his preaching is "not with words of human wisdom lest the cross of Christ be emptied of its power."

> For the message of the cross is foolishness to those who are perishing, but to us who are being saved it is the power of God. For it is written: "I will destroy the wisdom of the wise; the intelligence of the intelligent I will frustrate."
>
> Where is the wise man? Where is the scholar? Where is the philosopher of this age? Has not God made foolish the wisdom of the world? For since in the wisdom of God the world through its wisdom did not know him, God was pleased through the foolishness of what was preached to save those who believe. Jews demand miraculous signs and Greeks look for wisdom, but we preach Christ crucified: a stumbling block to Jews and foolishness to Gentiles, but to those whom God has called, both Jews and Greeks, Christ the power of God and the wisdom of God. For the foolishness of God is wiser than man's wisdom, and the weakness of God is stronger than man's strength.
>
> Brothers, think of what you were when you were called. Not many of you were wise by human standards; not many were influential; not many were of noble birth. But God chose the foolish things of the world to shame the wise; God chose the weak things of the world to shame the strong. He chose the lowly things of this world and the despised things—and the things that are not—to nullify the things that are, so that no one may boast before him. It is because of him that you are in Christ Jesus, who has become for us wisdom from God—that is, our righteousness, holiness and redemption. Therefore, as it is written: "Let him who boasts boast in the Lord" (1 Corinthians 1:17-31).

Our Fear of Shame

Are you ashamed of your faith? Be honest. We humans do not like to be humiliated, and one of the greatest fears people have is to be thought stupid. Consequently, many Christians move timidly through the passageways of life, hoping no one will notice God's seal of ownership on them.

It reminds me of the young man who joined the army. His pastor sat him down before he left for basic training and warned him, "Wally, the army can be a rough place. The men are vulgar, hard drinkers, and use filthy language. Many will mock you for your faith in Christ. If you pray and read your Bible, you may be persecuted, but remember, we'll be praying for you here at church."

"Thank you, Pastor," the new recruit replied. "I'll do my best."

The soldier went off to his camp and was gone for several months before coming home on leave. At church, the pastor came up to the soldier and said, "Wally, we prayed for you every week that God would bring you safely through. Tell me, did you suffer a lot of persecution?"

The soldier smiled and said, "Well, no, Pastor. They didn't persecute me at all."

"You're kidding!" the pastor said, surprised. "When I was in the army, every Christian faced incredible persecution. How did you manage to avoid it?"

"It was easy, Pastor," the young man replied. "They never found out I was a Christian."

Jesus meant it when He said, "Whoever disowns me before men, I will disown him before my Father in heaven" (Matthew 10:33). It may not even be open denial, but rather, an inward shame that dishonors the Lord. Jesus addressed that problem too: "If anyone is ashamed of me and my words, the Son of Man will be ashamed of him when he comes in his glory and in the glory of the Father and of the holy angels" (Luke 9:26).

No one likes to be embarrassed or thought poorly of by his family, friends, neighbors, or fellow workers. But there comes a time when each of us must stand firm for the truth no matter what others think.

Reasons for Our Confidence

Let me share with you five reasons Christians have no reason to be ashamed of God.

His Sovereignty   God is the highest power in all the universe. He is not *a* god among many; He is the only God that exists. As Moses declared: "Acknowledge and take to heart this day that the LORD is God in heaven above and on the earth below. There is no other" (Deuteronomy 4:39).

He is the absolute Ruler of the universe (1 Chronicles 29:12) and He does not need permission from anyone to do what pleases Him (Job 9:12; Psalm 135:6). The book of Daniel confirms this: "He does as he pleases with the powers of heaven and the peoples of the earth. No one can hold back his hand or say to him: 'What have you done?'" (4:35).

God's sovereign nature includes His omnipotence, omniscience, and omnipresence. *Omnipotence* means that God is all-powerful. There is nothing too hard for Him to do, as we are told in Job 42:2: "I know that you can do all things; no plan of yours can be thwarted." Jesus said, "With God all things are possible" (Matthew 19:26).

By the way, don't get caught up in the foolish argument that God is not omnipotent if He can't create a rock too big for Him to pick up. Part of God's character is that He is self-consistent. Nothing in His Being contradicts itself.

God's omnipotence is reason enough to have full confidence in Him, and it will always amaze me that some of His people believe God can get them to heaven, but in the meantime, there is little He can do to heal them from their "psychological" diseases.

In addition to being omnipotent, God is *omniscient*—that is, He knows everything. David writes, "Great is our Lord and mighty in power; his understanding has no limit" (Psalm 147:5). John writes plainly, "[God] knows everything" (1 John 3:20).

Jesus said, "Are not two sparrows sold for a penny? Yet not one of them will fall to the ground apart from the will of your Father. And even the very hairs of your head are all numbered" (Matthew 10:29-30). The point of this amazing statement is that God knows even the minute and seemingly insignificant details of His creation. It means that He knows you and me by name and what we need before we even ask Him (Matthew 6:8).

God's omniscience means that He knows the pain we feel, the fears that cripple us, the bitterness that plunges us into darkness. It means that God is never taken by surprise and that our emergencies do not confound Him, because He knows the future (Isaiah 42:9).

God knows our secrets (Psalm 44:21) and what goes on in the dark (Daniel 2:22). He knows what is in our hearts (Luke 16:15) and our minds (Psalm 94:11). He can see straight into our inner being (1 Chronicles 28:9) and knows our thoughts and motives (Proverbs 16:2), and there will come a day when God "will expose the motives of men's hearts" (1 Corinthians 4:5). That's a frightening concept in itself.

God understands every law of physics, every mathematical formula, every aerodynamic principle. He has a flawless understanding of anatomy, every medical procedure, every medicinal substance, and therapeutic procedure. He can name every creature, extant or extinct. He comprehends the fine points of atomic theory and the relationships between matter, energy, time, and space. And, yes, He knows how to mend the damaged mind and wounded heart.

There is, quite simply, *nothing* that God does not know.

Another glorious fact of God's sovereignty is His *omnipresence*. That is, God is present in all places at all times. As David writes, "If I go up to the heavens, you are there; if I make my bed in the depths, you are there" (Psalm 139:8). When the Russian astronaut laughingly reported that he had not seen God in space, he revealed his own blindness, not the absence of God. While he did not see God, God certainly saw him, for we are told, "'Can anyone hide in secret places so that I cannot see him?' declares the LORD. 'Do not I fill heaven and earth?' declares the LORD" (Jeremiah 23:24).

My wife and I are wonderfully comforted to know that when we are separated from our children by thousands of miles as they study in another city or we travel in a foreign land, our heavenly Father is right there with them at the same precise moment He is with us at our location. Sovereign, omnipotent, omniscient, omnipresent. How can we possibly be ashamed of the omni-King of glory?

His Righteousness   Not only is God the sovereign King, but unlike earthly dictators who are motivated by a lust for wealth and brutal power, He is also righteous—that is, He is just toward all without prejudice or partiality. The psalmist tells us "The LORD is righteous in all his ways and loving toward all he has made" (Psalm 145:17). His righteousness, of course, is multifaceted and includes other qualities such as holiness, integrity, and judgment.

What a contrast there is between our just and loving God and the wicked idols of demonic religions that rule by ignorance and fear. What a difference between the utter darkness of evil and the brilliant light of our heavenly Father. John writes, "This is the message we have heard from him and declare to you: God is light; in him there is no darkness at all" (1 John 1:5).

Though the unbelieving world scoffs at God, there will come a day when He will be glorified universally. "I will show the holiness of my great name, which has been profaned among the nations, the name you have profaned among them. Then the nations will know that I am the LORD" (Ezekiel 36:23). The result of this universal knowledge of God's righteousness is defined by John when he writes, "Who will not fear you, O Lord, and bring glory to your name? For you alone are holy. All nations will come and worship before you, for your righteous acts have been revealed" (Revelation 15:4).

I would be ashamed to worship a deity who was immoral, unfair, unholy, and unjust, but our heavenly Father is without flaw, as is His Word. David writes, "As for God, his way is perfect; the word of the LORD is flawless (Psalm 18:30).

What an awesome combination—sovereignty *and* righteousness! How could we ever be ashamed of Him?

His Love   A third reason we should never be ashamed of our heavenly Father is His unlimited and incomprehensible love. No god in any other religion can come close to the purity and mercy that is showered upon humanity by the God of Scripture. His love is seen from the earliest chapters of Genesis through the concluding verses of Revelation.

Jeremiah writes, "The LORD appeared to us in the past, saying: 'I have loved you with an everlasting love; I have drawn you with loving-kindness'" (Jeremiah 31:3). God's unending love is not His response to our innate worth, but an integral part of His immutable character. He loves us because it is His very nature to love: God *is* love (1 John 4:16).

His love, by the way, is not dependent upon our love for Him. On the contrary, human love is a response to and a poor reflection of His self-initiated love. "We love because he first loved us" (1 John 4:19). The truth of His primary love is wonderfully illustrated in the love God showed to the little nation of Israel. "It was because the LORD loved you and kept the oath he swore to your forefathers that he brought you out with a mighty hand and redeemed you from the land of slavery, from the power of Pharaoh king of Egypt" (Deuteronomy 7:8).

God's love is not a response to our being lovable, for Paul writes, "God demonstrates his own love for us in this: While we were still sinners, Christ died for us" (Romans 5:8). The thought is repeated in Ephesians: "Because of his great love for us, God, who is rich in mercy, made us alive with Christ even when we were dead in transgressions—it is by grace you have been saved" (Ephesians 2:4-5).

Of all the qualities that remove shame, love is perhaps the most powerful, as this story illustrates: A beautiful young woman by the name of Ruth rushed into her burning house to save her little daughter, Anna, and in so doing, her face was horribly disfigured by the flames. As little Anna grew older, she was embarrassed by the scars on her mother's face, as other children ran away in fear or laughed cruelly. Anna began to hurry home from school so that other children would not see her mother meet her on the sidewalk.

One day, Ruth's sister Jean came to visit and as Ruth was in the kitchen making some tea, Anna looked longingly at her aunt's beautiful face with perfectly smooth skin and said, "Aunt Jean, I wish Mama looked like you. You are so beautiful!"

Jean sat Anna on her lap and with tears in her eyes said, "Anna, your mother *is* very beautiful. In fact, people used to say she was the most beautiful girl in our family. But do you know how your mother's face was burned?"

"No, Aunt Jean," Anna replied, shaking her head. "Mama never told me."

"When you were a little baby, your house caught on fire. Your mother was burned when she ran back into the house to save you from the flames. She protected you with her hands and arms and her own face was left unprotected from the fire. Her face is a constant reminder of her love for you, Anna."

For a moment little Anna sat quietly as tears filled her big blue eyes. Then she slipped down from Jean's lap and ran into the kitchen and threw her arms around her mother. "Oh, Mama!" she cried, "I didn't know! I didn't know! I'm so sorry! Please forgive me!"

"For what, child?" her mother asked as she picked Anna up and held her close.

"For not loving you like you loved me. You took my place in the fire!"

Her mother smiled through tears and hugged Anna tightly. "Anna, my little baby," she said, "I would do it all over again!"

From that day on, little Anna proudly walked beside her mother, whose face carried the scars of love.

That's the glorious essence of the gospel: God loves us though we are full of the cancer of sin. John writes that God loved humankind so much "that he gave his one and only Son, that whoever believes in him shall not perish but have eternal life" (John 3:16).

He loves us so much that He is willing to adopt into His own family all who wish to be included. "How great is the love the Father has lavished on us, that we should be called children of God! And that is what we are!" (1 John 3 :1).

Only when we learn to love Him from the depths of our being will we be free from the crippling effects of shame.

His Eternal Plan of Salvation   A fourth cause for confidence in God is His eternal plan of salvation, which He had in mind for us before the beginning of time (1 Corinthians 2:7; Titus 1:2). Paul exhorts us not to "be ashamed to testify about our Lord" (2 Timothy 1:8) as he points out that God "has saved us and called us to a holy life—not because of anything we have done but because of his own purpose and grace. This grace was given us in Christ Jesus before the beginning of time" (2 Timothy 1:9).

God anticipated every problem before it ever arose, even to our need of being saved. The crucifixion of Christ was a necessary part of God's plan to redeem us from the curse of sin. That's why Peter told the people of Israel that Jesus "was handed over to you by God's set purpose and foreknowledge; and you, with the help of wicked men, put him to death by nailing him to the cross" (Acts 2:23). Though they were still responsible for their own sinful rejection of Christ, "they did what [God's] power and will had decided beforehand should happen" (Acts 4:28). It was all part of His plan and it was all predicted in writing. "The Scripture foresaw that God would justify the Gentiles by faith, and announced the gospel in advance to Abraham: 'All nations will be blessed through you'" (Galatians 3:8).

This profound truth has great implications for our puny faith. If God was able to anticipate our need for salvation before we were even created, how can we be so foolish as to doubt that He has anticipated and provided for our every need in this life? That's why 2 Peter 1:3 is such a blessed promise: "His divine power has given us everything we need for life and godliness through our knowledge of him who called us by his own glory and goodness."

Part of the joy of being a child of God is knowing that He is never surprised and *nothing* can hinder His plans. Paul writes that God "works out everything in conformity with the purpose of his will" (Ephesians 1:11). What He has determined will take place. Job said it well: "I know that you can do all things; no plan of yours can be thwarted" (Job 42:2).

How can we possibly be ashamed of so great a God? Those who doubt God's ability to take care of our every need are like the Pharisees Jesus diagnosed so clearly: "You are in error because you do not know the Scriptures or the power of God" (Matthew 22:29).

His Inevitable Victory   One final reason God's people must never be ashamed of their heavenly Father is the fact that God's victory over sin, sorrow, sickness, and death are already assured.

You may not believe that right now, especially if you are going through a time of trial and testing. It may seem to you as though God's promise of victory is a cruel hoax designed to increase your pain. According to the Scriptures, it's all in our focus.

Have you ever noticed that pain is lessened when we focus our minds on something else? This is especially true if we concentrate on something pleasant or urgent. Perhaps it's music or laughter, an important assignment, or the thought of a loved one. But for a few moments, we may find relief from the agonies of body and soul.

Think about it. An injured football player can continue to play when he sets his mind on the end zone. After the game is over, his pain may become so intense that he passes out. A soldier may be riddled with bullets and yet feel no pain as he carries a fallen comrade to safety. His mind is focused on getting home safely. That's exactly what God tells us to do in order to deal with our pain—focus on the goal, our heavenly home.

Peter writes, "Now for a little while you may have had to suffer grief in all kinds of trials. These have come so that your faith—of greater worth than gold, which perishes even though refined by fire—may be proved genuine" (1 Peter 1:6-7). This is a side point, but extremely important: We never know what kind of faith we have until it is tested by unpleasantness. It takes no faith at all to rejoice and trust God when things are going well, but disappointment, sorrow, betrayal, disease, and divorce all have a way of showing our faith for what it is—good or bad.

Let me ask you: Do you *really* believe that God is going to give you the victory? Or have you bought the lie that we have been left here on earth without the resources needed for a joy-filled life of inner peace? Jesus dispels that false and depressing thought when He says, "In me you may have peace. In this world you will have trouble. But take heart! I have overcome the world" (John 16:33).

Maybe you are thinking, *But I can't see Jesus, or touch Him. I'm hurting in this very real and evil world. Don't give me empty religious talk when I'm in such pain!* But dear friend, focusing our faith on Jesus is anything but empty. Peter says, "Though you have not seen him, you love him; and even though you do not see him now, you believe in him and are filled with an inexpressible and glorious joy, for you are receiving the goal of your faith, the salvation of your souls" (1 Peter 1:8-9).

Don't let the hollow philosophies of the world (Colossians 2:8) get you down. John writes, "This is the victory that has overcome the world, even our faith" (1 John 5:4).

WHERE IS OUR FOCUS?

It's all in our focus. The Bible tells us how to build our faith when it says to "set your *hearts* on things above" (Colossians 3:1), "set your *minds* on things above, not on earthly things

(Colossians 3:2), and "fix [your] *eyes* on Jesus" (Hebrews 12:2). That's why we are warned not to focus on our earthly problems, but to look ahead to the victory already won in Christ. We're going to examine these important principles for regaining our faith in chapter 13. This will require some thoughtful reading, but if you really want to believe again, it will be worth your time, so stay with me.

Answers to Prayer

Dr. David Miller hung up the phone and yelled, "Yes!" He hurried into the kitchen where Darla was fixing supper. "That was Robert Everett, honey!" he said with obvious excitement.

"What did he say, David?"

"He said the police have picked up six members of the gang, and that two of them have verified Jason's story. Robert said he thinks there's a good possibility that Jason might spend less than a year in a reformatory, and maybe—just maybe—he might even be paroled. He said that because of Jason's age and that he had never been in trouble before, and now that he's cooperating, the prosecutor is going to recommend leniency!"

"Oh, praise God!" Darla exclaimed. "But will he have to testify in court?"

"I'm sure he will," David said as he put his arms around his wife, "but the police have promised to protect him—and us. Whatever happens, though, we've got to trust the Lord, Darla. This could be what it takes to cripple these gangs. Maybe something good can come out of this tragedy after all!"

"Oh, but David, I am scared," Darla admitted as she leaned her head on her husband's chest. "What if the gang comes after us—or Faith?"

"I'll do my best to defend our family, honey. You know that. I would hate to shoot anyone, but if they were trying to harm you or Faith, I wouldn't hesitate!"

That evening, as they sat in their family room, they heard a car stop out front, and then the sound of breaking glass followed by a whooshing roar, footsteps running away, a car door slamming shut, and tires squealing.

"Dad!" Faith shouted from upstairs, "The house is on fire!"

"Out back!" David ordered Darla. "Get Faith and go out the back way!"

He dialed 911. "Someone just fire-bombed our house!" he said. "Send the fire department and the police!"

Soon, sirens filled the air as fire trucks and police converged on their quiet little street. The Miller's neighbors stood on the sidewalks watching as firemen quickly brought the blaze under control.

. . .

A few blocks away, Dr. Arthur Wilson blinked as he heard sirens rush by. A war of emotions still raged within between his loneliness and pride, his scientific training and his growing awareness of God. He suddenly turned, walked purposefully to the basement stairs, and hurried down to the storage room. He flipped on the lights, and there in a back corner, under several boxes, he saw an old metal trunk. It had a faded label on it that read, "Dad's Things."

He moved the boxes and stacked them one by one into another pile. He knelt before the trunk, opened the latches, and pushed the lid back. He paused for a moment, took a deep breath, and lifted out his father's old army uniform with a sense of reverence. He dug down past several boxes until he found what he was looking for.

He pulled out a gold-colored box about two inches deep, seven inches wide, and ten inches long. He stood to his feet and carried the box upstairs to his chair, turned on the light, and sat down. He tilted his head slightly, then opened the box and took out his father's Bible. Arthur had not touched it since the day his mother had packed it away in the trunk after his father died.

The Bible was worn from use, and as he flipped through the pages, he paused from time to time to see the verses his father had underlined years before. Here and there were handwritten notes explaining the meaning of a verse or its significance to his dad's life.

Arthur settled back in his chair and opened the Bible to the very front. "In the beginning, God. . . ." He smiled slightly, and shook his head in amazement that he was actually reading the Bible. He decided that he would approach it in a radically new way—with true objectivity and intellectual honesty. With that in mind, he determined to use a rationally acceptable filter to analyze each statement of Scripture: *Does this violate any proven law of science, or does it merely contradict a currently prevailing theory?*

As he read the biblical account of creation through this new analytical parameter, he was surprised to discover a startling integrity of logic founded on a primary assumption—the existence of an all-powerful being. *It's all in where you begin*, Arthur thought to himself.

He continued to read hour after hour, unaware of the passing of time. He moved from the stories of man's fall into sin to the catastrophic worldwide flood. *This could account for the extinction of dinosaurs!* he thought with excitement. He had been impressed with the rapid geologic layering during the flooding which followed the Mount St. Helen's explosion and how large canyons were formed in a matter of hours rather than thousands of years. *A worldwide flood of biblical magnitude could account for the Grand Canyon, the upheaval of the ocean floors, and even some of the continental drift,* he reasoned.

He moved on ahead in his father's Bible to a section that looked particularly worn through constant use—the book of Psalms. In the very first chapter, he read, "Blessed is the man who does not walk in the counsel of the wicked or stand in the way of sinners or sit in the seat of mockers. But his delight is in the law of the LORD, and on his law he meditates day and night."

He recognized himself in the description of the mocker and was cut to the heart. He skipped on down to the second psalm and read, "Why do the nations conspire and the peoples plot in vain?" He saw that he and his fellow atheists were part of the group who took their stand against the Lord, wanting to break off the chains of God and "his Anointed One." *It's not that the evidence denies God. It's that we simply don't want to submit to Him*, Arthur admitted to himself.

He stopped on Psalm 14, at another passage his father had underlined, and he read out loud, "The fool says in his heart, 'There is no God.' They are corrupt, their deeds are vile; there is no one who does good." For a moment Arthur felt his heart harden and his neck stiffen in reaction to these strong words. *I'm not really that bad, am I?* he thought. Then he said to himself, "Yeah, the truth is, I really *am* that bad. That's why I've been so cruel to Susan."

Coming to Psalm 19, he read, "The heavens declare the glory of God; the skies proclaim the work of his hands." Arthur looked up from his reading. At that moment, it was as though God ripped away a blindfold from Arthur's eyes and he received his sight.

"Oh, my God!" he cried out, as he fell to his knees, "It's all true! You *do* exist. I've been so blind! How could I have been such a fool?" In deep sorrow, he wept tears of conviction and repentance. "Can you ever forgive me? Oh, dear *God*, can you ever forgive me? I am so sorry. I do believe!"

In deep bitterness of soul, Arthur felt that his sin was too great to be forgiven. *I have blasphemed and raged against God*, he despaired. *I have caused others to disbelieve. I have destroyed my marriage and hurt the only woman who ever truly loved me. I don't deserve to be forgiven!*

By now it was nearly 2:00 in the morning, and his sense of hopelessness grew moment by moment as his life flashed through his mind like a horror film. His willful choice to reject God, his mockery of Christians, his disrespect for the Bible, his continually cursing tongue, his dishonoring of his parents, and the heartbreak he had caused Susan all flowed through his memory like a raging toxic stream.

He had no idea where to turn to find hope, and he momentarily considered ending his life, but Susan's voice seemed to echo somewhere in the back of his mind, saying, *God loves you, Arthur.*

Suddenly he thought of Michael Rollins, and not realizing what time it was, he picked up the phone and dialed. The phone rang several times before a weary voice answered.

"Hello?"

"Michael?"

"Yes? Who is this?"

"It's me, Michael! Arthur Wilson!"

"Arthur?" There was a pause as Michael collected his thoughts and sat up on the edge of the bed. "What's wrong, Arthur? You sound troubled."

"I'm more than troubled, Michael!" Arthur said, his voice tense with fear. "I've got to talk to someone—right now!"

"Of course, Arthur. Calm down and tell me what's going on."

"Not over the phone. I've got to see you, Michael. I have so many questions and they can't wait. Can I drive over to your house?"

"Tonight?" Michael asked incredulously.

"Yes, Michael! Tonight! I've got to have some answers tonight!"

"Well . . . of course, then, Arthur. Come on over. I'll be waiting for you."

Oh, thank you, Michael!" Arthur said with deep relief. "I'll be over in half an hour."

When Michael hung up the phone, Ellen rolled over in bed, her eyes nearly closed with sleep, and asked, "What's the problem, Michael?"

"I don't know for sure, honey," he said as he yawned and stretched, "but I think God may be answering our prayers regarding Arthur Wilson."

"Why don't we pray right now?" Ellen asked.

"Okay, hon," Michael agreed. "Unless I'm mistaken, I'm going to need all the wisdom God can give me."

They prayed for several minutes, then Michael put on his robe and went downstairs, Bible in hand. He switched on the lamp in the front room and turned to Romans 1:16: "*I am not ashamed of the gospel, because it is the power of God for the salvation of everyone who believes.*"

"Oh, dear Lord," he prayed, "please prepare Arthur's heart to listen, to understand, and to bow his heart before you. Humble him and help him to understand his need this very night, I pray. Thank you, Jesus."

About forty minutes later, Michael heard a car drive up and park in front of the house. A car door opened and then shut quietly and footsteps hurried to the front door. A gentle tap let Michael know that Arthur had arrived.

When Michael opened the door, Arthur blurted out, "Oh, I'm so sorry, Michael! I didn't realize how late it was until I pulled up out front! I thought it was only about 10:00 P.M. But you're awake, and I'm here, so can we talk anyway?"

"Slow down, Arthur," Michael laughed as he welcomed him inside. "I am so pleased you felt you could call me. Come on in to the front room and sit down. What kinds of questions bring you out at this time of night? Or morning, as the case may be."

"Michael!" Arthur exclaimed as he sat down, his eyes red with fear and weariness, "I finally see it all so clearly! You were right!" He held up his father's old Bible and said, "There *is* a God, and I *know* it! But I'm afraid I've committed a sin so great God can't forgive me. Can I still be saved?"

"Praise the Lord!" Michael shouted.

Arthur blinked, his eyes wide with confusion. "What do you mean?"

"Arthur, we have been praying for this moment ever since we first met you!"

"But can I really be saved, Michael? I have rejected God for so long, will He still forgive me?"

"Oh, yes, Arthur!" Michael answered with deep conviction. "God is always willing to forgive. He says, 'whoever comes to me I will never cast out!'"[55]

"But how can I be saved, Michael? I don't even know how to approach God."

Michael smiled and said, "Let me show you what God says." He pointed at Arthur's Bible and asked, "Would you like to see it in your own Bible?"

Arthur nodded. "It was my father's Bible."

"Then let's use it. I can't think of anything that would have pleased your father more, can you?"

"No," Arthur admitted, "Dad would love to see this."

"First, I want you to turn to Romans 3. Read what it says there in verses 10 through 18."

Using the table of contents, Arthur found Romans and turned to the third chapter. He began to read: "There is no one righteous, not even one; there is no one who understands, no one who seeks God. All have turned away, they have together become worthless; there is no one who does good, not even one. Their throats are open graves; their tongues practice deceit. The poison of vipers is on their lips. Their mouths are full of cursing and bitterness. Their feet are swift to shed blood; ruin and misery mark their ways, and the way of peace they do not know. There is no fear of God before their eyes."

Arthur looked up with pain in his eyes. "Except for the part about shedding blood, that's a perfect description of my life," he said.

"Look at verse 23," Michael directed.

"For all have sinned and fall short of the glory of God," Arthur read. "Again, that's me all the way!"

"Now flip over a few chapters to Romans 6, verse 23, and read that."

Arthur quickly paged over, found the passage, and read, "For the wages of sin is death, but the gift of God is eternal life through Christ Jesus our Lord." He looked up quickly and said with total sincerity, "I want that more than anything in the world! But how? I still don't understand."

"Well, Arthur, I know of another professor who asked the very same question years ago. Let's move back to the book of John, chapter 3, and you'll see what I mean."

Arthur turned to the table of contents again and then found the book of John and turned to the third chapter.

"Read verses 1 through 7, Arthur," Michael suggested.

Arthur read with a spiritual hunger deeper than Michael had ever seen.

"Now there was a man of the Pharisees named Nicodemus, a member of the Jewish ruling council. He came to Jesus at night and said, 'Rabbi, we know you are a teacher who has come from God. For no one could perform the miraculous signs you are doing if God were not with him.'

"In reply Jesus declared, 'I tell you the truth, no one can see the kingdom of God unless he is born again.'

"'How can a man be born when he is old?' Nicodemus asked. 'Surely he cannot enter a second time into his mother's womb to be born!'

"Jesus answered, 'I tell you the truth, no one can enter the kingdom of God unless he is born of water and the Spirit. Flesh gives birth to flesh, but the Spirit gives birth to spirit. You should not be surprised at my saying, "You must be born again."'"

Arthur looked up, his face still troubled. He shook his head and said, "I still don't get it."

"Well, don't be embarrassed, Arthur. Neither did Nicodemus. The point is, just as people must be born physically to enter this world, so we must all be born spiritually in order to enter the spiritual world."

"But exactly what did Jesus mean by being 'born again'?"

"He explained it in verse 16," Michael said with a twinkle in his eye. "Go on. Read it."

"For God so loved the world that he gave his one and only Son, that whoever believes in him shall not perish but have eternal life." Arthur looked up, his head cocked slightly to the left. "Do you mean all I have to do is believe that Jesus died and I'm saved?"

Michael shook his head gently. "No, Arthur. James tells us that the demons of hell themselves believe the *facts* about God.[56] Head knowledge alone will never get anyone to heaven."

"Then what does it mean 'to believe'?"

"It means to place the full hope of your eternal destiny squarely on His sacrifice for your sins, Arthur. It means that you not only believe in your head that Jesus died for your sins,[57] but you are trusting in nothing else to get you to heaven.[58] It means that you have full confidence in what God says[59]—that His Son's death is full payment for every sin we have ever committed."[60]

Arthur looked up, hope beginning to fill his heart as he understood the simple message of the gospel for the first time in his life.

Michael added, "In Acts 16, a desperate man asked Paul and Silas, 'Sirs, what must I do to be saved?' Do you know what Paul replied, Arthur?"

"I'm not sure of the wording, but I can guess. He must have said that the man needed to believe in Jesus to be saved."

"Exactly! He said, 'Believe in the Lord Jesus, and you will be saved—you and your household.'"

"And that's all there is to it? Just 'believe'?"

Michael looked Arthur squarely in the eyes. "What is there left for us to do, Arthur, except believe? God has already done all the rest!"

"But still, I feel I should have to *do* something, Michael. I mean, this seems almost, well . . . too easy."

"It wasn't easy for Jesus, Arthur. He spent hours on the cross in horrible agony for my sins. For yours. No, it isn't too easy. But anything we would add to His finished work would only cheapen it."[61]

Arthur nodded, understanding. "All I have to offer Him is my sin. Of course! If I could work my way into heaven, it would mean Jesus' death was pointless. But I can't."[62]

Michael smiled and nodded in agreement. He waited patiently for Arthur to make up his mind.

Arthur finally looked over at Michael and said, "I want to settle this thing here and now. What should I do?"

"I suggest you just tell Jesus what's on your heart."

"You mean pray? Out loud?"

"Why not? You used to curse out loud, didn't you?"

Arthur smiled sheepishly and said, "Yes, and I'm ashamed of it!"

"Then don't keep being ashamed. You're going to have to learn to take a firm stand for Jesus, and you might as well begin right now."

Arthur nodded. "Okay."

Instinctively he closed his eyes, and clasped his hands. "Oh, Lord," he said hesitantly, "I'm new to this, but I now understand that You exist and that You love me. And I want to tell You . . . I love You, too! I believe with all my heart that You died for my sins and that You rose from the dead to guarantee eternal life to every person who believes.[63] By faith right now in Your written Word, I accept Jesus as my own Savior." Arthur's voice began to tremble with emotion, and tears of joy streamed down his face. "Oh, Jesus! I am so sorry for having rejected You all these years! I submit my entire life to You this very moment. Thank You for loving me enough to die in my place and thank You for forgiving me!"

Both Michael and Arthur remained silent in the holiness of the moment, with heads bowed. Finally, they looked up and Arthur's face broke into a smile of joy and peace. They stood and embraced as brothers in Christ.

"Thank you, Michael, for taking the time to help me! I'll never forget this moment!"

"No, and neither will I, Arthur!" Michael said with a broad smile. "Welcome to the family of God!"

Arthur turned to leave. "I know you need to get to bed, Michael. But before I go, am I still invited to dinner on Friday night?"

Michael's eyes opened wide in surprise and he smiled again as he said, "Of course, Arthur! That's one more answer to prayer!"

12

A Greater Submission to Our God

THE BIBLE IS ABSOLUTELY clear that God has revealed Himself to every human in at least two ways: His creation and our consciences. Romans 1:20 says, "Since the creation of the world God's invisible qualities—his eternal power and divine nature—have been clearly seen, being understood from what has been made, so that men are without excuse."

Paul goes on to say that we also have the witness of our conscience telling us there is a sovereign Lawgiver:

> Indeed, when Gentiles, who do not have the law, do by nature things required by the law, they are a law for themselves, even though they do not have the law, since they show that the requirements of the law are written on their hearts, their consciences also bearing witness, and their thoughts now accusing, now even defending them (Romans 2:14-15).

The point is, the only way humans can deny the existence and love of God is by an active choice of the will.

IS "ALL TRUTH GOD'S TRUTH"?

An unfortunate twisting of this biblical concept of "general revelation"—that is, God revealed outside of Scripture—is the over-used and abused phrase, " All truth is God's truth." There is, perhaps, no more dangerous threat to the dike of accurate biblical doctrine that holds back the floods of heresy than this psychological plea to accept all "truth" as God's.

Larry Crabb has written, "Truth is truth, whether scientific truth or theological truth, whether found in the psychologist's laboratory or in the Bible student's library."[64] Psychologists, however, rarely address *how* one determines what is true, and that question is essential because "scientific" research, findings, and theories are in a constant state of flux. Even more appalling is Dr. Crabb's next sentence: "To speak of biblical truth as somehow more authoritative than scientific truth is really absurd. Truth has authority over error, not over another truth."[65]

I couldn't disagree more. Biblical truth must have primacy over *every* other "truth," for man's "truth" one day is found to be false the next.

The consequences of such foolish thinking are enormous. Pastor Tom Watson points out, "Using the 'all truth' philosophy, anything can be proclaimed as truth. For example when Focus on the Family introduced a tape by New Ager Norman Cousins, the announcer made these statements:

> We are fully aware that Norman Cousins does not come from an evangelical Christian perspective, but all truth is God's truth. If it's true, it came from God, and the next twenty minutes we feel are true and valuable and will make a contribution in your life.

"Cousins's teaching was one of holistic health that one can control pain, bleeding, and infection through a mental process. James said, 'This wisdom is not that which comes down from above, but is earthly, natural, demonic' (James 3:15 NASB)."[66]

A dear pastor friend of mine recently commented on the phrase "all truth is God's truth" by saying, "I agree. And all grass seed is grass seed. You can buy it in a clean container at the garden shop or you can go to the stable and separate it from horse manure."

From a proper source you will get consistent quality in grass seed, while from the stable you will get some grass and some weeds. When you're picking seed out of manure, you never quite know what you're getting. And in the same way, when you're picking through the world's systems to find "truth" you never quite know what you're getting.

The question is, why would *any* Christian paw through the filth of "hollow and deceptive philosophy" (Colossians 2:8) to find a few seeds of truth when God has already revealed in His Word everything pertaining to life and godliness (2 Peter 1:3)?

DATA IS NOT THE SAME AS TRUTH

The concept "all truth is God's truth" is seductively appealing until one realizes that *data is not the same as truth.* To arrive at truth, a person must interpret the data in accordance with reliable principles of rational analysis. In the physical realm, we must rely upon scientific method (which we discussed earlier), and in the spiritual arena, we must follow consistent biblical *hermeneutics* (a fancy word for "system of interpretation").

Let me illustrate. A psychologist and a biblical counselor may observe the same person who is exhibiting classical symptoms of depression—exhaustion, loss of appetite, sense of hopelessness, apathy, social withdrawal, insomnia, and so on. Both counselors can ask questions to collect more data. In the end, however, they will probably arrive at different conclusions about the root problems and the treatment required because they will analyze the data according to their system of interpretation.

You might well argue, "But the truth is, the person is depressed." Granted. But is that the level of truth people are speaking of when they cry out, "All truth is God's truth"? I don't believe so. I think they are pleading the case that foundational life-altering truths are just as available from the world as from the Word. And that is where I disagree.

Think carefully about what Larry Crabb said: "To speak of biblical truth as somehow more authoritative than scientific truth is really absurd. Truth has authority over error, not over another truth."[67] His statement is representative of the thinking of those who wish to integrate psychological theories with biblical principles to form a "truth" superior to the Scriptures alone.

We would do well to ask the same question Pilate asked Jesus: "What is truth?" (John 18:38). He was responding to Jesus' ministry statement, "For this I came into the world, to testify to the truth. Everyone on the side of truth listens to me" (John 18:37). He had defined truth earlier in the book of John when He said, "I am the way and the truth and the life. No one comes to the Father except through me" (John 14:6).

To suggest that all "truth" is equally authoritative borders on heresy, dear friend, and I urge all Christians to exercise extreme caution when listening to or reading books by "experts" who argue that "all truth is God's truth."

ENOUGH TRUTH FOR JUDGMENT, BUT NOT FOR SALVATION

The sad limitation of "general revelation" is that it removes all excuses about not knowing God, but it cannot provide enough information to be saved or sanctified.

We are accountable for what we know about God, and the physical world tells us about His infinity, His power, and His goodness (Romans 1:20). The vastness of the universe reveals God's infinity and eternal nature; it is so immense that we must measure distances in light years. From the macroscopic view of the cosmos to the microscopic complexity of molecules and atoms, God's limitless nature is so obvious that to deny His existence is the result of willful and active choice.

Like His infinity, God's awesome power is also clearly revealed by nature through the destructive force of nuclear reactions, the deafening roar of Niagara Falls, and the explosive energy of surging volcanoes. From the mighty winds of hurricanes, to the brilliant flashes of lightning, to rolling ocean tides, God's measureless power is plain to see.

Yet even from the signs of nature, God's gracious character is shown with crystal clarity. Jesus said that God "causes his sun to rise on the evil and the good, and sends rain on the righteous and the unrighteous" (Matthew 5:45). God's material provision for all people is a testimony to His love—even for those who despise Him. He "provides food for the raven" (Job 38:41) and even notices when a sparrow dies (Matthew 10:29). All of His care and providence show His love and gentleness to an undeserving world.

That is why God says that we are "without excuse" (Romans 1:20), and if we are without excuse, we will be held accountable for our lives, whether or not we choose to submit to His authority. Paul writes, "each of us will give an account of himself to God" (Romans 14:12), and Peter adds this warning: "They will have to give account to him who is ready to judge the living and the dead" (1 Peter 4:5).

SPECIAL REVELATION IS REQUIRED

God has given us enough information in the pages of nature to reveal His existence, but for salvation, we need "special revelation"—that which God Himself has revealed to us in the Scriptures. Without this special information, we are hopelessly lost. As Jeremiah writes, "Even the stork in the sky knows her appointed seasons, and the dove, the swift and the thrush observe the time of their migration. But my people do not know the requirements of the LORD" (Jeremiah 8:7). The result of this spiritual ignorance is that "they go from one sin to another; they do not acknowledge me" (Jeremiah 9:3).

Have you ever wondered why people are so incurably evil? Why is there so much anger, violence, pain, and sorrow? Why do people persecute one another in the name of religion? Jesus explained it quite simply: "They will do such things because they have not known the Father or me" (John 16:3). Jeremiah is not as gentle in his assessment: "My people are fools; they do not know [God]. They are senseless children; they have no understanding. They are skilled in doing evil; they know not how to do good" (4:22).

To remedy this problem, God has given us the written Word. Paul writes, "All Scripture is God-breathed [or inspired] and is useful for teaching [doctrine], rebuking, correcting and training in righteousness" (2 Timothy 3:16).

The Bible is God's "special revelation." It tells us about the origin of the universe, how man came to exist, our purpose on earth, why we suffer, the process of inner healing, and how we can live forever. It explains the past, present, and future of all humanity. None of these things can be understood by "general revelation" alone, so it became necessary for God to communicate these truths to humans through the prophecies that are recorded in Scripture.

THE REQUIRED RESPONSE OF FAITH

Many people who are intellectually honest enough to admit the existence of God are still uncomfortable with the fact that God requires each human to make a choice of faith. It is not enough to know that God *is*, for He also demands a personal response. Moses referred to this obligation when he said to his people, "This day I call heaven and earth as witnesses against you that I have set before you life and death, blessings and curses. Now choose life, so that you and your children may live" (Deuteronomy 30:19).

The majority of humans foolishly choose death over submission to God, and what's amazing is that God allows us to go the direction we choose. Joshua said, "If serving the LORD seems undesirable to you, then choose for yourselves this day whom you will serve" (Joshua 24:15).

In His mercy, God often gives us a prolonged period of time to make this most important decision of our existence. But there eventually comes a moment when we must decide what we are going to do about God. Elijah brought Israel to a moment of decision when he said, "How long will you waver between two opinions? If the LORD is God, follow him; but if Baal is God, follow him" (1 Kings 18:21).

Perhaps that same choice is now confronting you. Having considered the concept of God's existence and the insurmountable evidence pointing toward Him, you must decide for yourself whether you will acknowledge Him as your own God. A liberating fact is that He will never force you to love Him, for He wants your decision to come freely from your heart.

There will come a day, however, when the freedom to choose will be over. Then everyone will acknowledge God as the King of the universe whether they wish to or not. It will be too late for the rebel to be saved, but he will be forced to his knees before Almighty God. "'As surely as I live,' says the Lord, 'every knee will bow before me; every tongue will confess to God'" (Romans 14:11).

But today, God's mercy still reigns, and He invites you and all others to "turn to me and be saved, all you ends of the earth; for I am God, and there is no other" (Isaiah 45:22).

WHAT SUBMISSION TO GOD INVOLVES

People have been asking this question from the beginning of time: What does God require? The prophet Micah anticipated that question when he wrote, "He has showed you, O man, what is good. And what does the LORD require of you? To act justly and to love mercy and to walk humbly with your God" (Micah 6:8).

Please note what the passage does *not* mention: painful ritual, mysterious chanting, monastic robes, official membership in a church, or any of the other trappings of man's religion. In every age and in every location, what God has always required is a loving walk with Him.

In keeping with that metaphor, may I point out the obvious? God has designed our walk to be bipedal, which, being interpreted, means we have two feet. And just as our physical walk requires the balanced cooperation between both feet, so our walk with God is a delicate balance of two foundational elements: *faith* and *obedience.* Our last chapter will deal with these essential parts of Christian living, but for now, it is enough to understand that both must come from the very core of our being—the heart.

In the New International Version, the word "heart" appears some 541 times, giving us some indication of how important the concept is. The King James Version uses the word 762 times. The reason this concept is so foundational is that the heart controls the rest of our existence. As Proverbs says, "Above all else, guard your heart, for it is the wellspring of life" (Proverbs 4:23).

For faith to be genuine, it must stem from an authentic conviction of the heart: "It is with your heart that you believe and are justified, and it is with your mouth that you confess and are saved" (Romans 10:10).

Jesus explained genuine heartfelt submission to God this way: "Love the Lord your God with all your heart and with all your soul and with all your strength and with all your mind; and, love your neighbor as yourself" (Luke 10:27). Love is the essence of a true walk with God, and it involves every portion of a person's being. The result of an all-encompassing love for God is that we will also love our fellow man.

But even more than that, we will delight in fulfilling God's will in and through our lives. Jesus was the perfect example of willing submission throughout His time on earth, but especially in the Garden of Gethsemane when He said to His Father, "If it is possible, may this cup be taken from me. Yet not as I will, but as you will" (Matthew 26:39).

Many mistakenly believe that submission to God will produce a life of boredom, misery, and loss, but nothing could be further from the truth. That's why Jesus said "Take my yoke upon you and learn from me, for I am gentle and humble in heart, and you will find rest for your souls. For my yoke is easy and my burden is light" (Matthew 11:29-30). Dear friend, turning our lives over to Jesus is the path to peace and joy, but you will never know that until you love Him enough to trust Him . . . and trust Him enough to obey Him.

New Beginnings

The parsonage was not damaged severely by the firebomb. Whoever threw it was either inexperienced or had only intended to frighten the Millers. For the remainder of the night the police posted a patrol car outside the home, giving Dave and Darla a measure of security. Still, they found it difficult to sleep.

The next morning, the police called with some good news. "One of your neighbors happened to be out in his yard when the firebombing occurred, Dr. Miller," an officer reported. "He got a good look at the car, and with his description and the first four numbers of the license plate we were able to track it down. We arrested four more members of the gang, and according to our information, that is about the entire group. The narcs at the local school tell us this was a pack of wannabees who had just gotten started. Too bad it ended with the death of an old man."

"You mean you think you got the entire gang?"

"We think so, but we can't be absolutely sure for now. We're going to continue providing protection for you until we know for certain. Anyway, I think you can relax a bit."

"Thanks, officer!" David said. "That means a lot to us."

Now that things looked as though Jason might not receive a long sentence, David Miller began thinking about the process of rebuilding his family. They had all been damaged by the events of the past few months, and their sense of pain and embarrassment still cut deeply whenever they happened to see a member of their church at the shopping center or on the street.

One evening as they were sitting in the family room trying to regain a sense of normalcy, Faith asked her parents, "Why would God allow something like this to happen to us?"

"What do you mean, Faith?" David asked.

"I mean, if God really loves us, and if we've been serving Him faithfully, how could He let Jason get caught up in something so terrible?"

Darla turned to David, awaiting his answer, as though she had been wondering the same thing.

David paused for what seemed a long time. Finally, he said, "You know, Faith, a few months ago, I think I would have said that Jason had a psychological problem—maybe attention deficit disorder, or something like that. But, I'm beginning to believe Jason's problem was just old-fashioned rebellion. Nobody made him join the gang, but he was afraid of looking uncool, and he was just plain scared of what the other kids might do to him if he didn't join up. I guess it doesn't really matter now. The end result was that he fell in with the wrong crowd."

"But I would think God could have prevented Jason from making such a stupid decision!" Faith argued.

"I suppose He could have, Faith, but God decided a long time ago to give each of us humans the freedom to choose whether to follow Him. Do you remember when Joshua said to his people, 'Choose for yourselves this day whom you will serve . . . but as for me and my household, we will serve the Lord'? Following God is a personal and deliberate choice each of us has to make."

"But look where we are now, Dad. Jason is in jail, you're out of work, the parsonage has been firebombed, and we're afraid to go out in public. I mean, where is God in all of this?"

Darla nodded in agreement and said, "And where are all the people from the church who said they would be here for us? Whenever they see me at the store, they almost run the other direction. Maybe they're afraid a gang member will see them with me. I don't know." Tears of hurt and anger filled her eyes. "I'll tell you the truth, David, I wish we could just forget the whole 'church thing' and move back out to Colorado. We could both get jobs, and we wouldn't have to play the role of spiritual leaders anymore."

"Is that how you see our work, Darla?" David asked, his heart aching with a deep sense of failure. Darla had always been a faithful partner in their ministry, but she had not always been enthusiastic about the pastorate. "Do you think we've just been role-playing? Doesn't our faith in God mean anything?"

Darla's lips trembled with emotion as she looked at David and said, "What *has* our faith in God done for us, David? We're middle-aged, have almost no savings put away for our kids' education or our retirement, you don't have a job, and we're here in this God-forsaken city! All around us there are unbelievers who drive new cars, have excellent health, and their children aren't in jail!"

David sat silently for a few moments and then reached for his Bible. Turning to Psalm 73, he read, "But as for me, my feet had almost slipped; I had nearly lost my foothold. For I envied the arrogant when I saw the prosperity of the wicked . . . Always carefree, they increase in wealth. Surely in vain have I kept my heart pure; in vain have I washed my hands in innocence."

He turned to Darla and said, "Is that how you really feel?"

She didn't answer but stared at the floor sullenly.

David began to read again, "If I had said, 'I will speak thus,' I would have betrayed your children. When I tried to understand all this, it was oppressive to me till I entered the sanctuary of God; then I understood their final destiny."

Darla began to weep as the Holy Spirit gently pierced through the bitterness of her heart. It was several minutes before she could speak. She looked over at her husband and whispered, "I'm sorry. It isn't God's fault all this happened. We didn't spend enough time with Jason. We didn't teach him to stand firm against peer pressure. And I have always acted like this when I don't get my way, haven't I?"

David looked down and didn't answer.

"We haven't been very good examples for our children, have we, David?" she asked again.

He looked over at her and said, "No, Darla, we have been as petty and unbelieving as the people we thought we were preaching to. Look at what David writes in verses 21-22: 'When my heart was grieved and my spirit embittered, I was senseless and ignorant.'"

"That's really the root cause of our problems, David, don't you think?" Darla asked.

"What?"

"Bitterness. I have struggled with disappointment, bitterness, and anger my whole life. Even when I was a kid, if I didn't get what I wanted, I pouted about it—and I'm still doing it! The trouble is, David, I don't know how to stop!" She began crying again.

David didn't know what to say. He looked back down at the Bible in his lap and silently read. Suddenly he stopped and smiled, then looked over at Darla and said, "The answer is right here."

She sniffed and dabbed at her eyes with a tissue. "What answer?"

"The answer for our anger and bitterness. It's right here in Psalm 73. Listen: 'You guide me with your counsel, and afterward you will take me into glory. . . . Whom have I in heaven but you? And earth has nothing I desire besides you. My flesh and my heart may fail, but God is the strength of my heart and my portion forever. . . . It is good to be near God. I have made the Sovereign LORD my refuge; I will tell of all your deeds.'

"Darla, our problem has been our focus. We're always looking at ourselves, our worries, our problems, our wants, and desires. We have never really learned how to focus on the Lord for our contentment."

Another verse flashed into David's mind and he quickly found Hebrews 3:1. "Fix your thoughts on Jesus," he read out loud. "That's the issue, Darla, at least it is for me. Look at the warning in verse 8: 'Do not harden your hearts.' And in verses 12 and 13 it says, 'See to it, brothers, that none of you has a sinful, unbelieving heart that turns away from the living God. But encourage one another daily, as long as it is called Today, so that none of you may be hardened by sin's deceitfulness.'"

Faith had been listening silently to her parents' conversation. Now she joined in. "It's like that passage describes us perfectly, Dad. We have become sinful and unbelieving. I don't remember the last time I sat down just to read the Bible for myself. I think my heart has become hard toward God."

Darla looked over at Faith through her tears and said, "Honey, I think we all have become hard in our hearts. Maybe God is using all of this trouble to bring us back to Himself. I know my faith in God has become so small that I'm afraid of the future."

David nodded in agreement. "Me, too, honey. I'm scared to death about how I'm going to support our family in a few months when the church gets tired of paying my salary. At my age, it isn't going to be easy to find another church or start a whole new career. But I guess this is when we find out whether our faith is real or not. I've preached about it for years. Now it's time to practice it."

. . .

Arthur spent the week examining his newfound faith. Even at work, he could barely concentrate on his research as thoughts about God flooded his mind. Wherever he turned his attention, he saw clear-cut evidence for the Creator. The sun, the stars, the ocean tide, the elegance of birds in flight—everything pointed to the majesty and power of God. And as he gazed through his powerful microscope, the intricate order of the DNA code confirmed the existence of a Master Mind.

On Friday, as Arthur was walking back from lunch to his office, Gene Powell stepped out behind him from a side hallway. "Hey, Arthur," he called out, like a child on the playground, "Have you booked any more debates lately?"

Arthur stopped in his tracks, turned around, and walked back toward Gene, who backed up defensively.

Arthur smiled and said, "As a matter of fact, Gene, I am thinking of doing another debate, only this time on the other side."

Gene laughed. "Right! I can just see you as a creationist! Look, I'm just razzing you."

"I know, Gene, but I'm dead serious about this." He took a deep breath and said, "Dr. Arnold not only beat me in the debate.

He convinced me. I've become a Christian, Gene. What do you think of that?"

Gene's mouth dropped open and for a moment he simply stared at Arthur in total disbelief. Finally, he said, "You're not serious, are you? You're just kidding me, right?"

Arthur smiled broadly at Gene's confusion. "No, Gene," he said, "I've never been more certain about anything in my life. I know there is a God, that He loves me, and that I'll spend all of eternity in heaven. I've found the ultimate cure for cancer, Gene—and He's called Jesus Christ. I'd love to tell you about Him when you have time." Arthur reached out and patted his colleague on the shoulder. "Well, I've got to get back to my office. See you later, Gene." Arthur turned and walked down the hallway, whistling cheerfully.

Gene stood there, as though paralyzed, until Arthur turned the corner into another hallway and disappeared from view. Gene nearly tripped over himself as he turned and hurried back to the lab. He pushed open the doors and said in a loud voice, "Come here, you guys! You won't believe what I just heard!"

Arthur walked into his office, still whistling. His secretary Jenny looked up from her keyboard and smiled. "You sure seem to be in a good mood, Dr. Wilson!"

"Well, I am, Jenny! Something happened to me Monday night that has changed everything."

Jenny sat back and said, "And just what happened?"

"Well, this is going to be hard for you to believe—it's hard for *me* to believe!—but I became a Christian."

Jenny's mouth dropped open, just as Gene's had, and she smiled as she stood to her feet and went over to Arthur. "Oh, Dr. Wilson! I am so happy for you! I have been praying for this day ever since I started working for you."

Arthur laughed. "So you're the one, eh?" He sat down on the edge of Jenny's desk and said, "Thank you, Jenny, for praying for me. I have never been happier and I have so much to learn—about God, about Jesus, about Christianity. I can hardly think of anything else. All I want to do is read the Bible!"

Now Jenny laughed. "I know! That's just how I felt when I first came to Christ. It was as though I had been blind my whole life and suddenly I could see."

"Exactly! Now I see God in leaves, flowers, a baby's hand, the human eye, and especially the genetic code. Everything in our physical world is like God's signature telling us He is here."

"How did all this happen, Dr. Wilson?" Jenny asked. "I mean, what brought you to the Lord?"

Arthur folded his arms in thought for a few moments, and then replied, "I think God has been working on me for years, Jenny, but I was so stubborn in my pride that I wouldn't give in. When Susan accepted Christ, it made me so angry I treated her even worse than I had before. It's no wonder she left me. Then as I prepared for the debate with Dr. Arnold, my research kept pointing to the existence of an Intelligent Being who made the universe."

Jenny smiled, encouraging Arthur to continue.

"When Dr. Arnold thrashed me in the debate, I was so humiliated I didn't want to show my face in public again. That's when Michael Rollins showed up here on Monday. You remember."

"Yes, of course."

"Well, Jenny, Michael helped me think through the whole issue of creation, and that night, I got my dad's Bible out of the basement and read it—*really* read it—for the first time I can recall. Suddenly, it all made sense to me. It was like a blindfold had been taken off my eyes, or my mind had suddenly been enlarged to understand truths beyond my physical senses. I called Michael and went over to his house, and he explained to me how I could have a fresh start in Christ."

"Oh—that is so wonderful, Dr. Wilson!" Jenny said. Then her smile faded a bit as she said, "Do you think they'll make it tough for you here at NCI?"

Arthur smiled and said, "Probably. But, in all honesty, I don't care. I finally know what is true and they can laugh all they want. It won't change my mind one bit!"

. . .

On Friday afternoon, Susan received a generous severance check in the mail from DoubleSoft, along with her termination notice. She smiled at the amount of the check, nodded her head, and said, "Uh huh!" The check was stamped with Billy Costas's signature. On the form was a box that read "reason employee was terminated." Neatly typed inside was the phrase, "mutual agreement between employer and employee that philosophical differences made continued association untenable." Susan shook her head and half-smiled at the lie. She returned the form to the envelope and filed it in a manila folder.

She was surprised—and pleased—that she was neither angry nor depressed about the callous way Billy had fired her. *Of course*, she admitted to herself, *the size of the severance pay helps ease the sting.*

She hurried to her bedroom to get herself ready and to lay out clothes for the evening. She had mixed feelings about dinner with Arthur at the Rollins's home. She was still full of bitterness toward him for his years of insensitivity and coldness, and she was genuinely fearful at the thought of returning to their loveless marriage. Still, she was unsettled by the fact that she felt a measure of excitement and hope.

What should I wear? she thought, as she applied her makeup and arranged her hair the way Arthur liked it. *The red dress? No . . . too flashy. The black suit? No . . . too formal.* She pulled one outfit after another out of the closet, looking for something she would feel comfortable in. She smiled at the irony of her nervousness. *Just what does one wear to be reintroduced to her husband?* she thought. She finally settled on a royal blue dress with lace trim around the neck and sleeves. She held a simple gold chain necklace to her neck. It set off the dress perfectly. Gold earrings completed the effect she was seeking—elegant simplicity to project a confidence she didn't feel.

. . .

Arthur stopped at the shopping mall on his way home from work. He went into a department store and found the men's clothing section. Looking through the jackets, Arthur said out loud, "What do you wear to confession?"

"I beg your pardon?" a salesman said as he stood up on the other side of the rack.

"Oh! Uh . . . nothing!" Arthur said with a sheepish smile. "I'm looking for a casual outfit, but one that would be appropriate in a business office. What can you suggest?"

The clerk showed him a smart-looking ensemble on a nearby display. It was a gray jacket with black pants, a white shirt with subtle black pinstripes, and a patterned tie with shades of black and purple. It was perfect. Arthur made the purchase and hurried home.

Later, as Arthur stood in front of the bathroom mirror shaving, he looked at himself and admitted that the years were beginning to show. His old insecurity welled up as he thought about Billy Costas. *Who am I kidding?* he thought. *I can't compete with Costas's good looks and money. Why would Susan even consider me now? Especially when I've been so unkind to her over the years?*

He dried his face off with a towel and went to the bedroom to get ready for dinner at the Rollins's. He hadn't felt this nervous since his wedding day, including his debate with Dr. Arnold.

She'll never be able to forgive me, he thought. *I know I don't deserve another chance. But even so, I have to tell her how sorry I am for all the pain I've caused her over the years. I owe that to her—and to God.*

He put on his new outfit and looked in the mirror. *I hope she'll like this*, he thought as he adjusted his tie. He noticed that his hands were cold and sweaty with tension, and he swallowed hard and cleared his throat.

"Hello, Susan," he rehearsed. "It's so good to see you." *Oh, wow! That is so corny!*

"Hi, Darling, I've missed you more than I can say!" *No, no, no! That will just make her angrier!*

"Susan! I'm a Christian now! Let's get back together!" *Oh, right! She'll love that one!*

Arthur didn't know what he would say when he first saw Susan again. All he knew was that he desperately wanted her to be his wife again and that he wanted them to have a Christian home. But he tried to keep his hopes in check, knowing that he had destroyed her love by his harshness over the years.

The time finally came for Arthur to drive to Michael and Ellen Rollins's house across town. As he drove, he found himself praying out loud. "Oh, Lord God," he said, "please guide my mind and tongue tonight as I meet Susan again. Lord, I know I don't deserve her and I surely don't deserve another chance to be her husband, but if You are willing to do a miracle—please do one tonight. Help her to be able to love me again."

When Arthur arrived at the Rollins's he saw Susan's car already parked out front. He gulped hard as his heart began beating faster. He parked behind her car and bowed his head in prayer again. *Please, Lord, give me the right words to say.*

He got out, straightened his jacket and tie, and walked up to the door and rang the bell. Michael opened the door a few seconds later. "Arthur! It is so good to see you again!"

"Thank you, Michael, for inviting me." He looked past Michael nervously to see if he could catch a glimpse of Susan.

"Come on in," Michael said with a broad smile.

Michael led Arthur to the living room, where Ellen and Susan sat talking. They stood and Arthur sucked in his breath sharply when he saw how beautiful Susan looked. She was even more attractive than he remembered and she looked stunning to him in her blue dress. He always loved seeing her in that color.

Susan's face was flushed with nervousness, and in contrast to her blond hair, it made her look all the more appealing to Arthur.

He walked over to Susan, not even seeing Ellen, took her hands and nearly whispered in a husky voice, "Can you ever forgive me?"

Ellen quietly moved over to Michael, winked at him, and led him out of the room.

Susan's eyes glistened with emotion, and her lips trembled as she tried to answer. "I . . . I . . ." and she began to cry.

Arthur didn't know what to do. "Oh, I'm so sorry. I didn't mean to make you cry." He took out a brand-new handkerchief and handed it to Susan. "Please. Can we sit down?"

Susan nodded as she wiped her eyes and they sat on the couch. The last thing she had wanted to do was to cry. She had wanted Arthur to see that she had done quite well without him, but instead, here she was with tears streaming down her face.

"I'm sorry," she finally said.

"Oh, no, Susan! I'm the one to be sorry! Please listen to me."

"All right," she said as she dabbed at the corners of her eyes, trying not to smudge her makeup any worse than it already was.

Arthur turned toward her and with an earnestness in his eyes said, "Susan, I cannot tell you how sorry I am for all the pain I caused you during our marriage. I was so incredibly selfish and insensitive, and I don't blame you for leaving me. I'm not asking you to come back to me, because I don't deserve you. But I am asking you to forgive me." His lips began to tighten with emotion as a tear escaped his left eye and slowly made its way down his face.

Susan was astonished. She had anticipated Arthur being somewhat formal, offering to take her back if she was willing to apologize and fulfill her wifely duties. Instead, he was taking all the blame.

"I don't know what to say, Arthur. A lot has happened since I left." She looked down in embarrassment and deep pain as she thought about her affair with Billy Costas. "There are some things you aren't aware of."

Arthur's heart sank. He had hoped that Susan's affair with Billy Costas was a thing of the past, but obviously it wasn't. He choked back his disappointment and tried to smile. "I realize we can't get back together, Susan," he said with deep pain on his face, "but I am still asking if you could ever find it in your heart to forgive me. I sinned against you so terribly."

Sinned? Susan leaned forward and looked at Arthur. "Did you say you *sinned* against me?"

"Yes," Arthur said, looking down in shame. "I am so terribly sorry for all the pain I caused you."

"But I've never heard you use the word *sin* before, Arthur."

Arthur nodded and said, "I know. But that's exactly what I did with all my unkind words and actions toward you." He took her hand again, looked straight into her eyes and said, "Won't you please forgive me?"

Susan's heart began to melt. "Yes, Arthur, I can forgive you. But I don't understand. What has happened to you?"

Arthur sat back on the couch and breathed out deeply. He finally looked at Susan again and said, "I have become a Christian."

Susan sat there stunned. She tried to speak, but no words would come. She swallowed hard and then said, "Are you serious, Arthur? Have you really become a Christian?"

Arthur nodded. "I can't blame you for not believing me. I can hardly believe it myself, but it's true. I have finally come to my senses and realize that there is a God and He loves me. And I love Him."

"Oh, Arthur!" Susan exclaimed with a joy she had never known, "I am so thankful to God! I have prayed so hard, but I never thought it would happen!"

Then, her face changed to a sad expression and she sat back. Tears began to flow down her face again.

"What's wrong, Susan?" Arthur asked.

She couldn't speak for a moment and just shook her head. Finally, when she regained her composure, she said, "Oh, Arthur, now I have to ask for *your* forgiveness."

"For what, Susan?" Arthur asked.

Again she paused, trying to maintain control of her emotions. "For being unfaithful to you," she finally said as her face turned bright red and she looked at the floor in total shame. "I got involved with my boss at work, and I am so terribly ashamed. I don't know how you could ever forgive me for being so wicked.

I don't know if I can ever forgive myself!" Her body shook with sobs as she grieved over her sin.

Arthur wanted to comfort Susan but was afraid he would offend her, so he sat there awkwardly as she cried. But as she continued to weep, he couldn't help himself. Compassion swept over his heart and he slid over next to her on the couch and put his arm around her and gently pulled her head to his shoulder. Tears streamed down his face and they cried together.

"It's okay," he whispered in her ear. "It would never have happened if I had been the gentle husband you deserved. I forgive you from the bottom of my heart."

He gently placed his hand under her chin and slowly raised her face to his. "I know that it's too little, too late, but Susan Wilson, I love you. I always will!"

A rush of joy filled Susan's heart when Arthur said the words *forgive* and *love*. The feeling of love she thought she would never recover for her husband suddenly flooded her very soul. She threw her arms around Arthur and kissed him.

"Oh, Arthur," she finally said as she lay her head on his shoulder. "This is too good to be true. Ever since finding Christ, all I have wanted was for you to understand and love Him, too. But I never thought it would happen. You seemed to hate God so much."

"I was trying to convince myself that God didn't exist," Arthur said quietly. "But this last Monday, I got Dad's old Bible out of the basement and started reading. And, Susan, it was like God suddenly opened my eyes. Everything became so simple, and for the first time, life made sense to me."

"I understand," Susan said. "That's what happened to me. But I lost hope, Arthur, and then I became bitter toward you, and I just decided I didn't care anymore. But I found out that the way of the world is even more painful. I don't ever want to go back that way again."

A flash of hope burst into Arthur's heart. He wanted to ask Susan a question, but was afraid to push Susan to come back home. He hesitated, then said, "Susan?"

"Yes, Arthur?"

"Are you in love with Billy Costas?"

Susan looked at Arthur and shame gripped her heart once again. Tears filled her eyes and she looked down at the floor, and finally back at Arthur. "No, Arthur. I thought we were in love, but I found out that lust was the only thing we shared. I have asked God to forgive me, but I still feel so defiled. I can only hope you will someday believe just how sorry I really am."

"Oh, I *do* believe that, Susan. And I hope you believe me when I say that I'm sorry for having been such a jerk."

Susan laughed softly. "I do, Arthur," she said.

They sat quietly

"Susan," he said again, "your forgiving me is more than I could hope for, and I'll understand if you say no, but . . ."

"Yes, Arthur?" Susan said as she looked Arthur in the eyes.

He swallowed hard in fear that she would reject him, but he finally said, "I want you to be my wife again. Would you be willing to even consider it?"

Susan smiled. "I didn't think God could ever help me love you again, Arthur," she said, "but He has. I want to be your wife. I want our home to be a happy Christ-centered home."

"Oh, so do I!" Arthur said with deep conviction. An idea suddenly formed in his mind. He took Susan's hand and fell onto one knee. In a voice deep with emotion he said, "Susan, will you marry me?"

Susan's heart leaped with joy and she smiled as she said, "Oh, yes!" She threw her arms around him and kissed him long and hard.

When he was able to catch his breath, Arthur said, "Susan, why don't we get married in your church? Let's make this a truly Christian marriage from the start."

Susan smiled and then a troubling thought came to her mind.

"What's wrong, sweetheart?" Arthur asked.

"Oh, Arthur! I don't know how I can go back to my church, after all my sin and—you don't know about this, but I was the one who reported Pastor Miller's son to the police. I'm the last person in the world he would want to see in church!"

"I doubt that, Susan, but that's a different question altogether. Right now, I want us to tell Michael and Ellen that we're going to have another wedding, and this time, as Christians!"

CHAPTER
13

A Greater Faith in Our God

FEW CHRISTIANS WOULD ARGUE that we have enough faith in our lives. Though we stand at the edge of the twenty-first century and have more Bibles per capita than any generation in history, modern Christians are generally a biblically ignorant group. Few Christians have read through the entire Bible even once in their lives, and an even smaller segment of Christendom has a grasp of biblical doctrine. Even elementary biblical knowledge is woefully lacking today, as few Christians can list the books of the Bible, quote the Ten Commandments, or name the twelve apostles.

Theological terms such as *incarnation, atonement, justification, regeneration,* and *sanctification* are meaningless to the majority of modern believers. I am not arguing, however, that Christians will automatically have a closer walk with God if they excel at Bible trivia or understand and utilize theological terminology. I'm merely pointing out that—for all practical purposes—we are a biblically illiterate generation.

WHY WE NEED INCREASED FAITH

A direct result of our scriptural ignorance is a weakened faith, and with such an anemic belief system, our marriages, our children, our morality, and our mental/emotional/spiritual well-being have been severely damaged. The simple fact is, we desperately need increased faith.

For Correct Doctrine

We need more faith in order to *believe correct doctrine*. Some biblical truths are difficult to understand, while others are impossible to fully comprehend, yet because they are clearly taught in the Scriptures, we must believe them. It is at this very point that the wise man, scholar, and philosopher of this age stumble (1 Corinthians 1:20). Unable to mentally grasp the relationship of time and eternity, the fact of the triune God, the reality of Jesus' miraculous works on earth, or the redemptive power of Christ's death on the cross, self-proclaimed intellectuals reject the gospel.

For Service

We need increased faith for *effective service*. Someone once asked Jesus, "What must we do to do the works God requires?" (John 6:28). Jesus' reply was unexpected: "The work of God is this: to believe in the one he has sent" (John 6:29). There is an intimate connection between faith that leads to correct doctrine and that which leads to effective work for the Lord. Paul writes about "the sacrifice and service coming from your faith" in Philippians 2:17. Unless we *believe* God and His Word, we will never be able to effectively accomplish what He has called us to do.

Perhaps you are asking just what it is that Jesus wants us to do. He tells us clearly in Matthew 28:19-20: "Go and make disciples of all nations, baptizing them in the name of the Father and of the Son and of the Holy Spirit, and teaching them to obey everything I have commanded you." Do you see the essential elements of the walk with God? Faith and obedience. John writes, "I know your deeds, your love and faith, your service and perseverance, and that you are now doing more than you did at first" (Revelation 2:19).

For Healing

We need faith *to be healed*. When a Jewish leader came to Jesus on behalf of his little daughter, who was at the point of death, Jesus said, "Don't be afraid; just believe, and she will be healed" (Luke 8:50). Physically, emotionally, mentally, and spiritually—we need the Master's touch, for "He heals the broken-hearted and binds up their wounds" (Psalm 147:3).

I am constantly amazed to see professing Christians turning to modern-day witch doctors for their mental health. These witch doctors in white smocks pretend to understand their clients' inner woes as they lead them into false memories and past lives, all the while promising them freedom but instead leading them into bondage.

Dear child of God, remember, Jesus "was pierced for our transgressions, he was crushed for our iniquities; the punishment that brought us peace was upon him, and by his wounds we are healed" (Isaiah 53:5).

What a miserable and powerless faith it is that mockingly asks, "Do you really believe that the Bible *alone* is able to heal people of their dysfunctions?" That, in essence, is the question seminary professors and college administrators ask me incredulously. Yet Jeremiah declares, "Heal me, O LORD, and I will be healed; save me and I will be saved, for you are the one I praise" (Jeremiah 17:14).

To Overcome Temptation

We need more faith in order *to overcome temptation*. Those who declare that homosexuals, prostitutes, and the "sexually addicted" cannot be freed without psychotherapy do not know the Word of God, or if they know it, they do not believe it, for Paul writes, "No temptation has seized you except what is common to man. And God is faithful; he will not let you be tempted beyond what you can bear. But when you are tempted, he will also provide a way out so that you can stand up under it" (1 Corinthians 10:13).

The writer of Hebrews says about Christ, "Because he himself suffered when he was tempted, he is able to help those who are being tempted" (Hebrews 2:18). It is faith in God's power and provision that enables His children to overcome temptation. That's why James writes, "Submit yourselves, then, to God. Resist the devil, and he will flee from you" (James 4:7). It is the confident awareness that "the one who is in you is greater than the one who is in the world" (1 John 4:4) that gives us power to prevail. Paul writes, "Take up the shield of faith, with which you can extinguish all the flaming arrows of the evil one" (Ephesians 6:16).

Quite simply, biblical faith can free God's people from *every* "dysfunction," *every* "addiction," and *every* "inner wound" without the help of psychotherapy.

For Peace of Mind

We need increased faith in order *to have peace of mind*. The Bible calls this "a good conscience" (1 Timothy 1:19). We are told how to do this: "Let us draw near to God with a sincere heart in full assurance of faith, having our hearts sprinkled to cleanse us from a guilty conscience" (Hebrews 10:22).

Perhaps the greatest cause for depression, anxiety, and the "psychosomatic" illnesses that accompany these "disorders" is a guilty conscience—knowing that we have wronged others and offended God. That's why Paul writes, "I strive always to keep my conscience clear before God and man" (Acts 24:16).

There is a quiet confidence in knowing that we have truly done our best in regard to others. In writing to the believers at Corinth, Paul said, "Our conscience testifies that we have conducted ourselves in the world, and especially in our relations with you, in the holiness and sincerity that are from God. We have done so not according to worldly wisdom but according to God's grace" (2 Corinthians 1:12). He connects a clear conscience to faith in 1 Timothy 3:9, where he tell us to "keep hold of the deep truths of the faith with a clear conscience."

Having a clear conscience involves having the "desire to live honorably in every way" (Hebrews 13:18) "so that those who speak maliciously against your good behavior in Christ may be ashamed of their slander" (1 Peter 3:16). We need faith to do that.

For Wise Decisions

We need more faith in order *to receive wisdom from God* in the real-life decisions we must make. James writes, "If any of you lacks wisdom, he should ask God, who gives generously to all without finding fault, and it will be given to him. But when he asks, he must believe and not doubt, because he who doubts is like a wave of the sea, blown and tossed by the wind" (James 1:5-6). Faith in God will guide us as we seek God's mate for our lives and search for wisdom to raise our children successfully. Biblical faith will guide us when we must choose a career or decide whether to accept a promotion and move to another city. It will help us to know what to do in the face of sudden crisis, disease, or terminal illness. It will help us to evaluate the issues of abortion and euthanasia. You see, God's Word is so very practical for the difficult questions we all must encounter.

To Please God

Ultimately, we need increased faith in order *to please God*. We are told, "Without faith it is impossible to please God, because anyone who comes to him must believe that he exists and that he rewards those who earnestly seek him" (Hebrews 11:6). Our primary motivation for increasing our faith should be to become more pleasing to our loving heavenly Father. I am absolutely convinced that the more we love God, the more we will delight in doing what He wants us to do. John writes, "The man who says, 'I know [God],' but does not do what he commands is a liar, and the truth is not in him. But if anyone obeys his word, God's love is truly made complete in him" (1 John 2:4-5).

THE DESIRE FOR INCREASED FAITH

The men who walked most closely with Jesus while He was on earth also realized their need for more faith. In Luke 17:5 they said to Jesus, "Increase our faith!"

The context for this desperate request is interesting, for it follows Jesus' teaching that we must forgive those who have sinned against us. You see, faith is most necessary in the dark and painful moments of our lives when uncertainty and fear grasp our hearts. It is easy to believe in God when everything is going well for us, for it takes little faith to rejoice when our health is good, when finances are abundant, and people like us. But our level of faith is most clearly revealed when things are not going well, when we are wracked with pain, lacking in financial resources, and suffer the bitter criticisms of those who despise us.

The desire for more faith is commendable. However, be forewarned: When we ask for faith we may not like the process it takes to produce it, for growing in faith may sometimes require difficult steps. That's why, quite frankly, I am reluctant to pray for faith, knowing that God takes our prayer seriously and may indeed bring circumstances into my life designed to increase my faith.

Remember Peter when he saw Jesus walking on the water? He said, "Lord, if it's you . . . tell me to come to you on the water." He didn't know what he was asking for. Jesus simply replied, "Come" (Matthew 14:28-29). Peter climbed out of the boat and started walking toward Jesus, and as long as he kept his eyes on the Master, he did the impossible—walking on water.

But then, just as you or I would have done, he became conscious of his circumstances and was understandably terrified. He immediately began to sink and he cried out, "Lord, save me!" (Matthew 14:30). Jesus reached out His hand to Peter and pulled him to safety. Then He said to Peter what He says to you and me: "You of little faith . . . why did you doubt?" (Matthew 14:31). In other words, "Peter, how big is your God?" And, as your friend, I now ask you: How big is *your* God?

We desperately need to grow in our faith, don't we? I do, and my guess is you do, too. But, if we ask the Lord to increase our faith, we need to be prepared to grow in our walk. Still, it will be worth the journey.

THE WAY TO INCREASED FAITH

We have examined the need and have expressed our desire for increased faith, but unless we learn *how* to strengthen our faith, we can easily sink into despair, feeling as though we will never succeed. Don't give up now, dear friend. The process we are about to look at is simple, but it is not always easy.

Jude writes, "Dear friends, build yourselves up in your most holy faith and pray in the Holy Spirit" (Jude 20). "Yes, yes!" we reply impatiently. "But *how*, Jude?" The best way to find out what Jude had in mind, of course, is to read his entire letter. Earlier he writes, "I felt I had to write and urge you to contend for the faith that was once for all entrusted to the saints" (Jude 3). And what does it mean to "contend for the faith"? It means to stand up for God's truth, to vigorously defend its accuracy, its content, and its doctrine, regardless of what others say or how politically incorrect it may be. This, of course, presupposes a solid understanding of the Scriptures.

Paul puts it this way: "Faith comes by hearing, and hearing by the word of God" (Romans 10:17, KJV).

There is no shortcut to spiritual maturity, and that is what increased faith is all about. Strong faith is not the result of momentary conviction, "going forward" in a public meeting, or "being slain in the Spirit." It does not come from "holy laughter" or speaking in tongues. It does not come from attempts to replicate the Pentecostal experience of Acts 2.

Rather, as Jesus explained, spiritual maturity comes from the daily disciplines of life. "If anyone would come after me, he must deny himself and take up his cross daily and follow me" (Luke 9:23). Note the three things Jesus requires: self-denial, self-discipline, and submission. Those are the very things the world holds in contempt, but are absolutely necessary for increased faith.

Self-denial means that we desire more to please God than to please ourselves. It means that we freely choose to give up our own desires and ambitions to honor the Lord. Self-discipline means that we force our minds, hearts, and bodies to do the things we may not wish to do but realize are necessary to please the Lord. Submission means that all that we are and have belong to God.

While spiritual disciplines may seem painful at first, they actually provide the peace of heart, soul, and mind that we long for. Jesus put it this way: "Take my yoke upon you and learn from me, for I am gentle and humble in heart, and you will find rest for your souls. For my yoke is easy and my burden is light" (Matthew 11:29-30). One of Satan's greatest successes has been to convince the world that submission to God produces sorrow and loss, but the exact opposite is true.

But still the question arises: *How* can we know what God wants us to do? For this we must turn once again to the passage that explains the power of God's Word: "All Scripture is God-breathed and is useful for teaching, rebuking, correcting and training in righteousness, so that the man of God may be thoroughly equipped for every good work" (2 Timothy 3:16-17).[68] The Bible tells us what God expects of us, rebukes us when we get out of line, shows us how to correct our problems, and trains us how to walk consistently with the Lord.

For biblical knowledge and insight, again, there is no shortcut. You will never comprehend the Scriptures until you discipline yourself to read them, meditate on them, memorize them, and apply them to your daily life. We are told to "fix these words of mine in your hearts and minds" (Deuteronomy 11:18). The purpose for saturating our hearts and minds with God's Word is "so [we] may obey it" (Deuteronomy 30:14) and to keep us from sin (Psalm 119:11).

Christian magazines, videotapes, music, and television programs must never displace the Scriptures in our lives. Christian novels—even those said to be based on the Bible—can never provide the depth of life-changing truths found in the Word of God. Christian books—yes, even books like this one—are miserable substitutes for the profound wisdom offered in the Scriptures. While all these things may supplement our spiritual growth, they must never replace the role of Scripture in our lives.

Do you realize that you can read through the entire Bible every 15 weeks if you were to spend about two hours per day reading the Word of God? One hour a day will take you through the Bible almost twice a year.

Let me ask you a soul-searching question: *How much time on average do you spend in God's Word each day?* Five minutes? Two minutes? The sad fact is, many Christians rarely open the Bible. And then they wonder why their level of faith is so low. It's really no secret, is it? Though Jesus said that "man does not live on bread alone, but on every word that comes from the mouth of God" (Matthew 4:4), most Christians are on a starvation diet when it comes to spiritual food.

"But, Ed," you might be saying, "what about people who listen to Christian radio speakers all day long for spiritual nourishment?" Much of what passes for "Christian" radio today is filled with dangerous error and outright heresy. Even if the teachings are true, getting our spiritual food from radio speakers is like sitting down to a meal of pre-chewed food. True life-sustaining nourishment comes when we feed on the Word of God for ourselves.

"But it is so hard to understand!" some people object. I'm not suggesting that searching the Scriptures is easy, but what worthwhile skill comes without effort? Those who wish to become concert pianists must dedicate years of determined practice, day after day. Those who want to become Olympic athletes must commit themselves to years of self-denial and training. When it comes to the most important skill in this world—understanding the eternal truths of God—we cannot expect mastery without expending any effort.

I am always amazed at the level of dedication people will pour into meaningless pursuits while neglecting the things that lead to everlasting life. I watched a television special recently about an endurance race in Canada where 70 five-member teams raced by horseback, on foot, by raft, and by bicycle, over a 350-mile wilderness course to prove their physical fitness. I'll admit, I was impressed by their willingness to endure pain, lack of sleep, and sheer exhaustion for the glory of finishing the race. But I wondered at the time, *How many Christians are willing to suffer similar pain to complete the spiritual race?*

Paul speaks of his fear of running "my race in vain" (Galatians 2:2). He urges us to "run in such a way as to get the prize" (1 Corinthians 9:24). With that word picture in mind, Paul said to the Christians in Galatia, "You were running a good race. Who cut in on you and kept you from obeying the truth?" (Galatians 5:7). The writer of Hebrews coaches us, "Let us throw off everything that hinders and the sin that so easily entangles, and let us run with perseverance the race marked out for us" (Hebrews 12:1).

Writing to his young trainee Timothy, the elderly Paul said, "I have fought the good fight, I have finished the race, I have kept the faith" (2 Timothy 4:7). Can we say the same? If so, the rewards are great, for Paul continued, "Now there is in store for me the crown of righteousness, which the Lord, the righteous Judge, will award to me on that day—and not only to me, but also to all who have longed for his appearing" (2 Timothy 4:8).

It is time to throw our practical atheism aside and to reclaim our spiritual birthright in Christ. It is time to declare our absolute allegiance to our heavenly Father. Until we do, the world will continue to ask, "How big *is* your God?"

Are you still seeking the joy and happiness God offers to us in His Word? Then join me in the last chapter as we look at the two essential elements for a victorious Christian life. Together they provide the powerful antidote to practical atheism and the sorrow of unbelief.

Joy Comes in the Morning

Arthur called out, "Hey, where are you guys?"

Michael and Ellen walked down the hallway from the family room and joined Arthur and Susan in the front room. "We just thought you two needed a little privacy," Ellen said with a smile. "Is everything all right?"

"Oh, yes!" Susan exclaimed as she took Ellen's hands. She looked at Arthur and said, "Do you want to tell them?"

Arthur nodded and with a wide smile said, "I've asked Susan if she'll marry me again, and by the grace of God, she said yes!"

"Oh! Yes!" Ellen exclaimed joyfully. "Congratulations, you two!"

Michael grabbed Arthur's hand and shook it enthusiastically. "Way to go, buddy!" he said. He turned to his wife and said, "Ellen, can you believe what God has done in less than a week?"

"But we've been praying for months, Michael!"

"That's true! And when God finally answers prayer, He really does it in a big way, doesn't He!"

Ellen turned to Susan and said, "Dinner is still warm, if you two are hungry."

They went to the dining room and Ellen and Susan brought out the food and they all sat down at the table.

"Arthur, would you mind giving thanks for the meal?" Michael asked.

Arthur hadn't prayed at a meal since he was a child. He hesitated, then said, "Yes, Michael, I'd like that." He bowed his head awkwardly and said, "Dear Father in heaven . . . I thank You for these dear friends . . . and for Susan. And, uh, I thank You for this food. But, uh, but, Lord, more than anything else, I thank You for opening my eyes to see the truth . . . before it was too late. Bless us now as we share this meal together. Amen."

They ate and laughed and talked through the meal with a deep spirit of joy. Arthur had never felt so much at peace, and he said, "I can't believe I waited so long to open my heart to Christ."

Michael smiled and said, "Just out of curiosity, Arthur, may I ask you, what *did* take you so long? What was it that held you back?"

"Mostly my pride, I think," Arthur answered candidly. "My stupid intellectual pride. But there was another thing, as I think about it—I rarely saw happy Christians until I met you folks. Except for you and Ellen, Christians always seemed so stiff and legalistic, you know? It was like they were trapped as Christians and wished they could get out, but were afraid if they did, they would go to hell. It probably was just my own twisted perception, but that's how it looked to me."

"I hate to admit it, Arthur, but I think that's how most people see Christians. It's a terrible testimony, because it makes God look like a cosmic killjoy. The truth is, when a person really understands the Word of God and knows Jesus personally, there is a deep sense of peace and happiness that the world just cannot provide."

"Do you know what I think it is?" Susan said. "I think most Christians have just enough religion to make them miserable and not enough to make them happy."

Arthur laughed and said, "That's it, exactly! And I don't want to be that kind of Christian. That's the way I was before I came to Christ, and I've had enough of it!" Looking at Susan, he said, "Life is short enough as it is, and I want the rest of our years together to be happy."

Ellen smiled at Susan and Arthur as they stared into each other's eyes like young lovers. "Our lives are happy in direct proportion to our loving obedience to God, Arthur," Ellen said. "There's no magic formula, no secret of success. It just takes a quiet, consistent, daily walk as we fill our hearts and minds with His Word, and apply it to every area of our lives."

Michael asked, "How soon do you want to renew your vows?"

Arthur looked at Susan with a twinkle in his eyes and said, "Just as soon as we possibly can! Do you think you could arrange for us to be married at your church, Michael?"

"I'm certain of it. We're in an awkward situation right now, though. Our pastor is on leave of absence to deal with a personal tragedy involving his son. Still, our associate pastor could do the ceremony. What date are you thinking about?"

"How about next week?" Arthur said, looking at Susan.

"How about *this* Sunday!" Susan said.

"Sunday? That's only two days away!" Arthur said. "I thought you ladies liked to have more time to plan these things."

"This time, darling, I want it to be as simple—and holy—as possible," Susan said.

Arthur looked at Michael. "Do you think a wedding could be arranged on such short notice?"

"Let me go find out." Michael got up from the table and went into the family room to call the associate pastor. He came back about five minutes later with a big smile on his face. "It's all set for Sunday afternoon at 2:00."

After dinner, Michael pushed back from the table and asked, "Arthur, do you know what devotions are?"

Arthur nodded. "In fact, Michael, I do. When I was a boy, Dad used to call us together as a family to spend a few minutes reading the Bible and praying before we went off to bed. Why do you ask?"

"I just wondered if you would mind joining our family tonight for devotions."

"I'd love to. How about you, Susan?"

"Of course!"

"I'll call the children down from their rooms," Michael said. "They're doing their homework." He went to the stairs, banged on the wall and yelled, "Kids, come on down for devotions."

"Michael! You don't have to yell so loud!" Ellen looked at Arthur and Susan and shrugged her shoulders. "Sorry."

Arthur laughed. "That's okay. I'm glad to see your family life in action."

The Rollins children came running down the stairs talking and laughing and went to the family room, where the adults joined them.

"I don't think you've met our children, have you?" Ellen said.

"No, I don't think so," Arthur replied. "They're a good-looking group, though!"

"Why, thank you, Arthur!" Michael said in mock surprise. "Most people tell us they're kind of homely—and that they look a lot like me."

"Aw, Dad!" Eric objected. "We look more like Mom! I guess we just lucked out."

They all laughed.

"Children, I'd like you to meet Mr. and Mrs. Wilson. And this is Stephen, our oldest. He's twelve and loves to jump his bike over tree stumps," Ellen said, pointing to their mischievous son with light blond hair. "And this is Elizabeth. She's ten and loves to sing and act in her own plays. Then there's Aaron. He's seven and already understands computers. And last in the line is our little Miriam. She's five and can already read."

"What beautiful children!" Susan said. "You are truly blessed."

They all sat down and Michael brought out his Bible and asked, "Which chapter of Proverbs are we in tonight?"

"Isn't today the fourteenth?" Stephen asked.

"Yep," Michael agreed.

"Then we're in Proverbs 14!" Miriam said excitedly.

"Proverbs 14 it is, then," Michael said as he turned to the passage. He read one verse at a time and asked the children, "What do you suppose that means?"

Arthur found himself listening carefully to each verse and the children's commentaries and discovered that he was deeply convicted by the simple truths of God's Word and the depth of the children's understanding.

He noticed that Susan's head dipped slightly when Michael read verse 1: "The wise woman builds her house, but with her own hands the foolish one tears hers down." His own heart was pierced by verse 6: "The mocker seeks wisdom and finds none, but knowledge comes easily to the discerning." When Michael read verse 27, Arthur smiled, nodded, and sighed with deep contentment. "The fear of the LORD is a fountain of life, turning a man from the snares of death."

When they finished the Bible reading, Michael asked, "Who wants to pray tonight?" To everyone's surprise, including his own, Arthur said, "I'd like to, Michael, if that's all right."

"Why, of course, Arthur!" Michael said with genuine delight.

They all bowed their heads and Arthur took Susan's hand in his. "Dear Father," he began with deep reverence, "thank You for the time we could spend tonight with this wonderful family. Thank You for their friendship and that Michael cared enough to share Jesus with me. Thank You that Ellen cared enough to minister to Susan when she was so lonely. And, Lord, thank You for bringing Susan and me back together at last. I am more grateful than I'm able to say. Bless this home and these dear people. Amen."

The children each gave their parents a hug and kiss, and hurried off to their rooms.

When they were gone, Arthur said, "It doesn't quite seem real."

"What doesn't seem real, Arthur?" Michael asked.

"Your family. I mean, it's just too perfect. I feel like I just witnessed the Cleaver family—only better."

Michael and Ellen laughed. "I know," Michael said. "We've been told that before, but what you saw is genuine. Don't get me wrong. That doesn't mean we don't have our disagreements and arguments. Our kids were on their best behavior, that's for sure, but truthfully, we do view our home life as a little preview of heaven. If parents love each other and their children and each one in the family is sincerely trying to be obedient to the precepts of Scripture, the inevitable result is a peaceful home."

They talked for a few more minutes, and then Arthur said, "We should be going. Thank you again for everything you've done."

Susan smiled and asked, "Arthur, aren't there some details about the wedding that we should take care of before we leave?"

"Like what?" he asked, drawing a complete blank.

Susan and Ellen laughed. "I can see why he needs you, Susan," Ellen said. "Arthur, are you going to have a best man? What about music? How many people do you want to invite? Things like that."

"Oh! I hadn't even considered those things," Arthur admitted. "I just thought we'd have a simple ceremony with a few friends."

He turned to Susan. "What would you like, honey?"

"I want to keep it simple, too, but I would be pleased if Michael and Ellen would stand with us. On such short notice, I don't know if we could get a musician."

"I'll take care of that, Susan, if you like," Ellen offered. "And we would be honored to stand up with you."

They walked to the front door and Ellen hugged Susan as Michael shook Arthur's hand. Arthur and Susan walked hand in hand to Susan's car. They stood beside her car in the darkness, the only light coming from the streetlight down the block and a half-moon overhead. Even in dim light, Susan looked absolutely gorgeous to Arthur. "I didn't get to tell you just how beautiful you look tonight. Did you choose that dress for me?"

Susan nodded shyly and smiled. "I know you like this color."

"Oh, yes," he said, "and it is beautiful on you." He reached out and touched the gold necklace that hung around her neck and asked, "Is that the necklace I bought you when we were in Chicago?"

"Why, yes, Arthur," she said, surprised that he remembered.

"It was always one of my favorites. Thank you for wearing it tonight."

"I wanted to."

He looked into her beautiful eyes, which reflected the dim moonlight. "May I kiss you?" he asked.

"Oh, please do," she said, and they embraced as the curtain inside the Rollins home parted slightly for just a moment and closed again.

"I hate to go back to my apartment without you," she finally said in a soft voice. "We are still married, you know."

"I know, sweetheart," Arthur replied, "but I want a fresh start in our new life together, and I think a Christian wedding would be a great way to mark its beginning. Don't you?"

"Yes," she agreed. "But I had no idea how much I actually missed you until tonight."

"It's only two days, and I have a lot of cleaning to do at the house before you can step foot inside!"

"Oh, Arthur, I'll help you clean."

"Not this time, Susan," Arthur chuckled. "I want you to be able to come home to a clean place. And you'll have a lot of packing to do at your apartment, won't you?"

"Yes, but I don't think I can get it all done tomorrow."

"No problem. We'll work on it next week. Tomorrow, you just rest and get yourself ready for Sunday. It's going to be a wonderful day!"

He kissed her again, and watched as she slid into her car. He gulped as he appreciated her feminine form, and then gently shut her door. She waved at him and whispered, "I love you" as she drove away.

Arthur got into his car, and with a heart floating with joy, he drove home.

. . .

The next day, Arthur began cleaning the house in earnest. He walked through each room with a large trash bag, gathering old magazines, potato chip bags, newspapers, and other clutter. Quickly he organized each room to look as close to normal as possible, but he soon realized he was hopelessly outmatched. There was no way he could make it look the way Susan managed.

He dusted and vacuumed, the way a man does, missing several key spots, but to him, it looked thoroughly clean. He went into the family room and began picking up books and periodicals to put them in the cabinet behind his chair. When he opened the cabinet, he saw the *Playboy* magazines and his heart dropped with a sense of deep conviction.

"Oh, these have got to go!" he said as he scooped them out and tore them into shreds before placing them in another garbage bag. He went to his bedroom, got down on his knees, and pulled out several magazines from under the bed and destroyed them as well. When he finished, he went into the kitchen to wash his hands. He knew he had passed a major test in his life and moved from "adult entertainment" to moral maturity. He determined before the Lord that he would never again purchase or read pornography.

He washed the dishes that had been sitting on the kitchen counter for weeks and then scrubbed the bathroom until it shined. By the time he was done, it was nearly dark outside. The phone rang and he was glad for an excuse to sit down for a few minutes.

"Hello?"

"Hello, Arthur," Susan's soft voice came across the line. "I just called to say I love you, and I can hardly wait until tomorrow."

"Oh, Susan! I am so glad to hear your voice! I'm almost done cleaning the house. I hope you won't be too disappointed. I just can't do as good a job as you do."

"I'm sure it will be fine," she said cheerfully.

"Susan, I'd like to go to church in the morning. Would you go with me?"

"Well, of course!"

"What time is the worship service?"

"It's at 10:45, I think. Are you going to pick me up?"

"I wouldn't miss the opportunity!" Then he realized he didn't even know where she was living. "How do I get to your place, anyway?"

They both laughed, and then Susan gave him her address and directions to her apartment.

"I'll be there about 10:15."

"I'll be ready," Susan said. "Good night, darling. This will be our last night apart."

"Thank God!" Arthur said. "I'll see you in the morning."

He hung up the phone and sighed with deep contentment.

. . .

On Sunday, promptly at 10:15, Arthur drove up to Susan's apartment building, and she walked out as soon as she saw his car. Arthur's heart jumped again as he saw how beautiful Susan was. He quickly got out, hurried around the car, and opened her door. She threw her arms around his neck and gave him a passionate kiss.

"Wow!" Arthur said with a big smile. "What will your neighbors think?"

"Who cares? If a woman can't kiss her own husband, who can she kiss?" she teased as she slid into the leather bucket seat.

Arthur shut her door and walked around the back of the car to his own side and got in. As they drove down the tree-covered street, he said, "Do you realize this will be my first time in a worship service since we visited Mom and Dad's church when you and I were in college?"

"Yes, I know, darling, and I couldn't be happier! I have prayed for this moment for so very long."

"I know you have, Susan, and I'm just sorry it has taken me so many years to wake up!"

They arrived at the church and walked inside just in time to see Michael and Ellen coming through the foyer from a Bible class.

"Michael!" Arthur called out.

Michael and Ellen hurried over to greet them. They introduced Arthur and Susan to several other couples and as the music began to play in the sanctuary, they went inside and sat about a third of the way back on the left side.

The minister of music led the congregation in singing and Arthur's heart responded with a sense of deep contentment and awe. He had come to worship his God and he sang every word from his heart. Susan looked over at him with surprise. She had no idea he could sing, and she reached for his hand and closed her eyes to hold in tears of joy.

A small praise group sang a worship song about the faithfulness of God and Arthur squeezed Susan's hand as though to say, "Amen!"

When the ushers came by to receive the offering, Susan almost expected Arthur to get up and walk out, as he would have done before. This time, however, he took out a check he had already written at home, folded it in half, and put it in the plate as it went by. Susan looked at him with raised eyebrows, and then smiled as she thought, *You just keep surprising me, Arthur!* And then, *Thank You, Father!*

"And now," the minister of music said, "before Pastor Chris comes with his message, the elders have a word for the congregation. Michael Rollins, will you come to the platform, please?"

Michael strode to the front of the auditorium and up to a microphone. "As you know, our pastor David Miller and his family have been going through a difficult time due to the arrest of Jason. In obedience to the Word of God, Dr. Miller stepped down as senior pastor until he could get his own home back in order. I'm here to announce today that Jason Miller has been paroled and the elders met with the entire family yesterday for several hours.

"It is our opinion that Jason has genuinely repented and is willing to come under the authority of his parents and the leaders of this church. With that in mind, we want to give the Miller family another month or so to rest and rebuild their own relationships. Then, if things continue to progress the way we anticipate, we will recommend to the church that Dr. Miller be reinstated as our pastor.

"You see, folks, we believe the Scripture that says God's 'anger lasts only a moment, but his favor lasts a lifetime; weeping may remain for a night, but rejoicing comes in the morning.' That's found in Psalms 30:5 and it certainly applies to this situation, doesn't it!

"Oh—and while I'm up here—I have one other announcement, and it is just as joyful. This afternoon, at 2:00, there will be a celebration of Christian marriage right here, as our friends Arthur and Susan Wilson renew their marriage vows."

Susan cringed for a moment, thinking the announcement might upset Arthur, but as she looked at him, she saw surprise, and then happiness that others could enjoy the wedding with them.

The congregation applauded the announcement with enthusiasm as the minister of music came to lead another song before the message. The associate pastor preached a powerful message of God's forgiveness and cleansing, and both Arthur and Susan felt as though he was speaking directly to them. Ellen penned a little note and passed it to Susan. It read, "We didn't tell him any details. Honest!"

As they listened, they felt the love of God sweep over them, and they experienced a deep comfort from the words of the Scriptures that said, "In him we have redemption through his blood, the forgiveness of sins, in accordance with the riches of God's grace."[69]

On their way out of the church, several people stopped them with a greeting and congratulations. "Welcome to our church!" they said. "We hope you'll come back regularly." And Arthur knew they meant it.

. . .

Susan and Ellen were in a back room listening to the music playing in the auditorium. Susan was dressed in a simple yet elegant antique cream and dusty rose-colored dress, set off by a strand of pearls that she had matched with earrings. She and Ellen would walk the aisle together and meet Arthur and Michael at the front.

The music paused briefly and then began again, louder. It was their signal to enter. Susan held a single rose in her hand. Ellen opened the door and Susan walked out, surprised to see more people than she had expected seated in the auditorium.

Susan looked down the aisle and saw Arthur standing at the front, tall and proud, waiting for her. He looked dashing in his dark double-breasted suit and his tie matched her rose perfectly.

Arthur closed his eyes and breathed deeply, then opened them again to drink in Susan's beauty as she walked down the aisle, her eyes locked to his. *I'm the most blessed man alive*, he thought as he smiled.

When Susan arrived at the front, Arthur extended his left hand and turned to face the pastor.

"Friends, this is a special wedding today," he said with a smile. "I am honored to be part of God's healing of two wounded hearts as Arthur and Susan Wilson are reunited today by renewing their vows.

"Arthur has just recently committed his heart to Christ and it was at his suggestion that this renewal ceremony is taking place. He wants to begin his new life in Christ by putting the Lord at the center of their home."

The pastor smiled and looked at Arthur as he said. "Arthur, do you take Susan to be your wife?"

"I do!" Arthur said firmly.

"Will you love her, comfort her, honor and keep her, in sickness and in health, in times of prosperity and in times of want, in times of success and in times of failure, and forsaking all others, will you be faithful and loyal to her so long as you both shall live?"

"I will," Arthur said as he looked lovingly into Susan's eyes.

"And Susan, do you take Arthur to be your husband?"

"I do," Susan said softly.

"Will you love him, comfort him, honor, keep, and obey him, in sickness and in health, in times of prosperity and in times of want, in times of success and in times of failure, and forsaking all others, will you be faithful and loyal to him so long as you both shall live?"

"I will," Susan said firmly and she meant it with all her heart.

"May I have the rings?" the pastor asked.

Michael took two rings out of his pocket and handed them to the pastor.

"Arthur, take this ring and place it on Susan's finger as you repeat after me: 'With this ring . . . I pledge my life and love to you. . . . I take you to have and to hold . . . from today on . . . for better or for worse . . . for richer or for poorer . . . in sickness and in health . . . so long as we both shall live...I will always be faithful to you. . . . I will be to you the husband . . . God commands in His Word. . . . I promise you this . . . in the name of the Father . . . and of the Son . . . and of the Holy Spirit.'"

Arthur repeated each phrase as he gazed into Susan's eyes. He had never been more serious about anything in his life except when he prayed to receive Christ.

"Susan, take this ring and place it on Arthur's finger as you repeat after me: 'With this ring . . . I pledge my life and love to you. . . I take you to have and to hold . . . from today on . . . for better or for worse . . . for richer or for poorer . . . in sickness and in health . . . so long as we both shall live . . . I will always be faithful to you. . . . I will be to you the wife . . . God commands in His Word. . . . I promise you this . . . in the name of the Father . . . and of the Son . . . and of the Holy Spirit.'"

"Now that you have made to one another this solemn promise, it is fitting to make this sincere and irrevocable vow to God. Repeat after me, but with your heads bowed in prayer, say this to God: 'Our Father . . . You have heard the vows . . . I have just made . . . to the one I love. . . . Now to You, O God . . . I promise . . . I will never revoke . . . my vows of marriage . . . no matter what the circumstance . . . or reason. . . . Help us both . . . to keep this vow. Amen.'"

Susan and Arthur held each other's hands tightly as they repeated the prayer and both looked up with tears in their eyes.

The minister continued, "By the authority vested in me as a minister of Jesus Christ, I pronounce you husband and wife. Arthur, you may kiss your bride."

Arthur embraced Susan unashamedly and kissed her two or three times. He couldn't take his eyes off of her.

The pastor interrupted Arthur's thoughts as he said, "It is my pleasure to introduce to you Mr. and Mrs. Arthur and Susan Wilson!"

The music started again, and Arthur and Susan walked back down the aisle to the exit as the audience applauded happily. Michael and Ellen followed behind, and then led them downstairs to the fellowship hall.

Susan was amazed that a reception had been organized in such a short time. "Why would they do this for me?" she asked Ellen. "They hardly know me!"

"Because, Susan, we want you both to know that you are loved, and we want you to be a real part of our church family."

Susan and Arthur smiled as she said, "Thank you for all you've done!"

. . .

A couple of hours later, Arthur and Susan were in their car, heading for a hotel overlooking the ocean. Michael and Ellen had even arranged for an overnight honeymoon, and when they arrived, they went directly to their room.

Inside, they embraced passionately and kissed each other again and again. "Oh, Arthur," Susan said in a near whisper, "this is sweeter than our first wedding by far!"

"Yes, darling," Arthur agreed, "it is, because this time, we got married for the right reasons and we both love the Lord. I can hardly believe God has been so good to me," he said with a deep and contented sigh. "I have never been happier."

"Neither have I, my darling," Susan said as she kissed him.

The went out onto their balcony, which faced south and looked out at the ocean as the sun went down to the west. Arthur put his arm around Susan as she leaned her head on his shoulder. As the lights of the city began to shine, they went inside, and drew the curtains.

14

A Greater Joy Because of Our God

"WHY SHOULD I WANT to be a Christian if becoming one makes people so unhappy?" Have you ever heard someone ask that question? I have heard it countless times in various forms, and it is a valid objection to our witness. You see, people are not drawn to negative Christians, even if we are technically correct when it comes to doctrine.

Over the years, I have known professing Christians who had a solid grasp of the Scriptures but whose gloomy personalities and clumsy social skills repelled Christians and non-Christians alike. They wondered why they were ineffective witnesses and tended to blame the rejection they experienced on the inherent evil of unbelievers. The truth was, people were repelled because this kind of Christian is, quite simply, repulsive.

THE WORLD'S NEED
FOR JOYFUL CHRISTIANS

The world needs joyful Christians. Instead, what people often see are angry, resentful whiners who complain about everything from politics to movies to the unbearable conditions at their workplace. Of course, there is much to be critical about in our post-Christian society, and Christians have as much right to be involved in the political process as the next citizen. Still, we need to learn how to be the salt of the earth and the light of the world without being ugly about it.

Instead of showing the world how to live a happy life in an imperfect world, we are often the chief complainers. Paul once wrote his friends in Corinth that "I should not be distressed by those who ought to make me rejoice" (2 Corinthians 2:3). In a similar way, the unbelieving world has a right to expect Christians to bring a measure of joy wherever they go.

I have some friends who do just that. When I see them come through the door, I can't help but smile because they are a joy to be with. They lighten my burdens and lift my spirit with their heartfelt laughter. They see the bright side of life and enjoy the gift and beauty of each day. I love to spend time with them.

On the other hand, I have encountered some Christians over the years who seem to radiate gloom wherever they go. It's as though they live with a dark cloud hovering overhead ready to pour a cold and dismal rain upon any unsuspecting victim they meet. They see the cloud in front of every silver lining and are determined that others share their vision. Paul would ask them, as he did the Galatians, "What has happened to all your joy?" (Galatians 4:15).

Of all people in the world, we Christians have the most reason to rejoice. We have a Father in heaven who loves us and has made a way for us to spend all of eternity with Him! Surely it must grieve the Lord for us to mope our way through life as though He has failed us.

As I read the Scriptures, I find God's encouragement to rejoice as a way of life. We are incredibly blessed! We have God as our constant companion, and He has promised, "I will walk among you and be your God, and you will be my people" (Leviticus 26:12). He is always with us, and we are told, "In the presence of the LORD your God, you and your families shall eat and shall rejoice in everything you have put your hand to, because the LORD your God has blessed you" (Deuteronomy 12:7).

Read the following verses and think deeply on them, for if you grasp their liberating truth, you may never be the same.

Glory in his holy name; let the hearts of those who seek the LORD rejoice (1 Chronicles 16:10).

Let all who take refuge in you be glad; let them ever sing for joy. Spread your protection over them, that those who love your name may rejoice in you (Psalm 5:11).

I will be glad and rejoice in you; I will sing praise to your name, O Most High (Psalm 9:2).

Rejoice in the LORD and be glad, you righteous; sing, all you who are upright in heart! (Psalm 32:11).

My soul will boast in the LORD; let the afflicted hear and rejoice (Psalm 34:2).

My soul will rejoice in the LORD and delight in his salvation (Psalm 35:9).

May the righteous be glad and rejoice before God; may they be happy and joyful (Psalm 68:3).

May my meditation be pleasing to him, as I rejoice in the LORD (Psalm 104:34).

This is the day the LORD has made; let us rejoice and be glad in it (Psalm 118:24).

I rejoice in following your statutes as one rejoices in great riches (Psalm 119:14).

May those who fear you rejoice when they see me, for I have put my hope in your word (Psalm 119:74).

THE CHURCH'S NEED
FOR JOYFUL CHRISTIANS

The church desperately needs people who will rejoice as a part of their worship of God. I'm not talking about phony laughter and excitement where whole congregations are instructed to behave in unusual ways as an evidence of the Holy Spirit's anointing on their lives. I'm talking about a genuine, heartfelt spirit of joy that permeates a person's entire being the more he understands the love and mercy of God.

We need to rejoice because of our salvation—that is, that we are destined to live eternally in the glorious environment of heaven with God and His children. Jesus told the disciples, "Do not rejoice that the spirits submit to you, but rejoice that your names are written in heaven" (Luke 10:20). This is the "joy in the faith" that Paul spoke about in Philippians 1:25.

Nonetheless, life for believers in Christ can be difficult. Jesus painted a realistic picture when He said, "In this world you will have trouble." But He also encouraged us with His following sentence: "But take heart! I have overcome the world" (John 16:33). You see, if we choose to obey the Lord, we will suffer. "In fact, everyone who wants to live a godly life in Christ Jesus will be persecuted" (2 Timothy 3:12).

That can be a depressing thought unless we remember that Jesus said, "Blessed are you when men hate you, when they exclude you and insult you and reject your name as evil, because of the Son of Man. Rejoice in that day and leap for joy, because great is your reward in heaven. For that is how their fathers treated the prophets" (Luke 6:22-23). According to Jesus, we should actually *thank* those who persecute us because they are investing in our future rewards. But more than that, it is truly an honor to join Christ in His suffering. That is why "the apostles left the Sanhedrin, rejoicing because they had been counted worthy of suffering disgrace for the Name" (Acts 5:41).

We need to rejoice for the sake of our testimony before the world. People are looking at us skeptically and asking, "Where is this God you keep boasting about? Why can't He give you happiness?" What a shame! Peter writes, "Always be prepared to give an answer to everyone who asks you to give the reason for the hope that you have. But do this with gentleness and respect" (1 Peter 3:15). Who in the world is going to ask you about "the hope that you have" unless they see in you a spirit of joy and peace?

Joyful Christians simply cannot keep silent about the goodness of God. Like Isaiah, we should "tell of the kindnesses of the

LORD, the deeds for which he is to be praised, according to all the LORD has done for us" (Isaiah 63:7), "for we cannot help speaking about what we have seen and heard" (Acts 4:20).

The church needs Christians who will rejoice with others in their triumphs and victories, and this presupposes a closeness within the Body of believers. When you love someone, you can't help but rejoice when God blesses him or her, just as Elizabeth's "neighbors and relatives heard that the Lord had shown her great mercy, and they shared her joy" (Luke 1:58). Today, many Christians are so disconnected from the daily life of the church that they sense no need to rejoice with others.

We live in dark and troubling days as we watch our civilization slide ever deeper into wickedness and rebellion toward God. If we focus on the encroaching darkness rather than the light of Christ's inevitable victory, we can become depressed and full of anxiety. It is for that very reason that we must follow Paul's command: "Rejoice in the Lord always. I will say it again: Rejoice!" (Philippians 4:4). Child of God, this is not optional for us; it is a wonderful obligation and opportunity.

OUR OWN NEED TO BE JOYFUL CHRISTIANS

There are some personal benefits to rejoicing we should consider.

First, joy is a foundational element of mental health, and in our psychologized society, people long for relief from their dysfunctions and disorders. Though the "experts" describe this need in many ways, what people are truly seeking is inner peace. Closely connected with Paul's command to rejoice is this promise: "The peace of God, which transcends all understanding, will guard your hearts and your minds in Christ Jesus" (Philippians 4:7). I encourage you to mark this passage in your Bible and underline the words "peace," "hearts," and "minds."

We also need to rejoice because it is best for our families. Our children and mates need the security and happiness that comes from a heart at peace with one's self and with God. Life is heavy out in the world, and the believer's home should be an island of tranquillity—an oasis of peace in an angry and confusing world.

I grieve for the families I counsel who are in a constant state of turmoil and anger because they have never learned how to rejoice in the Lord. I have watched children run away from home because there was so much tension in their family they felt they had to get away. I have heard parents say that they could hardly wait until their children were old enough to leave home so there would be some peace and quiet once again.

Oh, dear child of God, it doesn't *have* to be this way. As we come to the close of this book, I want to share with you the secret of happiness. It is simple but so very powerful, and if you will commit yourself to this two-part process, you will discover a joy you never thought possible.

THE SECRET TO BECOMING A JOYFUL CHRISTIAN

I have yet to meet the person whose primary ambition was to find happiness who accomplished that goal. Listen to me carefully: If you have learned nothing else in this entire book, think deeply about this: *You will never achieve happiness by seeking it, for happiness is the by-product of a life lived according to God's unchanging principles.*

On our radio and television broadcasts, we use an old gospel song for our musical theme. It's called "Trust and Obey," and the chorus goes this way:

Trust and obey,
For there's no other way
To be happy in Jesus,
But to trust and obey.

As we discussed earlier in this book, faith is the foundation for our walk with God. "Trust in God" is another way of saying the same thing, for trust is a firm confidence in "the integrity, ability, character, and truth of a person or thing"[70] Isn't that a wonderful definition of faith in God? Compare the words *trust* and *faith* in the dictionary, and you will see just how closely linked the two concepts are.

There is a wonderful promise connected with trust found in Proverbs: "Trust in the LORD with all your heart and lean not on your own understanding; in all your ways acknowledge him, and he will make your paths straight" (Proverbs 3:5-6). I just *love* that passage!

Perhaps the hardest time to trust in the Lord is when the future seems uncertain and we have no idea what is about to happen or how we will face the problems that press in upon us. Isaiah counsels us, "Let him who walks in the dark, who has no light, trust in the name of the LORD and rely on his God" (Isaiah 50:10).

Dear reader, you will never experience genuine and lasting happiness until you learn to trust in God. But there is another essential element for real happiness, and it is one that many turn away from. It is obedience to God. This second part of joyful Christianity is the natural fruit of the first—faith in God. When we have learned to trust in our great and merciful God, our loving response is obedience.

The psalmist puts it this way: "Trust in the LORD and do good; dwell in the land and enjoy safe pasture" (Psalm 37:3). Do you see the two parts of a peaceful life? "Trust in the LORD" and "do good"—trust and obey!

Joshua relayed a glorious promise to us in regard to faith and obedience: "Do not let this Book of the Law depart from your mouth; meditate on it day and night, so that you may be careful to do everything written in it. Then you will be prosperous and successful" (Joshua 1:8). Have you ever connected prosperity and success with faith and obedience? That connection is clearly taught in the Word of God: "I gave them this command: Obey me, and I will be your God and you will be my people. Walk in all the ways I command you, that it may go well with you" (Jeremiah 7:23).

Of course, God wants our obedience to be a genuine response of love. Even in the Old Testament that was very clear: "The LORD your God commands you this day to follow these decrees and laws; carefully observe them with all your heart and with all your soul" (Deuteronomy 26:16).

It might surprise you to discover that the Lord is not nearly as concerned about our religious rituals as He is heartfelt obedience. King Saul thought God would be impressed with a religious ceremony, even though his heart was full of rebellion. Samuel sadly told him, "Does the LORD delight in burnt offerings and sacrifices as much as in obeying the voice of the LORD? To obey is better than sacrifice, and to heed is better than the fat of rams" (1 Samuel 15:22).

Joy Is Related to Our Faith

We have examined at great length why we need to increase our faith. As we conclude our study, let's review some basic principles of faith.

Faith Is Believing God   We can look up definitions in unabridged dictionaries, read books by "word of faith" teachers, and listen to television evangelists explain their secrets to health, wealth, and fame, but the simple truth is, faith is simply believing God. In Galatians 3 Paul writes, "Consider Abraham: 'He believed God, and it was credited to him as righteousness'" (Galatians 3:6). To know whether we have faith we only need to find out if we believe in God's character and power and whether we believe what He says.

It is important to understand that faith is not believing in our *faith*. Contrary to the unbiblical doctrines of many "faith teachers," our words have absolutely no power in and of themselves. God responds to our hearts, not to the formulation of our prayers. He is not a captive genie who appears when we rub the magic Bible and say the right words in the right order with the right tone of voice.

Faith is not working up a holy sweat and trying to "believe real hard." That's why Jesus gave an unexpected answer when His disciples asked Him to increase their faith (Luke 17:5). He replied, "If you have faith as small as a mustard seed, you can say to this mulberry tree, 'Be uprooted and planted in the sea,' and it will obey you" (Luke 17:6). In other words, it isn't the amount of faith you have, it is the One in whom you have placed your faith. Very simply put, faith is believing God.

Faith Is Obeying God   We can say that we believe God, but real faith is seen by what we *do*, not by what we say. James writes, "What good is it, my brothers, if a man claims to have faith but has no deeds?" (James 2:14). Years ago, a tightrope walker stretched a cable across Niagara Falls and moved from one side to the other with incredible courage and skill. Then he walked across the falls again, this time with a wheelbarrow. The crowd who watched with sweaty palms applauded wildly when he returned. He looked at their admiring faces and asked, "How many of you believe I could place a person in this wheelbarrow and take him across the falls?" Nearly every hand went up. Then he asked, "Who will volunteer?" And every hand went down. None of them had enough faith in the acrobat's skill to risk his life.

That is exactly how most of us believe in God. We claim to have faith, but our lives don't show it. When the opportunity comes to get in God's wheelbarrow, we put our hands down fast. James says, "In the same way, faith by itself, if it is not accompanied by action, is dead" (James 2:17).

We don't trust God for our happiness, our healing, or our future because we would rather trust ourselves. It shows in what we do—or don't do. Real faith is living a life of childlike obedience from day to day, regardless of circumstances or feelings. And the only way to do His will is to know what God wants. And the only way to know what God wants is to study His Word with a heart ready to obey.

Faith Is Trusting When It's Dark   Paul writes, "We live by faith, not by sight" (2 Corinthians 5:7). Sometimes, we just cannot see what God has in mind and life makes absolutely no sense at all. Everything seems dark and mysterious. That's exactly when we must trust in our loving God.

Pilots have learned that they have to trust their instruments when flying in dark and foggy conditions They must maintain their altitude, heading, and speed without the benefit of sensory feedback. Those who depend upon their own senses can become disoriented and are in great danger of crashing, taking their own lives and the lives of their passengers. Isaiah reminds us, "Who among you fears the LORD and obeys the word of his servant? Let him who walks in the dark, who has no light, trust in the name of the LORD and rely on his God" (Isaiah 50:10). Is everything in front of you dark and foggy? Do you have absolutely no idea what to expect? Then it's time to believe, because faith is trusting God when it's dark.

Faith Is Trusting When God Delays   There are other times when God seems to take forever! Yet part of the discipline of faith is waiting. Listen to what David writes: "Wait for the LORD; be strong and take heart and wait for the LORD" (Psalm 27:14). That doesn't mean that we sit idly doing nothing, but that we continue obeying God even when it seems as though He has delayed coming to our aid. The rule is this: We are to do what we know is God's will and when we don't know what that is, we are to wait.

I have experienced God's delays. When we were wanting to build our worship center, we purchased a large parcel of land. About eight minutes after we signed the contract, a recession fell on Colorado and finances dried up. We were obligated to maintain our payments, yet we could not begin construction. For some twelve years we waited and prayed and continued to preach the gospel. During this time some of our weaker members said, "Just walk away from it! We're never going to build! Give the land back to the bank!"

But we had promised we would make our payments—and we knew that to do so was God's will, since His Word tells us to honor our contracts. Though it was extremely difficult, that's exactly what we did, and God turned things around and blessed as we waited and waited. I am forever grateful to those in our congregation who did not give up, but trusted and waited on our gracious Lord. Now we are in our first auditorium and are completing our education buildings as well.

Sometimes we become frustrated when we see unbelievers succeed financially and are able to complete their projects with little delay. I am always amazed that banks will lend to bars, restaurants, and stores that are likely to fail, yet they are incredibly reluctant to help local congregations that rarely default. Do you know what God says? "Be still before the LORD and wait patiently for him; do not fret when men succeed in their ways, when they carry out their wicked schemes" (Psalm 37:7).

We are also to wait on the Lord emotionally. That means we can be at peace even though God seems to have put us on hold. We must remember what Isaiah wrote: "The LORD longs to be gracious to you; he rises to show you compassion. For the LORD is a God of justice. Blessed are all who wait for him!" (Isaiah 30:18). You still don't *feel* at peace? Then turn to Psalm 130:5 and learn from David: "I wait for the LORD, my soul waits, and in his word I put my hope." That's where we must go when we have to wait—God's Word! He has provided wonderful resources for comfort, assurance, patience, and joy.

Sometimes we must wait for years, or even a lifetime. The saints of Hebrews 11 "were all commended for their faith, yet none of them received what had been promised" (verse 39). Did God lie to them? No, for God's promise of the coming Messiah extended beyond their lifetime. Yet they continued to wait and believe. So must we.

Faith Is the Victory We live in a sin-cursed world with all of its suffering, sorrow, disease, disappointments, and "dysfunctions." We are affected by our culture, our personal environment, our friends and family. Sadly, in many cases, Christians are becoming more like the world and less like Christ. As Paul warns, "Do not be misled: 'Bad company corrupts good character'" (1 Corinthians 15:33).

God intends for His children to impact the world rather than allowing it to mold us. Paul admonishes, "Do not conform any longer to the pattern of this world, but be transformed by the renewing of your mind" (Romans 12:2). He clearly explains what he means when he writes, "Do not be overcome by evil, but overcome evil with good" (Romans 12:21). That is possible only through faith in God. John tells us, "Everyone born of God overcomes the world. This is the victory that has overcome the world, even our faith" (1 John 5:4).

Dear child of God, are you influencing the world around you for Christ? Or is the world pressing you into its mold? The source of victory, according to the Scriptures, is faith in the character, power, and Word of God. Faith is the victory.

Joy: The Choice Is Ours

Do you really want to be happy and free? Do you want to have power over the "addictions" and "dysfunctions" that seem to control your every waking thought? Do you want to see your marriage restored and your children brought into productive maturity? Do you want cleansing from wrong decisions of the past and a sense of peace with God and yourself? Then, dear friend, you must learn this simple lesson and apply it daily: Trust and obey, for there is no other way to be happy in Jesus, but to trust and obey.

No one can make you do it. God Himself has chosen not to force us into obedience, but to give us the freedom to make this all-important decision for ourselves.

HOW BIG IS YOUR GOD?

As we close this book, I want to ask you one last time: How big is *your* God? And what is He like? Is He the confused and insufficient god of "Christian" psychology? Is He the powerless and limited god of "theistic" evolution? Or is He the all-powerful, all-knowing, ever-present, loving God of the Scriptures?

We *can* regain faith in our mighty God, and it is worth the effort! If God *is* God, and we are His children, then let's live like it!

———

A New Home in Christ

Arthur and Susan Wilson awoke in each other's arms. Their love for the Lord had deepened their love for each other and they were anxious to return to their home and begin a new life together.

As Susan showered and dressed, Arthur could not take his eyes off of her. She blushed at his attention like a new bride, but she enjoyed every moment of it. She had never before experienced the holiness and purity of a godly marriage, and she rejoiced that God had cleansed and redeemed their home.

They ate a leisurely breakfast that was delivered to their room, compliments of the Rollins. Then they packed their overnight bags and went out to their car and drove back toward Bethesda.

On the way, Susan turned to her husband and said, "There's something I have to take care of, Arthur, at the police station."

"What do you mean, Susan?" Arthur asked.

"Well, I told you that I had reported Jason Miller to the police."

"Yes?"

"But, I lied to them at first and told them I couldn't identify anyone. Now I need to go clear that up. It has bothered me every day since it happened, and I want a totally clear conscience before the Lord."

"I understand, Susan. Let's take care of it right away." He drove directly to the police station and they went inside.

Susan went to the reception desk and said, "I need to speak to detectives Gustafson and Aker," she said tensely.

"And what shall I tell them this is about?" the secretary asked.

"It concerns the Czezak slaying," Susan replied.

Soon Gustafson and Aker appeared and ushered Susan and Arthur to a conference room.

"I'm surprised to see you again, Mrs. Wilson," Patricia Aker said with a slight smirk playing at the corner of her mouth. "What is it you want to see us about?"

Susan's face was red with embarrassment, but she forged ahead. "I came to clear my conscience. You were right about me when I was here the last time, Ms. Aker. I was lying. I told you I had not recognized Jason at first, when the truth was I knew it all along. I was simply reluctant to report it at first because Jason was my pastor's son. But when Mr. Czezak died, I knew I had to come forward. That's the simple truth. I am ashamed, but I felt I had to tell you."

George Gustafson sat in his chair without expression on his face. Patricia Aker lit up a cigarette and blew a blue-gray stream of smoke overhead. She hacked with a dry cough, and finally said, "Well, Mrs. Wilson, this is highly unusual, as you might expect. We knew you were lying, of course, but there was no way to prove it. Now with your confession, we could charge you with filing a false report."

"I know that, ma'am," Susan replied softly, "and I'm willing to face whatever penalty there is." Arthur took Susan's hand and held it. He noticed that it was cold and wet with tension.

Detective Gustafson sat up, cleared his throat, turned to Ms. Aker and said, "Patricia, I think it would take more time to fill out the papers than it's worth. This lady eventually did the right thing and it resulted in the gang being broken up."

Patricia Aker looked irritated at her superior, but didn't respond.

Turning to Susan, Gustafson continued, "What you did was wrong. You know that, don't you?"

"Oh, yes, sir, I do!" Susan said sincerely.

"All right, then. Don't ever let it happen again. Do you understand?"

Susan stood to her feet and said, "I understand completely. And thank you, Mr. Gustafson—I mean *Detective* Gustafson!"

Gustafson smiled at Susan's nervousness. "Go on!" he said. "Get out of here."

"Yes, sir!" Susan said, and she and Arthur quickly exited the building.

In the car, Susan leaned back in the seat and sighed with relief. "Oh, Arthur! I'm so glad that's over! But I'm glad I went in. One thing I've been learning from Ellen is for me to be happy, I truly have to be obedient to the Lord, and when I sin, I've got to confess it as quickly as possible to get back on track."

Arthur reached over and patted Susan on the knee. "Well, I'm proud of you, Susan," he said with a smile. "Now, can we go home?"

"Yes, Arthur," she said sweetly. "We can go to *our* home! Oh, that sounds so good!"

They drove up to the house and pushed the garage door opener. The door slid up and they drove inside. Arthur unlocked the door to the family room and opened it for Susan. She walked in and looked around with delight. "Oh, Arthur, it seems like it's been so long since I've been here."

"It *has* been a long time, sweetheart," Arthur said. "Much too long. But you're finally home!"

She walked from room to room, enjoying the comfort of finally returning to her own nest. She couldn't help but notice that a woman's touch was needed, but she said, "Arthur, you really cleaned the house beautifully! Thank you so much!" She threw her arms around him and kissed him again and again.

Arthur held Susan close and whispered, "I never want to let you go!"

She smiled and closed her eyes. "Isn't God good, Arthur?"

"Yes, my dear," Arthur said quietly, "and I'm so glad He's the head of our home! I just can't believe it took me so long to wake up. I wasted so many years."

Susan put her finger to Arthur's lips and said, "I know. Me, too. But that's behind us now. Let's just make sure we live for Him from now on."

They rocked back and forth, totally content, at peace with each other, the world around them, and with God.

Notes

1. *Newsweek*, March 3, 1997, p. 45.
2. All names are by random selection and do not necessarily represent any specific individual.
3. Dr. Tana Dineen, *Manufacturing Victims* (Montreal: Robert Davies Publishing, 1996), p. 250.
4. Ibid., p. 23.
5. Lyle E. Bourne, Jr. and Bruce R. Ekstrand, *Psychology, Its Principles and Meanings* (New York: Holt, Rinehart and Winston, 1979), p. 23.
6. Ibid., p. 28.
7. Jerome Kagan and Julius Segal, *Psychology, An Introduction*, 6th ed. (New York: Harcourt Brace Jovanovich Publishers, 1988), p. 72.
8. Ibid., p. 73.
9. Ed Bulkley's book, *Only God Can Heal the Wounded Heart* (Eugene, OR: Harvest House, 1995), deals with this process at great length.
10. *Software Toolworks Illustrated Encyclopedia*, Grolier, Inc., 1991.
11. Ibid.
12. *American Heritage Electronic Dictionary*, Houghton Mifflin Company, 1992.
13. For a more complete explanation of this passage, see pages 217–44 of *Only God Can Heal the Wounded Heart* (Eugene, OR: Harvest House, 1995).
14. *American Heritage Electronic Dictionary*, Houghton Mifflin Company, 1992.
15. For a more complete treatment of the process of change, see chapter 14 of *Why Christians Can't Trust Psychology* (Eugene, OR: Harvest House, 1994), pp. 307–32.
16. *American Heritage Electronic Dictionary*, Houghton Mifflin Company, 1992.
17. For an in-depth analysis of this growing problem, see *Only God Can Heal the Wounded Heart* (Eugene, OR: Harvest House, 1995).
18. Copies of radio and television interviews with Dr. Breggin are available from Return to the Word, 1-888-463-7967.
19. For a study of the root sin of bitterness, see *Only God Can Heal the Wounded Heart* (Eugene, OR: Harvest House, 1995).
20. For a study of False Memory Syndrome, see *Only God Can Heal the Wounded Heart*, or the Return to the Word video interview of the Rutherford family.

21. Diane Dungey and Janet Hallman, "Willow Creek disavows ex-pastor's retreat for men, chastises nudity," *Daily Herald*, Monday, September 30, 1996, p. 1.

22. Ibid.

23. This story was documented in the Return to the Word newsletter, Spring 1996, and is posted on the Internet under "Biblical Counseling." This quarterly *Biblical Counseling Newsletter* is available free by calling Return to the Word at 1-888-463-7967.

24. Mark Pendergrast, *Victims of Memory* (Hinesburg: Upper Access Press, 1996), pp. 472–73.

25. Ibid., p. 477.

26. A statement by Dr. Paul Meier with Dr. James Dobson on "Focus on the Family." See our reply in our Fall 1996 newsletter, available on the Internet under "Biblical Counseling."

27. *Why Christians Can't Trust Psychology* (Eugene, OR: Harvest House, 1994), pp. 312–50 and *Only God Can Heal the Wounded Heart* (Eugene, OR: Harvest House, 1995), pp. 217–49.

28. *American Heritage Electronic Dictionary*, Houghton Mifflin Co., 1992.

29. For an extensive study of this issue, see Joe Dallas's book *A Strong Deception* (Eugene, OR: Harvest House, 1996). Three taped radio interviews with Joe are available from Return to the Word, 1-888-463-7967.

30. *American Heritage Electronic Dictionary*, Houghton Mifflin Co., 1992.

31. *Rocky Mountain News*, December 27, 1996, p. 4A.

32. Ibid., p. 6A.

33. Ibid., p. 4A.

34. Ibid.

35. Ibid.

36. Ibid.

37. Ibid.

38. *Newsweek*, December 30, 1996/January 6, 1997, p. 17.

39. Ibid.

40. John Kryer was a main character in the books *Why Christians Can't Trust Psychology* and *Only God Can Heal the Wounded Heart.*

41. *Why Christians Can't Trust Psychology* is the first book in this series, published by Harvest House, 1993.

42. You can order a taped interview with this gentleman from Return to the Word, 1-888-463-7967.

43. The Rutherford story is available on two videocassettes from Return to the Word, 1-888-463-7967.

44. You can order a series of three audiotapes regarding the psychologizing of the Assemblies of God from Return to the Word, 1-888-463-7967.

45. *Chemical and Engineering News*, April 9, 1973, p. 1, as quoted by Jerald Tanner, *Views on Creation, Evolution and Fossil Man*, Modern Microfilm Company, 1975, p. 1.
46. Michael J. Behe, *Darwin's Black Box* (New York: The Free Press, 1996).
47. Henry J. Morris, *The Troubled Waters of Evolution* (San Diego, CA: Creation-Life Publishers, 1974), pp. 11–12.
48. Associated Press, November 27, 1959, as quoted by Morris, Ibid., pp. 12-13.
49. James Beck, "Christian Anti-Psychology Sentiment: Hints of an Historical Analogue," *Journal of Psychology and Theology*, 1992, vol. 20, no. 1, p. 6.
50. Ibid., p. 7.
51. Ibid.
52. Ibid., p. 8.
53. *Parade* magazine, December 1, 1996, p. 18.
54. *American Heritage Electronic Dictionary*, Houghton Mifflin Co., 1992.
55. John 6:37.
56. James 2:19.
57. 1 Corinthians 15:3; Hebrews 9:15; 1 Peter 3:18.
58. John 3:15; 3:36; 5:24; 6:40; 11:25; 12:46; 20:31; Acts 10:43; 3:39; 16:31; Romans 9:33; 10:9; 2 Timothy 3:15; 1 John 5:1.
59. Isaiah 40:8.
60. Romans 3:25; 1 John 2:2; 1 John 4:10.
61. Isaiah 64:56.
62. Ephesians 2:8-9.
63. 1 Corinthians 15.
64. Larry Crabb, *Understanding People: Deep Longings for Relationship* (Grand Rapids, MI: Zondervan, 1987), p. 40, as quoted by Tom Watson in *The Evangelical Eroding of the Deity of Christ*, published by Countryside Bible Church, 1995.
65. Ibid.
66. Tom Watson, *The Evangelical Eroding of the Deity of Christ*, published by Countryside Bible Church, 1995, p. 22. This is available from Return to the Word, 1-888-463-7967.
67. Ibid., p. 40.
68. For an in-depth treatment of this passage, see *Why Christians Can't Trust Psychology* (Eugene, OR: Harvest House, 1993).
69. Ephesians 1:7.
70. *American Heritage Electronic Dictionary*, Houghton Mifflin Co., 1992.

OTHER BOOKS BY ED BULKLEY

Only God Can Heal the Wounded Heart

Many Christians genuinely desire to overcome hurts that stem from past experiences. Pastoral counselor Ed Bulkley offers biblical solutions that promise true freedom and genuine inner peace for those who hurt.

Why Christians Can't Trust Psychology

Where should Christians go to heal the deep hurts in their hearts? Some say we need the Bible plus psychology; others say the Bible alone is sufficient. Here's both sides of the issue with biblical answers.

OTHER HARVEST HOUSE READING

Totally Sufficient
by Ed Hindson and Howard Eyrich

Experts ranging from counseling to science to ministry explore why the Bible holds all the answers for life and faith. Their solid insights enable people to minister to Christians who find it difficult to turn to God in the midst of trials or unmet needs.

Women Helping Women
by Elyse Fitzpatrick and Carol Cornish

A one-of-a-kind counseling resource written for every woman who desires to help guide other women from the chaos of life's storms to the calm of God's promises. For each major life issue covered in this book, you will find a concise overview, a clear biblical perspective, and practical guidelines from qualified experts. Woman will find renewed strength and skills to help their sisters in Christ as they discover how God's Word can change a heart like nothing else can.